NEW CENTURY BIBLE

General Editors

RONALD E. CLEMENTS

M.A., B.D., PH.D. (Old Testament)

MATTHEW BLACK

D.D., D.LITT., D.THEOL., F.B.A. (New Testament)

Ezekiel

NEW CENTURY BIBLE

Based on the Revised Standard Version

EZEKIEL

JOHN W. WEVERS B.A., Th.D.
Professor of Near Eastern Studies, University of Toronto

OLIPHANTS

OLIPHANTS
MARSHALL, MORGAN AND SCOTT
116 Baker Street
London W1M 2BB

© Thomas Nelson and Sons Limited 1969
assigned to Marshall, Morgan and Scott 1971
First published 1969
Reprinted 1976

ISBN 0 551 00755 9

The Bible text in this publication is from the Revised Standard Version
of the Bible, copyrighted 1946 and 1952 by the Division of Christian
Education, National Council of the Churches of Christ, and used by
permission.

PRINTED IN GREAT BRITAIN BY
BUTLER & TANNER LTD, FROME AND LONDON

CONTENTS

LISTS OF ABBREVIATIONS

ANEP	*Ancient Near East in Pictures relating to the Old Testament*, edited by J. B. Pritchard, Princeton, 1954
ANET	*Ancient Near Eastern Texts relating to the Old Testament*, edited by J. B. Pritchard, 2nd ed., Princeton, 1955
AV	Authorized Version
BH, BH³	*Biblia Hebraica*, edited by R. Kittel, 3rd ed., Stuttgart, 1937
D	Deuteronomic Code or School
E	Elohist Document
FRLANT	*Forschungen zur Religion und Literatur des Alten und Neuen Testaments*
G.	Septuagint Greek Version
H	Holiness Code
Herod.	Herodotus
Hithp.	Hithpaʿel verbal stem in Hebrew, reflexive
IDB	*Interpreter's Dictionary of the Bible*, 4 vols., Nashville, 1962
J	Yahwist Document
JSS	*Journal of Semitic Studies*
JV	Jewish Version
MT	Masoretic
Ni.	Niphʿal verbal stem in Hebrew, generally passive
N.T.	New Testament
O.T.	Old Testament
P	Priestly Code or School
Pi.	Piʿel verbal stem in Hebrew, intensive
RSV	Revised Standard Version
RV	Revised Version
S.	Syriac (Peshitta) Version
Sym	Version of Symmachus
T.	Targum
V.	Vulgate Version
Vers.	All the ancient Versions

ABBREVIATIONS OF THE BOOKS OF THE BIBLE

OLD TESTAMENT (*O.T.*)

Gen.	Jg.	1 Chr.	Ps.	Lam.	Ob.	Hag.
Exod.	Ru.	2 Chr.	Prov.	Ezek.	Jon.	Zech.
Lev.	1 Sam.	Ezr.	Ec.	Dan.	Mic.	Mal.
Num.	2 Sam.	Neh.	Ca.	Hos.	Nah.	
Dt.	1 Kg.	Est.	Isa.	Jl	Hab.	
Jos.	2 Kg.	Job	Jer.	Am.	Zeph.	

APOCRYPHA (*Apoc.*)

1 Esd.	Tob.	Ad. Est.	Sir.	S 3 Ch.	Bel	1 Mac.
2 Esd.	Jdt.	Wis.	Bar.	Sus.	Man.	2 Mac.
			Ep. Jer.			

NEW TESTAMENT (*N.T.*)

Mt.	Ac.	Gal.	1 Th.	Tit.	1 Pet.	3 Jn
Mk	Rom.	Eph.	2 Th.	Phm.	2 Pet.	Jude
Lk	1 C.	Phil.	1 Tim.	Heb.	1 Jn	Rev.
Jn	2 C.	Col.	2 Tim.	Jas	2 Jn	

SELECTED BIBLIOGRAPHY

Only a few basic works out of a vast number of published works are listed below·

(a) PROPHECY IN GENERAL

G. Hölscher, *Die Profeten. Untersuchungen zur Religionsgeschichte Israels*, 1914, Leipzig.

B. Duhm, *Israels Propheten*, 2nd edn, 1922, Tübingen.

E. Fascher, *Prophētēs. Eine sprach- und religionsgeschichtliche Untersuchung*, 1927, Giessen.

F. Häussermann, *Wortempfang u. Symbol in der alttest. Prophetie. Eine Untersuchung zur Psychologie des proph. Erlebnisses (Beihefte z. Zeitschr. f. d. alttest. Wissensch. 58)*, 1932, Giessen.

A. Jepsen, *Nabi. Soziologische Studien zur alttestl. Literatur u. Religionsgeschichte*, 1934, Munich.

A. Heschel, *Die Prophetie*, 1936, Krakow.

—— *The Prophets*, 1955, New York.

H. Birkeland, *Zum herbräischen Traditionswesen. Die Komposition der proph. Bücher des A. T. (Avh. utg. av Det Norske Videnskaps-Akademi i Oslo II, 1938)*, 1938, Oslo.

H. H. Rowley, 'The Nature of Old Testament Prophecy in the Light of Recent Study,' *Harvard Theol. Rev.* 38 (1945), 1ff. (reprinted in *The Servant of the Lord*, 2nd edn, 1965, Oxford, 97ff.).

S. Mowinckel, *Prophecy and Tradition. The Prophetic Books in the Light of the Study of the Growth and History of the Tradition (Avh. utg. av Det Norske Videnskaps-Akademi i Oslo II, 1946, 3)*, 1946, Oslo.

G. von Rad, *Die Theologie der proph. Überlieferungen Israels (Theol. des A.T., Bd. II)*, 1960, Munich (Eng. trans. by D. M. G. Stalker as *Old Testament Theology*, vol. II, 1965, London).

E. Jenni, *Die alttest. Prophetie (Theol. Studien 67)*, 1962, Zürich.

J. Lindblom, *Prophecy in Ancient Israel*, 1963, Oxford.

(b) COMMENTARIES ON EZEKIEL

C. H. Cornill, *Das Buch des Propheten Ezechiel*, 1886, Leipzig.

A. B. Davidson, *The Book of the Prophet Ezekiel (The Cambridge Bible for Schools and Colleges)*, 1892, Cambridge.

A. Bertholet, *Das Buch Hesekiel (Kurzer Handkomm. z. A.T. 12)*, 1897, Freiburg.

R. Kraetzschmar, *Das Buch Ezechiel (Gött. Handkomm. z. A.T. III, 3, 1)*, 1900, Göttingen.

H. A. Redpath, *The Book of the Prophet Ezekiel (Westm. Commentaries)*, 1907, London.

H. Schmidt, *Die grossen Propheten (Die Schr. des A.T. II, 2)*, 1923, Göttingen.

J. Herrmann, *Ezechiel (Komm. z. A.T. 11)*, 1924, Leipzig.

A. Bertholet, *Hesekiel, mit einem Beitrag v. K. Galling (Handb. z. A.T. I, 13)*, 1936, Tübingen.

G. A. Cooke, *A Critical and Exegetical Commentary on the Book of Ezekiel* (*International Critical Commentary*), 1936–7, Edinburgh and New York.

I. G. Matthews, *Ezekiel* (*An American Commentary on the O.T.*), 1939, Philadelphia.

J. Ziegler, *Ezechiel* (*Echter-Bible* 6), 1948, Würzburg.

A. van den Born, *Ezechiël* (*De Boeken van het Oude Testament* xi, 1), 1954, Roermond.

S. Fisch, *Ezekiel* (*Soncino Books of the Bible*), 1950, London.

G. Fohrer, *Ezechiel, mit einem Beitrag v. K. Galling* (*Handb. z. A.T.* I, 13), 1955, Tübingen.

W. Zimmerli, *Ezechiel* (*Bibl. Komm.: Altes Testament* 13), Lfgn. 1–12 publ. thus far, 1955–65, Neukirchen.

W. Eichrodt, *Der Prophet Hesekiel. Kapitel 1–18* (*Das A.T. Deutsch* 22.1), 1959, Göttingen.

(c) SPECIAL STUDIES ON EZEKIEL

H. St. J. Thackeray, 'The Greek Translators of Ezekiel,' *Journ. of Theol. Stud.* 4 (1903), 398ff.

G. Jahn, *Das Buch Ezechiel auf Grund des Septuaginta hergestellt*, 1905, Leipzig.

J. Herrmann, *Ezechielprobleme*, 1908, Leipzig.

G. Hölscher, *Hesekiel, der Dichter und das Buch*, 1924, Giessen.

M. Burrows, *The Literary Relations of Ezekiel*, 1925, Philadelphia.

C. C. Torrey, *Pseudo-Ezekiel and the Original Prophecy*, 1930, New Haven.

J. Smith, *The Book of the Prophet Ezekiel*, 1931, London.

V. Herntrich, *Ezechielprobleme* (*Beihefte z. Zeitschr. f.d. alttest. Wissensch.* 61), 1932, Giessen.

C. Kuhl, 'Zur Geschichte der Hesekiel-Forschung,' *Th. Runds.* N.F. 5 (1933), 92ff.

O. Procksch, 'Fürst und Priester bei Hesekiel,' *Zeitsch. f.d. alttest. Wissensch.* 58 (1940/1), 99ff.

W. A. Irwin, *The Problem of Ezekiel*, 1943, Chicago.

N. Messel, *Ezechielfragen* (*Skr. utg. av. Det Norske Videnskaps-Akademi i Oslo* II, 1945, 1), 1945, Oslo.

A. van den Born, *De Historische Situatie van Ezechiels Prophetie*, 1947, Bruges.

C. G. Howie, *The Date and Composition of Ezekiel* (*Journ. of Bibl. Lit.* Monograph Series 4.), 1950, Philadelphia.

G. Fohrer, *Die Hauptprobleme des Buches Ezechiel* (*Beihefte z. Zeitsch. f.d. alttest. Wissensch.* 72), 1952, Berlin.

K. Elliger, 'Die grossen Tempelsakristeien im Verfassungsentwurf des Ezechiel (42, 1ff.)', *Beitr. z. hist. Th.* 16 (1953), 79ff.

H. H. Rowley, 'The Book of Ezekiel in Modern Study', *Bull. of the John Rylands Library* 36 (1953), 146ff. (reprinted in *Men of God*, 1963, London, 169ff.)

H. Gese, *Der Verfassungsentwurf des Ezechiel* (*Kap. 40–48*) *traditionsgeschichtlich untersucht* (*Beitr. z. hist. Th.* 25), 1957, Tübingen.

H. G. von Reventlow, *Wächter über Israel. Ezechiel und seine Tradition* (*Beihefte z. Zeitsch. f.d. alttest. Wissensch.* 82), 1962, Berlin.

INTRODUCTION

1. GENERAL ARRANGEMENT OF THE BOOK

The book of Ezekiel more than any other book in the canon of the Latter Prophets yields evidence of intentional arrangement and a single editorial mind. This is not only apparent from the general fourfold division of the book by which chapters 1–24 contain pre-586 B.C. materials, chapters 25–32, the collected oracles against foreign nations, chapters 33–39, post-586 oracles mainly dealing with restoration hopes and conditions, and chapters 40–48, the ideal cult of the future, but also from the language of the book. Words, phrases and even sentences characteristic of the book occur again and again. Examples are **the hand of the LORD was upon . . . 1.3; the word of the LORD came to me, 3.16; Son of man, 3.17; the glory of the LORD, 3.23; rebellious house, 2.5; scatter to (all) the winds, 5.10; detestable things, 5.11; abominations, 5.11; my eye will not spare, 5.11; I, the LORD, have spoken, 5.13; spend . . . fury, 5.13; vent . . . fury, 5.13; set your face toward, 6.2; mountains of Israel, 6.3; Behold, I . . . am against, 5.8; shall know that I am the LORD, 6.7; idols, 6.4; nations . . . countries, 5.5; scattered through the countries, 6.8; I will stretch out my hand against, 6.14; I will . . . pour out my wrath, 7.8; prince, 7.27; stumbling block of . . . iniquity, 7.19; what is this proverb that you have, 12.22; Because . . . therefore, 13.8; prophesy and say to those who, 13.2.** Whether such recurring phrases signal a single author or simply the thorough work of an editor cannot be answered easily.

(a) *The chronological arrangement*
Sixteen dates are given in the book, though only fourteen passages are involved; in two cases, 1.1–2 and 40.1, a double dating, i.e. dating according to two calendric systems, obtains. These are listed in the table below.

As indicated above the double date notations in 1.1–2 and in 40.1 are references to single dates. Thus the enigmatic **thirtieth year** of 1.1 can be disregarded. If the four divisions of Ezekiel are

	Year	Month	Day	
1.1	30	4	5	
1.2	5	(4)?	5	June 593
3.16	at the end of seven days			June 593
8.1	6	6	5	Aug./Sept. 592
20.1	7	5	10	Aug. 591
24.1	9	10	10	Jan. 588
26.1	11	—	1	587/586
29.1	10	10	12	Jan. 587
29.17	27	1	1	Apr. 571
30.20	11	1	7	Apr. 587
31.1	11	3	1	June 587
32.1	12	12	1	Mar. 585
32.17	12	(1–G.)	15	Apr. 586
33.21	12	10	5	Jan. 585
40.1	25	1	10	Apr. 573
40.1	(fourteenth year after the city was conquered)			

taken as separate units it will be seen that the first date given in each division fits into a chronological scheme, i.e. 1.2, 26.1, 33.21, and 40.1 (as 5th, 11th, 12th and 25th years respectively).

Within chapters 1–24 the five dated sections are also in strict order. It should be noted in passing that the dates apply only to the section for which it was presumably originally intended rather than to all the materials which follow up to the next date. Thus the date in 1.2 applies to the vision of 1.4–3.15: that of 3.16, probably to the symbolic acts of 4.1–5.4 (cf. commentary on 3.16–27); that of 8.1, to the Temple vision of 8.1–11.25; that of 20.1, to 20.1–44, and that of 24.1 (though probably editorial in origin), to 24.1–14. The other materials are left undated.

In the oracles against the nations the situation is not straightforward. Chapters 26–28.19 are a collection of oracles against Tyre, whereas chapters 29–32 all concern Egypt. The only dated oracle against Tyre occurs in chapter 26, but it is later than the first dated

oracle in the second collection (29.1). Possibly the editor had over-
riding reasons for placing the Egyptian oracles last in the collection.
In any event, the oracles against Egypt are chronologically ordered
with one exception. The oracle dated by 29.17 is much later than the
rest. The oracle recognizes the failure of Nebuchadrezzar's siege of
Tyre and promises compensation in the form of Egyptian plunder.
The editor may well have felt the need of keeping it as close to the
Tyre collection as possible and thus placed it immediately after the
first oracle against Egypt.

The last dated section is 32.17. In MT the month is lacking, and it
might be argued that in view of its position the editor felt that the
twelfth month was meant, i.e. fourteen days later than the date of
32.1. In the commentary, however, the reading of G. **in the first
month** was accepted as original. If that is correct its placement at
the end of the Egyptian oracles was dictated by its contents. The
descent of the multitude of Egypt into Hades logically should end
the section.

The final division of the book, chapters 40–48, has only one date,
and that at the beginning. It was probably intended by the editor
to refer to the entire division, though originally it referred only to
the vision of the new Temple.

It is clear that the chronological pattern is an intentional editorial
one; the arrangement is one that has been imposed on the materials.

(b) *Inner Logic of the Arrangement*

Since only fourteen sections in the book are dated, other criteria for
ordering the materials must have been used by the editor. Certain
of these are immediately obvious. Chapters 40–48 contain all the
materials concerning the ideal cult of the future. The framework is
the original vision of the new Temple found in chapters 40–42, 43,
44, and 47. But the materials within the divisions are at times
so disparate that the pattern of arrangement is not clear. The first
three chapters deal with the Temple, its measurements, plan and
decoration, followed in 43.1–12 by its consecration, and the details
concerning the altar and its consecration (43.13ff.) The closing of
the outer east gate (44.1–5) symbolizes that the glory of Yahweh

will perpetually remain in the Temple, now to be central to restored Israel both geographically and spiritually.

With verse 5 the ordinances of Yahweh's Temple begin. First of all, admission to the Temple and its cult is detailed, more particularly as this concerns cultic personnel, i.e. Levites *v.* Zadokites. The chapter ends with various rules concerning priestly conduct and privileges.

Details concerning the cult might be expected to follow (the descriptions of various sacrifices do occur in 45.13–46.15), but, surprisingly, a summary statement about the allotment of the Holy Land first occurs (45.1–8) along with regulations dealing with weights and measures (verses 10–12). This summary of 48.8–22 has been placed here by the editor to correct any impression left by 44.28 that priests, though without possession in Israel, should be homeless; they are to dwell within the holy district.

The particular interest of the tradition concerning the provisions for sacrifices shown in 45.13–46.15 is the place of the **prince.** This gave rise to the placement of 46.16–18 after verse 15, since these deal with inheritance laws involving the prince. The chapter closes with a description of the Temple kitchens, made necessary by the sacrificial requirements of the Temple ordinances.

The end of the original vision begins the last part of the book. What the central place of the sanctuary is to mean for land and people is symbolized by the living waters flowing from the Temple eastwards. How the land is to be allotted in the ideal future is finally shown in 47.13 *ad fin.*, an ideal land with an ideal city with an ideal holy name (48.35).

The third division, chapters 33–39, constitutes a collection of oracles dealing with the promised restoration of Israel to Palestine. It may at one time, possibly together with chapters 40–48, have circulated as an independent collection, since it is prefaced by a statement on the nature of the prophet office. On the other hand, the editor of the book has so successfully incorporated it as part of the larger unit as to make this uncertain. Thus 33.1–20 is closely related to chapter 18, and 36.1–15 is the positive counterpart to chapter 6.

The restoration oracles themselves, chapters 34–39, evidence no

obvious arrangement. Chapter 34 deals with Yahweh's intention to
judge the wicked shepherds, verses 1–16, and with his distinction
between good and bad sheep, verses 17–31. Chapter 35 is a collection
of oracles against Edom probably placed immediately before 36.1–15
because 36.5 mentions Edom in particular as the object of Yahweh's
wrath. Edom had acted in vengeful fashion at the time of Judah's
misfortunes, and the restoration to favour of the mountains of
Israel, 36.1–15, must involve Edom's desolation. 36.16–38 presents an
overall theological statement explaining the rationale of the exile
and of the promised return as well as a description of the restoration.

The only vision in the division follows in 37.1–14; it is clearly
intended as a message of encouragement to the despairing exiles, but
why it should be placed immediately after 36.16–38 is not evident.
Since the promise in the vision concerns the whole house of Israel,
the symbolic act of 37.15–28, in which the two sticks symbolizing
the northern and southern kingdoms are joined as one, follows
naturally. More problematic is the next section, 38.1–39.20, but the
logic of the compiler seems clear. The enemy from the north had
been predicted by Jeremiah. This is here projected under the name
Gog, as still unrealized, into that future age. Gog will, however, be
completely defeated by God's restored people. This is part of
Yahweh's setting his glory among the nations (39.21). The concluding verses of the division restate in summary fashion Yahweh's
good intentions to restore Israel. It is evident that though a common
theme does obtain in chapters 33–39, no clear principle of arrangement can be fully traced.

The arrangement in the oracles against the nations, chapters 25–32,
is also largely formal rather than based on content. Chapters 29–32
contain the oracles against Egypt, whereas 26.1–28.19 are various
oracles against Tyre to which a separate oracle against Sidon has
been attached. These may at one time have been a separate collection
since a restoration oracle occurs at the end, 28.24–26. The division
begins with various oracles directed against Israel's more immediate
neighbours. It thus builds up to a climax progressing from the small
states and tribes surrounding Palestine to Phoenicia and finally to
Egypt, which to Israel symbolized uniquely the house of bondage.
Chapters 1–24 are a compendium of pre-586 materials, beginning

with a description of the inaugural vision in the first person and ending with the expected arrival of news that the city and Temple had fallen. The six dated sections naturally prejudge their ordering, but most of the sections are undated. These latter are chapters 6, 7, 13–19, 20.45–chapter 23 and 24.15–27. The concluding 24.15–27 describe a symbolic action which rendered concrete the immediate involvement and reaction of the exiles to the imminent disaster of Jerusalem's fall, and especially in view of the final two verses logically conclude the division.

The last dated oracle (cf. 24.1) refers to an allegory, a literary form not indigenous to prophecy. It is hardly accidental that most of chapters 15–23 also deals with literary types not native to the institution. Thus chapter 15 is an allegory as well; chapter 16 uses an old 'rags to riches' story as basis for a diatribe; chapter 17 uses an animal fable; chapter 18 begins with a *māšāl*; chapter 19 contains two dirges in allegorical form; 20.45–21.8 also interprets an allegory, and chapter 23 is an extended allegory. Chapter 22 is a diatribe on the bloody city and is thematically joined to chapter 23 which condemns the harlotrous city. 20.1–44 is presented in oracular form, but is none the less unusual. The elders gather to inquire of Yahweh. But instead of an oracle the prophet is told to **let them know the abominations of their fathers.** The theological review of Israel's history which follows is unique and it is not surprising that the compiler placed it in this part of the collection. Thus the arrangement of chapters 15–24 appears to have been made on formal grounds.

The undated sections in chapters 1–14 comprise chapters 6, 7, 12–14 and there is no discernible pattern of arrangement. All centre in the theme of judgment, and cluster about the vision of Temple idolatry in chapters 8–11. Certain parallels may be drawn to sections in chapters 33–39. Chapter 6 is addressed to the mountains of Israel and finds its counterpart in 36.1–15. Chapter 7 proclaims the coming of the end and rather vaguely parallels the promise of restoration in 36.16–38. Chapter 12 details actions symbolizing the coming exile and the certainty of its coming which might find its positive counterpart in the symbol of the joining of two sticks in 37.15–28. Chapter 13 is a collection of oracles against false prophets which is later paralleled in 34.1–16, a judgment on wicked shepherds, whereas chapter 14

deals with religious syncretists and the assurance that only the wicked
will be punished, which reminds one of a similar distinction made
in 34.17–31. Whether these are intentional parallels may seem
dubious.

It is clear, however, that not only do the divisions of the book
give evidence of literary arrangement, but that a single mind
imposed some pattern (largely formal) on the book as a whole as
well. This is especially evident from the relations between the vision
account of chapters 8–11 and that of chapters 40–48. The former
describes the departure of the glory of Yahweh from the Jerusalem
Temple eastwards and the destruction which that departure entails.
The latter shows the glory of Yahweh re-entering the ideal Temple
of the coming restoration from the east, followed by the closing
of the gate of entry, thereby showing that Yahweh will never again
leave his people.

(c) *Outline of Contents*

FIRST SECTION. CHAPTERS 1–24 PROPHECIES OF JUDGMENT
A. **1.1–3.15.** *Ezekiel's inaugural vision and prophetic call.*
(a) **1.1–28.** The vision of the glory of Yahweh.
(b) **2.1–3.11.** The commission.
(c) **3.12–15.** The end of the vision.
B. **3.16–27.** *Editorial expansions on the commission.*
C. **4.1–5.4.** *Prophetic actions.*
D. **5.4b–17.** *Commentary on the prophetic actions.*
E. **6.1–14.** *The mountains of Israel addressed.*
(a) **6.1–7.** The mountains of Israel.
(b) **6.8–10.** A remnant will remember.
(c) **6.11–14.** Alas for Israel.
F. **7.1–27.** *The end has come.*
(a) **7.1–4.** Poem A.
(b) **7.5–9.** A parallel version.
(c) **7.10–27.** Poem B.
G. **8.1–11.25.** *A vision of temple idolatry.*
(a) **8.1–4.** Ecstatic transport to the Jerusalem Temple.
(b) **8.5–18.** Visions of cultic abominations.
  i **8.5–6.** The image of jealousy.

2. THE NATURE OF PROPHECY

(a) *Oral character*

From Part I it might be concluded that the Book of Ezekiel is a purely literary product. Indeed, the book does show the impress of a logical mind intent on a literary production.

Prophets, however, were not writers in the study, but rather impassioned speakers in the market-places, and Ezekiel was no exception. The word of Yahweh which came to him was oral. The introductory oracle formula is 'Thus *says* Yahweh'. The prophet is told to **prophesy . . . say** (6.2–3; 13.2; 34.2; 36.1), **speak . . . say** (14.4; 20.3; 33.2), **propound a riddle . . . speak an allegory . . . say** (17.2–3), **Say now** (17.12), **take up a lamentation . . . say** (19.1–2), **preach . . . prophesy** (20.46; 21.2), **declare to . . . say** (22.2–3), **set your face (against), prophesy, say** (25.2–3; 29.2–3; 35.2–3; 38.2–3), **raise a lamentation . . . and say** (27.2–3; 28.12; 32.2). Once he was told to write the name of the day (24.2), but this was simply to give occasion for uttering an allegory (24.3). On another occasion (37.15–16) he is told to write on two sticks and join them, but this was to make graphic the oracle accompanying the action (cf. 37.19ff.). In 21.18–23 the prophet symbolizes Nebuchadrezzar's coming against Jerusalem by drawing a parting of the ways, probably in the sand, with signposts pointing the ways to Rabbah and to Jerusalem. It is obvious that writing is completely subsidiary to the prophetic office, is in fact irrelevant to it.

Ezekiel did not differ in this respect from the earlier prophets. Like his earlier contemporary, Jeremiah, he may have had a scribe to record some of his sayings—dated oracles would certainly give that impression—but such records would only be resorted to as aids to memory. The spoken word remained primary until the end of the prophetic movement in the late postexilic age.

(b) *Visions*

Four sections of the book are described in the commentary as visions: the inaugural vision in 1.1–3.15, the vision of the abominations in chapter 8–11, the vision of the revivified dry bones in chapter 37, and that of the new Temple in chapter 40–48. It seems likely that 11.1–13 is a separate vision paralleling chapter 8 (cf. commentary, p. 92). Materially these represent four critical points in the prophet's life and thought: the first forms the basis for his prophetic work since it was his call experience; the second (including that of 11.1–13) epitomizes the message of doom prophecy before 586 B.C.; the third lies at the heart of the immediately post-586 restoration prophecy; and the final one records the prophet's dreams for the future age.

These visions are all ecstatic visions. Each is introduced by the technical phrase 'the hand of Yahweh was upon me', describing entrance into the trance state, whereas the technical term for ecstasy as such is 'visions of God'. Unlike Isaiah's vision in Isaiah 21, which records the nightmarish reactions of the prophet (cf. also Hab. 3.16), there is no hint of any personal response on the part of Ezekiel (but see 11.13).

The vision has certain points in common with the dream state. In both the categories of time and space are voided. Ezekiel, though physically in Babylon, is suddenly in Jerusalem, or on a very high mountain (40.2) or in the midst of the valley (37.1). In both, scenes can change rapidly and illogically. Thus in the vision of abominations after the people of Jerusalem are slaughtered by the swords of the angelic executioners, the angelic scribe takes fire from the altar in order once again to destroy the city (chapters 9–10). Time categories are shortened so that the moment doom is prophesied it is brought to pass in the case of Pelatiah (11.13). In the vision of the new Temple the heavenly guide leads the prophet through the Temple complex stopping to measure everything in detail. Physically this would have taken considerable time, but in a vision this might be as in the dream a momentary experience.

The vision is, however, not to be equated with the dream. The vision experience includes awareness of entrance to and departure from the ecstatic state (cf. 8.1 with 11.24b). Furthermore, the vision state did not occur during sleep but **as I sat in my house, with the elders of Judah sitting before me** (8.1).

It should also be noted that the vision is closely related to the prophetic office. Except for the final vision which in essence is somewhat distinct from the others (cf. the Medinah with the earlier Meccan utterances of Muḥammad), each vision account contains relevant interpretative oracles which are intended to convey some divine message to the prophet and/or the audience. The inaugural vision only becomes meaningful through the call to service in 2.1–3.11. The vision of abominations becomes a means of communication through the intermittent dialogue in chapter 8–9, whereas the parallel 11.1–13 contains a lengthy oracle in verses 5–12. Similarly the vision of the dry bones in chapter 37 becomes a relevant message to the exiles through the concluding interpretation in verses 11–14.

The vision thus normally contains dialogue. Whether such dialogue between God and prophet is automatically part of the vision experience or is a later reflection on its meaning is not always clear, since a purely visual vision is certainly possible (as in chapter 1 as distinct from 2.1–3.15, or as in chapters 40ff.). But even the somewhat literary and artificial vision of the new Temple contains an auditory direction to the entranced prophet to communicate what he is seeing in turn to the house of Israel (40.4).

In fact, this passage portrays the way in which the vision became a prophetic revelation. The vision is an individual experience but its telling is a prophetic revelation. At the end of the vision of abominations the prophet states **I told the exiles all the things that the LORD had showed me** (11.25). Whether he similarly told the exiles about the inaugural vision (cf. 3.15) or simply his immediate disciples is not known.

(c) *Symbolic actions*

Prophetic messages may be communicated by means of some dramatic action to render the import of the message more concrete. Symbolic acts on the part of prophets are attested from earliest times. Such acts were often sufficiently bizarre to call special attention to them on the part of the audience, and though often accompanied by interpretative oracles were normally perfectly clear as to their meaning.

Such actions being divinely ordered were effective actions. When Ezekiel acted out successively the raising of a siege against Jerusalem, the famine conditions in the city, and the disastrous outcome of the siege (4.1–5.4), it served as a divine word and was equally effective. Of particular importance to their effectiveness is the prophetic awareness of being ordered by Yahweh to act out the drama, cf. 4.1–3, 9–12; 5.1–4; 12.3–6, 18; 21.19–20; 24.16–17; 37.16–17.

Since all the dramatic prophetic actions in Ezekiel concern future events, their accounts lost some of their relevancy after the events actually took place, and details of interpretation either in the light of the events or of later history were often added. The result is sometimes bizarre. Thus to a simple action depicting the siege of a city on a 'brick' in 4.1–3 were added interpretations concerning the length of the exile for the two kingdoms. The result is confusion, with the prophet seen lying on his left side for 390 days and then on his right side for another forty, an impossible feat in view of the second stage of the drama in 4.9–12. Similarly in 12.2–16 later events changed the account of the original symbolic act. The prophet had been ordered to prepare an exile's baggage and carry it out at dusk as a symbol of what was shortly to happen to the inhabitants of Jerusalem. When the city actually fell Zedekiah tried to escape from the falling city, was captured, blinded and taken in chains to Babylon. These details were added to the account with the result that in the final tradition there is a mixture of details applying to exiles in general and to 'the prince in Jerusalem' in particular. For details of analysis cf. commentary, p. 99.

To serve as effective warnings such actions were often highly unusual. When Ezekiel's wife suddenly dies he is ordered to engage in no mourning rites whatsoever, contrary to custom (24.16–17). Naturally this caused comment and the prophet explains with telling effect that this action typifies conditions soon to obtain when the sanctuary falls and their sons and daughters are killed by the sword (verses 19–24). Ezekiel thus becomes **a sign** to them (verse 24*a*). The action of shaving the hair from head and beard (5.1–2) and dividing it into three parts, one to be burned, one to be hacked by the sword, and one to be scattered to the wind, depicted the outcome of the coming siege far more impressively to the prophet's audience than any words of his might have done.

Usually such symbolic acts were, however, accompanied by an interpretative oracle. When Ezekiel took two sticks, one labelled **For Judah** and another **For Joseph** and joined them together into one stick (37.16–17), he explains the meaning of the act by means of an oracle of restoration (verses 19–22). In 21.18–23 the distinction between act and oracle is not formally made, but it is clear that verses 19–20 describe the action to be performed by the prophet and verses 21–23 explain its meaning. Even when the act originally stood by itself as a clear message, later traditionists would make extensive commentary on it, as 5.4*b*–17 shows.

(d) *Prophetic speech*

Though the symbolic act could occasionally be used with extraordinary effect, the spoken word or 'oracle' remained the common means of prophetic communication. Even the symbolic act was prophetically considered to be 'the word of Yahweh'. This is proven by the fact that all literary sections in the book except accounts of visions are introduced by the formulaic 'The *word* of Yahweh came to me'. Oracles are further introduced by the introductory formula 'Thus says Yahweh'. The oracle normally is also formulaically concluded throughout the book. These are of three kinds: the oracle conclusion 'says Yahweh', the affirmation formula 'I, Yahweh, have (spoken)', or the recognition formula 'And you/ they shall know that I am Yahweh'.

Mowinckel in *Prophecy and Tradition* (pp. 46–47) has convincingly shown that the oracle indigenous to prophecy is essentially of two kinds: prediction and command. These in turn may also contain a motivation motif of some kind. The prediction may be causally conditioned, and the command may contain a threat (i.e. a 'Do this lest . . .' type of command), or a motivation (i.e. a 'Do this and you shall . . .' type).

In the realization of these two primitive types, various types of oracles occur in Ezekiel. Often the true oracle incorporates some other literary form not indigenous to prophecy but used by the prophet to render his message more effective. And finally non-prophetic forms are used in non-oracular contexts and can therefore not be called prophecy.

1. Oracular forms are varied; the commentary distinguishes judgment and restoration oracles, commands, disputations, demonstration oracles, situation oracles, recitals, diatribes and woe oracles.

The *judgment oracle* commonly begins with **Behold I, even I,** and continues either with 'am against . . .' or with the future active verb, which tense is then usually sustained throughout the oracle. Illustrative of the former is 21.3–5 (ending with an affirmation formula), and of the latter, 6.3*b*–7 (ending with a recognition formula). These illustrate the simple prediction oracle basic to the institution of prophecy. The term 'judgment' oracle is of course prejudicial of the content, since oracles of promise, *restoration oracles* in the commentary, are formally exactly the same type. In fact 36.9–12 is introduced by the same formula as the former judgment type: 'Behold I am for you,' now rendering *'l* as 'for' rather than 'against' as elsewhere. An example of a simple restoration oracle parallel to the second type described above is 34.11–15.

Commands in Ezekiel are seldom found within the oracles themselves (as in 21.6), but usually occur prior to the oracle and introductory to it. These are normally orders to the prophet to prophesy. In judgment prophecies they commonly begin with the vocative 'Son of man' and continue with the idiom 'set your face towards . . . (and prophesy . . .) and say' (6.2–3; 20.46–47; 21.2–3; 25.2–3; 29.2–3; 35.2–3; 38.2–3). Other instances of commands are the divine impulses to perform symbolic acts (cf. Part 2 (c) above, pp. 14f.).

The most common type of oracle in Ezekiel is the prediction (usually of judgment) along with a motivation preceding it. This is the *demonstration oracle*. Examples may be found in 13.8–9, 10–16, 22–23; 16.36–42, 43; 25.3–5, 6–7, 8–11, 12–14, 15–17; 26.1–6; 28.2–10; 29.6b–9a, 9b–12; 35.5–9, 10–12 and 36.2–7. Such oracles begin with a 'Because' clause and end with a 'therefore' statement. The former contains the reason for the judgment, i.e. the castigation giving rise to and basic to the judgment. The latter may be amplified by an introductory oracle formula; it is then a complete oracle in itself.

The castigation can also stand alone as a prophetic *diatribe* or *invective*. Two such are found in 16.44–52 and 22.3–12. In these the object of the invective is scathingly denounced but no actual judgment oracle as a 'therefore' clause obtains. It is a statement of condemnation by itself which statement is itself an unexpressed judgment. In the former no formal introduction or conclusion formulae occur, but the latter example has both. Another diatribe occurs at 22.24–30, but this is followed by a 'therefore' clause. It is not a true demonstration oracle since the 'therefore' clause is in past tense rather than a prediction of judgment, nor is the 'therefore' judgment formulaically introduced; it is a typical invective. Invectives are statements of present condition or in past tense and may issue in an imperative; cf. 16.52.

A related type is the *woe oracle*, of which 13.3–7, 18–19 and 34.2–6 are examples. This is a technical form of prophetic invective introduced by 'Woe to . . .' and usually involves some societal class— in the above examples, false prophets, prophetesses and wicked shepherds of Israel, respectively. Like the diatribe they are descriptive and normally in past tense.

The *recital*, like the diatribe, is not necessarily marked by oracle formulae, though they may occur. They are formally, however, quite distinct in that the diatribe is an oral castigation of wrong whereas a recital details past judgments of Yahweh, and are thus hortatory in character. In 36.16–21 the recital contrasts Yahweh's judgments on Israel by means of the exile (due, of course, to Israel's sins) with the present exilic condition, which condition constituted a profanation of the holy name. The recital then becomes the occasion for the following restoration oracle. The recital itself contains no oracular formulae, unlike 20.3–26. Here the recital is enjoined by 'let them know the abominations of their fathers' (verse 4) and the recital which follows is both formulaically introduced and concluded; it details Yahweh's relations with his sinful people in pre-Canaan days. It should be noted that the recital here too issues in two 'therefore' statements, verses 27–29 and verses 30–31 (only the second being relevant to the occasion for the recital; cf. verses 1–4*a*).

The recital in 20.3–26 was a response to a particular situation to which the prophet reacted and reminds one of the *situation oracle*. In the latter some general situation is first given and an oracle of some kind pertaining to the situation follows as a solution to the inherent problem. In 14.1–3 the general situation is given as the coming of idolatrous elders to seek an oracle from Yahweh through the prophet. In the oracle that follows in verses 4–5 and 7 (verse 6 is a later accretion) gives the solution. In 29.18 the situation is one in which Nebuchadrezzar had worked as Yahweh's instrument against Tyre for years without success. The oracle that follows in verses 19–20 promises divine compensation for the unpaid king through Egyptian spoil. A similar situation plus oracle obtains in 22.17–22. The present form of 30.21–26 is related to this same type, but this is due to an editorial union of two originally distinct oracles; for details cf. commentary, pp. 232f.

A final oracular form is the *disputation oracle*. The disputation sets forth some popular proverb which is then disputed by an oracle or an extended discourse. In 33.24 the false claim of those who remained in Judah to the land is quoted, and verses 25–29, formulaically introduced, refute this in two stages. Verses 25–26 refute the claim on moral grounds, and verses 27–29 refute it absolutely by a judgment oracle. In 12.22 a popular saying is quoted suggesting that prophecy is ineffective. This is refuted by a relevant oracle (verses 23–25) predicting the imminent fulfilment of Yahweh's word. Verses 26–28 are a parallel disputation in similar terms. Chapter 18 represents a longer and more complex form of disputation. Again a popular proverb is cited and then refuted, but in a lengthy argument setting forth the principle of personal responsibility as illustrated by a variety of individual cases. For the possible origin of this type of argument in Israel's cult, cf. commentary, pp. 139ff.

2. Borrowed types used in oracles. Oracles of prediction and command were native to prophecy but literary forms from other realms of life were often adapted to the oracular form. The adaptation might be extremely slight or intimately subject to the oracular form. The *lament* in chapter 19 has no oracle formulae whatsoever; the prophet is simply told to take up a lamentation. On the other hand, a borrowed type can be used as the basis for an oracle.

An example of the reverse, i.e. the adaptation of the oracle to the borrowed form, occurs in 14.13–23. The oracle is a justification of Yahweh's acts of judgment against Jerusalem (verses 21–23; verses 22–23a are, however, later accretions). Formally it is neither a command nor a prediction, though it is introduced as an oracle and ends with recognition and conclusion formulae. Verses 13–20 constitute a *legal peroration* on divine justice put into the form of casuistic law, and dictates the form of the oracle in verse 21.

Effective use is sometimes made of secular *poems* by the prophet. The difficult sword song in 21.9–17 is one such. It consists of two strophes, the first describing the keenness and glitter of the sword, and the second, its destructive potential. Though the original poem has received a number of accretions and its text is corrupt (cf. commentary, pp. 164ff), the adaptation of the poem as an oracle is still clear. The poem is introduced by an introduction formula and concluded by an affirmation formula. It is then prophetically adapted as a judgment oracle, i.e. a divine judgment, by the addition of verse 17.

Another poem taken from secular life and adapted to prophetic use is found in 24.3b–5. It is a poem from the kitchen, calling on the cook to put on the pot, fill it with water, put in the mutton and boil it well. This poem is then used as a *māšāl*, **allegory,** or extended simile (cf. commentary on chapter 17 and 12.22). The poem is then allegorically applied to the Jerusalem situation. Yahweh will stoke the fire and boil the inhabitants of Jerusalem. Unfortunately later traditionists confused the poem and its interpretation (verses 3*b*–5, 9–10) with another allegory and its interpretation, in which the city is compared to a rusty pot in the form of a woe oracle (verses 6f., 11).

Still another poem borrowed by and adapted by the prophet is found in 31.3–9, a poem describing the downfall of the cosmic tree and originally used in the cult. The myth is obviously related to the tree of life in the Garden of Eden tradition (for the original text of verse 3, cf. commentary, p. 235). It was then ironically adapted to the pretentious Pharaoh and his multitude by prefacing the poem by the query **Whom are you like in your greatness?** A prose oracle (verses 10–13) applies the poem allegorically. The oracle is, however, without a concluding formula.

In fact Ezekiel is extremely fond of the *māšāl* form. These *mᵉšālîm*, 'similes', are of different types, animal and plant stories, fables, allegories, but all are in some way applied to the contemporary situation. Chapter 15 is an allegory setting forth first of all the uselessness of the wood of the vine and then the even greater uselessness of the partially charred vine. Verses 6–8 in proper oracular form then apply the second part of the allegory to the already decimated Jerusalem populace. In chapter 16 the prophet uses an old story of a foundling cared for by a prince. When she is mature he marries her and decks her with riches (verses 4–14), but she becomes a wilful harlot (verses 15–25). The story is adapted to the Jerusalem situation throughout by the use of the second person. The narrative is initially defined as in chapter 20 as a 'making known her abominations'. The allegorized fable is then introduced as an oracle. The story is thereafter fully applied by means of a demonstration oracle (verses 35–43). The text of chapter 16 (cf. commentary) is strongly influenced by chapter 23 which is a true allegory. The two kingdoms are here portrayed as two harlot sisters whose harlotries symbolize various political intrigues and alliances. Unlike most allegories this one is not interpreted but issues in a judgment oracle (verses 22–27), though without formal conclusion.

The adaptation of the *māšāl* in chapter 17 is somewhat more complex. The fable about two great eagles, a cedar and a vine (verses 3–9) is identified as an allegory (*māšāl*) and a **riddle** (cf.

commentary) but introduced as an oracle. Verse 9 is an adaptation of the fable but within terms of the fable itself. The fable is then succeeded by a new word of Yahweh (verses 11–15; verses 16–18 are secondary), which interprets the fable in terms of Zedekiah's perfidy. The interpretation is then succeeded by an oracle of judgment on the prince.

The *lament* or *dirge* is a well-defined type of poem in direct address and past time. Usually the second hemistich of each line is shorter than the first. A number of these obtain in Ezekiel, but their adaptation to the oracular form is superficial and often completely abandoned. They are usually identified as a *kînāh*—**lamentation.** One such is placed within an oracle against Tyre (26.15–18). The oracle is introduced by a formula and predicts that a lamentation will be raised, which then follows in verses 17–18 but without conclusion formula. That the lament is quite foreign to prophecy is evident from the total lack of conclusion formulae in all the laments in the book.

32.1–16 is defined in verse 16 as a lament, but the designation is correct only for verse 2, which is followed by a complete oracle of judgment (verses 3–8). Two long laments against Tyre obtain in chapter 27 and 28.11–19. Both are introduced by an unnecessary introduction formula (contrast 32.1–2 and 19.1). Chapter 19 is a lament for the two exiled princes of Israel; in fact the chapter has two laments, verses 2–9 and verses 10–14. These laments are unusual in that they are in allegorical form; cf. commentary. The lament is taken from the context of political life; in Ezekiel they mourn the downfall or passing of Pharaoh, the king of Tyre, the Tyrian state, and the exiled Judean princes. It should be said that the dirge in chapter 27 has a *commercial document*, listing the customers of Tyre and their wares, inserted between the two parts of the dirge (verses 12–25a) which is of course not part of a lament. Its origin is unknown; it is hardly original with Ezekiel.

Somewhat related in content but distinct in form to the lament is the *wailing*, of which 32.18–28 (verses 29–32 are accretions) is the only attested example in the O.T. Whereas the lament is in the second person, the wailing refers to the departed in the third person. The type may find its origins in the wailing for the dead. Unfortunately the text has been badly preserved; for a suggested analysis, cf. commentary, pp. 244ff.

3. Non-prophetic writings. Actually the *lament* and the *wailing* are both non-prophetic forms, though the former was sometimes introduced by an oracle formula, and the accretions to the wailing (32.31–32) contain conclusion formulae. Other types of writing quite unrelated to prophecy but found in the book are *commercial documents* (mentioned above), *historical narratives* (33.21–22), and in chapters 40–48 various types of *laws, normative sacrifices, priestly regulations, architectural designs*, and pseudo-*geographical descriptions*. Since these latter are all in the context of a plan for a cultic Utopia which are not prophetic in origin or character they are only listed here.

3. FROM THE PROPHET TO THE BOOK

From Parts 1 and 2 it will appear that the work of the prophet Ezekiel cannot simply be equated with the book of Ezekiel. The book is a carefully arranged collection of materials which represents the end product of a long tradition which began with the words spoken by the prophet.

The manner in which the books of the prophets were collected and codified has been admirably presented in Mowinckel's *Prophecy and Tradition*. As insisted on in Part 2 (a) above (pp. 11ff.), the prophets themselves were speakers not writers. The sayings of the prophets were remembered and passed on by the disciples of the prophets during an indeterminate oral stage of tradition history. These sayings were however not passed on as immutable holy givens but as relevant messages, which meant that the original sayings were often modified by explanatory phrases or even by the addition of new sayings amplifying, changing or correcting the original.

Such an oral stage of traditional growth need not have been unilinear; that is to say, various collections of the sayings of a prophet may have been in existence at the same time. The presence of so-called doublet versions in Ezekiel (which Kraetzschmar tried to explain as two literary versions woven together) is probably best explained in this way.

Eventually these sayings would be collected in some literary form, but such collections were not made to create a final version in book form but rather as aids to memory. An editor was in the end responsible for the general arrangement of the materials. In some cases such an editor worked with earlier partial compilations; in others the inner arrangement of the entire book was his responsibility. But even with the product of the final editor the history of tradition did not end. Literary accretions by the scribes who recopied the work enlarged it, as the shorter text of G. amply attests for Ezekiel. Only when the work is fully accepted as canon does its text become sacrosanct, and copyist changes after such times are unintended errors.

(a) *Time and place of Ezekiel*

The fountain head or father of any prophetic book is the original prophet. Biographical information about Ezekiel is sparse, but the time and place of the prophet are clearly given. He was of priestly descent and his priestly interests are evident throughout the book. He was, however, first of all a prophet in the classical tradition. Since a number of his prophecies are dated, including his inaugural vision, it appears that he began his work in 593 B.C. and continued until at least 571 B.C., the date of his last dated prophecy (29.17). These traditional dates have occasionally been challenged (e.g. by Zunz, Seinecke, Winckler, Smith, Berry, Torrey, Burrows, Messel), but these contrary views have received little support. The evidence for the approximate correctness of the traditional date for Ezekiel's work seems overwhelming. The situations portrayed for chapters 1–24 fit the last years of Jerusalem's existence better than do any other period. Jerusalem is still standing, but its imminent fall is predicted. Some are already in exile (i.e. the 597 B.C. deportation), and the prophet expects the complete end to Judah's political existence shortly. Clear references to the final rulers of Judah (Jehoahaz, Jehoiachin and Zedekiah) presuppose the traditional dates. The oracles against the nations also fit into this traditional pattern. The siege of Tyre by Nebuchadrezzar, reference to Egypt's fence-sitting propensities, the failure to take Tyre, all these are relevant precisely to the assigned period. The post-586 B.C. materials all presuppose the exilic situation, and the restoration prophecies were relevant particularly before the return. Even the idealistic cult of the future is basically sixth century in origin, since there is no proven influence of the actual Zerubbabel Temple on chapters 40–48. Accordingly the commentary is based on the acceptance of 593–571 B.C. as the dates of Ezekiel's work.

Not as easily disposed of is the problem of the place of the prophet's ministry. Again the traditional picture is straightforward; the prophet as part of the 597 B.C. deportation lived and prophesied in exile, **in the land of the Chaldeans by the river Chebar** (1.3), **at Tel-abib** (3.15). All his prophecies are thus Babylonian in origin.

This traditional picture has been vigorously attacked (especially by Herntrich, but cf. also Bertholet[2] and Matthews). It is alleged that the prophecies of chapters 1–24 have relevance only in a Jerusalem setting and that like Jeremiah, Ezekiel was a Jerusalem prophet. (Variants of this position are that Ezekiel lived in a town near the capital or that he was a Jerusalem prophet up to the fall of Jerusalem in 586 B.C. and was then exiled.) All reference to a Babylonian setting are the work of Babylonian redactors. Herntrich maintains *inter alia* that none of chapters 25–32 and 40–48 is the work of Ezekiel. Similarly the vision of the glory of Yahweh in chapter 1 is secondary. Reference in 8.1–4 and 11.24–25 to ecstatic transport is all secondary as well as all of chapters 9 and 10. Naturally the references in 24.26–27 and 33.21–22 to news of Jerusalem's fall coming to Babylon are considered unoriginal; in short every reference to an exilic background is denied to Ezekiel.

Though all this might seem highly arbitrary Herntrich has strong reasons for his point of view. Many of the oracles of chapters 1–24 are relevant to Jerusalem and Judah rather than to the exiles. The symbolic acts, the denunciations of Jerusalem and Judah and of the mountains of Israel, pertain to the situation in Palestine rather than to Babylon. In fact, in chapter 16 the prophet is told to **make known to Jerusalem her abominations,** which seems odd for a prophet in exile (cf. also 21.2, 6). Again and again prophecies are directed to 'the house of Israel', which is called a 'rebellious house'. The most natural meaning of the term would be the inhabitants of Palestine. After all, in contrast to those remaining, the exiles were good figs according to Jer. 24. Furthermore Ezekiel betrays an intimate acquaintance with what is going on in the Temple in chapters 8–11. And finally chapter 11 from a Babylonian setting would demand clairvoyant powers on Ezekiel's part which would be unnecessary if he were physically present in Jerusalem.

None the less the position in this commentary, is taken that the traditional setting is historically correct. Chapter 11 does not demand powers of second sight on Ezekiel's part at all. The statement in verse 13 that Pelatiah died immediately in response to the oracle is itself part of a visionary experience; visions are not to be confused with history. The intimate knowledge of conditions in Jerusalem does seem puzzling, but contacts between Babylon and Jerusalem and consequent news of Jerusalem events in Babylon were possible. The Book of Jeremiah mentions correspondence between the areas precisely during this decade. Ezekiel, due to his priestly background, would have had vivid recollection of the Temple structure and cult.

Furthermore, though the hopes of Israel's future were centred on the exiles, the exiles considered themselves part of the house of Israel. The principle of the solidarity of the people was firmly rooted in Hebrew thought. Corporately they were part of the rebellious house. As a matter of fact little is known of the religious and ethical sensibilities of the 597 exiles apart from the Jer. 24 reference (which is, however, addressed to Jerusalem). But if the tradition given in Ezekiel as to the place of Ezekiel's ministry be accepted, a great deal of information does obtain. It is reasoning in a circle to say that denunciations of those who come to enquire of Yahweh must refer to Jerusalem elders, since the materials do not apply to a Babylonian situation, when the information concerning conditions in the latter rest solely on the materials which are being dealt with. In a sense the exiles considered themselves still part of Jerusalem society, and invectives against the society are far from meaningless to an audience which optimistically expected to rejoin that society physically in short order.

Nor is it correct to maintain that a message directed to a society demands the physical presence of the prophet. No one would suggest that oracles against the nations in Isaiah, Jeremiah and Ezekiel imply long journeys throughout the Near East on the part of the prophets concerned. These oracles affected Israel as a whole and were never sent to those nations. Even though one or two prophecies are directed to Jerusalem and Judah, this does not mean that Ezekiel was actually there.

The position of Herntrich and his followers raises far more difficulties than it solves. When major parts of the book are denied the original prophet, not on internal grounds, but because they do not fit a radical theory, serious doubts about that theory should be raised. If the difficulties which are to be met by such a theory can be solved in some other way, that is usually to be preferred.

(b) *The oral tradition*

The position is taken throughout the commentary that the original words of the prophet were passed on orally by the school of Ezekiel. In the course of this transmission the oral text grew by accretion. Though accretions in the oral stage cannot often with confidence be distinguished from those that are literary, some probably can. Thus the addition of a restoration oracle or statement to an oracle of judgment is probably oral. When oracles predicting ruin for Jerusalem became obsolete by the events of 586 B.C., the tendency existed to bring such judgments up to date either by an amelioration of the judgment in the light of later events or by a restoration statement giving hope to the contemporary audience. An example of the former appears in 14.22–23a. Thematically Ezekiel states in terms of casuistic law that only the righteous shall escape the coming judgment. Such ancient heroes of righteousness as Noah, Daniel and Job would by their intercession be able to save no one but themselves. The matter is then made relevant to the Jerusalem situation, a city totally wicked, by an oracle stating that judgment on it will quite rightly cut off from it man and beast. But not all the inhabitants were cut off in 586 B.C., and the school of Ezekiel 'corrected' the oracle by means of an exceptive clause.

Oral accretions can also be noted in connection with symbolic actions. A good illustration may be found in 12.1–16. The original action was fairly straightforward. Ezekiel acts out the going into exile. When asked what this means, he states that this is symbolic of their future. But the fact is that two answers are given to the question in verse 9 (verses 10 and 11)—the later tradition (verse 10) applies the action to Zedekiah. Once the exile had taken place details concerning Zedekiah's fate were known; he fled by night through a break in the city wall but was captured, blinded by Nebuchadrezzar at Riblah and taken captive in chains to Babylon. These later events were then added by the school of Ezekiel both to the interpretation (verses 12–14) and to the action prescribed. Thus verse 5 and the references in verses 6–7 to darkness, covering the face, not seeing the land and digging through the wall are a second layer of tradition bringing the original account up to date.

Another such is the account in 4.1–5.4a. The original drama consisted of three acts portraying in succession the miniature picture of a city besieged, the famine rations at the height of the siege, and finally the grim outcome of the siege. The manner in which oral traditions accrue to an original simple statement can be seen by examining the text of the first act. The original action is depicted in verses 1–2. Ezekiel is to take a mud brick and portray a city on it. Then miniature siege-works and camps are to be built around it. This was obviously meant to represent what was shortly to happen to Jerusalem. Verse 3 adds to this the placing of an iron plate between the prophet and the city. This represents a second stage of tradition quite alien to the original, viz. Ezekiel's intransigent attitude towards Jerusalem. If this comes from Ezekiel it was added later; it is more likely to be a later reflection of the school of Ezekiel. For the literary character of verses 4–8, cf. commentary, p. 59.

The second action is equally clear. The original action is described in verses 9a, 10–11 (verse 9b is a literary accretion based on verses 4–8). The point of the action is again obvious. During the siege people will scurry for grain in order to alleviate their hunger, and water will also be under ration. But these conditions were no longer of interest or relevance after 586 B.C. Later traditionists were more concerned about exilic conditions, more particularly its ritual uncleanness; thus verses 12–15 add materials more relevant to the later scene.

The last action is found in 5.1–2. Ezekiel's shorn hair is dispersed in

three parts: by fire, sword and wind. To Ezekiel this symbolized
the complete destruction of the citizens of the city. But events
proved otherwise and not all were killed. So the school of Ezekiel
'corrected' the action by the addition of verse 3—a few were to be
saved. A still later stage is reflected by verse 4a, which depicts the
fate of the saved few.

(c) *Literary stage of tradition history*

It is impossible to determine when the prophetic traditions were
first written. There is abundant evidence, however, for literary
accretions. Levels of literary accretion can often be identified by a
scramble in number, gender and/or person. In the superscription
to the inaugural vision (1.1–3), the original account was told in the
1st person; since the cryptic **thirtieth year** of verse 1 needed
clarification, another statement in the 3rd person was added to make
it all intelligible (verses 2–3a).

Change in gender often indicates literary accretions. Thus in
1.4–14, where the living creatures of the vision are being described,
references should be feminine since *ḥywt* is feminine. Masculine
references are later levels; accordingly verses 7–8 and much of
verses 10–11 can be taken as a later tradition (for details, cf. commentary, pp. 41f.). In the commentary on the symbolic acts of 4.1–5.4
(5.4b–12) different levels of tradition can be identified by the change
in number, gender and person. Probably the earliest materials are in
the singular; verses 5–6a are the invective in 3rd feminine singular
and verses 8–12 are the judgment in 2nd feminine singular. Verse 6b
is a later accretion, since it is in 3rd plural, and so is verse 7 which is
in 2nd masculine plural.

A similar case is to be found in 6.1–7. The original oracle is a
judgment oracle. It is of course in the first person—Yahweh himself
will destroy. Verse 4a ill fits its context since its verbs are passive,
as are those of verses 6–7a. These passages constitute a later literary
accretion.

(d) *The editor*

The next stage in the history of tradition is the work of the editor
who collected the traditions and ordered them along the lines

described in Part 1 above. The discussion there led to the conclusion that a single individual must have been responsible rather than an editorial school.

But the editor was more than a collector and arranger of materials. His work also represents a level of tradition. In the process of arrangement, traditions had to be amplified and changed to fit the editor's conception of the book. This can sometimes be identified by a failure to understand the intent of a tradition. For example, in the account of the arrival in Babylon of news of Jerusalem's fall in 33.21–22 it is stated that Ezekiel had been in a trance involving dumbness the preceding evening; the dumbness had passed by the time the news arrived. Another tradition interpreted the dumbness as a long period which had been predicted (24.25–27). The editor used this to conclude the first division, inserting chapters 25–32 between the two accounts, which at an earlier stage had probably been together. The editor further tied these accounts to that of the commission to prophesy by the addition of 3.24b–27 in which the commission is changed to one of perpetual dumbness—because Israel is a rebellious house. The result is certainly far from the original account.

Again the hand of the editor is clear in 3.16b–21. The collection of restoration prophecies in chapters 33ff. began with a statement on the prophetic office under the symbol of a watchman on the city wall whose duty was to warn the city against imminent attack. The original commission (2.1–3.11) of the inaugural vision had been a commission to play the role of doom prophet (cf. the call of Isaiah in chapter 6 and of Jeremiah in chapter 1). The editor apparently felt this to be an incomplete description of Ezekiel's function as prophet and included a florilegium of quotations from chapter 33.

(e) *The scribal period*

There is no certainty whatsoever as to the time of the editors' activity, though it is likely that he was active in exile rather than in post-exilic Judah. Since there is no evidence that the traditions represented in chapters 33–48 show any awareness of the post-exilic Temple or of the conditions in Judah after the return, it would seem likely that he did his work before the end of the sixth century.

The formation of a book of Ezekiel did not however end the growth of tradition. This becomes apparent on comparing the ancient versions with MT. The text of G. is usually shorter, but often attests an earlier stage in the history of tradition. V. and S. are too late to constitute evidence for tradition growth (though they are sometimes useful for text criticism, whereas T. is too paraphrastic to be much help). For the versions the commentary of Cornill is still the most thoroughgoing study, though its textual conclusions are often over rash. On the whole this last stage of traditional growth is not as creative as the earlier ones. The post-editorial accretions attested by their absence in G. are often verbose, unimportant glosses and doublets. Not that every instance of a shorter text attests an earlier tradition; G. was a fairly literal translator, but he occasionally paraphrases when the text is difficult, and sometimes changes the text intentionally in accordance with a different point of view.

For the history of tradition between the time of the editor and that of G. (early 2nd century B.C.) little can be said. That the Hebrew textual growth continued after G. to result in MT must mean a period of growth prior to it, as well seems plausible. A few traditions which seem to reflect post-exilic times must be post-editorial.

One curious evidence of scribal activity is that of marginal themes. Chapter and verse divisions did not exist for ancient MSS., and to help readers, scribes often placed a word or phrase on the margin summarizing or signalling the content of the adjacent section. Inadvertently scribes often copied these into the text. The commentary points out a substantial number of such themes.

4. FROM THE BOOK TO THE PROPHET

Oral and literary accretions have often obscured and even changed the words of the original prophet, and any attempt at recovering them remains necessarily tentative. Nevertheless the attempt must be made, and it remains to discuss the principles of analysis which served as guides for the attempt made throughout the commentary.

(a) *Formal characteristics*

Normally any artistic creation follows its own rules of composition
and style. A letter shows the characteristics of an epistolary style; a
bill of sale, of legal style; a sermon, that of the pulpit. So also
prophetic materials. The oracle begins with an introductory formula
and ends with one of three formulaic conclusions: an oracle conclusion, a recognition or an affirmation formula. If the text of an
oracle has more than one introduction and/or conclusion formulae,
only one of each can normally be original.

Parenthetically it should be pointed out that the term 'section' is
used to indicate segments of the book formally introduced either as
a vision (**the hand of the LORD came upon me,** 1.3; 8.1; 37.1 and
40.1) or by the formula **The word of the LORD came to me.**

A striking illustration of an original oracle heavily commented
on is 36.1–15. The introductory oracle formula occurs seven times
verses 2, 3, 4, 5, 6, 7, and 13), whereas concluding formulae occur
three times (verses 11, 14, and 15). Other formal characteristics also
recur. Thus the command **prophesy, and say** occurs in verses 1,
3, and 6, and the imperative **hear the word of the LORD,** in verses
1 and 4. Since it is a demonstration oracle a second introductory
formula might be expected to begin the 'therefore' clause, but the
oracle should have no more than two. The conclusion in the commentary that verses 1, 2, 5, 8–9, and 11 represent the original oracle
is fully consonant with the requirements of the oracle.

The characteristics of the literary type should also be kept in mind
(cf. the discussion in Part 2 above, pp. 11–22). The original demonstration oracle in 36.1–15 should begin after a formulaic introduction
(as in verses 1, 2*aα*) with a single 'because' clause to be followed by a
single 'therefore' clause. MT, however, contains **Because** in verses 2,
3, and 13, while **therefore** occurs in verses 3, 4, 5, 6, 7, and 14.
Obviously the original oracle has received various layers of accretion,
verses 2 and 5 probably representing the original demonstration
oracle.

(b) *Consistency of language*

Under Part 3(c) above (p. 28) reference has already been made to
the jumble of number, gender, and person in various sections

throughout Ezekiel. This fact is usually evidence of accretions. One might expect an original oracle to be more or less consistent linguistically. In 6.3–7 a simple judgment oracle obtains of the **Behold I, even I, will . . .** type. The oracle should be in the 1st person throughout, except for the expected 2nd plural subject of the recognition formula at the end, and the verbs should be active. Verses 4*a*, 6, and 7*a* are in the plural passive, however, and represent accretions to the original text.

The application of this principle may be illustrated in 10.1–7. This passage is part of the Temple vision of chapters 8–11 which has been strongly influenced by details from and the language of chapter 1. Each of the seven verses mentions **cherubim,** but verses 2, 4, and 7 use *krwb*, the singular collective, whereas verses 1, 3, 5, and 6 use *krwbym*, the regular plural. When it is then seen that it is precisely these latter verses which are strongly influenced by the inaugural vision while the former make a consistent narrative, it is clear that verses 2, 4, and 7 are the original account.

The original oracle against the false prophets in 13.3–9 can be recovered by applying the test of linguistic consistency. Formally the oracle is a woe oracle which is naturally continued as an invective and concluded with a judgment oracle. The woe oracle (verse 3) must, of course, be in 3rd plural since the class being condemned must be identified. The remainder should consistently be in 2nd masculine plural. Verse 4 is, however, addressed to Israel in 2nd singular, whereas verses 6 and 9 are in 3rd plural; these are later accretions, and the original account is found in verses 3, 5, 7*a*, and 8 (for the secondary character of verse 7*b*, cf. commentary p. 105).

(c) *Historical probability*

Every prophetic message was relevant to the contemporary situation, and as circumstances changed such messages would be updated by means of additions to the text (either in the oral or in the written stage). If MT shows an awareness of specific historical details later than the original oracle such materials must be later. In 4.1–8 the original command to depict a city under siege is found in verses 1–2 (cf. Part 3 (b) above, pp. 26ff.). Verses 4–6 are intended to symbolize the length of the exile. The 390 years probably represent the chronology of the Deuteronomic historian by which the period from the division of the kingdom to the fall of Jerusalem was meant (cf. commentary on 4.4–5). Since his work was not completed until *c.* 560 B.C., the tradition here is likely later. Verse 6 represents a later tradition of a forty-year exile for Judah i.e. *c.* 547/6 B.C. Nor is the tradition of verses 4–6 historically likely. That the prophet should lie on one side for 390 days and finally turn over to the other to lie in that position for another forty days can hardly be considered as something actually carried out. The tradition of verse 8 makes it even more ludicrous by the imposition of divine cords on the prophet rendering him immobile for the period. The conviction that these traditions are later literary products is inescapable.

In Part 3(b) reference was made to oral accretions to the original account in 12.1–16. The account originally referred to an imminent exile, but the end text has detailed references to Zedekiah's fate which presuppose knowledge of the events depicted in 2 Kg. 25.4–7 (cf. also Jer. 39.4–7 and 52.7–11). At a later stage, probably shortly after the events, the traditions concerning the prince's ill-fated attempts to escape from besieged Jerusalem, his capture, blinding and exile, were added to an account which referred to the exile of Jerusalem's citizens in general.

Chapter 17 contains a fable (verses 3–10) about two eagles (Nebuchadrezzar and Hophra), a cedar (the Davidic house), the topmost twig (Jehoiachin) and a lowly vine (Zedekiah), and an interpretation of the fable (verses 11–21). The original account is to be dated well before the fall of Jerusalem, probably in 588 B.C. when the siege of the city was imminent. But parts of the interpretation reveal an exact awareness of Zedekiah's fate in 586 B.C. in terms similar to the accretions in 12.1–16. This applies to verses 16–18 as well as to verses 20 and 21, both of which are post-586 B.C. traditions.

(d) *Consistency of thought*

A reasonable inner consistency of conception might be expected of any single composition. Thus in chapter 17 it is immediately apparent that the second interpretation of the fable (verses 22–24) is secondary, since it does not really interpret the details of the fable at all but proclaims a faith in Yahweh's ultimate restoration of the Davidic dynasty. This principle can also be applied to the account of the fable itself. Fables are animal stories, but verse 9bβ introduces people, an alien element. A later traditionist added this detail to show that Babylonians overthrew the prince with little effort. Verse 10 is also inconsistent. In the original fable Nebuchadrezzar was a great eagle, but this tradition transforms him into an east wind. It is clear that verses 9bβ–10 are later accretions.

Often passages with similar figures or messages strongly influenced each other in the history of tradition. Chapters 16 and 23 both use the figure of the harlot to characterize and condemn Judah, but originally had quite separate themes. Chapter 16 is a diatribe against Jerusalem's cultic sins, whereas chapter 23 condemned the city for its political alliances. When reference is made in chapter 16 to harlotrous relations with other nations in verses 26–29 it is clearly inconsistent with its message and is a later accretion dependent on chapter 23. Similarly a reference to idolatry would be inconsistent in chapter 23, and verse 7b is therefore secondary. In the original fable of chapter 16 only one foundling (Jerusalem) and her fate is described. Chapter 23 is, in contrast, based on an allegory dealing with two adulterous sisters (Jerusalem and Samaria). But 16.44–52 no longer deals with Jerusalem alone, but with her sisters, Samaria and Sodom, a later tradition taking its point of departure from chapter 23 and in content inconsistent with the original judgment. This tradition does not predict judgment but rather invites Jerusalem to exercise patience in bearing her shame. The remainder of the chapter (verses 53–63) is also inconsistent with the diatribe. Verses 53–58 continue the exhortation to shame, but promise restoration of the sisters to their former estate. The last part (verses 59–63) takes up this latter theme in conventional terms. Obviously these traditions have completely abandoned the original account for independent messages.

In the lament over the ship of Tyre in chapter 27 the application of this principle can help to recapture the original poem. Verses 12–25a are, of course, not part of the poem at all; they represent a trade list inserted to explain the last phrase of verse 9. The figure of Tyre as a ship is sustained throughout the original poem, which is in two

parts. The first part describes the construction and manning of the
ship and the second part describes the wreck of the ship and the
resultant lament over it. Verse 9*b* bizarrely has the ships of the sea
in the ship; the figure has been abandoned for that of the actual
harbour of Tyre, and is a later accretion. Verses 10–11 are also
secondary, since these describe the manning of the city's defences
rather than the ship (as consistently in verses 8–9*a*). In the second part
verse 27 is probably an accretion; the men and wares are described
as going down with the ship which anticipates verse 34. Verse 33
also seems inconsistent to its context; both verses 32*b* and 34 refer to
the destruction of the ship, whereas verse 33 discordantly describes
Tyre's international trade in former times.

(e) *Conciseness*

The true oracle in its original form was concise, even bordering on
the cryptic. Such oracles, whether of prediction or command, were
often only a single sentence. Obviously oracles could be and
were often longer, but the tendency towards conciseness remained.
This principle is to be applied only to the oracle; other literary
types, recitals, perorations, laments, do not reveal this same
tendency.

Admittedly the application of this principle cannot be as objectively
applied as those above, but if used with common sense it can be a
most helpful guide.

In the history of tradition original oracles tended to become longer
by explanatory accretions. This can be objectively demonstrated
by comparing MT with G. When MT represents the longer text,
this is often the product of a later tradition history. These accretions
are commonly attempts to clarify and sometimes to correct the
shorter tradition.

Thus if an oracle in MT seems verbose and repetitive, it is likely
that it represents a text commented on by traditionists. 34.1–10 is
an oracle against wicked shepherds of Israel. Formally, like 13.3–7,
it is a woe oracle followed by an invective and a 'therefore' clause
at the end. MT, however, has two 'therefore' clauses, verses 7–8
and 9–10. Verses 7 and 9 are identical and obviously only one
can be original. Verse 8 recapitulates the content of the invective,

adds nothing new, is not a judgment oracle at all, and so the conclusion that verses 9–10 rather than verses 7–8 are original is unavoidable.

In the commentary on 37.15–28 it is argued that the original account is to be found in verses 15–20. But even this account is verbose. The interpretative oracle in verses 19–20 shows accretion. Verse 20 is simply a variant to verse 17 and is not interpretation at all. The last part of verse 19 refers simply to the stick of Judah. From this it would appear that the stick in verse 16a was simply designated **For Judah**; the words **and the children of Israel associated with him** are an explanatory accretion to avoid any misunderstanding of the term as tribe rather than as kingdom. The same thing is true for the second stick both in verses 16b and 19a where a similar accretion is added by way of explanation; in fact in verse 16b a further explanation of **For Joseph** is added, a fact which RSV recognized by placing it in parentheses.

(f) *Other linguistic criteria*

Any reader who is sensitive to Hebrew style will recognize later accretions by a change in style. In the oracle against the proud king of Tyre in 28.1–10, verses 3–5 are clearly not part of the oracle; this is clear from the introductory *hnh* which is stylistically intrusive in the 'because' part of a demonstration oracle as well as by its prosaic contents. RSV recognized this by placing it between dashes. Similarly in the lament that follows (verses 11–19), the list of stones in verse 13 is stylistically out of place. In the descriptive poem on the cosmic tree in 31.3–9, verse 5·is stylistically jarring; it begins with '*l-kn*—'therefore'. This judgment is enhanced by the occurrence of Aramaic words in the verse, whereas the rest of the poem is in excellent Hebrew.

Change in style and vocabulary is also helpful in the analysis of chapters 40–42. The visionary style with which chapter 40 begins consistently makes use of the angelic guide whose principal duty is to measure various parts of the Temple complex in the sight of the prophet. With verse 38 the visionary style comes abruptly to an end and a purely descriptive passage begins. In verse 45 the guide speaks rather than measures, whereas with verse 47 the original vision is resumed to continue through 41.5. Verses 6–11 are a purely architectural description and cannot be part of the vision. The visionary style is again resumed in verses 13–15a (on other grounds considered secondary), whereas the remainder of the chapter is again a descriptive passage. 42.1–14 are also descriptive, though introduced in a visionary style, but this is imitative; dimensions are given in verse 2, but as descriptive statements, not as measurements of the guide. The concluding overall measurements in verses 15–20 are in a visionary style, but the language of MT is stylistically different. The present text is a later reworked version of an original text which cannot now be recovered.

5. THE WORDS OF THE PROPHET

None of the principles of analysis discussed under Part 4 above can be applied absolutely but must always be used with discretion. Nor is it possible to do more than give tentative conclusions as to the original prophetic materials. It is accordingly with some hesitancy and many questions that the following list of passages is given as original to the prophet. A * after a verse indicates that only part of it is original to the prophet.

1.1, 3b*, 4*–6, 9a*, 11*, 13*, 15*, 16*, 18*, 19, 21b*, 22, 26–28; 2.1–7, 8a, 9–10; 3.1–12, 14–15; 4.1–2, 9a, 10–11; 5.1–2; 6.3, 4b, 5b, 7b; 7.1–4, 10–20a, 25–27*; 8.1, 3, 5–7a, 8*–11, 12*, 13–16, 17*, 18a; 9.1–2, 3b, 4–6, 8–11; 10.2, 4, 7, 18a, 19ba; 11.1–7a, 8, 13, 23; 12.1–4, 6*, 7*, 8–9, 11, 17–18, 19*, 20–23, 25–28; 13.1–3, 5, 7a, 8, 10, 13–14, 17–19a, (20–21)?, 22–23; 14.1–5, 8, (9–11)?, 12–21, 23b; 15.1–7ba; 16.1–5aa, 5b–8a, 9–12, 14a, 15, 23a, 24, 25aβ–b, 35–36a, 37aa, 39–41a; 17.1–6a, 7, 9a–ba, 11–15, 19; 18.1–25, 30–32; 19.1–6, 7b, 8, 9*; 20.1–26, 30–31; (20.45–21.3, 5)?, 21.8–10a, 11*, 14–18, 19*, 20*, 21–23*, 24*, 25–27; 22.1–3, 4b–7, 9–12, 17–19aa, b, 20; 23.1–4a, 5–7a, 9–10a, 11, 14b–17, 19–20, 22–23a, 24a, 25aβ–b, 27; 24.1–7, 9–11, 15–17, 18aβ–21, 24; 26.7–14; 27.1–9a, 25b, 26, 28–32, 34–35; 28.1–2, 6a, 7–8, 11–13*, 14–16a*–b, 17, 18b, 20–22a; 29.1–4*, 5*, 6–9a, 17–20*; (30.2–4, 6*)?, 30.20–

22, 24; 31.1–6, 6–9*, 10, 11*a*, 12–13; 32.1–3*, 4–8, (17–28)*;
(33.1–9)?, 33.21–22, 25–30*, 31, 32*a**, 33; 34.1–4, (5–6*)?, 9–15;
36.1–2, 5, 8–9, 11, (17–23)?; 37.1–12*aa*, 14–16*, 17–19*; 39.1–4,
6; 40.1–37, 47–41.4*a*; (42.15–20)*; 43.1–2, 3*b*–6*a*, 7*a*; 44.1–2*;
46.9; 47.2–3*, 4–5*, 6*a*, 8*.

THE BOOK OF

EZEKIEL

EZEKIEL

FIRST SECTION 1.1–24.27 PROPHECIES OF JUDGMENT

A. EZEKIEL'S INAUGURAL VISION AND PROPHETIC CALL 1.1–3.15

This combination of vision and call finds its clearest parallel in the call of Isaiah. In both a vision of the enthroned Deity obtains; in both there are present heavenly winged creatures in the service of the Deity. In both there is some symbolic preparation for the prophetic ministry: in Isaiah the cleansing of the lips by fire, and in Ezekiel the eating of the scroll. In both there is a commission to a people who will pay no attention to the message. Much later the combination of heavenly vision and the commission to preach was to mark Paul's conversion experience on the road to Damascus (Ac. 9).

Some scholars have tried to separate chapter 1 from chapters 2 and 3 as being of quite separate authors. Bertholet speaks of the strong difference between the spiritual atmosphere of the two call visions. It might indeed appear that the conception of God in chapter 1 is much more sophisticated than that in the account of the eating of the scroll. But this kind of distinction could also be employed in Isa. 6. There too there is a lofty vision of an exalted Lord on the throne, but, in the actual commissioning of the prophet, God and man speak on terms as master and servant. Yet no one would suggest that the Isaiah account must be attributed to two authors.

(a) THE VISION OF THE GLORY OF YAHWEH 1.1–28

This is one of the most difficult chapters in the O.T. Not only is the symbolism difficult to understand, but the text has suffered considerably from accretions of traditions from Ezekiel's successors. It was in turn used to expand the great ecstatic vision of chapters 8–11 and reciprocal influence further conflated the text of this chapter. One thing is certain: the original text was much shorter—and much clearer!

Many attempts at finding the original text have been made. Some have tried to find a poem, a testimony to real ingenuity. Thus Hölscher leaves only verses 4, and 28*aa*, *b*; all the rest is secondary. Irwin believes that there is nothing in the chapter from Ezekiel. Herrmann limits the original material to verses 4–5, 27–28. Matthews suggests verses 4, 5*a*, 22*aβ*, 26–28*aa* as containing the original poem. Of those scholars mentioned who find some Ezekiel material in this chapter all start from the assumption that only a theophany of a natural thunderstorm could be original. The remainder, with its bizarre symbolism, is rejected on the *a priori* ground that it must have been a normal experience rather than an ecstatic vision.

A much more scientific approach is a study of the text for objective marks of later layers of tradition. Zimmerli has done this with great acumen by examining the bewildering misuse of gender throughout the chapter, though oddly enough he did not apply the same standard to verses 15–21, which he rejects out of hand. For the latest expansions of the text G. must be used with care. G. represents a text somewhat earlier than MT and is often shorter. Many times its shorter text will be an excellent witness to a late stage in the text development.

Verses 1–3 clearly show two superscriptions. Since verse 1 is told in the 1st person and verses 2–3 are in the 3rd person, one must be earlier than the other. In verse 3*b* both G. and S. read for **upon him,** 'upon me'. The account of the vision then proceeds throughout as a 1st person account; thus verse 1 and verse 3*b* as G.S. have it constitute the original superscription. A later traditionalist, possibly the final editor, added verses 2–3*a* in order to bring the date into line with the Jehoiachin dating system used throughout the book.

Verses 4–14 represent the most difficult textual situation. Verse 4 has been expanded slightly as can be seen from the repetition of 'from the midst of it' (omitted in RSV) and **in the midst of the fire.** MT has after **great cloud** 'and a fire flashing about and brightness round about it', i.e. the cloud. RSV has transposed the two to make sense. In any event **and in the midst . . . bronze** is secondary. Verses 5–6 are both original. The reference is to living creatures, which is feminine in Hebrew. But verses 7–8 are secondary since all references are masculine. In verse 9 only **touched one another** is original and must originally have come after verse 6, i.e. referring to 'four wings'. The rest is secondary as is verse 10, again masculine (except for **four** 2° and 3°, for which see below). In verse 11 the original feminine is found in **were spread . . . bodies,** and the remainder is secondary (masculine) along with verse 12. In verse 13 **like torches** (*kmr'h hlpdym*) may be a gloss on the preceding; the following clause certainly is, as its awkward syntactic structure shows. Verse 14 is a late addition as its absence in G. shows. The original version of verses 4–14 thus contained verses 4–6, 9*a*★, 11★, 13★. Beginning with verse 6*b* this could be rendered as follows: 'and each had four wings, the one touching the other, stretching upward, each having two touching, and each two covering their bodies. And the likeness of the living creatures was an appearance as burning coals of fire and lightning flashes were going out from the fire.'

Most of the expansions were stimulated by the desire both for fuller description and for symmetry. Thus the creatures had to have feet and hands and the four faces had to be individual and facing on a square. For further details, cf. the commentary below.

Verses 15–21 concern the wheels accompanying the creatures and again the textual accretions can be identified in similar fashion. Again there is a scramble of gender references. Verse 15 probably has some minor expansions: **living creatures, upon the earth** and 'of their faces', but is in the main original. Since the reference is now to wheels the gender must be masculine. Verse 16 has some expansions as well, but is in the main straightforward. Verse 17 uses feminine suffixes and is secondary. Verse 18 is corrupt at the beginning but with the help of G. can be restored. Except for one word **beside them,** verse 19 is original. But verses 20–21 use masculine suffixes to refer to the living creatures. Only the concluding clause may be original.

Thus the original probably was something like this. 'And I looked and behold a wheel beside the living creatures, one each to the four of them. The appearance of the wheels was like the shining of chrysolite and their construction as though there was a wheel within a wheel. And I looked at them and their rims were full of eyes round about. And when the living creatures went the wheels would raise themselves, for the spirit of the living creatures was in the wheels.'

In verses 22–28 the original is much easier to find. There can be little doubt that verses 22, 26–28 represent the *raison d'être* of the entire vision. The living creatures sustain the throne of the glory of Yahweh, while the wheels give it mobility. Verse 23 is repetitive of verse 11 and is prosaic in this context. Verses 24–25 give the context for lowering the wings which in turn is dependent on verse 23. Furthermore the voice should hardly be heard until the end of verse 28. Verses 23–25 are thus later expansions to the text.

1. The first words of the book present an insoluble problem. What is meant by **thirtieth year**? Various suggestions have been made: of Manasseh's reign, of Nabopolassar's, from Josiah's reform, but these are pure guesses. The first simply denies all the historical statements in the book and should be dismissed out of hand; the second is incorrect since he was dead; and the last is a guess. There is no evidence that the D Reform was ever used as a calendric system, nor is it likely. Others have suggested that it marked his age, i.e. the prophet was thirty years old. This is only possible if the Hebrew is disregarded. Another suggestion is that it signifies the date of publication of the completed book. Some MSS. in antiquity did append a colophon giving such information, but at the end of the text. Our text must have been intended to date the inaugural vision. Others have admitted defeat and amended the text but without any versional support. Thus 'thirtieth' has been changed to 'third' or 'thirteenth'. The former would be the third year of Zedekiah, but this would not be the fifth of Jehoiachin's captivity. The latter would be the date of Nebuchadrezzar's reign, but this should on the Babylonian calendar be the fourteenth year. Furthermore the calendric system of the book relates only to Judean events. Kimchi makes it the thirtieth year of the jubilee, not a very helpful suggestion since it is unknown whether a jubilee year was ever more than an ideal before Ezekiel's time. Ezekiel must have meant something, but no one today knows what it was. If some word such as 'of my life' were inserted it would be clear, but there is no evidence for it. The exact dating of prophetic oracles was not characteristic of early prophecy (as Amos, Hosea, Micah, and Isaiah), but becomes more prominent in Jeremiah and is well attested in the post-exilic prophecies of Haggai and Zechariah. For a good parallel, but with a king's name inserted, cf. Hag. 1.1; 2.1.

among the exiles seems to contradict 3.14–15, where the prophet goes to the exiles; it merely signifies location rather than his presence in public. The river **Chebar** (*Chobar* in G. and V.) is known from cuneiform inscriptions as *nāru kabari*, a canal flowing near Nippur and into the Euphrates near Erech, mod. *Shaṭṭ en-Nīl*. The canal left the Euphrates near Babylon and the area near Nippur would have been well suited for an exilic colony. 'opened heavens' as a place for prophetic visions is unique for the prophet. In chapters 8–11 and 40–48 the glory of Yahweh is located in the earthly sanctuary. The latter is, however, only the earthly dwelling-place of the Deity in line with the D concept, whereas the actual home of the Deity was in the heavens. In later thought visions of God were tied to the opening of the heavens as in late Judaism (3 Mac. 6.18; 'seven heavens' in Test. Levi 2–3) and in N.T. (Mt. 3.16–17; Mk 1.10–11; Lk. 3.22–23; Ac. 7.55–56; 10.10–16; Rev. 4). **visions of God** is a technical term for an ecstatic vision in which the prophet sees the Deity (cf. also 8.3; 40.2; 43.3). It occurs only with 'God', never with the personal name 'Yahweh', and is always plural in Ezekiel.

2. Fortunately the mysterious dating system of verse 1 is here translated into the usual dating system of the book, i.e. dating from Jehoiachin's captivity. The exact date of his captivity is now known from the *Babylonian Chronicle* as 22 April 597 B.C. It is not clear whether 597 is then the first year or the zero year of the captivity; thus the date is 593 or 592, probably the former. The month is not given, but it is probably the fourth, thus about June. Jehoiachin is here called king even though no longer ruling. He was officially recognized both by the Babylonians and in Judah as the king of Judah even though in captivity, and Zedekiah was simply his regent rather than king in his own name. Thus a Judean calendric system based on Jehoiachin's reign such as the Book of Ezekiel uses throughout (except for 1.1) is quite proper.

3. G. correctly omits **there** and has 'upon me' for **upon him**. The statement is here in the 3rd person, the mark of a secondary hand. The name **Ezekiel** is literally 'may God strengthen', and is attested of only one other person in O.T. (1 Chr. 24.16—RSV Jehezkel, also of a priest), and occurs elsewhere only at 24.24 in an oracle. Whether **the priest** pertains to Ezekiel or to his father Buzi (of whom nothing further is known) cannot be determined. The **land of the Chaldeans** is Babylonia. Hebrew throughout preserves the older form *kaśdîm*. **hand of the LORD** is used throughout Ezekiel for extraordinary divine influence. At 3.14; 8.1; 37.1,and 40.1 as here it signifies ecstatic vision. Its use in 3.22 is dependent on its use in 1.1–3.15 and is secondary (cf. commentary *ad loc.*). At 33.22 extraordinary divine action is indicated since the hand of Yahweh removed ecstatic dumbness enabling the prophet to speak.

4. In **with brightness round about it**, 'it' must refer to cloud. In MT **and fire flashing forth continually** intervenes, which is awkward. Possibly the transposition of RSV is correct. The rest of the verse is an expansion adding the detail of shining bronze. The vision is triggered by a storm in the heavens. Reference is made to a stormy wind, a huge cloud, and fire, i.e. lightning. If this took place in June it was a highly unusual weather phenomenon. Theophanies commonly were associated with a storm cloud: Hab. 3 presents a theophany in these terms; Elijah expected Yahweh to appear in the storm, 1 Kg. 19.11 (cf. also Job 38.1; 40.6). Yahweh's appearance in a great storm is best described in Ps. 18.7–15(MT 8–16). As a parallel to Ezekiel's vision of the divine throne carried by the living creatures, Ps. 18.10(MT 11) says 'He rode on a cherub'. **north** should not be pressed for esoteric meanings. Storms usually rose in the west and passed through the north. It is, however, appropriate in the light of the Jerusalem tradition that Yahweh's holy mountain was in the far north (cf. Ps. 48). The word *hhšml*, occurring only here and at verse 27 and 8.2 may be a borrowed word probably from the Akkadian *elmešu* referring to some precious metal. G. renders it by *ēlektrou*, 'electrum'.

5. The appearance of living creatures human in form. The use of vision words such as **likeness** and **appearance** is characteristic of the chapter as is the use of the number **four.** There are four creatures, with four faces and wings, as well as four wheels. Four was a favourite number of the prophet; thus four abominations, chapter 8; four plagues, 14.12–20. The abstract term **living creatures** for angelic ministrants is used only by Ezekiel. It is undoubtedly rooted in the old Hebrew conception of Yahweh as the one 'who sits enthroned on the cherubim' as part of the full cultic name of Yahweh used to designate the Ark (2 Sam. 6.2), as well as in the prayer of Hezekiah in the Temple (2 Kg. 19.15; cf. Ps. 80.1(MT2)). In the enthronement liturgy the phrase symbolizes Yahweh's enthronement (Ps. 99.1). So too the Ezekiel school representing later traditions in chapter 10 identified the living creatures of chapter 1 as 'cherubim'. The basic symbolism here is quite clear; the living creatures are the heavenly ministrants who are to bear the throne (cf. verse 26) on which sat the glory of Yahweh. Their general appearance was human (not too carefully borne in mind by the later expanders of the text in verses 7–8).

6. The notion of a four-faced creature is not attested earlier in the O.T. Some have thought that the idea was pagan in origin, but this is unnecessary. The notion is a necessary concomitant to the wheels going in any of four directions. Since the creatures are throne-bearing their movement too must be forward in any of the four directions and four faces, bizarre though it might seem, become necessary. Four rather than the six wings of Isaiah's seraphim (Isa. 6.2) are here indicated. Apparently the two with which the face was covered, signifying reverence in the presence of God, were unnecessary since the creatures were under, not facing, the throne.

7. The text is obscure. The Hebrew says 'their feet were a straight foot . . .'. There is also no antecedent for **they.** G. has 'their legs were straight, and their feet winged (reading *knp* for *kp*—'sole') and emitting sparks like the flashings of bronze and their wings were light', which is based on a consonantal text only slightly different from that of MT. What was originally intended is impossible of recovery. The tradition evidently pictured the creatures as animal-like men of some sort.

8. G. omits **their wings** as a late gloss. In fact the three words rendered by **And the four . . . thus** look like marginal glosses. But verse 8*a* also presents a vague picture. How many human hands did the tradition feel each creature had? The addition of **on their four sides** may be symmetrical, but it is confusing. Was there a pair of hands for each side, i.e. eight? Each creature had four wings, i.e. two pairs, which would mean one on each side, so probably only four hands were envisaged, i.e. two pairs.

9. Verse 9*a* is omitted by G., but this does not make it a later expansion, since

G. is the result of parablepsis due to homoeoteleuton. The first four words in MT are original and **their wings** is a gloss made necessary by the expansion between verses 6 and 9. Verse 9*b* is borrowed from the context of the wheels in verse 17. The meaning is that when the living creatures went the wheels would go straight ahead without having to shift direction, as is clear from the suffixes which are feminine for **when they went** (i.e. living creatures), but masculine for the rest, i.e. **the wheels.**

10. As a whole this is an expansion on verse 6*a*, but reflects more than one layer of tradition. The word 'to the four of them' occurs three times, but 'them' is masculine only the first time. Note that the Hebrew has neither **in front** nor **at the back,** and the confusion will be evident. The instances of 'to the four of them' must be a series of marginal glosses, and the references to **right** and **left** represent midway traditions. Had the editorial process been allowed to continue, doubtless 'front' and 'back' would have been added eventually. Verse 6*a* originally must have thought of four human faces, but the later tradition identified these as **man, lion, ox,** and **eagle.** The four are probably chosen for their dignity, according to Jewish tradition: man as God's highest creation; the lion as the king of wild animals; the ox, among domestic animals; and the eagle, among birds. The imagery is borrowed in Rev. 4.7, but with a differing order. Early Christian writers interpreted the four faces as the four evangelists.

11. G. omits the first sentence; it was a late marginal gloss identifying the subject-matter of verse 10. The next phrase **And their wings** is a similar gloss made necessary when verse 11 became separated from verse 9*a* by expansions. The remainder, with slight changes ('*yš* to *wl'yš* and *wštym* to *štym*), can be rendered as above.

wings . . . spread out above rather than to the sides—was this possibly due to the prophet in his trance looking upward rather than horizontally, since one pair touched respectively the wings of the neighbours, and the other covered the body? The last is related to the vision of Isa. 6, 'with two he covered his feet', whereas the former reflects the static position of the cherubim in Solomon's Temple (1 Kg. 6.27).

12*a* is the same as verse 9*bβ*; cf. commentary above, whereas verse 12*b* is a further expansion on verse 12*a* with the last phrase, a copy of verse 9*ba*.

13. The text has suffered both from expansions and corruptions. For *wdmwt*, 'and the likeness of', G. and RSV have **in the midst of,** but MT makes good sense. A series of three expansions occurs after **burning coals of fire,** viz. 'like the appearance of torches' (intended to explain the figure of coals of fire), 'it (i.e. the fire) was going back and forth between the living creatures' (an added detail which is inconsistent with the fact that the creatures themselves are being described) and 'the fire had brightness' (which also disrupts the context). For the original text, cf. the translation above. The fiery character of the living creatures may reflect the seraphim of Isa. 6, who were undoubtedly fiery winged creatures of some sort.

14 is a very late expansion (later than G.), probably an explanatory comment on the last phrase of verse 13. The writer forgot, however, that the creatures were to hold up the throne rather than dart about.

The wheels accompanying the living creatures **15–21**

The roots for Ezekiel's conception of a chariot for the divine throne may depend on an anthropomorphic conception of Yahweh as king. The kings of Israel and Judah rode in chariots as a sign of royal dignity (1 Kg. 22.35; 2 Kg. 9.27; 10.15). In the vision of Habakkuk, Yahweh rides on a chariot of victory (Hab. 3.8), whereas in Isa. 66.15 Yahweh rides 'chariots like the storm wind' to effect judgment. Throughout the Near East the notion that the Deity rode on a chariot was widespread; cf. the 'chariots of the sun' in 2 Kg. 23.11. It is quite unnecessary to insist on Babylonian influence.

15. G. omits **at the living creatures** and 'of their faces' as later glosses. The phrase **upon the earth** is also an expansion on the presumption that the wheels should be on the ground (cf. verse 19), whereas the original vision was up in the clouds. There are four wheels, one beside each creature, thus at the four corners.

16. Omit in verse 16*a* **and their construction** and in verse 16*b* **their appearance,** with G., as well as 'and one likeness to the four of them'. That the last is not original is clear from 'them', which is feminine, whereas 'wheels' is masculine. **chrysolite** is a dark green stone, whereas a yellow colour is expected. Probably beryl or topaz is meant. **a wheel within a wheel** probably means two wheels at right angles; it could then run in all four directions without turning.

17. This is clearly the interpretation intended by this tradition; without turning they could go in any of four directions. The secondary character of the verse is clear from the mixture in gender.

18. A corrupt text at the beginning: lit. 'their backs (error for "rims"), and they had height and they had fear'. Both 'backs' and 'height' seemed like doublets for an early marginal notation, viz. *gbtm*, 'their rims'. By reading *w'r'h* for MT *wyr'h* with G., the text becomes 'And I looked at them'. The last word 'to the four of them' is again feminine and a gloss showing that it was true for all four. **full of eyes:** probably intended to show that the glory of God was all-seeking, just as the mobility of the wheels taught the omnipresence of Yahweh.

19. Only one word is secondary; **beside them** by its mistaken suffix shows that it is not original. The wheels and the creatures move in perfect harmony.

20. This, along with verse 21, is a repetitive expansion on verse 19 with the exception of the concluding clause **for the spirit . . . wheels,** which gives the reason for the harmonious movement. G. has a somewhat different but equally difficult text. RSV follows G. in not rendering the repeated *šmh hrwḥ llkt* (RV 'thither was the spirit to go'). The 'spirit of the living creatures' simply refers to the living impulse. The wheels were alive with the life of the creatures and thus synchronized their movements. The preposition *'l*, 'upon, against, concerning', is here intended as *'l*—'to, towards'. These two prepositions are completely confused in MT of Ezekiel, possibly due to Aramaic influence on copyists of the book.

The throne and the glory **22–28**

Verses 23–25 are later expansions referring to the living creatures, whereas the original vision has moved on to the platform and the throne.

22. MT has a double reading 'over the heads of the living creatures', a conflation of two texts. The plural is preferable. G. omits *hnwr'*, 'fearsome', before **crystal** as a late gloss. Also a later tradition is **above their heads**, which is a gloss on *mlm'lh*, 'upwards'. Above the creatures was what looked like a platform (**firmament**, a word elsewhere used of the sky, but here of a flat surface).

23. A series of expansions, the latest of which (not in G.) repeats the words 'each creature had two wings covering (them)', which RSV sensibly omitted.

24. G. omits the late glosses represented in **like the thunder . . . host.** The first of these is borrowed from 10.5.

26. Omit **over their heads,** which was copied from verse 25. Omit *'lyw*, 'upon it', as a minority reading and RSV (at end of verse). For **sapphire,** better 'lapis lazuli'. Cf. Exod. 24.10 for this verse. The description of the being on the throne as **a likeness . . . form** is an attempt to avoid anthropomorphic terms.

27. G. omits as a late explanatory gloss the words **like the appearance of fire enclosed round about.** The description of the divine being is that of two degrees of brightness, the upper half of **gleaming bronze** (cf. commentary on verse 4), and the lower, of **fire.** The gloss wrongly introduces the fire to the upper as well.

28. That the description is made in terms of light is clear from the comparison to the rainbow with its light spectrum. Ezekiel avoids a direct description by referring to **the appearance of the likeness of the glory of the LORD.** Yahweh is thus not described nor directly named. The term 'glory of Yahweh' is here used in a special sense. The term 'glory' may mean 'honour' and thus reputation in a purely secular sense (cf. Job 19.9, Prov. 3.16). As applied to Yahweh it can thus mean God's honour, as Prov. 25.2. By extension it can mean the honour due to God (Mal. 1.6; 1 Sam. 6.5; Isa. 42.12). God's glory then can appear in natural phenomena (Ps. 29.3); here 'glory' means God manifest, and it is something that can be declared (Ps. 19.1 (MT 2)). The evidence of God's presence, i.e. His glory, can fill the earth (Isa. 6.3), and is the hope for the future (Isa. 40.5). But in Ezekiel, as well as in the P writings dependent on him, the term 'glory of Yahweh' has a special meaning. It indicates a special presence, a manifestation of the brightness of his being. It can thus leave the Temple (11.23) and later return to the renewed Temple (43.4). In Ezekiel the glory is always seen in ecstatic vision and not by ordinary vision. The light which marks the special presence is also seen in the P use of the term, e.g. Exod. 24.17. As in Isaiah the vision issues in the prophet's falling on his face, i.e. the position of worship and obeisance. Only then comes the commission.

(b) THE COMMISSION **2–3.11**

In contrast to chapter 1 the text of the commission has received little expansion, as an analysis quickly shows. Here and there minor glosses have been added to the text, for which see commentary below.

The section easily divides into a number of sub-sections, each of which begins with the vocative, **Son of man,** often preceded by **And he said to me.** These are (i) 2.1–2. Introductory command to stand at attention; (ii) 2.3–5. Commission of the prophet to Israel, that rebellious house; (iii) 2.6–7. Do not be afraid of them, but speak out boldly; (iv) 2.8–10. Do not be like rebellious Israel; here are your oracles of lament and mourning and woe; (v) 3.1–2. Eat the scrolls; (vi) 3.3. The prophet obeys; (vii) 3.4–9. Israel will not respond, but I will harden you; (viii) 3.10–11. Now take over the commission, and preach to the exiles.

A comparison with two earlier prophetic commissions, those of Isaiah and Jeremiah, shows that each part belongs to the account. Aside from the introductory command to listen, each section has a counterpart in the earlier accounts. Section (ii) reflects the commission in Isa. 6.9, 'Go and say', and in Jer. 1.7, 'to all to whom I send you go, and whatever I command you speak'. Section (iii) is paralleled in Jer. 1.8; 'Be not afraid of them' as well as in verse 17b. Sections (iv), (v), and (vi) combine the symbolism of the scroll completely covered with words which is to be eaten. For symbolism accompanying a commission, cf. Isa. 6.6–7 and Jer. 1.11–12, 13–14; more particularly, cf. God's statement to Jeremiah in Jer. 1.9, 'I have put my words in your mouth'. Section (vii) finds its parallel in Isaiah's commission in 6.9–12 and to a lesser extent in Jer. 1.19; whereas (viii) may partly reflect Jer. 1.17.

An examination of the internal structure of the section confirms its general integrity. The double role of the prophet, viz. oracles *against* Israel but *to* the exiles, is made clear by the use of the introductory oracle formula in an unusual way, i.e. simply to denote oracles from Yahweh in general (at 2.4 to rebellious Israel and at 3.11 to the exiles). The use of the phrase is here formal, without actual content; it is part of his commission to speak oracles.

A unity of theme also emerges in the use of the term **rebellious house** which occurs at 2.5, 6, 7, 8, and 3.9, thus in sections (ii), (iii), (iv), and (vii). Only in the introduction, the eating of the scroll, and the final (and ultimate) commission is it lacking. It would be irrelevant in sections (i), (v), and (vi), and is intentionally missing in (viii) to distinguish between the mediate and immediate audience. The house of Israel is rebellious; it is to be hoped that the exiles are not, for they are the hope of the future.

It might be suggested that sections (iv) and (v) are doublets and that one is secondary. Both contain the command to eat what Yahweh has given, viz. the scroll. It is fully possible that verse 8b is a secondary expansion of that text based on section (v).

2.1. Son of man: used throughout the book as an introductory term of address by Yahweh for the prophet. In the face of the vision of the glory of God in chapter 1, this term is contrastive, emphasizing the lowly creaturely character of the prophet (cf. Ps. 8.4(MT 5)). Prior to Ezekiel the individual personality and individuality of the prophet played a greater part. With Ezekiel begins the trend to anonymity among the prophets broken only by Haggai and Zechariah. The rendering **with you** must be correct, though MT has 'ōṯāḵ (normally 'you' as direct object). The two forms of 't are confused throughout the book and may, like the confusion of 'l and 'l, show Aramaic influence either at the editorial or copyist level.

2. when he spoke to me: an expansion lacking in G. The Hebrew *'t mdbr* is impossible; either *'t hmdbr* or *mdbr* must be read, probably the latter, i.e. 'one speaking' instead of 'him speaking'. RSV is based on an emendation proposed by Cornill and accepted by *BH* of *'t* to *'tw*, which is just as bad Hebrew as MT. What is meant is an unidentified (but recognized from the context) speaker. The form *middabbēr* is unusual (cf. 1.28), though the Hithp. is not impossible. Mention of the activity of **the Spirit** reminds one that the prophet is still in an ecstatic vision.

3. Glosses are partially attested in G. in **to a nation of rebels** and **have transgressed against me.** G. has 'house' rather than **people**; the use of plural modifiers might make MT preferable, though usage in Ezekiel is normally 'house'. Ezekiel's new office is solely based on Yahweh's commission (cf. Isa. 6.8, Jer. 1.7; Am. 7.15). **Israel** is for Ezekiel a generic term comprising all Israel from its inception onwards, as is clear from verse 3*b*. So too Israel can be termed rebellious, since its history has been one of sinful rebellion against Yahweh. The exiles are part of that Israel and share in its guilt corporately (cf. Isa. 6.5), even though themselves not rebellious.

4. Verse 4*a* is a late expansion on verse 3*b* and is not in G. The usual name in MT of Ezekiel is 'Lord Yahweh'. G. testifies, as is now known from Pap. 967, to a single name throughout. Apparently 'Lord' as the perpetual *Qerê* for 'Yahweh' crept into the text, and only 'Yahweh' should be read throughout Ezekiel. The introductory oracle formula, **Thus says the LORD,** denotes the divine source of words that follow. Here and in 3.11 the prophet is enjoined to use the formula in speaking to the people; in other words, Ezekiel is to speak Yahweh's words only.

5. The certain outcome of Ezekiel's prophetic activity is Israel's recognition of the fact that Ezekiel was a prophet—this due to his use of the introductory formula; cf. also 33.33. (For the more usual form of the recognition formula, cf. 6.7.) This recognition is an inexorable result independent of Israel's willingness or refusal to listen; cf. also 3.11.

a rebellious house is applied to the house of Israel indicating the certain refusal to listen which Ezekiel may expect. Israel the chosen is by its own choice become a rebellious, and therefore rejected, house.

6. nor be afraid: G. witnesses to 'nor be dismayed' (*tḥt*) as a better text. **briars and thorns are with you:** Ezekiel is counselled not to be afraid, even though his situation will be painful ('briars, thorns, scorpions').

7. With G.S. and many Hebrew MSS. read (as RSV) **house** with **rebellious.** The opening clause reinforces the interpretation given above of the significance of the introductory oracle formula in verse 4 (and 3.11).

8. Probably only verse 8*a* is original, a warning against prophetic identification with the Israel of the new name, **rebellious house.** Such identification would involve not hearing what Yahweh is saying.

9. Omit **lo** with G., and change *bw* (in it, masc.) to *bh* (in it, fem.), which is necessary since the reference is to **hand** (fem.). The divine word which the prophet is warned to obey becomes a symbolic act. The prophetic word is now seen (as well as heard), i.e. an outstretched hand containing a scroll.

10. G. omits **on it.** The scroll is unusual in being written on both sides; scrolls were normally smoothed on one side only for a writing surface. The word for **lamentation** is here masc. plural (apparently a variant plural for the usual *kynwt*, fem. plural). The three words signify not the contents of the fearful judgments of Yahweh written on the scroll but rather the reactions they will certainly promote.

3.1. G. omits the gloss based on the same tradition as Jer. 15.16 **eat what is offered to you** (lit. 'what you find'). Ezekiel is given the double command to eat the scroll and to prophesy, the latter being dependent on the former. The symbol of eating the scroll signifies devouring the words written on it, i.e. receiving the word which he must then mediate to the people.

2. G. rightly omits *hz't*, i.e. 'this' (scroll), as does RSV.

3. RSV by its euphemism fails to render the Hebrew adequately. MT has for the command: 'Son of man, make your belly eat and fill your stomach with this scroll which I am giving you.' Ezekiel is not just to swallow the scroll, but must assimilate it, digest it. This will make him a true prophet. RSV, following G.V., rightly adds 'it' to **then I ate.** For the word of God being sweet as honey, cf. Ps. 19.10(MT 11); 119.103.

4. speak with my words means using Yahweh's exact words.

5. but to the house of Israel is (Hebrew does not have 'but') probably a corrective gloss. For **people of foreign speech and a hard language,** cf. Isa. 33.19; Jer. 5.15. Ezekiel develops the theme of Israel's great stubbornness at length in chapter 23.

6. S. omits **of foreign . . . language** rightly; it was probably copied from verse 5. For *'m l'*, 'if not', G.V. read *'m*, which the sense requires. Peoples who cannot understand Hebrew, i.e. the prophet's language, would be even more responsive than the rebellious house. This section is really a commentary on the phrase 'a rebellious house'. Jer. 1.5*b* is a striking contrast to verses 5–6 here.

7. Israel's hardness of heart was a typical theme of all the major prophets; as part of the initial call to service, cf. Isa. 6.9–10. G. misread *mṣḥ* **forehead** as *mṣḥ*— 'strife'.

8. God promises Ezekiel that he will make him 'harder for the truth than the people are against it. There may be an intentional play on the prophet's name; Ezekiel means 'may God harden'.

9. Like adamant: G. misread *kšmyr* as *wtmyd*, 'and continually', and omitted **have I made your forehead.** If the latter is an expansion, verse 9*a* must be connected with verse 8*b*.

10–11. The specific call. In practice, the prophet can only speak to the exiles among whom he lives. Though he has eaten the divine words, his prophetic office will be that of mediator of Yahweh's words that will continue to come to him. For verse 11*b*, cf. commentary on 2.4.

(c) THE END OF THE VISION **12–15**

The section has been expanded somewhat by a later tradition. Verse 13 is dependent ·on the expansions in chapter 1 and therefore must be later than the original account (cf. commentary on 1.23–25). The passage is a reminder that not only the vision of chapter 1 but also the commission itself was part of the ecstatic experience. Scholars who believe that Ezekiel's ministry was in Jerusalem rather than Babylon take this entire section as secondary; cf. Introduction (pp. 23ff.). For small expansions to the text, cf. commentary below.

12. **arose:** based on an emended text. MT reads for **and . . . place,** 'Blessed be the glory of Yahweh from his place,' which though attested by Versions is peculiar Hebrew. The suggested emendation changes *brwk* ('blessed') to *brwm*, and makes good sense. The divine spirit lifted up the prophet to take him away when suddenly he hears behind him a great noise caused by the movement of the glory of God. **its place** is indefinite, not the Jerusalem Temple as in chapters 8–11, but apparently in the opened heavens of 1.1.

13. A later expansion explaining the words **the sound of a great earth-quake** in verse 12, partially on the basis of 1.23–24. A still later copyist expansion repeated the phrase commented on, at the end of the verse. For verse 13*a*, cf. 1.9, 11.

14. Possibly G.'s omission of **in bitterness** attests its later addition. On the other hand, it may be a word play on 'rebellious', i.e. *mr* and *mry*, in which case the meaning should not be pressed. Certainly original is **in the heat of my spirit,** which here does not mean anger (as 'in bitterness' might suggest), but rather excitement or exaltation. This is clear from the qualifying phrase that follows: 'the hand of Yahweh upon me' always signalizing for Ezekiel the ecstatic state.

15. RSV omitted 'and who were dwelling there' after **Chebar.** It seems more likely that **who dwelt by the river Chebar** (and) is the expansion, since a later writer might well amplify the text on the basis of 1.3 but hardly by the phrase left out by RSV. Apparently Ezekiel returned to his home still in a trance condition. **Tel-abib** has not been identified, though the term *til abubi* in Assyrian Annals of Tiglath-pileser and in Cod. Hamm. refers to mounds covering ancient cities. The exiles apparently occupied such ruins; cf. also Tel-melah and Tel-harsha at Ezr. 2.59; Neh. 7.61. The prophet was **overwhelmed** for a week, i.e. did not prophesy, still being dazed by the tremendous experience he had undergone.

B. EDITORIAL EXPANSIONS ON THE COMMISSION 3.16–27

This section represents two distinct insertions into the original text between verse 16*a* and 4.1. Verse 16*a* gives the date of the next event, which refers to 4.1–5.17. It has because of the insertion of verses 16*b*–21 and 22–27 been shortened, though something like verse 16*b* must have stood there. The Hebrew of verse 16 shows that *b* was the beginning of a section. RSV, as G., has smoothed over the difficulties. MT says more or less: 'And it happened at the end of seven days—and the word of Yahweh happened to me saying.' MT shows the equivalent of the dash, indicating a break.

The first insertion is verses 16*b*–21. It is a florilegium from chapters 18 and 33 probably made by the editor. These chapters picture the prophet under the symbol of a watchman on the walls who must warn the populace of danger. Since this is an aspect of the prophetic office, the editor felt it appropriate to insert a short statement of Ezekiel as watchman in connection with 2.1–3.11. Its secondary character can be seen by comparing verse 17 with 33.7; verse 18 with 33.8; verse 19 with 33.9; and verse 20 with 33.13; 18.24.

The second insertion presents two problems. Verses 22–24a seem to have little to do with what follows. In fact they seem like a brief summary of 1.1–2.2. On **the hand of the LORD**, cf. commentary on 1.3. The presence of the glory of Yahweh may be the reflection of later traditionists desirous of inserting references to it wherever it might seem appropriate. Verse 24a is taken almost literally from 2.2. The passage seems highly arbitrary in view of what follows. Why should the prophet be called out to the plain in order to be told to stay home, unless it is simply to give occasion for another reference to Yahweh's glory once again? Furthermore, original references to Yahweh's glory (the sight of which demanded ecstasy, hence the introductory words of verse 22) are of two kinds: the introductory vision of chapter 1 in which the picture of the heavenly throne on the platform is mandatory, and that in which the glory is related to its presence or absence in the Temple, chapters 8–11; 43.4. But here the glory **stood**. It is thus clear that verses 22–24a are an accretion.

The second problem concerns verses 24b–27. Normally Yahweh's commands begin with the vocative **son of man** or **and you, son of man** (cf. commentary on 2.1), but this does not come until verse 25. Possibly verse 24b is thus later than verses 25–27. It is, however, the content of the enjoinder which poses the difficulty. The prophet is to be rendered dumb until such time as Yahweh will open his mouth to speak an oracle. This is tied to the original commission since the same terms for the prophet's speech occur in 2.4–5; 3.11. It is thus a further reflection on the original commission. On the other hand it must also be understood as preparing for 24.27 and 33.22, where the end of dumbness is recorded as coincident with news of the fall of Jerusalem in 586 B.C. seven years later. But this cannot possibly be the case, since these seven years were the main period of prophetic activity in the sense of 2.4–5; 3.11. The statement in 24.27 must refer to a temporary ecstatic dumbness, and hardly to a period of seven years. The passage is a later expansion to prepare for 24.27 and 33.22.

17. An exact copy of 33.7, except for the omission of 'And you' at the beginning; cf. *ad loc.*

18. Cf. 33.8. This verse is somewhat expanded by adding **and you give him no warning, wicked** in the phrase 'wicked way', and **in order to save his life**.

19. Cf. 33.9, which has for **and he does not … way,** the words 'from his way to turn from it and he does not turn from his way'. The two words *mrš‘w* ('from his wickedness') and *hrš‘h* ('wicked' in the phrase 'wicked way') (omitted in G. both here and in verse 18) are glosses. Verse 20 reflects the thought of 33.13, but is recast by the editor to parallel the form of verse 18; cf. also 18.24, 26. The writer adds, however, a note by attributing to Yahweh the stumbling-block which results in the judgment of the once righteous. To him Yahweh's control of all human destiny was an article of faith. The stumbling-block is the divinely imposed test (cf. Gen. 2.16–17) on the righteous. God even leads the righteous into temptation (2 Sam. 24.1, Mt. 6.13). The prophet's commission must in spite of the origin of the stumbling-block be one of warning all men against sin.

21. MT has 'warn him the righteous man'; with G. and RSV omit 'him'. MT repeats 'the righteous man' after the phrase **not to sin.** Originally this was probably a marginal notation. This verse is related to verse 20, as verse 19 is related to verse 18.

22. Cf. 2.1. **there,** a gloss added after G., which does not have it. The word *bḳ'h* really means a cleft, hence a valley. Since Ezekiel's house was on Tel-abib the alluvial plain surrounding the tells could easily be called valley (cf. also 37.1–2); the reference in 8.4 is dependent on this verse (and chapter 1 as ultimate source).

23. Here the glory of Yahweh appears without accoutrements. For the phrase **like . . . Chebar,** cf. 10.15, 20, 22, and 8.4. For the last clause, cf. 1.28*b*.

24a. Cf. 2.2.

25. The tying-up of the prophet in this verse gives a clue to the source of verses 25–27. In 4.8 Yahweh ties up the prophet so that he cannot turn round during his lying on one side to symbolize the duration of the 'siege', i.e. the exile. Thus the period of dumbness is to last for 390 days, again proof that the relation of this passage to 24.27 and 33.22 is artificial and editorial. The purpose of the cords is here given as keeping Ezekiel to his house, but this contradicts 4.8.

26. It is doubtful whether an actual dumbness could have been intended here. What is meant is that the prophet is to speak only the oracles given him by Yahweh. As in the case of 4.4–8, this section is a literary creation rather than reflecting an actual state of affairs. The dumbness will make it impossible for the prophet to act as 'reprover'. This is a contradiction of his prophetic office as given in the original commission in 2.7 and 3.4–9.

27. Does this verse mean that on occasions the prophet's silence will be broken? The tradition apparently noted the incongruity of a seven-year (or 390-day) silence, and makes allowance for exceptions. This may well be a later expansion by someone who wanted to allow for such exceptions and at the same time relate it more closely to the original commission in 2.4*b*–5*a* and 3.11. That the writer is not Ezekiel is also evident from the departure from the idiom 'and whether they hear or refuse to hear' in verse 27*ba*.

C. Prophetic Actions 4.1–5.4

This section is part of a larger complex since no introductory formula occurs. The section begins at 3.16; cf. commentary *ad loc.* There is abundant evidence for different layers of tradition accruing to the original prophecy. (i) Three prophetic actions depict the siege of Jerusalem and its outcome (4.1–3; 4.9*a*, 10–11; 5.1–2), whereas two actions portray the exile and its conditions (4.4–6, 8; 4.12–15). The former must have been enacted before the fall of Jerusalem; the latter, afterwards. (ii) Later accretions apply details of one type indiscriminately to the other. Thus verse 9*b* adds a detail from the exile symbolism to the action showing conditions within the city under siege. Similarly verse 7 applies details from the first action to 4.4–6, 8. (iii) The prophetic application may be widely separated from the action interpreted. Thus 4.16–17 are applicable not to verses 12–15 but to verses 9*a*, 10–11.

This process of accretion can only be detailed in part. The original oracles were in three parts: (i) 4.1–2, an action portraying the siege of the city; (ii) 4.9*a*, 10–11, an action depicting the famine conditions within the besieged city; and (iii) 5.1–2, an action symbolizing the outcome of the siege. 4.3, though not part of the original, was added to (i) probably by Ezekiel himself. Verses 16–17 is a divine oracle interpreting (ii), separated from it by a later addition (verses 12–15), which depicts the uncleanness of exilic life. Since verse 14 is a reaction to the command in verse 12, it would appear that verse 13 is subsequent to verse 12. 5.3–4 qualifies the absoluteness of the judgment portrayed in 5.1–2, and is later.

4.4–8 represents an accretion, probably written about 547 B.C., the time of Deutero-Isaiah's call to prophesy. The end of the exile is envisioned as close at hand; the people have been in exile almost forty years. But this section also grew gradually. From verse 9*b* it is clear that verse 6 is later than the tradition of lying for 390 days on one side only. Originally there may have been no reference to **left** side at all in verse 4. Verse 5 was then added, whereas verse 6 is still later, in fact later than the addition of verse 9*b* to 9*a*. Verse 7 is inserted to tie this section to the preceding. This may well have been the work of the final editor to whom the framework of the book is due.

Prophetic actions were enacted to symbolize some message dramatically. Earlier prophets often used such actions to imbue their words with greater realism. Isaiah walked about Jerusalem 'naked and barefoot' for three years as a warning to its inhabitants not to rely on Egypt and Ethiopia (Isa. 20); Jeremiah buried a linen waistcloth and later recovered it 'spoiled' to pictorialize the eventual spoilage of the pride of Jerusalem (Jer. 13.1–11); Ahijah tore a new garment into 12 pieces, 10 of which he gave to Jeroboam, thereby showing the coming disruption of the kingdom (1 Kg. 11.29–39). Most bizarre of all prophetic actions was Hosea's domestic experience in Hos. 1 and 3, an experience which became the text for his prophetic work. Of prophetic action 4.3*b*β rightly says, **This is a sign for the house of Israel.**

Prophetic action has often been compared to magic, but the comparison is quite inadequate. Magic attempts to effect an action by enacting such symbolically. But prophetic action was never thought to bring about that which is symbolized. Rather it was the dramatic depiction of some divine intent; it is itself a divine word, an oracle; it is a prediction rather than a coercion of an event.

There can be little doubt that the three actions commanded in 4.1–2(3); 4.9*a*, 10–11, and 5.1–2 were literally carried out successively, probably in Tel-abib (cf. on 3.15). The last action was clearly done in public view. The second concerned his diet, but must have been publicly performed for it to be a dramatic message.

The later actions (4.4–6 and 4.12–15) constitute a different *genre*. These are literary creations, sermons rather than dramatic performances. This is obviously true for verses 4–6. The prophet could hardly have lain on one side for 390 days tied with divinely placed cords to make movement impossible, and then for forty days on his other side. The prophetic figure was neither fakir nor cataleptic as has often been proposed. Furthermore, if this passage is purely literary in origin, the same can be suggested for verses 12–15, since this too is a later product dealing with exilic conditions.

4.1. even Jerusalem: a gloss; cf. 'the king of Assyria' in Isa. 7.17. The prophet is told to take a mud **brick**, not 'tile' as AV. Mud brick was extremely common in Babylon, not only being almost the only available building material, but also used for writing. The brick was made of soft clay, the sides being flattened. A stylus was used to make marks on the surface and such inscribed tablets would then be baked in ovens to make them hard. Building bricks were only baked in the sun.

2. Delete the last occurrence of **against it** with G. A complete siege of the city is to be portrayed in miniature, probably around the brick since there would hardly be room on it. The **siegeworks** is to consist of a **siege wall, a mound, camps,** and **battering rams.** The difference between the first two is unknown; they refer to an earthen mound built by besiegers, probably for two reasons. Cities were built on hills and were walled. An earthern mound would permit the attackers to fight on a level with the defenders, and at the same time serve as a protection for the archers. For 'battering rams', cf. *IDB*.

3. The prophet portrays here Yahweh's iron determination to carry out his intent to destroy the city. The plate occurs elsewhere as the griddle upon which the cereal offering could be prepared (Lev. 2.5); it was thus a household cooking utensil, here used to represent an impenetrable and unbreakable wall between the prophet and the city; for a similar figure, cf. Jer. 1.18.

4–5. punishment: the exile; symbolically this is to be borne by the prophet. RSV has corrected the Hebrew to **I will lay . . . upon you** from 'you shall lay . . . upon it', i.e. upon your sides. Thus Ezekiel is to place the guilt upon his own side. Probably better is the change to **and you shall bear** (*wnś't* for *wśmt*) **the punishment . . . Israel** (delete '*lyw*, 'upon it', as gloss). The original meaning of 'house of Israel' is uncertain. If **left** is not original, the phrase meant the southern kingdom. But then the 390 years is no longer clear. The 390 years seems to be based on the chronology for the separate kingdom of Judah of the D historian, who wrote *c.* 560 B.C. From the division of the kingdom to the fall of Jerusalem adds up to 393 years. Or does the writer have in mind the cultic apostasy of the northern kingdom as beginning with the reign of Jeroboam I? In the latter case it would be preferable to insist on the basic meaning 'guilt' or 'iniquity' for *āwōn* rather than **punishment.** Then 'house of Israel' in verse 5 must mean the northern kingdom. In G. in both verses 5 and 9, 390 is changed to 190, and the number 150 is inserted in verse 4. The forty days of verse 6 are thus taken as part of the 190; thus the point of departure is 150 years before the fall of Jerusalem, i.e. the deportation of much of the northern kingdom by the Assyrians in 734 B.C.

6. Delete **a second time** with G.S. A forty-year exile for Judah from 586 B.C. dates the writer as writing in the time of Cyrus, whose victory against Lydia awakened Jewish hopes for release from exile. In Hebrew **right** means S. and **left** N. The representation of a year by a day (i.e. seven years for a week) eventually became common in apocalyptic writing, e.g. Dan 9.24–27.

7. An editorial expansion to tie verses 4–6 to verses 1–3. RSV interprets MT 'against her' as **against the city.** For **arm bared** cf. Isa. 52.10, where Yahweh is prepared to save. It symbolizes constant readiness, in this passage for the prophetic act.

8. An echo of 3.25, but here Yahweh places the cords on the prophet. This must be earlier than verse 6, since **days of your siege** involves both 390 days on the left, and forty on the right side.

9. The gathering of various available grains in order to make bread is intended to show the scarcity of food in the besieged city, rather than a violation of the laws not to mix seed (cf. Dt. 22.9; Lev. 19.19*b*). The first four grains are also listed in 2 Sam. 17.28. **millet** occurs only here, but the word is known from Akkadian and Aramaic. Verse 9*b* is a later addition, since the prophet could hardly be expected to prepare a meal to last 390 days.

10–11. The food is to be strictly rationed; 20 shekels would be approximately 8 or 9 oz. **once a day,** for Hebrew 'from time to time'; it might better be rendered 'at fixed times'. Water was also rationed; a **hin** (originally from an Egyptian word *hyn* or *hnw*) was approximately one gallon. Thus the daily ration allowed was about $\frac{2}{3}$ quart.

12. Food during the exile will be unclean. That it was not part of verses 9*a*, 10–11 is clear from the designation **barley cake.** Animal droppings mixed with straw were commonly used for fuel in the Near East where wood was costly and scarce, but human dung was revolting.

13. G. deletes **their bread** and **whither I will drive them,** which is preferable.

14. For **Lord GOD,** cf. commentary on 2.4. For the prohibitions against Israelites' eating **what died of itself,** cf. Dt. 14.21; for **torn** flesh, cf. Exod. 22.30 (MT 31). **foul flesh** according to P was food from a peace-offering left over to the third day, and hence an 'abomination' (Lev. 7.18; cf. 19.7).

16–17. S. omits **and with fearfulness** and **and in dismay** rightly; they are glosses from 12.19. These verses apply verses 11–12 to the Jerusalem situation.

5.1–4. The original prophetic action is contained in verses 1 and 2. The action represents the complete destruction of the populace of Jerusalem as outcome of the siege. The concept of the remnant in verse 3 is a later corrective added after the fall of Jerusalem. That it is a later accretion is evident from the vagueness of the antecedent in **from these.** Verse 4 refers to fire as well as verse 2, but it can hardly have the same meaning. In verse 2 it refers to the fate of Jerusalem in defeat; in verse 4, to the general destruction of some survivors. Verses 3–4 are thus literary postscripts to the original oracle.

1. For the symbol of shaving of hair as sign of enslavement, cf. Isa. 7.20; more commonly it is a sign of shame (2 Sam. 10.4–5), or mourning (Isa. 15.2; Jer. 41.5–6; 48.37; cf. Ezr. 9.3). The use of balances for dividing the hair is not to be pressed; it merely symbolizes the division into thirds.

2. Delete **and I will . . . them,** as editorial insertion from verse 12. Yahweh's judgment is part of the interpretative oracle that follows, not part of the prophetic action. **fire** represents death through the deprivations of the siege; the **sword,** death by actual slaughter during the razing of the city; and **scatter,** annihilation by exile from the homeland. The **midst of the city** refers to the model of 4.1–2. For **when the days . . . completed,** cf. verse 4.

3. from these, literally 'from there', probably referring to the city. Binding a few hairs is a symbol for protection from harm.

4. The final clause does not fit the context. G. has instead 'and you shall say to all the house of Israel', which properly introduces verses 5ff. Originally the words 'from it [not 'there', as RSV] a fire will come forth into all the house of Israel' probably preceded 'when the days of the siege are completed' in verse 2. The antecedent of 'it' is then 'midst (of the city)'. The entire clause represents an accretion to verse 8 stating that Jerusalem's fall meant the destruction of the entire house of Israel. Eventually a copyist erroneously conflated the two clauses from verses 2 and 4 at the end of verse 4.

D. COMMENTARY ON THE PROPHETIC ACTIONS 5.4b–17

This section in its present form illustrates a complicated growth of prophetic traditions. Its language is full of formulas favoured throughout the book: 'Therefore, because, as I live, I, Yahweh, have spoken, they shall know that I Yahweh. . . . Thus says Yahweh.' Different layers are evident from the change of person, thus verses 5–6a are 3rd fem. singular, verses 8–12, 14–15, and 17aβ, 17b are 2nd fem. singular, verses 6b, 13, and 16a are in 3rd plural, and verses 7, 16b, 17aa are in 2nd masc. plural.

Formally the commentaries on the three prophetic actions seem contained in verses 7–8, 9–10, and 11–12; verses 13–17 are an appendage which has no obvious connection with 4.1–5.4, and must be analysed separately.

The earliest materials can be recognized by the use of the singular, the invective of verses 5–6a being in the 3rd person, and the judgment of verses 8–12 in the 2nd person. Verse 6b (**by rejecting . . .**) is in the 3rd plural and represents a later accretion. Verse 7 is in the 2nd plural, and is probably earlier than the 3rd plural additions, verse 6b constituting a summary of verse 7. Even within the 2nd fem. singular materials there is evidence of traditional growth. Verse 10 with its introductory **Therefore** hardly fits after the judgment of verse 9b.

In the appendage the earliest materials are found in verses 14–15. Verse 13, in the 3rd plural, is a later summary conclusion to verses 4b–12 as is clear from the recognition formula in verse 13b. Verses 16 and 17 are mainly in the 2nd plural, though the latter part of verse 17 reverts to the singular (only the first **you** is plural). That they are later accretions is clear from the loose subordinate structure of verse 16, and the concluding affirmation formula of verse 15 being repeated at the end of verse 17.

4b–5. For the introductory formula, cf. note on verse 4. For **Lord God,** cf. on

2.4, as also for verses 7, 8, 11. **nations, countries,** terms commonly used by Ezekiel for heathen peoples and lands respectively. Jerusalem at the centre of the world is not simply a mark of provincial pride, but the result of divine election, the 'place Yahweh chose to put his name there' (Dt. *passim*). For the **centre of the nations,** cf. 38.12. Later Deutero-Isaiah used this notion as redemptive theme for the future day of Yahweh.

6. This unique position of favour has been used as occasion for exceptional wickedness. Israel has rebelled against Yahweh's ordinances (casuistic law) and statutes (apodictic law). Israel is pre-eminent in position and in wickedness.

7. Its secondary character is clear both from the repetitive nature of its contents and the recurrence of the introductory oracular formula (already in verse 5). RSV follows a minority Hebrew reading in verse *b*. Better to read with MT 'and have not (even) acted according to the ordinances of the nations that are round about you'. Israel shared casuistic or case law (ordinances) with the Near East in general, whereas apodictic or categorical law (statutes) was a form of law indigenous to Israel.

8. Here the introductory oracular formula may be original since judgment is proclaimed. RSV rightly has **judgments** with G. for the Hebrew 'ordinances'. **Behold . . . against you,** is particularly characteristic of Ezekiel (13.8, 21.3 (MT 8); 26.3; 28.22; 29.2, 10; 35.3; 38.3; 39.1; cf. also 13.20, 30.22, 34.10, and 36.9).

10. RSV has smoothed the text. The Hebrew has 'sons' for **their sons.** Probably **their** should be omitted throughout. Cannibalism is elsewhere attested as the extremes to which the famine of a besieged city might drive the besieged (cf. 2 Kg. 6.24–30); as evidence for divine punishment for disobedience, cf. Lev. 26.27–29; Jer. 19.6–9. The prediction does not necessarily reflect acquaintance with actual siege conditions, but is simply a figure for the extremities of the siege. The last clause is somewhat at variance with verse 2 which it echoes, since it is not the remnant but a third that is to be dispersed.

11. I will cut you down is based on an early (T.) conjecture. The Hebrew 'I will withdraw', i.e. my presence, is to be preferred as more in harmony with the succeeding parallel clauses.

12. Interpreting the action of verse 2. 'Fire' is interpreted as both **pestilence** and **famine,** which led G. to change the text to read four quarters rather than three thirds. Furthermore the last two (**sword** and **scatter**) are transposed probably because of the mention of 'sword' in the last clause. G. is a striking example of the continuance of traditional growth at a late date.

13–17. G. has a shorter text tradition, often an earlier stage than MT. Thus in verse 13 **I will vent** and **and satisfy myself** are not attested. In verse 14 **and an object . . . you and** appears as a late addition which G. partly attests by a doublet translation, 'and your daughters [i.e. cities] about you', for the Hebrew word *sbybwtyk*, 'round about you' (cf. *wbnwtyk*, 'and your daughters'). The addition probably comes from verse 15. In verse 15 G. has only two words for the four: **reproach, taunt, warning, horror,** and for **in anger . . . chastisements,** simply

'in the execution of my anger'. In verse 16 G. rightly omits **which . . . upon you.**
The longer Hebrew text probably represents later amplifications to the text.

13b. The first occurrence of the recognition formula so common to the book.
When events predicted take place people will recognize Yahweh as the source of
revelation.

14–15. Closely related to the recognition formula is the affirmation formula at
the end of verse 15. That Yahweh identifies himself as the one who has spoken is
the pledge that the judgment given will certainly take place. RSV correctly follows
Versions in **you shall be** for Hebrew 'it shall be'.

16. Reference in famine and breaking the staff of bread is to the fire of verse 2
as interpreted in verse 12. RSV changed MT 'against them' to **against you.** The
change of persons represents difference in source.

17. Two layers of tradition apparent in change from plural 'you' to singular
'you' in verse 17aβ. The list of plagues differs completely from that in the primary
tradition in verse 2; here they are famine, wild beasts, pestilence, bloodshed, and
the sword. For the affirmation formula, cf. on verse 15.

E. THE MOUNTAINS OF ISRAEL ADDRESSED 6.1–14

The recognition formula occurs four times in the chapter (verses 7, 10, 13, 14). The
material after verse 13a is an editorial attempt to tie the material of the chapter
together by references to the first section. Thus reference to idols and altars occurs
in verses 4–6; desolation and waste echoes verses 4, 6. **high hill** and **green tree** are
reminiscent of the editor of Jeremiah, and **pleasing odour,** of P. The chapter thus
consists of three separate sections tied together by an editor (verses 1–7, 8–10,
11–13a). Its placement after chapters 4–5 was probably due to the recurrence of the
triad, sword, famine, and pestilence, in verses 11–12 (cf. 5.12). The reference in
verse 11 to **all the evil abominations** may be evidence of the editor's attempt to
tie this section to section (a), the reference being to cultic malpractices, whereas the
woe prophecy concerns people rather than abominations.

Section (b) is the latest layer since exilic conditions are presupposed. For details
of text and literary history, cf. below.

Section (a) is an oracle against the high places which embodies several accretions.
In verse 3 **to the mountains, valleys** seems secondary, but cf. 36 6. Verse 5a
is absent in G. and shows its secondary nature by the use of the 3rd plural; it is an
adaptation from Lev. 26.30. The style of verses 4a, 6–7a with its use of the passive
(statives and Niphal forms) instead of 1st singular active as well as the shift in
addressee from the mountains to the people of Israel indicates a later stratum. The
original oracle is contained in verses 3–4b, 5b, and 7b.

(a) THE MOUNTAINS OF ISRAEL **6.1–7**

2. set your face toward and **mountains of Israel:** favourite phrases in the
book. The former may originally (as Zimmerli) have implied actual visual contact
on the part of a seer in order to effect a prophetic word as in the case of Balaam
(cf. Num. 23.13 with 24.2), but this primitive notion is not valid here. In Ezekiel

it simply means 'turn attention to'. The latter term intends the whole land of Israel (cf. chapter 36), but is used to focus on Israel's cultic sins.

3. For **Lord God** here and at verse 11, cf. 2.4.

3–4. The paraphernalia of illegitimate cult is comprised of **high places, altars, incense altars,** and **idols.** High places had been declared illegitimate places of sacrifice by the adoption of D by Josiah as breeding places for syncretistic cult. Josiah's reform in 622 B.C. became ineffective, however, after his death, and Jehoiakim's reign marked a return to former practices. High places were so called because of their usual location, though this was not essential; cf. Jer. 7.31 and its reference to high places in the Hinnom valley. The word *ḥammān*, occurs only here and in verse 6 in Ezekiel. G. made a guess at its meaning by the vague *temenē* 'sacred place'. Jewish commentators interpreted it as 'pillars to the sun'. The word is now known from archaeological finds as meaning an incense altar or stand, numerous specimens having been found in Palestine and Syria. *Gillûlîm* is a particularly favourite term for **idols** in Ezekiel. The term is obviously one of ridicule, a pun on *gēlālîm*, 'dung pellets', thus 'dung-idols'. Its vocalization is on the analogy of *šiḳḳûṣîm*—'detestable things'. Though the mountains are addressed it is the populace that must be intended since Yahweh is to bring a sword. The purpose of casting the slain before the idols was to defile the high places and render them unfit for cultic use; cf. Josiah's burning of bones on illegitimate altars on the occasion of his reform (2 Kg. 23.15–20).

5. Verse 5a is an amplification either of verses 4b or 5b. Verse 5b is parallel to 4b, as are the two clauses of 4a to each other.

6–7a. G. represents a shorter and earlier text by omitting **and ruined, and destroyed,** and **and your works wiped out.** The Hebrew word *wy'šmw*, 'and be held guilty', is a mistaken spelling for *wyšmw*, 'and be ruined', as S.T.V. **your works** may refer generally to Israel's cultic practices, or probably more specifically to the idols which they have made (cf. Isa. 44.9–20).

(b) A REMNANT WILL REMEMBER 6.8–10

The purpose of this section is to show that the judgment of the preceding oracle is not Yahweh's final end for Israel. Those who escape will learn to confess their judge in their exilic home, and to loathe their former abominations.

8. MT represents a conflation of two traditions *whwtrty* and *bhywt*, G. preserving the latter. Either one is possible Hebrew, but not both. The first tradition would be '*But I will leave* some among you who escape the sword among the nations', and the second, '*when there will be* some among you who . . .'. For the former construction, cf. 12.16, whereas the latter construction parallels **and when you are scattered** in verse 8b.

9. A corrupt Hebrew text. RSV has changed Hebrew 'I have been broken' to **I have broken** correctly (though G. attests *nšbrty* by its mistranslation *omōmoka*, 'I have sworn', presupposing *hšb'ty*). G. also omits **which has departed** and **for the evils . . . committed,** probably rightly. Render: '. . . whose heart which turned like a harlot from me and whose eyes turned like a harlot after their idols

I have broken', a zeugmatic construction recognized by RSV. The phrase 'turned like a harlot' (RSV—euphemistically **turn wantonly**) is a vivid figure made famous by Hosea to denote idolatry. To **remember** God is to confess Him. This involves verse 9b, viz. self-loathing for idolatry.

10. G. again represents a shorter tradition, viz. the simple recognition formula: 'And they shall know that I, the LORD, have spoken.' The phrase **not in vain** is however, germane to the passage since the effectiveness of Yahweh's speech is demonstrated by the exile's confession and self-loathing. The remainder **that I would . . . them** is probably an accretion.

(c) ALAS FOR ISRAEL 6.11–14

11. G. omits **evil** rightly, since the Hebrew text is impossible; possibly the original text was even shorter, omitting **of all the evil abominations.** The word **for** represents the relative pronoun '*šr*, which can then be correctly rendered 'which (shall fall . . .)'. G. changes the order to sword, pestilence, and famine throughout (also in verse 12), but this is hardly original. For the word '*ḥ*, 'alas!', cf. also 21.15 (MT 20), 'ah!'; it should not be changed to *h'ḥ*—'aha!' (as 25.3; 26.2; 36.2), as many suggest. The clapping of hands and stamping of feet are usually symbols of malicious joy as at 25.6, but they are ironic. If '*ḥ* is changed to *h'ḥ* this would continue the irony.

12. G. omits **and (he) that is left** rightly. It was probably intended to interpret *whnṣwr* 'and he that is preserved', which could also mean 'and he that is besieged', which misinterpretation G. preserved.

13aβ, b, 14. G. shows the fluid state of the text by 'your' for 'their' in **their slain, their idols,** and **their altars** and by 'you' for **they** in the last clause, but following the 3rd plural elsewhere. G. also shows an earlier stage of the text by the absence of **on all the mountain tops** and **and under every leafy oak.** The dimensions of the land are defined from south to north as **from the wilderness** (south of the Negeb) **to Riblah** (in Syria on the Orontes, cf. 2 Kg. 23.33; 25.6; Jer. 52.9), and not 'from the wilderness of Diblatha' as MT and Versions, which is impossible as vocalized in MT.

F.   THE END HAS COME 7.1–27

Chapter 7 is one of Ezekiel's greatest poems, but the text is difficult—in fact, some passages defy any attempt at translation, and it has suffered from numerous accretions. The first problem lies in verses 2–9. It seems clear that there are two versions of a single short poem. Both verses 4 and 9 end with the recognition formula showing the end of a section. Verse 2 finds its parallel in verse 5; verse 3 in verse 8; and verse 4 in verse 9. G. may well help to unscramble the text here. It has inserted, between verses 2 and 3, the phrase 'the end has come' followed by verses 6–9. After verse 4 all of verses 5–6 is omitted except the introductory oracular formula 'therefore thus says the Lord' to introduce verse 10. This peculiar rearrangement of text is of course incorrect, but it does suggest that verses 5–9 are the later doublet of the original poem, and that verse 10 begins a new oracle expanding in detail the theme set forth in the introductory poem.

A comparison of the short poem (verses 2–4) with the long poem (verses 10–27) will immediately show a basic stylistic difference. Poem A (as well as its doublet in verses 5–9) is mainly in the 1st person, whereas Poem B is mainly in the 3rd person. The only materials in the 1st person are verses 20*b*–22, 24, and 27*ba*. These are probably to be taken as later amplification and commentary on the original poem. Other parts of the poem have also had accretions and G. often by its shorter text is evidence for an earlier stage in the history of the text. Thus in Poem B the following verses are shorter in G.: verses 11, 12, 13, 14, 16, 19, 20, 23, 24, and 27. Details will be presented below.

The poem deals with the 'day of Yahweh' as a day of darkness for Israel. The end has come. Yahweh's patience with Israel is at an end. The theme of an end time in Am. 8.2 is dramatically taken up and carried to its full conclusion. Later apocalyptic writers, especially Daniel, were to translate this into a day of vindication, just as Deutero-Isaiah did for the term 'day of Yahweh', but Ezekiel belonged to the classical doom prophets who saw for sinful Israel a catastrophic end. The poem, though undated, must have been composed prior to the fall of Jerusalem. It was intended, as so many of his oracles, to show his exilic audience that the future of Israel lay with them and not with those who remained in the land of Israel. These Ezekiel believed to be completely doomed to destruction.

(a) POEM A 7.1–4

2. G.S. add 'say!' after **son of man.** An imperative of some kind is expected. For **Lord GOD**, cf. 2.4. The term **land** (*'dmt*) **of Israel** occurs only (seventeen times) in Ezekiel. The prophecy concerns the land, and more particularly its inhabitants. The direct address throughout refers to the land, except for the recognition formulas at verses 4 and 9 which concern the inhabitants. The 3rd plural use refers to the people. For the **end** coming, cf. Am. 8.2. The prophetic rationale has it that wickedness stores up seeds of inevitable destruction. Ezekiel, like Amos, feels that nothing can avert that impulse towards doom. The term for land in **four corners of the land** is *'rṣ* and means 'the earth'. The full expression refers to the universe, but should not be pressed. For Ezekiel the end of Israel had cosmic implications. The expression is common in Assyrian texts, where when combined with 'heaven' it means the entire universe.

3. The coming of doom is morally conditioned as the terms **anger, judge,** and **punish** show. Yahweh's anger is personified as a divine messenger of destruction, which had been held back until the land's iniquity reached a certain height. A favourite term of Ezekiel for Israel's sin is **abominations,** emphasizing Yahweh's repugnance and loathing for the unclean and impure.

4. For verse 4*a* cf. 5.11; usually **you** is omitted as G. and 5.11; 8.18; 9.5, 10 *et al.* RSV gives an incorrect interpretation in **while . . . midst.** Ezekiel does not here allow for repentance as a way of avoiding punishment. What is meant is that

Israel's abominations will be allowed to run their inevitable course. Verse 4ba might be rendered 'for I will place your ways upon you and your abominations will continue in your midst'.

(b) A PARALLEL VERSION 7.5–9

5. MT has 'Disaster, even a disaster'. RSV is based on a minority reading of '*hr* for '*ht* (as T.).

6. A corrupt text. The last clause in RSV cannot be correct. The verb **comes** is feminine and the subject, 'end', is masculine. The first word in verse 7 repeats *b'h*, 'it comes'. The word is probably a dittograph, and **Behold** should be moved to the beginning of verse 7. Also peculiar is the verb **it has awakened.** To say that the end has awakened when thematically it has come seems odd. MT represents a pun, *hḳṣ/hḳyṣ*, and may simply be a scribal error, a dittograph but in *plene* form, later revocalized as a verb. Delete and read 'the end has come against you'.

7. The translation of this verse is mainly guess-work. The word *hṣpyrh*, **doom,** as in verse 10, occurs elsewhere only at Isa. 28.5, but with the meaning of 'crown'. V. renders by *contritio*, and G. omits. AV's 'the morning' is based on the Aramaic *ṣpr'* and is wrong. On the basis of Arabic, 'cycle' or 'turning' has been suggested. 'Destruction' has been suggested from Akkadian. The word 'doom' (not 'your doom') is as good a guess as any. The end of the verse is also obscure. MT simply has 'a tumult' for **a day of tumult.** The word *hd*, **joyous shouting,** occurs only here, but is probably attested by G. G. has 'neither with tumults nor with pangs' (*ōdinōn*, possibly by inner Greek corruption for *ōdōn*, 'songs'), but omits **upon the mountains.** Originally it may simply have been 'a tumult (i.e. of battle) without joyous shouts (i.e. of defeat rather than victory)'. It is thus descriptive of a day of Yahweh, which is darkness and not light (cf. Am. 5.18).

9. Cf. commentary on verse 4. **who smite** should read 'the one who smites'.

(c) POEM B 7.10–27

10. This poem also began with an introductory formula; cf. notes above. **Behold it comes,** impossible since the verb *b'h*, 'it comes', is feminine, and its subject *ywm*, 'day', masculine. Delete **it comes.** For **your doom,** cf. on verse 7. **injustice,** based on *hammuṭṭeh* for MT *hammaṭṭeh* 'the rod'; cf. Num. 17.8 (MT 23); cf. on 9.9. It is then a pun on **rod** in verse 11. The day of Yahweh is a day of harvest, a reaping of the fruits of injustice and arrogance (or **pride**). For the day of Yahweh, cf. Zeph. 1.14–18.

11. Completely corrupt and defying reconstruction. For verse 11a G. has 'And he shall break the rod of the wicked'. The remainder of the verse is unintelligible.

12–13. *Trade will cease.* Both verses are badly preserved. G. lacks **for wrath . . . multitude** in verse 12, a late addition. Verse 13 has also been enlarged by later tradition. G. omits **while they live . . . turn back.** The phrase 'while they live' is an attempt to render three Hebrew words literally 'still alive their life'. This addition actually misconstrues the original meaning. Neither buyer nor seller will react emotionally in Yahweh's day, for all will be alike; all will be together in

Sheol (cf. Job 3.13–19). The original text is supported by the final clause, which may be rendered 'as for one whose life is in his iniquity, they shall not be able to hold on to it', i.e. all sinners shall die. As for the remainder of the text omitted by G., where MT has 'for vision [probably a mistake for **wrath**] shall not return upon all their multitude', this is also an addition to the original poem. Practically the same words occur at the end of verse 12 and verse 14.

Yahweh's day will be one of defeat in warfare 14–16

14. G. omits **but none . . . multitude** (though *polemos* 'war, battle', does occur at the beginning of verse 15). The last clause is in the 1st person and thus an accretion. But the text of verse 14a is also corrupt. The first verb is plural and the second singular. The word for **all** looks much like that for 'weapons', which, with trumpets, are accoutrements for battle. Change *whkyn hkl* (**and made all ready**) to *hkynw hkly* and render verse 14a: 'The trumpet is blown; weapons are prepared, but none goes out to battle.'

15. Sword, pestilence, and famine are used by Ezekiel to describe the punishment which Israel is to undergo, 6.11–12; cf. 5.16–17. Verse 15b is an explanation of a, but may be at odds with the intent of the figure. The words represent a siege rather than its outcome. One going outside the walls would be slain, whereas a tight siege caused famine and plague to rage within.

16. Omit with G. **like doves of the valleys,** and with S. change *hmwt* (**moaning**) to *ymwtw* ('they will die'). Then verse 16b reads: 'All of them will die, each in his iniquity.' There is to be no remnant, no escape from the consequences of their wickedness.

A day of terror and mourning 17–18

17. Terror will overtake them rendering them enfeebled. G. renders verse 17b more correctly as 'their thighs shall be stained with moisture', a mark of extreme fright.

18. sackcloth, baldness, signs of great distress and mourning; cf. Isa. 15.2–3; 22.12. **horror** refers to the emotion with which the hopeless here meet the prospect of death, whereas the veil of **shame** signifies the loss of standing in a community and hence of the prospect of honourable life.

Wealth will be useless on that day 19–20a

19. G. does not have **their silver and gold . . . LORD,** a later accretion. Silver and gold will lose their value, in fact will be proven worse than useless; they were the cause for the wickedness which is now bringing on destruction. The term *ndh*, **an unclean thing,** signifies menstrual impurity (cf. 18.6; 22.10).

20a. An elaboration on the statement that silver and gold become a stumbling-block. The text needs some correction. Omit **and their detestable things** with G. as a late comment on **abominable images.** The first clause in the verse is singular throughout in MT. Thus MT reads: 'As for the beauty of its [i.e. of silver and gold] ornament one used it for vain glory.' S. simplifies as RSV by reading the plural. The silver and gold, beautiful ornaments though they be in themselves, have been moulded into idols. **used for vainglory** here means used as objects of pride, i.e. idols of gold and silver.

20b–24. This section uses the 1st person and was not part of Poem B. It is prose, whereas the poem is in poetic form. The use of the 3rd plural pronouns is peculiar. The words **them** and **their** always refer to the Israelites, whereas **they** refers to the invaders. Verse 20b is probably a later commentary on *a*, as the repetition of **an unclean thing** shows. The fragment in verses 21–24 is so specific in its detail that it must date from after 586 B.C. by someone (possibly the prophet) who knew of the pillaging and destruction of the Temple and city.

21. foreigners, wicked: the Babylonians.

22. The Temple was not inviolate, because Yahweh intentionally hid himself from the people. **my precious** (or secret) **place** refers to the Temple in general, but more particularly to the Holy of Holies; cf. V. *arcanum meum*.

23. and make a desolation: apparently based on G. 'and they shall effect confusion', rather than the obscure Hebrew 'Make the chain!'

24. Verse 24a is a late tradition absent in G. **their holy places** is based on a revocalization of MT's *mᵉkadᵉšēhem* ('those sanctifying them') as *mikdᵉšēhem* (G. V. also). Technically there was only one legitimate holy place according to D, but the Judeans had many shrines as well.

The conclusion to Poem B **25–27**

Textually only verse 27 shows later accretions. **The king mourns** is not in G. and was added to explain **the prince** which is Ezekiel's favourite term for the Judean ruler. A prosaic commentary in the 1st person is also evident in **and according . . . judge them.** The poem ends appropriately with the recognition formula, which again gives point to the poem, viz. that the divine purpose of the judgment is recognition of Yahweh.

25. peace, wholeness in every way, physically (health), economically (prosperity), and socially (solidarity). Instead of this human ideal there will be **anguish,** undoubtedly because of the siege.

26. For disaster upon disaster, cf. the story of Job (chapter 1). **rumour** means evil report. For verse 26b, cf. Jer. 18.18 where the passage is, however, secondary, with the change of **vision** to 'word' and **elders** to 'wise'. The prophetic word was often visual (cf. 1.1). The unspoken conclusion to **they seek . . . prophet** is 'but there is none', since it is parallel to the next two clauses. The term *twrh,* **law,** is better rendered 'instruction'. The priest was the ancient custodian of sacred traditions and both through this accumulated tradition and through priestly means of ascertaining the divine will, such as the ephod, Urim and Thummim, and the lot, he was the means for explaining *torah.* The **prophet** or visionary was a more direct and inspired medium of revelation. The **elder** in contrast to youth (Isa. 3.5) was wise in experience and had standing in the community.

27. prince: Ezekiel's usual designation for Zedekiah. Both prince and populace are terror-stricken.

G. A Vision of Temple Idolatry 8.1–11.25

These four chapters constitute a single section. At the beginning of chapter 8 the prophet is ecstatically transported to Jerusalem, and not until the end of chapter 11 is he returned to Chaldea, where he informs his exilic audience about all the things he has seen.

The section has been extensively expanded as can be seen upon analysis. It includes the following accounts: (a) ecstatic transport to the Temple (8.1–4); (b) visions of the cultic abominations perpetrated in and near the Temple (8.5–18); (c) Yahweh's command to his messengers to destroy the city (9.1–11); (d) the man clothed in linen ordered to destroy the city with fire (10.1–7); (e) vision of the cherubim and the wheels (10.8–17); (f) Yahweh's glory leaves the threshold and hovers above the cherub (10.18–19); (g) the cherubim again (10.20–22); (h) vision of twenty-five wicked counsellors near the Temple (11.1–13); (i) an oracle of restoration from exile (11.14–21); and (j) the full departure of Yahweh's glory and the prophet's return to Chaldea (11.22–25).

The first and final sections constitute the setting for the entire vision which thematically concerns the idolatry of the Jerusalemites and their punishment. Thus sections (b), (c), and (d) are the heart of the vision along with (f). Sections (e) and (g) are attempts to tie this vision with the inaugural vision in chapter 1, as can be seen from the repeated insistence that the cherubim were the same as those living creatures seen by the River Chebar (10.15, 20, 22). Section (h) may be a doublet account of 8.16–18; in any event, it is inappropriate in its context. The sins detailed in chapter 8 are all cultic abominations, whereas this section simply condemns the leaders for misguided optimism. The oracle in verses 5–12 could be by Ezekiel, but it does not belong here. Section (i) is completely out of context. There is no room for restoration prophecy in this chamber of horrors. For accretions even within the original sections (especially in section (d)), cf. commentary below.

Objection to section (h) is sometimes raised on the logical basis that according to chapter 9 the wicked are destroyed and in chapter 10 the city burned by fire. It would then be illogical to begin again at the east Temple gate with twenty-five wicked men and the detailing of the death of Pelatiah. Since time and space are inconsequential in a vision, this argument should not be pressed. Nor is the death of Pelatiah a case of second sight. It is also part of the vision.

The marks of an ecstatic vision are all present in the account. The prophet feels himself transported by the hair and eventually returned, presumably in like fashion. He sees the glory of God and heavenly messengers and hears them converse. The terms used to describe the ecstatic experience are intentionally vague (cf. 8.1–4). Though this is the outstanding case of ecstatic vision in the O.T., it stands in the line of classical prophecy. Micaiah saw a heavenly vision and heard a divine dialogue (1 Kg. 22.17–22); Elijah was thought customarily to be transported by the spirit (1 Kg. 18.12; 2 Kg. 2.16); Elisha was endowed with second sight (2 Kg. 5.26;

6.8–14). Isaiah's inaugural vision in which he saw the Lord sitting on a throne in the Temple and heard supernatural dialogue is an excellent parallel (Isa. 6). Amos saw the Lord standing with a plumb-line beside a wall (Am. 7.7) and again standing upon an altar (Am. 9.1).

This vision has sometimes been taken as proof that Ezekiel prophesied in Jerusalem rather than in Babylon. It is argued that the relevancy of the vision pertains only to Jerusalem, something which is true for much of chapters 1–24. A prophet's audience need not, however, be present. Isaiah and Jeremiah, as well as Ezekiel, prophesied against foreign nations (cf. chapters 25–32; Isa. 13–23; Jer. 46–51), but they were hardly present. Furthermore, Ezekiel's real audience was exilic. The exiles are not to pin any hopes on Jerusalem's future; it is corrupt and must be destroyed.

For the parallel to this vision of Yahweh's departure in the vision of his return to Jerusalem and the Temple in chapters 40–48, cf. on 43.1–12.

(a) ECSTATIC TRANSPORT TO THE JERUSALEM TEMPLE 8.1–4

1. The date of the vision is given as a year and two months after the inaugural vision (1.1–2). G. changes the month to fifth, probably under influence of **the fifth day.** This would be August–September in 592 B.C. Critics have suggested that G. is original and MT an editorial change to allow for the 390 days of 4.5, 9, plus the seven days of 3.16. The date would then be editorial. This cannot be right, however, since an editor would also have allowed for the forty days of 4.6. This would make 437 days. A lunar year consists of 354 days, which, plus two months, would make 414 or 413 days. The date is thus not the product of an editor who knew the accretions in 4.5–9, and must be original. The vision took place in his house in the presence of Judean elders. Apparently the social structure of Judah carried over to the exiles (cf. 2 Kg. 6.32). For **Lord GOD,** cf. on 2.4. The last clause is a regular idiom for entrance into an ecstatic state (cf. 1.3; 40.1 and 11.5).

2. This interrupts the account of the transport and may not be original, being an adaptation of 1.26b–27 (cf. 40.3). The **man** can hardly be Yahweh, since Yahweh appears in the vision as His 'glory', cf. verse 4; 9.3; 10.18; 11.22, 23. On the other hand, the agent of transport is identified as the divine spirit in verse 3. RSV adopts **man** for MT 'fire' rightly, as G. (*'yš* for *'š*), cf. 1.26b. Visionary language is clear from the avoidance of actual description by such phrases as **form that had the appearance, what appeared to be,** and **appearance of brightness** (cf. on chapter 1).

3. This is the first instance of ecstatic transport by the hair; cf. Bel and the Dragon (verses 36, 39) where Habakkuk is thus transported to Babylon. G. omits **of the inner court,** which if correct makes the first location the north gate of the city (possibly the Benjamin Gate, Jer. 37.13); the second, the outer or great court, 1 Kg. 7.12; the third, the entrance of the north Temple gate; and the last, in the inner court, 1 Kg. 7.12. Actually MT has only 'of the inner' with the word 'court' being added in RSV *ad sensum*. Ezekiel is aware that these are **visions** (not a vision as G.) **of God,** and not a physical transport. Problematic is the concluding phrase

where was ... to jealousy. One would hardly expect mention of the phrase until Ezekiel is told to view the abomination in verse 5. **seat** may refer to a recessed niche in the gateway in which an image was placed. The words **which provokes to jealousy** are probably an editorial explanation for the image of jealousy. Various conjectures as to its meaning have been proposed, but none is fully convincing. The editorial gloss may well be correct, i.e. an idol of some kind which provokes Yahweh to jealousy.

4. Reference to the presence of the divine glory is unexpected since it was in the Temple, hardly at the north gate. The allusion to the inaugural vision shows that the verse derives from the author of 10.15, 20, 22. G. adds *kurios* before **God of Israel,** but this is not correct. Only two designations for the divine glory are attested throughout: 'glory of the God of Israel' and 'glory of Yahweh', but not a conflate of both.

(b) VISIONS OF CULTIC ABOMINATIONS 8.5–18

(i) *The image of jealousy* 5–6

In each of the four vile abominations Yahweh speaks to the prophet and brings him to a new place. G. wrongly omits reference to the image of jealousy and misread *hmzbh*, 'altar', as *hmzrḥh*, 'the one towards the east', i.e. north-east. The offensive idol stood in the gateway, probably in its niche (cf. verse 3).

6. G. attests a shorter text omitting **that the house of Israel,** i.e. simply having 'they are committing great abominations here'. There is no antecedent for 'they', but it clearly refers to the Jerusalemites. **to drive me far** is an incorrect rendering of *lrhkh*, which means 'to be far off ', thus, 'at a distance'. Yahweh is not yet driven off from his sanctuary; his glory leaves voluntarily at 11.23 at the end of the vision. It is rather the people who are engaging in idolatrous cult at the north gate of the city outside the Temple precincts. The final clause also occurs at the end of the next two visions.

(ii) *Idolatrous imagery* 7–13

This passage contains certain difficulties. The area in which seventy elders are engaged in idolatrous worship must have been fairly large. All the other abominations were openly performed. But the prophet is brought to a hole in the wall near or at the door of the court. Then he is told to dig in the wall even though a hole already exists. Only after this is a door found. Here, according to MT, the men were worshipping wall pictures of various idols in the dark. G. omits the phrase **in the dark** in verse 12 as well as all of verse 7*b*. It does have a version of verse 8, but without the two references to a wall. All these are later accretions based on the account in 12.1–8.

7. It has often been suggested that the courtyard where this takes place is at the north gate of the palace within the Temple complex. This would fit with Ezekiel's procession from the city wall to the inner Temple court.

9. G. rightly omits the gloss **vile**; cf. on 6.11. In the original text this immediately follows verse 7*a*.

10. Precisely what the cultic aberration consisted of is not clear. Scholars have suggested Babylonian cult, Egyptian influence, a secret *hieros gamos* ceremony, or a vegetation-deity rite. What is clear is that images were engraved, probably in relief, on the wall. RSV represents MT inadequately. MT says: 'engraved on the wall was every form of creeping thing and cattle, loathsome things, and all the idols . . .'. G. does not have 'every form . . . cattle', probably reading 'all loathsome things and all the idols . . .'. The phrase, though secondary and based on Dt. 4.15–18, is a correct interpretation. What was particularly revolting was the disregard of the proscription of images in Yahweh's cult, especially animal forms of deity. For **idols,** cf. on 6.4.

11. That seventy elders, as representative of the whole people (in Exod. 24 they with Moses, Aaron, Nadab, and Abihu see God in the covenant making ceremony; in Num. 11.16–25 they are to be specially consecrated with a measure of the spirit in order to share in the government of the people with Moses), were involved was particularly shocking. To 'stand before' means to serve cultically. Why one of the elders should be singled out is not clear unless it was to call attention to the decay which had set in in the house of Shaphan, who first read the 'book of the law' to the righteous Josiah (2 Kg. 22.8–10). The verb 'to stand' occurs twice but in different senses, and it is possible that the reference to Jaazaniah is an accretion. G. omits **of the cloud,** probably rightly.

12. MT has 'his rooms of carvings', which G. has in the singular 'in their hidden chamber', reading *mśkytw* quite differently. Could the text possibly mean each man performing cultically in the room of idols? Apparently the elders who should be the guardians of Yahwism now excuse their forsaking Yahweh's worship by accusing Yahweh of having already abandoned the land.

(iii) *Women bewailing Tammuz* **14–15**

The third scene is at the north gate of the Temple. **Tammuz** was a Sumerian (at least 3rd millennium B.C.) deity (Dumuzi), the brother and consort of Inanna (Ishtar in Akkadian; Ashtoreth in the O.T.), who in Semitic times was a vegetation deity. Annually in the summer, the dry season, he died and descended into the underworld. Then his sister would mourn for him and finally go down to bring him back to life. This was the period of rains and consequent renewal of fertility. During the month Tammuz (July) women bewailed the death of the fertility god. V. translates Tammuz into Adonis as his Syrian counterpart quite properly. The substitution of cultic wailing for a dead fertility god for the cult of the living Yahweh and that within the courts of his Temple was an abomination.

(iv) *Worship of the sun* **16–18**

16. Ezekiel is finally brought into the inner court of the Temple itself. The door of the Temple (i.e. of its nave) would be leading out to the porch (or vestibule); cf. 1 Kg. 6.3. Between it and the altar (probably the bronze altar; cf. 2 Kg. 16.10–16) in the court were twenty-five men, for which G. has twenty men. Possibly MT's twenty-five is an adaptation of 11.1, and thus a later reading. The final **toward the**

east is a later gloss unattested by G. The worshippers turn their backs upon Yahweh's Temple (cf. Jer. 32.33) and their adoring faces to the rising sun. Josiah had destroyed the cultic paraphernalia of sun worship at the time of the D Reform (2 Kg. 23.11), but this had again revived under Jehoiakim.

17. G. omits the expansion **and provoke me further to anger.** Possibly the preceding clause **that they should fill the land with violence** is an earlier gloss. The point of all these abominations is that they are cultically aberrant, whereas **violence** refers to social evils. The original question refers simply to the abominations. What **put the branch to the nose** means is obscure. G. interprets by *muktērizontes*—'turning up the nose', i.e. sneer. The problem is the meaning of *zmrh* which occurs elsewhere simply as 'vine branch' (15.2 and Num. 13.23). In Isa. 17.10 it designates slips of the vine set out for a strange god which some consider to be the vegetation god, thus possibly involving some idolatrous rite. Others have called on Egyptian or Persian parallels, and some have even thought of it as a phallic symbol, which is completely fantastic in this context. Traditional Jewish exegetes thought of some obscenity. When all is said and done, G.'s explanation is simplest and safest.

18. G. omits verse 18*b*, a reflection of 9.1. In view of the people's disregard for Yahweh, He will now vent His wrath on them.

(c) YAHWEH ORDERS THE SLAUGHTER OF THE WICKED **9.1–11**

The scene is now set for judgment. The narrative is fairly straightforward. The messengers of destruction gather to receive instructions. The scribe is given advance instructions to mark the faithful; the remaining messengers are to destroy the unmarked beginning at the Temple area itself. The prophet is appalled and tries to intercede, but Yahweh is not to be swayed. The scribe then returns reporting the completion of his assignment. Two major interruptions show later expansions of the text. Verse 3*a* introduces the presence of the glory of God, probably in order to show that it had left the Holy of Holies to stand at the threshold to make 10.18 possible. But 10.18 does not presuppose a prior stage, since Ezekiel would not view the glory of God departing from the Holy of Holies until it crossed the threshold. The second expansion is verse 7. The six messengers had already begun to carry out their orders when they were again given orders to defile the Temple and fill the courts (not 'court' as in the original account) with the slain. For minor accretions, cf. below.

1. Yahweh speaks with the voice of thunder; cf. Ps. 29.3–9 ('loud voice'). The verb *krbw* can hardly be Pi. imperative here since that would render the verb transitive (so RV). If MT correctly vocalizes the word (*kārᵉḇū*) it must be Qal perfect, i.e. 'have drawn near, are at hand'. G. supports this, though in the singular; RSV presupposes an emendation, *kirḇū*, as Exod. 16.9. **executioners** is a mistranslation as well. The word *pḳdwt* means 'overseers', 'those in charge', here in an evil sense. Yahweh makes an impressive announcement: 'Those who have charge over the city are at hand.' **each . . . hand** is probably an expansion based on verse 2, 'every man . . . hand'.

2. Seven men appear on the scene from the north. These are to be the divine messengers of judgment. For Yahweh's destroying angels, cf. the J Exodus story (Exod. 12.23), the story of the evil census in the time of David (2 Sam. 24.16), and the slaughter of Sennacherib's army (2 Kg. 19.35). The passover story in Exod. 12 has a number of parallels to this account. A distinctive mark, the blood on the lintel, saved a household from death; the slaughter was throughout the land, and it was effected by a destroying angel. The number 'seven' for the angels who carry out the divine judgment first occurs here, later becoming popular (cf. Tob. 12.15; Rev. 8.2, 6; 15.6–8; 16). They came through the north gate of the Temple, rebuilt by Jotham (2 Kg. 15.35); cf. Jer. 20.2, where it is called the 'upper Benjamin Gate'. The area between the porch and the altar (made by Ahaz, 2 Kg. 16.10–15) was occupied by the sun worshippers (8.16–18), and the bronze altar was directly to the north of the Ahaz altar (2 Kg. 16.14). Six of the angels bore a weapon. **for slaughter** really means 'his club' or 'battle-axe'. The word *mpṣ* literally means 'a shatterer'. G. translates by *pelux*—'axe' and omits 'his weapon'. **linen** was the clothing for priests. Priests were charged with instruction (cf. on 7.26), and writing was undoubtedly common among priests. **writing case** is literally 'case of the scribe'. The word for 'case', *ḳst*, is an Egyptian loan-word. It was a small case carrying writing implements and the materials for making ink. In Babylonia it was a leather case containing the stylus. It is the former which is meant here. G. misunderstood the word for scribe *hspr* as *hspyr*—'sapphire'.

3. For **the glory of . . . God,** cf. on 1.28. The glory is here shown as resting on the cherubim (MT singular but collective). This may be compared with the evidence of divine glory in the cloud filling the Temple (1 Kg. 8.10–11).

4. Omit **the LORD** as G. The consecution **through the city, through Jerusalem** contains a doublet; probably the latter is the gloss, though G. omits the former, possibly by parablepsis. The angelic scribe is to put a preserving mark on the foreheads of the righteous; cf. the mark on Cain's forehead (Gen. 4.15). The word for 'mark' in Hebrew is *tāw*, the last letter of the alphabet which in the old Canaanite script was an X. Thus it means to put an X on the forehead. Reference to the seal on the forehead of the redeemed in Rev. 7.3–4(cf. Rev. 14.1) is undoubtedly based on this passage. The early church took the *tāw* as the symbol of the cross and thus as a specifically Christian symbol. The two words in Hebrew rendered **who sigh and groan** are alliterative: *hanneʾenāḥîm wᵉhanneʾenāḳîm.*

5–6. the others: the six remaining. All those unmarked are to be killed, but those having the X are to be spared. The distinction is reminiscent of the Exodus story; cf. also Abraham's question in Gen. 18.23. The judgment is begun at the Temple itself, no longer valid as an asylum (cf. 2 Kg. 11.15), and then proceeds throughout the city. G. renders the last sentence 'and they began with the men who were inside the house', i.e. the sun worshippers of 8.16. Since these are not called elders, the word *hzḳnym* ('the elders') may be secondary.

7. G. misread *hḥṣrwt*, **courts,** as *hḥwṣwt*, 'streets'. The latter part of the verse is confused. **Go forth** is overly abrupt, and the verb is immediately repeated (G.S. have the verb but once). Read instead, 'Go forth and smite the city.'

8. For **Lord God**, cf. on 2.4. **and I was left alone** is unattested in G., and may be an explanatory gloss. Though Ezekiel seldom shows mercy for the people of Jerusalem, here as intercessor he shows himself in the old prophetic tradition of Amos (Am. 7.2, 5) and Jeremiah (Jer. 8.18–21; 14.7–9, 19–22) and Moses (Num. 14.13–19). **all that remains** is more lit. 'all the remnant'. The populace had already been severely decimated by the deportation of 597 B.C. Ezekiel's more normal interest centres on the remnant already in exile.

9. God will not listen to the intercession of his prophet (cf. Jer. 7.16; 11.14; 14.11–12; 15.1), because their guilt is too excessive for a stay in punishment. The condemnation is unexpectedly based not on their cultic sins, as might be expected, but on social sins, again in line with the eighth- and seventh-century prophetic emphasis, and may be secondary. **blood** is commonly used in Hebrew for bloodshed and violence, whereas the word *mṭh* (only here, but cf. on 7.10) signifies that which is bent, thus 'perverse', i.e. injustice. G. has a doublet here, 'injustice and impurity', the latter a misreading of *mṭh* as *ṭm'h*.

10. For verse 10*a*, cf. on 5.11. It also occurs in verse 5.

11. Nothing is said of the return of the six, since they are unnecessary to the next stage in the vision. The scribe must return to be addressed in 10.2. Coming immediately after the preceding statement it dramatically recalls the remnant who are not destroyed, as an important supplementary reply to the prophetic intercession of verse 8.

(d) YAHWEH ORDERS DESTRUCTION BY FIRE **10.1–7**

It has been objected that this section could not be part of the same vision as chapter 9 since the destruction of the wicked has already been effected, and this destruction would be one of those with the mark, i.e. righteous. But an ecstatic vision is not to be construed as a logical consecution of events. Jerusalem is to be destroyed by sword and by fire and both are in this way successively portrayed.

Two distinct strands of composition are apparent in this section. Each verse mentions the cherubim; in verses 2, 4, and 7 it occurs in the singular collective, but in the remaining verses in the plural. Furthermore, the point of view of the latter is a reflection of the inaugural vision in chapter 1. The later writer is attempting to tie in the cherubim as being the living creatures of chapter 1 (cf. verses 15, 20). 10.1 is clearly based on 1.26; verse 5, on 1.24. 10.6 is an attempt to identify the **whirling wheels** (*glgl*) of this vision with the 'wheels' of chapter 1 (*'wpn*), whereas verse 3 simply amplifies the vision by depicting the exact location of the cherubim. Thus verses 2, 4, and 7 remain as the original vision. For smaller expansions within these verses, cf. commentary.

1. The gradual growth of this expansion is illustrated by G., which represents a shorter text. MT has 'like the appearance of the form of a throne appeared above them'. G. omits 'like', 'of the form', and 'appeared'. 1.26 makes no mention of cherubim (rather of living creatures; cf. commentary *ad loc.*).

2. This followed directly on 9.11. G. and RSV both omit 'and he said' (after 'linen') rightly. Also secondary is **from . . . cherubim**. G. failed to identify the man clothed in linen as the one in 9.11, simply calling him 'a man dressed in a robe'. **cherubim** is ultimately derived from the Tigris-Euphrates valley; the Akkadian *kāribu* means 'intercessor' for men with the gods. In Hebrew they were winged creatures in Yahweh's service who guarded his honour. They were the guardians of the Holy of Holies, where they symbolized the throne of the invisible deity. In the original vision only those cherubim from within the Temple were seen. To the ecstatic prophet they were the guardians of the holy fire. Admittedly this was not in the adytum, but such logic does not guide the visionary. Why these guardians of the fire should be mounted on whirling wheels is not known. Apparently the two cherubim were thus mounted on either side of the fire and above it. Possibly the altar itself was portable. Fire is often the symbol of purification. In Isaiah's call experience a seraph took a burning coal from the altar in order to touch the prophet's lips (Isa. 6.6–7). Here the divine messenger is to give handfuls of such coals in order to put fire to the city and destroy it. To 'go in' means into the Temple.

3. Its secondary nature is apparent from its awkward relation to verses 2 and 4. The man had gone in to the Temple to the cherubim, but here they are standing on the south side, i.e. in the court. All the activity in chapters 8 and 9 had been on the north and east sides. It also does not fit with verse 4, since a cloud fills the court, whereas in verse 4 it fills the house but the court is bright.

4. This is the first mention of the glory of Yahweh in the original vision. For the term, cf. on 1.28. The glory of the divine presence now appears accompanied with cloud and brightness prepared to leave the sanctuary. It has left the cherubim which still have a task to perform, viz. to give the divine messenger of destruction his means for destroying the city. For the cloud filling the house as a sign of the divine presence, cf. 1 Kg. 8.10–11. The twin phenomena are also reminiscent of the pillar of cloud and the pillar of fire in the wilderness, also symbols of the divine presence (Exod. 13.21–22). For the appearance of **brightness**, cf. on 1.27–28.

5. For the original description of the noise made by the wings, cf. on 1.24.

7. G. omits **from between the cherubim**, but has the other accretion **that was between the cherubim**. Both are in the plural and not part of the original narrative. As guardians of the fire it is appropriate that one of them should actually give the fire to the destroying angel who then left the Temple to perform his destructive duty.

(e) THE CHERUBIM AND THE WHEELS **10.8–17**

This entire section is a series of expansions based on chapter 1 added to ensure the identity of the cherubim with the living creatures of the initial vision. At times the expansions have become textually corrupt and the result is most peculiar. Only by comparing the text with its source in chapter 1 can some sense be made of it. Verses 9–12 and 16–17 seem on the whole to represent a picture based on 1.15–21. Thus verse 9 represents parts of 1.15–16, the differences being due to the intro- duction of the cherubim. Verse 10 is a reflection of 1.16; verse 11 amplifies 1.17

(note that verse 17*b* is added to explain pedantically what is meant by the preceding clause); verse 12 reproduces the content of 1.18. Verse 16 is parallel to 1.19, and verse 17 is equal to 1.21. Verse 8 is a gloss based on 1.8, but intended to explain how a winged cherub in verse 7 could stretch out a hand. This is probably an expansion of the text divorced from the main accretion in verses 9–12, 16–17. verse 15*a* is a clumsy reflection of verse 19 and quite out of place here. It was added in view of verse 16. Verse 15*b* makes explicit the identification of the cherubim as the living creatures of chapter 1, and verse 13 assures the reader of the identification of the wheels ('*wpn*) as 'whirling wheels' (*glgl*), which is backward indeed. It does demonstrate that verse 13 is later than the main expansion since the latter uses the term '*wpn* as does chapter 1, whereas the original vision used *glgl*. Verse 14 reflects 1.10, but in so doing misapplies it. In the original context the four-facedness applies to the living creatures, but here it applies to the wheels. That this absurdity was not intended in the narrative as a whole is clear from verses 21–22, where the four faces apply to the cherubim.

8. G. changes the verb to the 1st person due to a failure to realize that the verb was Ni. (i.e. passive, 'was seen', or **appeared**) and its subject, *tbnyt* (cf. on 1.8).

9. MT repeats the words **one beside each cherub** to show distribution; G. omits the repetition through haplography.

11. the front wheel renders *hr'š* which means 'the head'. The writer must have thought of the cherubim.

12. Similarly here the writer mistakenly had the cherubim in mind since the Hebrew has 'and all their bodies and their backs and their hands and their wings'. The word for 'backs' also means **rims,** and that for 'hands' **spokes.** Both G. and RSV omit 'and all their bodies', and RSV also omits 'and their wings', thereby making the reference to wheels possible. The last two words in MT are also difficult (*l'rb'tm 'wpnyhm*, i.e. 'to the four of them, their wheels'). RSV tries to preserve this meaningless reading. The last word must have been a marginal annotation showing what the verse was all about.

14. G. omits the entire verse, showing the late character of the addition. The author carelessly changed the first face from 'ox' (cf. 1.10) to **cherub.**

16. In adapting 1.19 to the present context the writer substituted from 1.17 the notion of the wheels not turning for their rising up with the cherubim. G. omits **from beside them**; that the phrase is a later expansion seems clear from the use of *gm* ('moreover', untranslated in RSV).

17. That this is borrowed from 1.21 is proved by **the living creatures,** which in this context should logically have been 'the cherubim'. It is the movement of the cherubim which controls that of the wheels.

(f) YAHWEH'S GLORY MOVES TO THE EXIT **10.18–19**

This section must be seen together with 11.22–23 as containing the conclusion of the actual vision, viz. the departure of the glory of Yahweh from the city. The insertion of 10.20–22 and 11.1–21 has given rise to expansions within the account because of the insertion. Thus 11.22 repeats word for word much of verse 19.

Obviously the original account would not have done so. The Hebrew of verse 19*b* reads 'and it stood' rather than **and they stood**: the reference is to Yahweh's glory, not to the cherubim. This shows that the remainder of the verse is an expansion made necessary by the intrusion of the cherubim which is foreign to the simple departure of the glory. If all references to the cherubim are taken as accretions, the original narrative stands out as verses 18*a*, 19 (**and it stood at the door . . . LORD**) and 11.23. It should be noted that the references to cherubim in this section and in 11.22 are all plural, an indication (in verses 1–7) of their secondary nature. The original narrative used only the singular in which the cherubim were guardians of the fire within the sanctuary. Their role as upholding the throne of the glory of Yahweh is secondary. Their introduction here was necessary because of their positioning in 9.3; thus the additions cannot be earlier than 9.3.

18. G. omits **the threshold of,** but this cannot be correct in view of verse 4.

19. The east gate was the most important gate since it faced the front of the Temple. This temporary stand at the eastern exit to the Temple simply signalizes the departure. The city has been destroyed by fire; the judgment has been completed; now the glory of Yahweh must leave, not to return until the new Temple is again ecstatically conceived in the final section of the book, chapters 40–48. The gate of entrance, so important to the Yahwist cult (cf. Ps. 118.19–20 and Ps. 24), now becomes the gate for Yahweh's symbolic exit.

(g) FURTHER EXPANSIONS ON THE CHERUBIM 10.20–22

The secondary character of this section is immediately obvious. It deals with the cherubim (in the plural); they are identified with the living creatures of chapter 1, and twice the statement of identity with the initial vision is made. The expansion at this point was occasioned by the introduction of the cherubim into section (f). This summarizes and concludes the editorial expansions based on chapter 1.

21. Repeats verses 14*a* and 8, adding only that each cherub had four wings. G. rationalizes this as pairs of wings changing 'four' to 'eight'.

22. G. attests an even further addition, having 'under the glory of the God of Israel' after **seen,** but omitting as a late gloss **whose appearance.** The word *w'wtm* (RV renders 'and themselves') makes no sense in its context. It could be a corruption of some kind. Possibly it was a marginal gloss with *mr'yhm*, i.e. 'their appearances and they themselves' referring to the equation of both the appearance and essence of the cherubim and the living creatures. Its eventual inclusion in the text created MT. The final clause is an exact copy of 1.12*a*.

(h) VISION OF THE WICKED COUNSELLORS 11.1–13

That this section is secondary to the original narrative is clear from its total lack of connection with the context. As at the beginning of the narrative, 8.3, the spirit transports the prophet to the Jerusalem Temple, although in chapters 8–10 he is already there. Nor is there any regard for what has already taken place, viz. the destruction of the city and its inhabitants and the glory of Yahweh departing from the Temple. Some in view of these considerations have suggested that it belongs with chapter 8, i.e. as a fifth abomination, but this is also incongruous. Chapter 8 is a literary whole, each vision proceeding gradually from the northern gate of the city until the inner court of the Temple is reached. Nor is the content of a kind with chapter 8, which deals with cultic sins, various forms of idolatry; this section deals with social and political evils. The judgment is also essentially different; in 11.1–13 it is an oracle of invective and judgment proclaimed; in the original narrative it is action visually perceived.

It is not argued that this is not a genuine product of Ezekiel, but rather that it is not part of the chapters 8–11 vision; it is a separate ecstatic experience in some ways parallel to 8.16–18. The setting of both is near the east gate of the Temple; in both a group of men is gathered and judgment is uttered. Verse 13 is a parallel to the account in 9.8.

This section has also received later tradition accretions. This is clear from the occurrence of an oracle conclusion formula in verse 8*b* and the double occurrence of the recognition formula in verses 10*b* and 12*a*. Thus verse 12*b* must be an expansion. But which of the three conclusions is the original one? Verses 9–10 seem to reflect the events of 586 B.C. Prior to the fall of Jerusalem Ezekiel had little hope for any remnant remaining outside the Chebar exiles. But here the princes are to be delivered into the hands of strangers, i.e. the Babylonians, and they will be put to the sword at the border, i.e. Riblah, Nebuchadrezzar's headquarters (cf. 2 Kg. 25.18–21). Since the original narrative is certainly pre-586, these verses must be an accretion. Verses 11–12*a* are an attempt to reintroduce the original reference to pot and flesh, but the application is based on the expansion in verses 9–10. Thus the original end of the oracle was with verse 8. With that oracle a small expansion based on the first accretion in verses 9–10 occurs, viz. the last clause indicating that the princes will be taken out of the city. The original narrative is therefore verses 1–7*a*, 8, 13.

1. The opening clause indicates a new ecstatic experience; cf. the more colourful 8.3. For **east gate,** cf. on 10.19. G. renders the number 25 as 'about 25'. Here an exact number is given and G. is wrong. The people mentioned are known only from this chapter. **Jaazaniah** also occurs for a different individual at 8.11. **which faces east** is often taken as a gloss, but Hebrew writers do repeat themselves. **princes of the people** refers to the ruling class often mentioned by Jeremiah (Jer. 26.10, 12, 16, 21; 36.14 *et al.*) of Judah, not necessarily royalty even in such passages as Jer. 24.8; 34.21, etc.

2. G. and S. add 'Lord' as subject of the first verb for clarity. Exactly what the devising of iniquity and giving wicked counsel consisted of is not certain. Apparently they misled the people. Since this narrative dates from the latter half of Zedekiah's reign Jeremiah's experiences with the princes may give some indication. In spite of Jeremiah's constant proclamation of certain doom on the wicked city, the princes optimistically advised the people of the city and Temple's invulnerability. Something like that seems intended here.

3. The verse consists of two parts, both of which are ambiguous. G. turns the first part into a question, 'Is not the time at hand to build houses?' This is a possible rendering of the Hebrew. It is then an optimistic assurance that the future is bright. It could, however, be taken as a sign of insecurity (as apparently RSV), i.e. the future is uncertain; they are in danger of being cooked in the pot, so let us make alliances against Babylon. The former is more likely to be what the princes intended. Then the second part (cf. the use of the same figure in a somewhat different way in chapter 24) would mean that the city as the pot will protect us, the princes who are the flesh in the pot, against outside attack. For the city is invulnerable. The falsity of the princes' interpretation of this proverbial saying is then shown in the oracle in verse 7.

5. And . . . Say: a late expansion on the command to prophesy. The phrase 'the Spirit . . . fell' in the sense of prophetic inspiration is hardly in keeping with the activity of the divine spirit in verse 1, nor is this phrase attested elsewhere of Ezekiel. It is rather 'the word of Yahweh came to me', which occurs at the head of almost every oracle. The oracle is directed generally to the house of Israel rather than specifically to the princes. **So you think** refers to the interpretation given to the proverb in verse 3*b*. For God knowing the inner thoughts, cf. Ps. 139.

6. A prophetic invective against the violence of the Jerusalemites. Whether the **slain** is to be taken literally or not is uncertain, but in any event the social and political iniquities are being castigated in terms of classical prophecy; cf. Isa. 1.21–23; Am. 2.6–8; Hos. 4.1–3; Mic. 3.1–3 as examples.

7. After the invective the judgment is announced with **Therefore** and the introductory oracle formula. For **Lord God**, as in verses 8, 13, cf. on 2.4. The **slain** here are those slain in warfare. The irony of the judgment is not only that it reinterprets the proverbial saying, but also the word 'slain', which in the invective referred to the oppressed but here to those killed by the sword. The evil practices of the rulers have brought on a situation in which the city walls will not protect but rather ensure the death of the inhabitants. The cauldron does not protect its contents; instead it holds its contents together for slaughter. The last clause is an expansion suggesting that the leaders will be brought out of the city for destruction by the sword. This is based on the events of 586 B.C. Versions attest a better text (as do many Hebrew MSS.) with its 'and you I will bring forth . . .'.

8. The end of the original oracle. The leaders' fear of the sword may refer to their attempts to gain Egyptian help against the Babylonians.

9. The leaders were brought out with Zedekiah to Riblah and there executed. The **foreigners** are the Babylonians. The expansion in verse 7*b* is probably based on this verse.

10. border: the ideal border of Israel, since Riblah lies in Syria near the entrance of Hamath, the traditional but seldom actual, northern border of Israel. The concluding recognition formula shows that this ends this particular expansion.

11–12a α adds nothing new, but makes explicit what is implicit, viz. that 'we are the flesh' can hardly be correct as far as the leaders are concerned, since they will be slain ('judged') at the borders. This tradition understood the saying in verse 3 in the sense of security, i.e. the way in which the leaders used it; cf. on verse 3. The omission of these verses in some G. MSS. is not original but due to parablepsis.

12aβb. This is a late expansion absent in G., probably borrowed from, and therefore later than, 5.7.

13. Part of the original narrative of verses 1–12. In the prophet's vision he sees his judgment immediately effective when one of the twenty-five men falls down dead. For the effectiveness of the prophetic word in similar circumstances, cf. 1 Kg. 13.20–25; 2 Kg. 7.1–2, 17–20; Jer. 28.15–17. But this situation differs in that Ezekiel is hundreds of miles away. The solution is simple when it is recalled that this is an ecstatic vision rather than actual event. Whether Pelatiah actually died at this time no one knows. It is certainly not a case of second sight as some have alleged. Ezekiel's reaction in the vision is a clear parallel to that in 9.8; cf. commentary *ad loc.*

(i) AN ORACLE OF REDEMPTION 11.14–21

This section originally had nothing to do with the vision of chapters 8–11; it is simply an oracle, as the introductory formula shows. Ezekiel's hope for the future is pinned not on those who remained in Judah and Jerusalem after the 597 B.C. deportation, but on the exilic band. This is the real Israel. Prior to 586 Ezekiel felt that Jerusalem and its inhabitants were all doomed to destruction; only occasionally is there a vague reference to a remnant. The insertion of this section is the work of the editor who tied this with verses 1–13 as a balance to the absolute gloom of the judgment on Jerusalem, more particularly as a divine response to the intercession of the prophet who despairs for the future of the remnant of Israel.

The section has grown from at least two or more traditional accretions. The oracle begins at verse 16 in the 3rd plural. The first layer of expansion can easily be identified by the change in suffix to 2nd plural (verse 17 and the second half of verse 19a). Verse 17 promises in direct address a return from exile and the gift of the land, something quite foreign to the original oracle the theme of which is presented in verse 16. Verse 18 must be subsequent to the expansion in verse 17, but constitutes another hand. The introduction of **for a while** in verse 16 also betrays the same mind. Concerning verse 19aβ, cf. commentary below. Another layer of tradition is in verse 21 and is based on the expansion in verses 17–18, but it is told in the 3rd plural. Its interest is in the correction of cultic affairs after the return of the exiles. Though it also deals with cultic evils, it may be yet a third layer since it deals with judgment, a notion foreign to the entire section. Only the concluding oracle formula at the end of verse 21 may be taken as original. The original narrative then is in verses 14–16, 19–20, and 21bβ.

Many scholars attribute this entire section on prejudicial grounds to post-Ezekiel scribes, or at least to a post-586 period in Ezekiel's career. Cooke, e.g. maintains, 'A prophecy of consolation is out of harmony with Ezekiel's tone at this period' (*ad loc*). But Ezekiel's audience was the exilic one; even his severe judgments directed against Jerusalem are intended to bolster the self-confidence of his actual audience. To suggest that a positive establishment of the divine covenant with the exilic remnant is out of line with his thinking at this stage is a superficial judgment. Doom prophets such as Isaiah and Jeremiah believed in a remnant with whom God would continue his good relations and Ezekiel is a member of that classical band of prophets. Neither can this section be dated after 586 B.C., since Jerusalem is still standing, as is presupposed in verse 15. After that event the land is referred to as 'these waste places in the land of Israel' (33.24), 'waste and desolate and ruined cities' (36.35), whereas in verse 15 Jerusalem is still inhabited.

15. G. omits **even your brethren** as a dittograph. **your fellow exiles** is based on G. rather than MT (*g'ltk*, 'your redemption'). Thus 'the men of your redemption' means those who will play the part of redeemer or avenger on your behalf. Such are one's close relatives. In view of the parallel **brethren** it is better to read 'men of your kindred'. It is, of course, the exiles who are being referred to. The notion that the exilic group constitutes the whole house of Israel is unusual. More commonly the term is used for those who remained in Palestine after the 597 B.C. deportation. But when so used it is in a context of judgment. The usage is fully in accord with Ezekiel's belief that the Judeans have rejected God's ordinances and are thus rejected from being the people of God. That designation can only apply in the future to the exiles. RSV rightly changes the verb *rhkw* from the imperative (cf. RV 'get you far') to the perfect (**They have gone far**). The statement of the Jerusalemites is in two parts both of which are false and are corrected by the oracle. The first is that the exiles by their exile are far from Yahweh's domain. This is based on the old conception that each land had its own deity. Absence from the land meant absence from its deity's effective protection and control. Being away from Palestine meant away from Yahweh's supervision. The second statement involves possession of the land. Yahweh's permitting the exile meant idle land free for those who remained. Canaan was the land given by Yahweh to Israel. The gift of the land was the seal of the covenant between God and his people.

16. For **Lord GOD**, as in verses 17, 21, cf. on 2.4. **though** in both cases should be changed to 'indeed'; the *ky* is asseverative. Yahweh affirms in this oracle that he was responsible for the exile. The verse is the prophetic correction to the first statement of the Jerusalemites, as verses 19–20 correct their materialistic view of the covenant. The exiles are not far from Yahweh, as is clear from the fact that he actually engineered their present lot, and in their present state is actually their sanctuary. The sanctuary is the concretization of the divine presence among a people. For the priestly prophet this involved a new concept of the relation between people and God to be expressed in a life lived without a physical temple.

17. Its secondary character is immediately recognizable from the use of the introductory oracle formula. The author gives a different kind of reply to the statement of the Jerusalemites, viz. a return from exile and Yahweh's gift of land to the returnees. It is they, not the present inhabitants, to whom Yahweh gives it for possession. G. normalizes the text by changing all the 2nd personal pronouns to 3rd plural. Another indication of different authorship is the use of '*mym* for 'peoples' rather than the usual *gwym* ('nations'), as in verse 16.

18. This statement seems much later than the proceding, probably after the return with its interest in cultic reform in the post-exilic age. **detestable things** and **abominations** are references to idols and other cultic aberrations, and recur in verse 21.

The new covenant between God and exilic Israel 19–20

Like P's view of the covenant (Gen. 17), God not only sets up his covenant but also provides all the qualifications for living under the covenant.

19. For MT 'within you' RSV, with numerous MSS. and Versions, reads **within them.** G. rightly reads 'another' ('*ḥr*) for **one** ('*ḥd*). God will give them new hearts and spirits. The **heart** to the Hebrews was not just the voluntary centre but also the mind, the intellectual basis for emotion and action, whereas **spirit** is the principle of life. **stony heart** implies intransigence and wilfulness, whereas **a heart of flesh** contrasts with it. By it is meant a new impulse to obedience (cf. also 36.26). The new spirit is God's spirit, since God is the source of all life (36.27).

20. The purpose for God's new work is given in verse 20*a*. **statutes** and **ordinances,** cf. on 5.7. For the covenant formula elsewhere in Ezekiel, cf. Ezek. 14.11; 36.28; 37.23, 27. It is particularly common in Jeremiah (Jer. 7.23; 11.4; 24.7; 30.22; 31.1, 33; 32.38) and also occurs in prophetic literature in Hos. 2.23 (cf. Hos. 1.9 for the negative counterpart) and Zech. 8.8. It always stands in the context of promise and is normally given as double sided as here. The formula is possibly a reflection of a covenant renewal ceremony as shown in Jos. 24.

21. The beginning of the verse is corrupt in MT and the Versions give little help. RSV probably gives the intended sense. For the last clause, cf. on 9.10.

(j) CONCLUSION 11.22–25

The end of the vision is the departure of the glory of Yahweh from the city. Because of the large insertions (10.20–11.21) a recapitulation of most of 10.19 was made by an editor. Originally 11.23 simply continued 10.19. The departure finds its counterpart in the return in 43.2–5.

23. mountain: the Mount of Olives overlooking the city across the Kidron from the east.

24. vision: technical term for the ecstatic vision; cf. 43.3 and in the plural at 8.3; cf. also 1.1. As at 8.3 it is the divine spirit who is responsible for the transport. The prophet returns to his normal state, presumably to the situation in 8.1.

25. Here the prophetic purpose of the vision experience is reached. The point of the vision is not a message to the inhabitants of Jerusalem, but rather to the exiles.

H.   THE EXILES SYMBOLIZED 12.1–16

This section is similar to 4.1–5.17 in that a prophetic message is acted out rather than spoken; only afterwards is an explanatory oracle given to make certain that the message of the symbolic action is understood. As with chapters 4–5, so here later accretions have amplified and changed the picture. At least two distinct accretions can be distinguished. Since the recognition formula occurs both in verses 15 and 16 it is unlikely that they represent the same stratum. Verses 1–15 throughout deal with the certainty of judgment, whereas verse 16 introduces a remnant from sword, famine, and pestilence, which reminds one of the tradition represented in 5.3; it is also at odds with the rest of the passage since only exile is pictured. It is the second expansion of the text. The first expansion is a larger one and is based on the events of 586 B.C. more particularly those which concerned Zedekiah. Verses 10–11 represent doublet answers to the question asked the prophet; one interprets the action simply as signifying what will happen to Israel, but the other relates it in some way to the prince, i.e. Zedekiah. Zedekiah and his princes had fled by night through a break in the city wall but were caught by the besiegers. Zedekiah was enchained and brought to Babylon, but was blinded beforehand (cf. 2 Kg. 25.4–7; Jer. 39.4–7; 52.7–11). Verses 12–14 reflect detailed knowledge of these events. Zedekiah will leave in the dark, dig through a wall, cover his face so as not to see the land, be taken, and brought to Babylon sightless. They must be, along with the conclusion in verse 15, a post-586 accretion to the text to which verse 10 serves as introduction.

When verses 1–7 are now read in the light of this analysis, evidence of expansion in the account of the action can be found. Verse 5 applies to Zedekiah rather than to the Jerusalemites as a whole. In verse 6 **and carry it out in the dark** as well as **you shall cover your face that you may not see the land,** and in verse 7 **I dug through . . . dark** are part of the same individual reference.

A few expansions of varying types may be recognized as well. At the end of verse 2 occurs the repetitive **for they are a rebellious house** and in verse 9 the attributive **the rebellious house.** Both seem out of place and were probably added later in accordance with its repeated occurrence in 2.1–3.15.

Thus the original account is clear. Except for minor expansions it comprises verses 1–4, parts of 6 and 7, 8, 9, 11. The original of verses 6–7 could be rendered as follows: 'In their presence lift (the baggage) on your shoulder for I have set you for a sign to the house of Israel. And I did just as I was ordered. My baggage I brought out as an exile's baggage by daylight, and at even I lifted (it) on my shoulder.'

2. The exiles are representative of the house of Israel and are thus called **a rebellious house.** They are blind and dumb since they cannot interpret the obvious signs of the times. Their blithe hopes for a short exile and an imminent return to an inviolate city had to be shattered. **eyes . . . see not** and **ears . . . hear not,** cf. Isa. 6.9; 43.8; Jer. 5.21.

3. G. rightly omits **and go into exile** as a copyist's dittograph (*gwlh wglh*). An **exile's baggage** (cf. also Jer. 46.19) would consist of only the barest necessities. **another place** is an indefinite location but outside Ezekiel's own house, possibly on the other side of the city since the whole point of the action was that it be done publicly and in broad daylight. **Perhaps** expresses doubt though also some hope. The doubt is substantial 'for' (not **though** as RSV; the phrase occurs many times in Ezekiel) they are a rebellious house.

4. Baggage would be assembled by day but the actual trek would begin at sunset in the cool of the evening.

5. wall: of a house rather than of a city. Walls in Babylon were made of sun-dried mud brick and could easily be dug through. For **go** Hebrew reads 'bring' (i.e. the baggage).

6. Lifting the baggage on to the shoulder indicated the start of the trek. **dark** occurs only once outside this section (also verses 7, 12) in Gen. 15.17 where it signifies the period after sunset. It must here mean dusk since people could still see what one was doing. The intent of **carry . . . in the dark** was escape rather than exile, cf. verse 12. Similarly **cover . . . face** was done as a disguise to facilitate escape. **that you may not see the land** was added to reflect the blinding of Zedekiah at Riblah, but cf. on verse 12.

7. with my own hands: not attested in G., and a late gloss. The first clause is a formula recurring in 24.18; 37.7. Hebrew has 'brought forth' for **went forth** as in verse 5.

9. For a similar query cf. 24.19.

10. For **Lord GOD,** cf. on 2.4. RSV has smoothed out the difficulties of the text, probably correctly. MT has no **concerns** and possibly '*l* must be inserted. For 'the prince, this oracle' G. has 'the prince and the leader', taking *hmś* ('oracle') as from the same root as *hnśy'* ('prince'), and therefore a word play. At the end MT has 'in the midst of them' without antecedent; is this a copyist's error based on **among them** in verse 12? If so, the phrase **who are in it** ('them') may be taken as secondary. The reference of the verse is to Zedekiah, called **prince,** because he was regent for king Jehoiachin (cf. on 1.2). Though tradition added **and all the house of Israel** in deference to the original tradition, the details in verses 12–14 show that it was only applying the symbolism to Zedekiah.

11. The asyndetous construction of **into captivity** (a synonym for 'into exile') shows its nature as a gloss. The change in pronoun is intentional. The sign is for the exilic audience; but what the prophet enacted will take place for the Jerusalemites. This verse is the explanatory oracle interpreting the action.

12. For **in the dark and shall go forth** G. read 'in the dark he shall bring forth', i.e. it. MT has 'they shall dig . . . and he shall bring (it) out'. Zedekiah went out through the breach made by others. MT is corrupt in the last clause. G. has 'in order that he might not be seen by an eye (i.e. anyone) and he might not see the land'. MT literally says 'because that he may not see by an eye, he, the land'. The opening particle must be wrong; it should be *lm'n* as G. MT seems to combine two readings: 'that he might not be seen by anyone' and 'that he might not see the land', the latter based on the expansion in verse 6. G. correctly interprets *yr'h* as Ni. ('be seen'), but then translates the later gloss as though the verb was Qal ('see'). For the events reflected by this verse and verse 13, cf. 2 Kg. 25.4–7; Jer. 39.4–7; 52.7–11.

13. For the picture of a net set, cf. 17.20 and 19.8. Verses 13–14 may be dependent on 17.20–21. Zedekiah will not see Babylon because he was blinded. This is the only allusion in the O.T. to his death in Babylon.

14. his helpers: rightly with G.S. for MT 'his help'. The word *'gpyw*, **his troops,** occurs only in Ezekiel and is a loanword from Akkadian, *agappu* (kappu), 'wing'. **scatter . . . wind** means exile among foreign nations. For the last clause, cf. on 5.2.

15. The recognition formula is part of the tradition which created verses 12–14 rather than the original one, since it is in the 3rd plural.

16. This reflects the same tradition as 5.3 but adds as the purpose for the survival their account of their abominations to peoples everywhere. Through their account heathen nations will recognize the justice of the exile and the righteous character of Yahweh who engineered it. The subject of **may know** is not the **few** as in RSV, but 'the nations' as G. understood.

I. ANOTHER SYMBOLIC ACTION 12.17–20

In form this short section is like verses 1–16; in both Ezekiel is told to do something followed by an oracle applying the action to the Jerusalem situation. Some have compared this section to 4.10–11 and considered this dependent on it. Both deal with eating and drinking under siege and defeat conditions, but the theme of 4.10–11 is scarcity of food during the siege, whereas here the stress falls on the emotions expressed. The accent must fall on **quaking, trembling, fearfulness,** and **dismay.** In verse 19 occurs an explanatory expansion. **concerning . . . Israel** was added to define the subjects of the oracle. The original account already defined these as the people of the land.

18. and with fearfulness: a gloss on **with trembling** based on verse 19. The parallelism with verse 18*a* shows that a single noun is required. The symbolic action which the prophet is to perform is quaking and trembling. The word *r'š* ('quaking') occurs elsewhere only of earthquakes, whereas *rgzh* ('trembling') occurs only here, although the root is well known.

19. For **Lord GOD,** cf. on 2.4. MT has 'its [i.e. Jerusalem's] land', which seems far-fetched. Better to read 'the land' as G., or with a variant Hebrew text **their land.** The usual meaning of **people of the land** is the common people as opposed to the ruling class (cf. 7.27). The explanatory oracle does not use the same words used in the symbolic action, but rather **fearfulness** and **dismay,** words implying shock and fear at the ruin and defeat of the land. The stripping of the land is due to the violence (cf. on 8.17) of its inhabitants. The ruination of the country is morally conditioned.

20. That the message of this section is addressed to the exiles is clear from the 2nd plural address in the recognition formula, though 3rd plural is used in the oracle.

J. MY WORD WILL BE PERFORMED 12.21–28.

Verses 21–28 illustrate a phenomenon common in prophetic literature. Prophets used materials more than once in different contexts as is the case here. Verses 21–25 and 26–28, though not doublets, are parallel accounts with related themes and at times identical language. Both deal with the certainty that Yahweh's word will be performed. Both oracles are cast into a similar literary mode, a rudimentary form of disputation oracle that Malachi was to develop more fully. A hypothetical case is set forth, i.e. statements of the people, to which the answering oracle gives crushing reply.

Some have seen in these oracles eschatological statements about an end time, which might seem strange to an Ezekiel who at this time was so preoccupied with judgments against Judah and Jerusalem. It is much more natural, however, to read these as warnings to the exiles against false hopes. Jerusalem's fate is assured, and the doom oracles which the prophet has spoken will shortly be fulfilled. The text has suffered little from accretions of later traditions except for verse 24. Both verses 24 and 25 begin with the causal particle *ky* (not 'but' as RSV in verse 25). The point of the divine rebuttal is that the words will be fulfilled because it is Yahweh who speaks and what he says happens (cf. Ps. 33.9). Verse 25 is the natural continuation of verse 23, whereas verse 24 is a pious expansion on the word **vision** in verse 23, suggesting that in the future there will be no misleading vision in Israel, which is hardly the subject of the original oracle.

22. The word for **proverb** in its original form was a 'simile', but it is also used of any pithy saying and even of extended wisdom discourses. The popular saying is rendered literally by RSV, but its meaning is not too clear. What the people are saying is that as time goes by prophecies gradually fall into disuse; so much time has elapsed since their utterance that the power of the word has become ineffective. The word for **vision** is not the same as that used in the ecstatic visions of chapters 1 and 8, but rather the word used in 7.26; it even occurs in superscriptions to designate prophetic collections as a whole (Isa. 1.1; Nah. 1.1; Ob. 1). It could be written down (Hab. 2.2) and was thus not simply visual. The term must here refer to Ezekiel's prophecies of doom.

23. For **Lord GOD**, as in verses 25, 28, cf. on 2.4. The divine rebuttal is a prediction that the proverb will fall into disuse because coming events will disprove its validity. G. misunderstood *hšbty* 'I have put an end to' as *whšybty* 'and I will turn back'. It probably represents the original tradition in reading the conjunction (cf. e.g. 11.17). The correct proverb is then given; in contrast to the popular proverb, this one is in the perfect aspect. **fulfilment** correctly interprets the Hebrew *dbr* 'word'. *dābār* means effective word, word which has lasting power (Isa. 55.11). Thus the time for the effectuation of every prophecy has arrived.

24. For **false vision** and **flattering divination,** cf. chapter 13. G.S.V. have 'among the sons of Israel' for **within . . . Israel.** It is difficult to decide which reading is preferable.

27. The popular statement which is to be refuted differs from the proverb in verse 22 though it has a similar effect. People are saying that Ezekiel's prophecies are not immediate but only concern the distant future.

28. Again the rebuttal is the divine pledge that his word will be immediately effective. The reply is almost identical with verse 25, but transposed, and with a plural subject ('my words') added instead of the neutral subject.

K.   AGAINST FALSE PROPHETS 13.1-23

The chapter consists of four parts put together because of common subject-matter. The first two concern false prophets, verses 1-16, and the last two false prophetesses, verses 17-23. The text of the chapter has suffered greatly in transmission and MT is often corrupt. For a parallel, cf. Jer. 23.9-22.

(a) **1-9.** Some scholars have tried to find two distinct accounts here which have been interwoven. Prophetic books were not put together in this way, but evolved first orally and later in written form through accretions to the original account and with care these layers of tradition can often be peeled off. In this prophetic invective, e.g., certain layers are immediately obvious. The invective and judgment occur in the 2nd plural, but verses 6 and 9 are in the 3rd plural though the recognition formula is in the 2nd plural again, probably as an editorial tag. The rest of verse 9 can also be recognized as a much later expansion from its contents. It is the period of the exile, thus after 586 B.C., as is clear from the judgment denying entrance into the land of Israel. Verse 6 is an expansion on verse 7a. Verse 7b is not in the 2nd plural and its absence in G. attests it as a late addition. Verse 4 is an address in the 2nd singular to Israel and represents still another tradition. Verse 3 is in the 3rd plural, but this is necessitated by its form. A 'woe oracle' is generally in the 3rd person (cf. verse 18). The original prophecy is represented in verses 1-3, 5, 7a, and 8. The end of the passage is recognizable from the oracle conclusion formula at the end of verse 8.

2. RSV follows G. in reading an imperative **prophesy** (following Israel) instead of the corrupt hnb'ym ('who prophesy') of MT. **to those . . . minds** in G. occurs in verse 3 instead of here. Read '(say) to them' with G. and one Hebrew MS.

3. For **Lord GOD**, as in verses 8, 9, 13, 16, 18, 20, cf. on 2.4. For **the foolish prophets** read with G. 'those who prophesy out of their own minds'. MT is the result of scribal error. This kind of false prophet is to be distinguished from the 400 in 1 Kg. 22.5-23 who were deluded by a false spirit. These prophets of Israel follow their own hearts, and their oracles are not from Yahweh, i.e. they have not **seen** anything. The relative clause is a late gloss unattested in G., probably on the preceding phrase. The clause itself may be corrupt since the syntax is peculiar. The woe oracle is peculiar to the prophets and often introduces an invective as here. Such an oracle always involves a doom oracle of some kind.

4. Probably an expansion on **breaches** of verse 5. The mention of **ruins** or uninhabited places shows that it may come from a time when Judah lay in ruins, i.e. after 586 B.C. G. rightly omits hyw ('have been'); render: 'your prophets are like . . .'. Foxes as lonely scavengers in waste places are an appropriate symbol for the place of false prophets in Israelite society.

5. G. misunderstood this verse, but along with S. and V. attests the singular for 'breaches'. It should be understood not as a reference to the destruction of Jerusalem but as a general one to time of trouble. The figure is that of warfare; when a wall is sprung the defenders must go up into the breach, i.e. quickly repair the break. The building of a wall (cf. 22.30) refers also to rebuilding, as in Am. 9.11. The city wall being made of loose stones without mortar had regularly to be repaired. **day of the LORD** is part of the figure and must not be pressed along lines of chapter 7. Here it refers in general to a time of crisis. In the real day of Yahweh when 'the end has come' (7.2), well-built walls will be of no avail against the divinely directed enemy.

6. divined correctly follows G. for MT 'divination of'. Divination was the art of foretelling the future by human devices rather than by divinely inspired oracle and was illegitimate among Israel (Dt. 18.14). True prophets never made use of divination. False prophets did make use of oracular formulae. Ezekiel maintains this use to be legitimate only to those who are commissioned by Yahweh; cf. Jer. 14.14; 23.21 for the same figure. The self-delusion of these prophets is such that they actually believe their own words.

7. Verse 7*b* is a late doublet on verse 6*b*.

8. After the invective comes the short but effective judgment after the introductory formula in the form of a demonstration oracle, i.e. in 'because ... therefore' form. This 'because' clause is stated in terms of verse 7*a* and the 'therefore' simply **Behold I am against you,** a favourite prophetic phrase. Such divine opposition was of course effective and sealed their doom.

9. my hand will be 'upon' is always used in Ezekiel to mean ecstatic vision (cf. on 1.3); most scholars on the basis of G. change *whyth* ('will be') to *wntyty*, i.e. 'And I will stretch forth my hand against.' This makes good sense, but since this is a later expansion Ezekiel's own usage is hardly determinative here. In view of the rest of the verse the reading of MT makes better sense. It means that Yahweh's power will be directed **against** these false prophets; this will appear as follows: 'they shall not . . .', etc., i.e. the triple privileges of citizenship in the true community of Yahweh's people, viz. participation in counsel, registration of one's name on the roll, and return to the promised land, will be denied them.

(b) **10–16.** In form this account is similar to the preceding; it too is a demonstration oracle with verse 10 constituting the 'because' clause, and verse 13, the 'therefore', along with the introductory oracular formula and the doom oracle. The passage presents two formulaic conclusions however: the recognition formula in verse 14 and the concluding formula in verse 16. Usually the one occurring earlier is original and that is also true here. Verse 16 is a statement of subject, probably a marginal statement showing what the passage is about, whereas the formula was added by the editor to end the section. Verse 15 is an expansion of verses 13–14. Verse 11 can be identified as secondary by its 3rd plural references whereas the 2nd plural is expected. It is a prosaic explanation of what happens to a whitewashed and poorly constructed wall when a heavy storm attacks it. Verse 12 is also intrusive; it must be subsequent to verse 11 since it is dependent on it. Neither verse 11 nor verse 12 fits as part of the invective of the 'because' element, whereas verses 13–14 fit perfectly. The original account is represented in verses 10, 13–14.

10. The opening repetition of **because** seems peculiar but also occurs at 36.3 and Lev. 26.43 (MT). G. throughout misunderstood *tpl*, **whitewash,** as the verb *tpl*, 'it will fall', thereby confirming the text. For **saying, Peace . . . peace** cf. Jer. 6.14; 8.11. This is not only gross negligence but leading people astray; cf. prophet as watchman 3.16–21; 33.1–6. For the false prophet as whitewashing with false visions and divinations, cf. 22.28. The word *ḥyṣ*—**wall** is used only here and in contrast to the heavy city wall or even house wall probably means a fence wall out in the open of loosely constructed stones, still common throughout inhabited areas around Jerusalem today. Daubing with whitewash in no way adds to its strength.

11. Most scholars on the authority of G. delete **that it shall fall,** but this removes the pun on **whitewash,** *tpl*, and 'fall', *ypl*. The last verb is transitive and should be rendered 'break (it) up'. MT has 'and you' after 'rain' which yields no sense. G. read it as 'and I will give'. Was this a gloss intended to show that the rain came from Yahweh? In any event, the word must be omitted with, RSV. The references to rain, hailstones, and storm are all based on verse 13.

13. The last phrase is literally 'and hailstones in wrath to destruction'. A verb is lacking and Cornill suggests plausibly that *lklh*, 'to destruction', is a copyist error for 'will fall'; cf. verse 11 which is based on this verse. The judgment continues the figure of the invective. Yahweh will send a violent storm to break down the bedaubed wall.

14. Here the word for **wall** is the usual word for house wall, also used in 12.5, 7. **when . . . midst of it** is an expansion as the feminine singular for 'it' shows. The feminine has no antecedent and may have been a marginal statement alluding to the fall of the city. The use of whitewash instead of mortar is what makes the false prophet a criminal, and in the destruction of the society which he has failed to strengthen he too will perish.

15. and I will say: more appropriately read with S. and T. 'and it will be said'. In view of verse 12 S. may represent the original text, having instead of the negatives the word 'where', i.e. 'Where is the wall and where those daubing it?'

16. This may well reflect a period after Jerusalem's destruction. It could almost serve as a title for verses 10–15.

(c) **17–21.** Similar in form to verses 2–8, except that it lacks the 'because' element. Verse 17 is parallel to verse 2; verse 18, to verse 3; and verse 20, to verse 8. The end is signalled by a recognition formula. With the exception of the woe oracle which is generally in the 3rd person, the entire passage is in direct address to the false prophetesses.

17. The women against whom Ezekiel is prophesying are not actually called prophetesses, but rather 'those women who play the role of prophet'.

18. wrists, lit. 'joints of my hands'; G. and RSV rightly omit 'my'. It can mean either 'elbows' or 'wrists', but here the latter is likely correct. Verse 18*b* is rightly a question (a statement in MT). The woe oracle is directed against female sorcerers. The paraphernalia of the sorcerer is listed as sewing magic bands for wrists and making shawls for heads. Whether these were worn by the sorcerers or their clients is not clear. That some spoken spell accompanied the use of these objects is clear, since in verse 17 they are said to act the role of prophet. Prophecy made use of effective word and action and thus involved life and death. Sorceresses far from being viewed as harmless cranks are actually involved in a struggle for souls, i.e. lives, of men. 'Hunting' lives is here contrasted with preserving lives. The term probably was some technical term for harming by magical means.

19. by your lies . . . lies is an expansion as is clear from the masculine form of 'your'. It was added to make explicit the false character of their words. Magic though strictly illegitimate in Yahwism was none the less believed to be an effective force. People died or were kept alive by the activity of these sorceresses. These evil people wielded their powers for small fees like their fellow false prophets (Mic. 3.5, 11).

20. Why RSV should use **Wherefore** instead of 'therefore' is not clear. It represents exactly the same word and is in the same context as verses 8, 13. **go free (like birds)** is based on a brilliant reconstruction by Cornill of the corrupt '*t npšym* ('the souls') in MT as '*tn ḥpšym* ('them free'). MT is impossible, and Cornill is surely correct. *lprḥwt*, here rendered as **like birds,** also occurs by error in MT after **hunt the souls.** The rendering is just barely possible, being based on an Aramaic root meaning 'to fly' and thus literally 'for things that fly'. Even more doubtful is the rendering 'like' for the Hebrew preposition *l*. G. has 'for scattering' probably reading *lprśwt*, but that is no better. The word remains obscure. Implied in the judgment is that the magic bands and shawls in some way imprison the lives of people. **you** and **your** in 'your arms', as well as **your** in 'your veils' of verse 21, are wrongly masculine.

(d) **22–23.** Formally this is a demonstration oracle. Verse 22 is the 'because' element showing the charge, and verse 23 the 'therefore', i.e. the judgment. This oracle is also directed against false prophetesses but not in the terms of the preceding. The charge is not that of binding souls by magical forces, but rather not functioning properly in the prophetic role as watchman (cf. 3.16–21 and 33.1–6).

22. G. attests that **falsely** is a late gloss. **disheartened him** is incorrect; MT says 'caused him pain'. God has not afflicted the righteous and yet these women dishearten him. The Hebrew represents a play on the two roots *k'h* and *k'b*. Contrary to proper prophetic practice they have encouraged the wicked in their wickedness and discouraged the righteous without cause.

23. The judgment entails rendering these prophetesses ineffective by denying them their evil powers. But the real purpose of the judgment is freeing Yahweh's people from their grasp. The recognition formula, as is the entire oracle, is in direct address.

L. JUDGMENT ON SYNCRETISTS 14.1–11

The exilic situation created a natural tendency towards syncretism. Yahweh worshippers had been taken from their homeland into exile by force. This was not

Yahweh's land and they were far from the single legitimate sanctuary at Jerusalem. How could they engage in worship in an alien land? This was the land of the Babylonian gods and their power was evident in the greatness of Nebuchadrezzar's empire. The temptation to engage in idol worship while at the same time not abandoning Yahwism must have been a constant temptation to the exiles. This is the situation to which Ezekiel here addresses himself.

The composition of this section has been viewed in a wide variety of ways, ranging from Irwin, who finds only parts of verses 3 and 6 original, to Zimmerli, who defends it in its entirety. One is immediately struck by certain formal characteristics. Verse 8 ends with the recognition formula and verse 11 with an oracle conclusion formula. Furthermore the introductory oracular formula occurs both at verse 4 and at verse 6. Verse 4 and verse 7 are also doublet versions.

If one begins with the statement of the situation being dealt with in verse 3, it is clear that the problem is what is to happen when an idolater comes to seek an oracle of Yahweh. The answer to that problem comes immediately in verses 4–5. Verse 6 is a call to Israel to repent and abandon idols, but it does not deal specifically with the problem, whereas verse 7 is a doublet on verse 4. The minor differences between the two verses are mainly small additions to verse 7, which is thus later. Verse 8 again deals with the situation in verse 3 and is an excellent continuation to verse 5. The section ends with the recognition formula.

Verses 9–11 constitute a peculiar problem in that they deal with a specific problem arising out of the situation described in verse 3, but it appears as a post-script after the oracle is completed. There is no good reason for not understanding it as precisely that—an afterthought by the prophet but necessary to a complete statement of the case.

1. The elders came to seek an oracle (cf. 20.1). Their sitting before the prophet (cf. also 8.1) is the position of an audience before king, wise man (teacher), or prophet awaiting a word.

3. Omit **at all,** which is based on a dittograph in MT. For **idols** as dung-images, cf. on 6.4. The elders are syncretists. Idols occupy their minds and fill their vision. For **stumbling block of their iniquity,** cf. 7.19. The problem is: Will Yahweh allow himself to be inquired of by such?

4. For **Lord GOD,** as in verses 6, 11, cf. on 2.4. The text in MT at the end of the verse is peculiar. The variant text in verse 7 simply has 'myself', whereas verse 4 has 'by it by the multitude of his idols'. G. shows still another tradition: 'by those things in which the mind is entangled'. Verse 7 probably is the original text and the rest are expansions restating the reason for Yahweh's answer. The form of the oracle is that of sacral law, especially as found in H (cf. Lev. 17.3, 8, 10, 13; 20.2). Except for Lev. 17.3 these references all include 'or of the strangers that sojourn in Israel' after 'house of Israel' as in verse 7, a variant form of the legal formula. Ezekiel as a priest was obviously well versed in priestly language. The answer to the problem posed in verse 3 is that no prophetic oracle will be forthcoming, but Yahweh himself will bring himself to answer (the verb is in the Ni.), viz. the judgment of verse 8.

5. This gives the purpose for Yahweh himself answering the idolater, viz. to strike terror into the hearts of all idolaters among the Israelites. **all** is a late gloss absent in G.

6. This is an expansion by a later writer reflecting on verse 5. The divine purpose behind laying hold of the hearts is that Israel may repent and abandon all idolatry. The concept of repentance is basic to prophetic thought from Amos and Hosea down to Ezekiel, but especially in Jeremiah. Here however it is an addition from the Ezekiel school.

7. who separates himself from me does not belong to this variant text to verse 4. It is a gloss from verse 5.

8. For **byword** MT wrongly has the plural. Again the language is borrowed from the divine penalties imposed in sacral law. For the first and third penalties, cf. Lev. 17.10; 20.3, 5, 6. The usual penalty for infraction was for 'that person to be cut off from among his people'. For the second penalty, cf. Dt. 28.37. The judgment is thus excommunication from the people of God.

9. A corollary of the general law imposed by the oracle in verses 4–5, 8 concerns the situation presented by a prophet who in spite of the sacral law forbidding a prophetic oracle none the less gives such. In such a case the prophet will be annihilated (a synonym here for 'cut off') from the people of God. Such a prophet is deceived. For Yahweh as the deceiver of prophets, cf. 1 Kg. 22.19–23 and Dt. 13.1–5 (MT 2–6).

10. For deluders and deluded suffering the same fate, cf. Jer. 14.15–16; 27.15.

11. This is not part of the original account. As a redemptive function for the preceding sacral law it is in character completely different from its parallel in verse 5. In content it comes closer to the mind of the writer of verse 6. For the covenant formula, cf. on 11.20. On the other hand, it presents a prophetic ideal which would be shared by all prophets. For **go . . . astray**, cf. 13.10 and 44.10; for **transgressions,** cf. especially 18.21–32. The priestly interests of Ezekiel and his school are evident from the statement that transgressions (conscious rebellion against divine law) render one unclean, i.e. defile one.

M. ONLY THE RIGHTEOUS SHALL ESCAPE 14.12–23

This passage should be compared to Jer. 14.19–15.4, a passage with which Ezekiel may well have been acquainted. After a national confession of sins in verses 19–22, which presumably is the prophet interceding for his people, an oracle is given by Jeremiah. In it Yahweh rejects prophetic intercession *per se*. Even though Moses and Samuel were to intercede for the peoples, Yahweh would remain intent on judgment. This judgment is then depicted as fourfold: pestilence, sword, famine, and captivity.

Ezekiel's oracle is similar in content to that of Jeremiah. Here too four successive judgments are depicted, viz. famine, wild beasts, sword, and pestilence. Instead of captivity Ezekiel has wild beasts, and the order is different. Instead of Moses and

Samuel, Noah, Daniel, and Job are used as examples of worthy intercessors whose words will not avail to avert the divine judgments.

In spite of these formal similarities, this passage is highly individual. Ezekiel's discussion is one on legal justice, whereas Jeremiah's oracle pinpoints Yahweh's determination to destroy. Ezekiel phrases his oracle in the style of casuistic law: 'when . . . then . . .' and logically demonstrates that Yahweh is dealing justly. The righteous will be saved, but the wicked will be destroyed (cf. Gen. 18.23–25). Ezekiel simply asserts that Yahweh's patience has gone beyond the point where he will listen to any pleas.

This passage is in two parts: verses 12–20 and 21–23. Not until verse 21 does the introductory oracle formula occur formally introducing the judgment. The recognition formula in an unusually amplified form sets forth the purpose of the entire passage, viz. the recognition that Yahweh will have acted justly when he destroys Jerusalem. Verses 13–20 constitute the legal peroration in which the case for Yahweh's justice is set forth. Inconsistent with the entire account is verses 22–23a. Noah, Daniel, and Job will be unable to save sons and daughters, but here some survivors from Jerusalem's destruction will do so. Obviously some member of the Ezekiel school after 586 B.C. realizing the actual state of affairs wanted to justify the existence of survivors within the framework of Ezekiel's argument.

13. Unusual is the lack of an imperative after the vocative. Yahweh apparently addresses the prophet alone; it is clear from the 2nd plural in the recognition formula in verse 23b, however, that the exilic community is the audience. The legal language is evident from the casuistic formula in the Hebrew: 'as for a land when it sins . . .'. The sin is defined as **acting faithlessly,** a phrase taken from priestly circles involving perfidy in respect to religious law. With one possible exception (Prov. 16.10) the phrase always refers to breaking religious law as a conscious act of treachery. Except for Jos. 7.1; 22.20 (?), and Prov. 16.10 no earlier or non-priestly use of the term of the phrase is attested. It is common in Ezekiel (Ezek. 15.8; 17.20; 18.24; 20.27 *et al*), P, and the work of the Chronicler. Such perfidy naturally involves divine judgment—**stretch out my hand against it.** The first supposed judgment is famine; for **staff of bread,** cf. 4.16. The verb **cut off** is the usual term in sacral law for excommunication; cf. on verse 8. The formula recurs in the third and fourth cases, verses 17, 19, but not in verse 15.

14. For **Lord God,** as in verses 16, 18, 20, 21, 23, cf. on 2.4. Noah, Daniel, and Job are here chosen in contrast to the great Israelite figures, Moses and Samuel, not as intercessors but as outstanding, non-Israelite examples of personal integrity. In contrast to the Gen. 18.22–33 account, the presence of righteous men in the city will not save it; only they would be spared. Noah, the hero of the Flood, is now attested outside Hebrew tradition as the theophoric element in Old Babylonian names. In the P tradition Noah was known as 'a righteous man, blameless in his generation' (Gen. 6.9). Daniel (or possibly Danel, to distinguish him from the Daniel of the Book of Daniel) was a well-known Phoenician hero not known from the O.T. outside of Ezekiel, but now known as the father of Aqhat in the Ugaritic poem of *Aqhat* as one who 'judges the case of the widow, espouses the cause of the orphan', I *Aqhat*, V. 8; cf. also 28.3. Job too was traditionally a man who was 'blameless and upright, one who feared God, and turned away from evil' (Job 1.1). Job, like the other two, was a non-Israelite, whose story was widely known. Each was known as an outstanding example of personal righteousness and because of it would in the hypothetical case under discussion be saved in the general destruction.

The second hypothetical case: wild beasts 15–16

15. The introductory particle is unexpected; probably *'w* for *lw* is to be read, i.e., 'or if'. Hebrew lit. has 'bereave' for **ravage**.

16. In contrast to the first case, verse 14, the 'then' clause contains the oath formula (together with the oracle conclusion formula) with an *'m* clause, i.e. 'that they would not save sons or daughters' (cf. also verses 18, 20).

The third case: the sword 17–18

Cf. chapter 21.

The last case: pestilence 19–20

Added incongruously are the words **with blood,** which is more commonly combined with the sword; but cf. 5.17.

21. The dénouement, the oracular judgment which translates the hypothetical cases of verses 13–20 into the actual threat against Jerusalem. The legal form is now abandoned for the doom oracle which is however closely tied to the preceding by **How much more when.** The causal particle **For** is omitted by G. probably due to parablepsis. In any event it is necessary to the argument. The legal idiom for excommunication is still retained in verse 21*b*, but now as judgment.

22. RSV correctly vocalizes *hmwṣ'ym* to mean **to lead out** (or better 'who bring out') instead of the passive form of MT. The destruction of Jerusalem did yield some survivors in spite of the absoluteness of Ezekiel's earlier statement. The purpose which Yahweh has in mind for these escapees is for them to serve as object-lessons. The Ezekiel school found this troublesome, as successive attempts at expanding the text show. The *'t* clause at the end (lit. 'even all that I have brought upon her') is syntactically intrusive; similarly the phrase 'behold they are coming forth to you' has been added to the first statement. RSV has smoothed out the difficulties but thereby changed the meaning. The verse actually begins with: 'And behold there are left in it.'

23a is also repetitive of verse 22*ba* and represents still another expansion. Verse 23*b* in the form of a recognition formula gives the *raison d'être* of the entire section. Yahweh's destruction of Jerusalem by the four judgments is completely justified.

N. PARABLE OF THE USELESS WOOD OF THE VINE 15.1–8

In form this passage is typically Ezekiel. After the vocative there is an address of some kind to be followed by the oracle of judgment. It shows some expansion,

however, in that the recognition formula occurs in verse 7*ba* and the oracle conclusion formula in verse 8*b*. The amplification of the recognition formula is
repetitive of verse 7*aa* and is probably a later accretion to the original text. Verse 8
completely abandons the original allegory and represents a similar addition.

The parable of the wood of the vine brings out the useless character of such
wood. Because of this it is only fit for the burning which is its inevitable lot. The
oracle of verses 6–7 applies the parable to Jerusalem. So Jerusalem will be con-
signed to the fire. This partial application has led Irwin to designate verses 6–8 as
secondary, as false commentary, in fact. But the prophet does not need to apply
the notion of uselessness to Jerusalem; this is an obvious reference which any hearer
would himself make. The real comparison is: as the wood of the vine is good for
nothing but fuel for the fire so Jerusalem is fit only for the fire.

2. The figure of the vine is a favourite one in the O.T., not only among the
prophets (Hos. 10.1; Isa. 5.1–7; Jer. 2.21), but in other works as well (Jg. 9.8–13
and Ps. 80.8–16 (MT 9–17)). Reference to the vine is often a symbol of fruitfulness
(Num. 13.23–24; Dt. 8.8); thus Israel is called a luxuriant vine that yields its fruit
in Hos. 10.1. Ezekiel, however, uses the vine stalks after the grapes are harvested.
Verse 2*b* shows a difficulty since the verb **is** is masculine and its antecedent **the
vine branch** is feminine. **wood** is, however, masculine, and if 'the vine branch'
is deleted the problem is resolved. Often suggested is taking 'wood' over into
verse 2*a*, i.e. 'wood of the vine branch', but if *hzmrh* means 'vine stalk' (cf. 8.17)
the result makes little sense since 'wood of the vine' and 'wood of the vine branch'
are the same thing.

3. Harvested vines are simply useless. Such a vine is too small for building
purposes, and it is too soft and crooked even to be used for a peg in the walls on
which to hang things.

4–5. Even less useful is such a vine stalk when its ends are burned and the
remainder charred.

6. For **Lord GOD**, as in verse 8, cf. on 2.4. It must be admitted with Irwin that
the application is not that Israel is useless, which is what the allegory itself stresses.
The prophet does not elaborate the central comparison logically. The point of
comparison that he does make is on an incidental point of the allegory, viz. the
burning of the vine stalks. Yahweh naturally consigns the useless vine to the fire,
and in the same manner he consigns Jerusalem to the flames (cf. Isa. 6.13). The fire
is a favourite figure for destruction in Ezekiel (Ezek. 5.2, 4; 10.2; 16.41; 23.47;
24.10–11).

7. The Hebrew has 'they have escaped' for **they escape**. The reference is to the
deportation of 597 B.C. of Jehoiachin and others, including Ezekiel. The remaining
Jerusalemites did escape, but in the coming attack there will be no escape. The
recognition formula is in the 2nd plural, i.e. the exiles. G. regularizes to 3rd plural,
but this is incorrect.

8. land desolate: cf. on 6.14, and for **acted faithlessly,** 14.13.

O. Jerusalem an Unfaithful Wife 16.1–63

This chapter and chapter 23 are extended diatribes against Jerusalem as an adulterous woman. In the history of tradition they have mutually influenced one another with the result that considerable expansion has taken place.

The marriage relation as a figure for the relation between Yahweh and his people was first used extensively by Hosea. Hosea's own domestic experience with an unfaithful spouse was used by that prophet as a symbol of Yahweh's tragic experiences with Israel (Hos. 2). Israel's harlotry consisted in idolatry, a harlotrous pursuit of the Canaanite fertility gods. Jeremiah, strongly influenced by the older prophet, also uses the marriage symbol to show the Yahweh–Israel relation (Jer. 2.2), and that of unfaithfulness to the marriage vow to elucidate Judah's sin (Jer. 3.6–14). Ezekiel elaborates and deepens the use of the symbol. In contrast to his predecessors Ezekiel does not admit a primeval period of blissful innocence; Jerusalem's origins were pagan. Nor is divine forgiveness of an erring bride contemplated, or even the possibility of a repentant wife. For Jerusalem he predicts destruction; only later events ameliorated this picture.

In this chapter Ezekiel takes an old story of a foundling baby who is cared for and eventually, when full-grown, taken to wife by a great prince, verses 4–14. But the bride in singular ingratitude used her new position and riches to play the part of a wilful nymphomaniac, verses 15–34. Accordingly Yahweh will condemn her to the judgment proper to an adulterous woman, verses 35–43. The remainder of the chapter abandons the original story and its application and is a sermonic diatribe more or less dependent on chapter 23 against a Jerusalem who is more harlotrous than her wicked sisters, Samaria and Sodom, verses 44–52. When the fortunes of the three wicked sisters are restored, Jerusalem's sense of shame will be awakened, verses 53–58. The future status of Jerusalem will then be that of an enduring covenant in which Yahweh's pardon will result in the city's remembering her former shame, verses 59–63.

Many modern scholars are agreed that the original prophecy is to be found only in verses 1–43. Not only is the figure of the original story completely abandoned in verses 44ff., but the concept of a restoration to the former estate is completely at odds with the judgment on the adulteress in verses 40–41a. Thus verses 53–63, which presuppose such a restoration, must represent later accretions. Verses 44–52 are also inconsistent with this total judgment but are an invective against Jerusalem calling her to a sense of shame. Its dependence on chapter 23 will be delineated later.

(a) the story of the foundling 16.1–14

As might be expected, the story, which is told in a form of poetic prose, shows few accretions. The minor accretions can easily be recognized by their prosaic nature. Thus in verse 5 **to do any of these things to you out of compassion for you** is an expansion on verse *aa*. In verse 8 **yea ... God** is a later expansion explaining what the actions in verse 8a really meant. In verse 13 **and your raiment ... cloth** is a repetitious expansion from verse 10, and verse 14b is an expansion intended to correct any possible misapprehension that the young woman's beauty was anything but God-given, whereas it is only verse 14*a* which is taken up by verse 15.

2. That the narrative is intended as a diatribe is clear from the imperative **make known.** G. with its 'witness to' misread *hwd'* ('made known') as *h'd*.

3. For **Lord GOD,** as in verses 8 and 14, cf. on 2.4. The oracle is in accordance with the directive in verse 2 addressed consistently throughout the chapter to Jerusalem as representing the rebellious house of Israel. This does not imply actual address since the prophet is in Babylon. As in chapter 15, it is intended for the exiles. They are to place no confidence in Jerusalem's future. The opening statement of the oracle is not part of the foundling story which begins in verse 4, but sets the tone for the opening of the story in verses 4–5. Jerusalem's origin is of mixed pagan origin. The word for origin means 'places of digging'; hence G. has 'root'; even better, render 'your roots'. These origins of Jerusalem are given as Canaanite, a mixture of Amorite and Hittite. Ezekiel makes no mention here of an Israelite period before Jerusalem's fall to David. As the capital its history and origins are symbolic of the people. Its origin as a Canaanite city were well known. **Amorite** is the name of the pre-Israelite inhabitants of Canaan in the Elohist (Gen. 15.16; 48.22). Amorites, or 'Westerners', were Semitic peoples now widely attested in cuneiform sources, especially those from Mari, an Amorite city state on the Euphrates. The Amorites were involved in overthrowing the third dynasty of Ur in the early twentieth century B.C., as well as the establishment of the first dynasty of Babylon, of which Hammurabi was the best-known ruler. In later centuries they occupied many important cities in Syria and Palestine. Eventually their dominance came to an end with the rise of the **Hittite** kingdom in Asia Minor. The Hittites were an Indo-European race; after the fall of the kingdom at the beginning of the twelfth century they scattered south into Syria and Palestine and assimilated with the local populace. They are attested in the O.T. particularly as living in Judah. Numerous references to Hittites in the patriarchal stories remain a mystery as far as their relations to the Hittites in Asia Minor are concerned. According to the Amarna tablets a ruler of Jerusalem was named Abdiḫepa. The theophoric element, *ḫepa*, refers to a Hittite goddess, indicating early Hittite influence in Jerusalem.

4. The word *mš'y* occurs only here and is completely unknown. The rendering **to cleanse you** or better 'for cleansing' is based on T. and fits the context. The details relating to care of the newly born infant are still practised among natives in Palestine. The infant is bathed in water, rubbed with salt and oil, and then tightly wrapped in strips for a week before it is again washed with water and anointed with oil and again wrapped up tightly. What the salt was intended for is uncertain; it may simply have been a cleansing agent.

5. The foundling not only did not receive the usual care of the new-born but was immediately abandoned in the open field. Female offspring among the bedouin are often unwanted and in the time of Muhammad were often abandoned in the desert sand.

6. your blood: MT has the plural, usually signifying shed blood. G. has singular (as does MT at verse 22). RSV omits MT's repetition of 'I said . . . Live', which is a dittograph. Yahweh in passing saw the new-born babe weltering in its birth blood and by a word of command gave continuing life to the child. **in your blood** does not modify **you** but **Live**. Ezekiel cleverly plays on the term 'blood'. To 'live in blood' means to live in health. As in Ps. 33 and Gen. 1 the divine word is active and its pronouncement brings into immediate effect.

7. RSV correctly presupposes the omission of *nttyk*, 'I gave you', and the change of *rbbh*, 'a myriad', to the imperative *rbby*, **grow up**. For **at full maidenhood** MT has 'in the finest of ornaments'. A slight emendation, *b't 'dym* or even better *b'dym*, 'to the (time of) menses' for *b'dy 'dyym* restores the intended meaning. In the parallel clause **hair** refers to pubic hair as a sign of maturity.

8. The girl is now full-grown and Yahweh notes in passing that she was sexually mature, i.e. **at the age for love,** and he took her to wife. The phrase **spread . . . skirt over** was the symbol for marriage (Ru. 3.9). Similarly, 'to cover the nakedness' is the symbol for the husband's protection of his wife, just as 'uncover nakedness' is the symbol for the loss of protection on his part in the case of unfaithfulness, verse 37. The expansion explains these symbols as the marriage covenant (cf. Mal. 2.14).

9. For **your blood,** cf. on verse 6. The term must refer here to the menses. Here the washing and anointing is taken from the realm of the rites of the new-born and adopted as a symbol of the preparation of the bride.

10. The meaning of *mšy* is uncertain. It is probably a loanword from Egyptian *mšj* meaning 'finely woven'. The rendering **with silk** is an incorrect Rabbinic tradition; silk was unknown in the Near East until considerably later. G. renders it as 'something woven of hair'; V., by *subtilibus*. **embroidered cloth** is rather variegated material, i.e. coloured stuff, much prized by women and used as robes for a queen, Ps. 45.14 (MT 15). The word for **leather** does mean some kind of leather, but it is not certain what kind was intended. It may be another Egyptian loanword, i.e. *čḥs*, 'skin, leather', just as *ss*, **fine linen,** is. All these are intended to represent the best in wearing apparel.

The bridal jewellery **11–12**

The **crown** is the bridal crown, though it presages her coming to regal estate at the end of verse 13.

13. G.'s omission of the final phrase is an error. The spelling *'klty*, **you ate,** represents an archaic spelling of the 2nd fem. singular, a spelling preserved throughout the chapter. **and your raiment . . . cloth** is a later tradition summarizing verse 10. Food provided consisted not only of honey and oil (cf. Dt. 32.13), but also of fine flour, a term particularly beloved of P, but also found in Gen. 18.6 as food for guests of honour and in 1 Kg. 4.22 (MT 5.2) as part of the royal provisions for Solomon's household. **came to regal estate** means that the foundling became a queen.

14. Only the first clause is original to the account. That she should be inter-

nationally famed for her beauty is the climax of the story which now sets the stage
for the invective of the next section.

(b) THE QUEEN BECOMES A HARLOT 16.15-34

This section has received numerous accretions to the original invective. Hölscher
is probably right in limiting the original account to verses 15, 24-25. In these verses
the charge is one of harlotry with any passer-by. Verse 15 must be original since it
takes up chiastically the terms **renown** and **beauty** and charges Jerusalem with
prostituting these to base ends. Verses 16-20 are a series of four charges each
introduced by 'you took'. These are a later attempt to treat the story as an allegory,
i.e. apply all the elements of the story to Jerusalem's history. The last of these is
however a charge which is not at all borne out by the story. This was of course
not necessary, but seems to have been the point of view of the traditionist. Within
verses 16-20 later traditions are also evident. Verses 18b-19, by not following the
pattern, shows its later character, viz. to add further details from the story.

Verse 21 is dependent on verse 20 and is thus subsequent to it. The last four letters
of verse 15 still show the original continuation, as they are also the first letters of
verse 23. This is probably the origin of the peculiar *lw yhy* at the end of verse 15.
The *wyhy* of verse 23 correctly continues the original account; thus verse 22 must
also represent a later accretion, a tradition which emphasizes ingratitude rather than
idolatry. Within verse 23 the words in parentheses are not original, but verses 24-25
are, continuing the protasis of verse 23a. Verses 26-29 introduce a historical record
of Jerusalem's various relations with surrounding nations (cf. chapter 23). Adultery
might be viewed as having relations with other nations instead of an isolationist
policy of simple reliance on Yahweh, but this is not how Ezekiel defined it here;
to him Jerusalem's harlotry was cultic wrong, i.e. idolatry. Within the tradition of
verses 26-29, verse 27 is a separate tradition with its note of judgment rather than
prophetic invective.

Verses 30-34 introduce still another tradition. The opening statement is difficult,
but verse 31a simply repeats part of the original oracle, verse 24, but then interprets
Jerusalem's sin as paying bribes, i.e. tribute to various nations, instead of receiving
such. Sin is thus purely political, and it is even later than verses 26, 28-29. Substantially the original invective is represented by verses 15 (except for *lw yhy*), 23a,
24, 25 (except for *aa*, which repeats verse 24b).

15. The abstract *tznwt*, 'harlotry', would normally not be possible as a plural
noun, and yet here and in verses 22, 25, 33, 34, 36 it occurs. Many would change
these with G. to the singular, but this can hardly be intended. The plural is used to
designate 'acts of harlotry' as distinct from the abstract 'harlotry'. For the unintelligible 'may it be his' at the end, and omitted by G.S. as meaningless; cf.
discussion above suggesting it as a scrambled form of the first word in verse 23.

16. Verse 16b is completely unintelligible: MT has four words which mean 'not
things coming (?), nor will it be'. It is doubtful whether RSV's **the like has never
been, nor ever shall be** can be correct, since the participle in the first clause is
feminine plural and the verb in the second is feminine singular. Verse 16a represents

the first application of a detail in the story by a later tradition, viz. on the garments of verse 10. Garments were used to make **gaily decked shrines.** The word for shrines is that for high places, but how the cloth could be used to make such is not clear. Possibly curtains for the high places are meant; cf. the curtains of 'blue and purple and scarlet stuff' in the P account of the desert Tabernacle (Exod. 36.8–13, 35).

17. The second in the series concerns the misuse of the gold and silver. **fair jewels** really means 'vessels of beauty' and refers to the ornaments of verses 11–12. These were melted and recast into male images, probably phallic symbols used in Canaanite fertility rites. On the other hand it may be a reflection of 23.14 where male images portrayed on walls are mentioned.

18. The misuse of the embroidered garments, verse 10, to clothe the images of verse 17 describes an idolatrous rite possibly hinted at in Jer. 10.9. Verse 18b and 19 show a different syntactical pattern and are later details added to describe the pagan sacrifices indulged in by Jerusalem. The incense is an added detail not found in the story.

19. A reference to food in general must have been the original form of the tradition as is clear from *wnttyhw* 'and you set it'. The singular suffix refers to 'my bread' and the intervening words are a subsequent gloss. For **pleasing odour,** cf. on 6.13. For **Lord God,** as in verses 23, 30, cf. on 2.4.

20. The fourth **you took** is a charge of child sacrifice (cf. 23.37). This practice is referred to as prevalent in the last decades of the northern kingdom (2 Kg. 16.3; 17.17), as well as during Manasseh's reign (2 Kg. 21.6). In the account of the D reform mention is made of Topheth in the Hinnom valley as the place where the Judeans sacrificed sons and daughters as an offering to Molech (2 Kg. 23.10). Eissfeldt (*Molk als Opferbegriff im Punischen u. Hebräischen u. das Ende des Gottes Molech*) has suggested that 'to Molech' really means for a votive offering. If so, that would solve the question of the identity of the elusive 'king' god. On the other hand, the Hebrew tradition by its vocalization unambiguously understood it to be an idol. In any event, child sacrifice was considered pagan in D (Dt. 12.31; 18.10), and was strictly forbidden in H (cf. Lev. 18.21; 20.2–5). The children were Yahweh's, **borne to me,** and to sacrifice them was an offence. The last two words of the verse are taken together with verse 21 in RSV; they mean 'were your harlotrous acts few (or small)?' It could be taken simply as a sarcastic question.

21. 'your sons' is preferable to **my children** of MT and RSV. **as an offering by fire** is lit. 'by causing them to pass through (the fire)'. The word recurs at 20.26; 23.37 and with 'the fire' at 20.31.

22. RSV rightly omits with S. *hyyt* 'you were' at the end of the verse. G. omits **your abominations and.** The first word *w't* is a scribal error for *z't* ('this'), as G. *touto* shows. The verse should begin 'Thus are all your harlotries. Nor did you remember.' The tradition charges Jerusalem with ingratitude. Verse 22b quotes fragments of verses 6–7.

23. G. reads for **your wickedness** 'your wicked deeds' rightly. Ezekiel reserves the singular for divinely wrought calamity. G. omits the late **woe, woe is you**

but attests the oracle conclusion formula, which is however probably also an accretion.

24. vaulted chamber and **lofty place:** meaning uncertain, but some illegal shrine must be intended. Possibly these are merely references to high places which the D legislation had rendered illegitimate. The word for lofty place is *rāmāh*, which may be a play on *bāmāh*, 'high place'. The word for 'vaulted chamber' is *gb* and occurs only in this chapter in this sense. The word means something rounded, thus possibly an artificially constructed hill on which cult was performed. G., not understanding the word, rendered it by 'brothel'. The prophet's hyperbole is evident from the words 'on every street' (**square**), lit. 'broad place'.

25. at the head . . . place: a repetitious gloss on verse 24*b*. **offering yourself** is a chaste rendering for the picturesque Hebrew, which might be rendered 'with your legs sprawled'.

26. Harlotrous pursuit of Egyptians refers to Israel's constant search for alliance with its powerful neighbour to the south against encroachment and attack by Assyria and Babylon; cf. 2 Kg. 17.4; 18.21, and for similar reliance in the last days of Jerusalem, 17.15–17; Jer. 37.5–7. **your lustful neighbours** is a euphemism for the coarser Hebrew 'your neighbours with the large members'.

27. An accretion subsequent to verses 26, 28–29. A judgment oracle is out of place here. The reference is apparently to the invasion of Judah by Sennacherib in 701 B.C. Sennacherib records in his Annals that he gave Hezekiah's cities to Ashdod, Ekron, and Gaza and diminished the land (*ANET*, page 288).

28. For *wtznym*, **yea, you played the harlot with them**, delete 'with them'. The two clauses are almost identical; verse 28*b* is probably a late repetitious gloss. Dependence on Assyria such as 2 Kg. 16.7–9 is here castigated.

29. The word 'Canaan' may also mean 'trader' and is here used as an adjective for the land of Chaldea (cf. 17.4). For relations with the Babylonians, cf. 23.14–18. For **Chaldea,** cf. on 23.23. The reference is probably to the politics played with Nebuchadrezzar in the last decade of Jerusalem's existence.

30. The first clause is difficult. The word for **your heart** occurs only here and is rendered thus because it is similar to *lbk*. But *lbtk* could be Aramaic, meaning 'your flame', thus 'your wrath', i.e. 'anger concerning you'. Then *'mlh*, **lovesick,** might be taken as a variant spelling of *'ml'* which in the Ni. could then validate the translation 'How filled with wrath am I against you', which makes excellent sense. The word for **brazen** occurs only here, but the sense of 'domineering' is probably correct since its root 'to rule' is well known.

31. Repetitious of part of the original oracle in verses 24–25. The last sentence introduces the theme of the tradition in verses 30–34, viz. that Jerusalem as an unnatural harlot paid rather than received the harlot's fees (cf. Gen. 38.15–18).

32. strangers: G. misread as 'wages'. This can hardly be correct since the point of the tradition is precisely that she did not receive fees but gave them. The entire verse could of course be a later tradition since it does not fit the context too well, whereas verse 33 follows verse 31*b* naturally.

33. The lovers are the nations with which Jerusalem sought alliances and the gifts are tribute. The vacillation between Egypt and Babylon during Jehoiakim's and Zedekiah's reigns may be intended.

34. S. attests a shorter text, omitting **none . . . harlot** and **therefore . . . different.** The resultant text is terser, but Hebrew writers were often prolix.

(c) THE HARLOT IS SENTENCED **16.35-43**

Again the original oracle of judgment has been expanded by later traditionists. The judgment is formally a demonstration oracle, i.e. a 'because . . . therefore' construction. After the usual introductory formulae the 'because' clause is given in verse 36. It has been amplified by two additional 'because' clauses which are clumsy in Hebrew. One refers to 'dung-idols' (cf. on 6.4), and the other to child sacrifice, which in the invective, verses 20-21, was seen to be secondary. Verse 37 introduces the judgment with the formulaic **therefore, behold, I** plus a participle. If the remainder of the passage is examined in the light of the original invective in verses 15, 23a, 24, 25*, the appropriate judgment recapitulating the vaulted chamber and lofty place is found in verse 39. The judgment there is left in the hands of the lovers. This continues through verse 41a. Thus verses 39-41a constitute the original judgment. Verses 38, 41b-42 show Yahweh himself effecting the judgment personally, and probably represent later accretions. Verse 37 has also been amplified by the Ezekiel school. The phrase **all those you loved . . . loathed** is explicative of the first line of the oracle and an unnecessary amplification. The remainder of the verse is again Yahweh acting as agent of judgment. What remains as original then accents the agency of the lovers as Yahweh's representatives in judgment; they are mentioned in the 'because' clause, as gathered by Yahweh, and as the agents of judgment. The original account is thus verses 35, 36a, 37aα (up to **pleasure**), 39-41a.

36. For **Lord GOD,** as in verse 43, cf. on 2.4. **your shame** is a homonym of the word 'your bronze'. The word is otherwise unknown. RSV is based on T., and in view of the parallel **nakedness,** probably correct. **laid bare** is based on reading *ḥśpk* for MT *ḥšpk*, 'poured out', but the verb is then active and should be rendered 'you laid bare (your shame)'. In view of the uncertainty of the meaning of the noun it is unwise to change the text. The change of *wkdmy*, 'and like the blood of', to *wbdmy*, **and because of the blood of,** with G., is necessary. The last clause refers to the blood of the children offered to the idols.

37. took pleasure in the sense of sexual pleasure is hardly warranted by MT *'rbt*, which means 'were pleasing, sweet'. Probably *'gbt* 'doted, lusted', as in 23.5, 7, 9, 12, 16, 20, was original; render: '(on whom) you doted'. For **uncover . . . nakedness,** cf. on verse 8.

38. upon you is based on the change of *wnttyk* to *wntty bk* as at 23.25. **blood of** is a copyist's error and should be omitted; 'blood of wrath and jealousy' makes no sense. The judgment of adulterous women was death (Dt. 22.22, Lev. 20.10), and that for bloodshed as well (Gen. 9.6, Exod. 21.12).

39. Yahweh will restore Jerusalem to her state as a foundling by means of the lovers, throughout the original prophecy unidentified. The bridal gifts he had bestowed will be removed (garments and jewels), and she will be left **naked and bare,** verse 7; of course the high places (cf. on verse 24) will be broken up and destroyed as well, not by reforming kings such as Hezekiah and Josiah, but by the lovers.

40. host: not a military host, *ṣb'*, but rather the assemblage, *ḳhl*, gathered as a council to whom judgment is given, 23.24. 'Stoning with stones' was the sentence imposed by the D legislation on a betrothed virgin caught committing adultery in the city (Dt. 22.23–24); later tradition extended this to all adulteresses (Jn 8.5).

41. The burning of houses with fire is a prophecy of Jerusalem's imminent destruction by fire. **many women** continues the figure; it means many nations, i.e. in the eyes of the world. Verse 41*b* is certainly secondary. To put an end to harlotry implies Jerusalem's repentance whereas the original sentence imposed death. The last clause must be later than verses 31*b*–34 on which it is based.

42. Later than verse 38*b*, since it is an explanatory tradition based on the words 'wrath' and 'jealousy'. For **satisfy my fury,** cf. on 5.13. It recurs in 21.17(MT 22); 24.13 and is characteristic of a later tradition in the Ezekiel school.

43. The word *h'*, **behold,** is in a peculiar position in MT, coming after *'ny*, **I.** Probably they should be transposed. The word should not be deleted since it is expected to introduce the 'then' clause in a demonstration oracle. The verse is a later tradition, however, since the invective is based on the secondary verse 22. RSV follows the minority reading and G.S.V. in adding the necessary 'your' in **your head.** RSV has taken verse 43*bβ* as belonging to the next section. It certainly does not fit after the oracle conclusion formula. It may have been a marginal comment on verse 51 which was later copied into the text at the wrong place.

(d) JERUSALEM AND HER WICKED SISTERS I6.44–52

This is a prophetic diatribe, quite different from the usual oracular style of Ezekiel. The comparison of Jerusalem's abominations with those of her sister cities, Samaria and Sodom, reminds one of the comparison between Jerusalem and Samaria in chapter 23. There is no judgment predicted, only a call to patience in bearing the disgrace. Usual prophetic formulae are lacking except in verse 48. The entire passage is a further development on the proverb in verse 3*b* by a member of the Ezekiel school after 586 B.C.; the city is already bearing the disgrace. Within the passage there may well be later accretions, particularly verses 49–50. Since Samaria's sins are adequately dealt with in chapter 23, a later traditionist added a note listing the various sins of Sodom.

44. For **proverb,** cf. on 12.22. The proverb is used to explain Jerusalem's tendencies towards evil inherent in the fact that her mother was also pagan; cf. the original proverb in verses 3 and 45.

45. your sisters: MT has 'your sister' but the du. *'ḥwtyk* must be read (not the plural *'ḥywtyk as BH³*). 'Daughters' refers to neighbouring cities, of which the 'mother' was the chief; cf. e.g. Num. 21.25; Jg. 1.27, where 'daughters' is rendered 'villages' quite correctly. The term **husband(s)** must not be pressed; it simply completes the figure of an unnatural married women.

46. Hebrew has 'left' for **north,** and 'right' for **south**; cf. on 4.4, 6. Samaria and Sodom, born of the same parents as Jerusalem, were symbols of wickedness. For the former's, cf. 2 Kg. 17.7–18; for the latter's, cf. Gen. 19. Samaria's wickedness consisted largely in her idolatry, whereas traditionally that of Sodom was sexual immorality (cf. Gen. 19.5–9).

47. The word *ḳṭ* is obscure. The word before it is *km'ṭ,* 'like a little, hardly, just shortly', and *ḳṭ* (not attested in G.S.) may be a copyist's error for *ḳṭn,* 'little', which would be a late gloss on the preceding word (RSV renders 'within a *very* little time'). The verse should be rendered: 'Had you not walked in their ways and acted according to their abomination when shortly you became even more corrupt. . . .'

48. For **Lord GOD,** cf. on 2.4.

49. The last clause is in the 3rd fem. singular, thus applying to Sodom only, i.e. MT has 'she did not aid'. The traditionist failed to adapt his expansion to the rest of the verse. The source of this tradition about Sodom's sin is unknown; it is not based on the Gen. 19 story. That other oral traditions were existent about the cities of the plain is clear from Hos. 11.8.

50. For **when I saw it** read 'as you have seen'. The old spelling of 2nd fem. singular perfect, which is used extensively in this chapter, is the same as the 1st singular.

51. For **your sisters,** as in verse 52, cf. on verse 45. The theme reflects that of Jer. 3.6–11. In the light of Jerusalem's sins, sinful Samaria and Sodom seem righteous.

52. This verse seems prolix. Possibly verse 52*b*, which begins like *a*, was simply a marginal summary of *a*, later copied into the text.

(e) JERUSALEM WILL BE ASHAMED IN THE NEW AGE 16.53–58

This section is closely bound to the preceding (cf. verse 54 with verse 52) and may be part of the same tradition. On the other hand, it may well be a further explanatory tradition on verse 52. The stress is placed on the shame Jerusalem feels in the restoration. Verse 55 is probably an amplification of verse 53, which was added to explain that the restoration of fortunes for the three sisters would be to their former estate. The judgment, as in verses 44–52, is simply an enduring sense of shame, in contrast to the judgment of the original oracle (cf. verses 35–41*a*).

53. The meaningless *wšbyt* (RV 'and the captivity of') is a copyist's error for *wšbty* (RSV 'and I will restore'), as is recognized by RSV and the Versions. **restore . . . fortunes** was particularly favoured by the prophets as an idiom denoting a divine promise of restoration in the indefinite future involving an end to a period of punishment. *šbyt,* **fortunes,** occurs only in the singular except here and in Zeph. 3.20.

54. becoming . . . them is ironic. Such consolation is also reflected in the tradition of 14.22–23*a*. This verse gives the divine purpose behind the promised restoration, viz. Jerusalem's constant sense of shame.

56. byword is lit. 'report, a thing heard' and therefore passed on. **your pride** is erroneously plural in MT, which is not attested elsewhere.

57. your wickedness: probably should be changed to the minority reading 'your nakedness'. For the singular of **wickedness,** cf. on verse 23. **like her** represents an emendation of MT's 'as even now' or 'as the time of'. MT means: before your nakedness was uncovered at the time of (your being) an object of reproach, i.e. the exposure coincided with Jerusalem becoming an object of scorn. **Edom** (*'dm*) correctly for MT's *'rm*, 'Syria'. **and for** (not in MT) **the daughters of the Philistines** is a gloss. Edom and her neighbours, i.e. Moabites and Ammonites, were traditional enemies (cf. 25.2–12). The accretion was added, though Philistia was hardly a neighbour, being mentioned along with the others in chapter 25.

58. penalty does not occur in the Hebrew 'you have borne them', but the verb is here used in a legal sense, as RSV understood.

(f) THE ENDURING COVENANT 16.59–63

This is still another accretion to the original oracle to which it is tied by reference to **days of your youth** (verse 60), and to verses 44–58 by such references as **be ashamed** and **your sisters** in verse 61. Reference to the new and lasting covenant which God will establish with his people also occurs at 34.25; 37.26, as well as at 11.19–20; 14.11 and 36.28 (cf. on 11.19–20). This section represents the final stage in the tradition history of this chapter.

59. For Lord God, as in verse 63, cf. on 2.4. **yea** is not attested in G. The asseverative *ky* preceding the introductory oracle formula is peculiar. By transposing it after the formula good sense is obtained. Verse 59 then is the 'when' clause for verse 60, the apodosis. By dropping the conjunction before the verb the opening words of the oracle become: 'When I have done to you as.' **covenant** is a reference to the marriage covenant in verse 8, one which Jerusalem had broken.

60. But Yahweh will remember it. 'Establish the covenant' is characteristic of P language (cf. Gen. 17.7). The everlasting covenant will take the place of the broken one.

61. I take with S. for 'you take' of MT. Israel's memory in the eternal covenant will be one of perpetual shame. The promise of complete restoration is here made of a fully restored Palestine in which the northern kingdom and the Dead Sea plain will be part of the redeemed community. In this Jerusalem will be the capital, and the sisters become daughter cities. The final phrase is not clear. Probably what is meant is that the incorporation of the sisters as daughters is not due to their pact with Jerusalem but through divine action.

63. This is placed after the recognition formula as an appendix to emphasize the roles of the two parties in this new covenant: Jerusalem to remember her shame and Yahweh to forgive.

P. A FABLE AND ITS INTERPRETATION 17.1–24

As in chapters 15 and 16 some kind of literary device, parable, allegory, story, is first presented and then application to the contemporary situation is made. The device here used is called both a *ḥydh* and a *mšl*. For the latter, cf. on 'proverb' in 12.22. Since it is here intended as an extensive comparison RSV renders the word by **allegory.** The former is rendered by **riddle,** but the word has somewhat broader connotation. Anything propounded in which the intended meaning does not lie on the immediate surface can be called a *ḥydh*. Thus proverbs, riddles, allegories, in fact anything told in a way that the intended implication must be inferred by the audience are included. In Ps. 78.2 it refers to a recital which indirectly teaches a lesson, whereas in 1 Kg. 10.1 it means difficult questions propounded by the Queen of Sheba. Here it refers to verses 3–10, which constitute a fable which is allegorically interpreted in the remainder of the chapter.

Fables are stories about animals and plants which act like human beings. In Jg. 9.8–15 Jotham tells a fable about the trees who wanted to anoint a king, but the olive, fig, and vine successively declined the honour. Finally the bramble consented by becoming a tyrant. As in this chapter the fable is applied allegorically, the bramble being the rebel king, Abimelech. In 2 Kg. 14.9 Jehoash scornfully rejects overtures from Amaziah by a short fable about a thistle seeking the daughter of a cedar for a wife and being trampled by a wild beast. Again details of the fable are carefully applied to the situation.

Ezekiel's fable concerns two eagles, a cedar, and a vine. The finer of the eagles is Nebuchadrezzar and the second one was Hophra of Egypt. The cedar's topmost twig was Jehoiachin, whereas the lowly vine planted by the first eagle was Zedekiah. For details of the fable, cf. below.

(a) THE FABLE 17.1–10

Only the latter part of the fable has received some accretions to the original account. Verse 6b may well be such an expansion intended as a summarizing conclusion to the first part of the fable, though this is not certain. It could indicate the period of quiet after Zedekiah's appointment by Nebuchadrezzar before his revolt. Verse 8 is an expansion explaining Nebuchadrezzar's action and its purpose in verses 5–6 rather than the logical development of verse 7. In verse 9 the last sentence is foreign to the fable and is really interpretation. People have no place in a fable. It is from a traditionist explaining that it really took little effort on the part of the Babylonians to overthrow Zedekiah. Verse 10 also introduces something alien; the first eagle is now an east wind. The tradition is later than verse 8 since it develops the idea of transplanting. The original account is found in verses 1–6a, 7, 9aba.

2. A word such as story, tale, fable would be preferable to **riddle.**

3. For **Lord GOD,** as in verse 9, cf. on 2.4. The great eagle is Nebuchadrezzar. **many colours** is the same as 'embroidered cloth' in 16.10; its basic connotation is 'variegated'. **plumage,** not understood by G.S. which have 'claws', but variegated claws could hardly have been intended. As the eagle is the king of the birds, so the cedar is the king of trees. Since the cedar was traditionally from **Lebanon,** Lebanon is used as a term of honour for the Davidic house in Jerusalem. The coming to Lebanon refers to Nebuchadrezzar's coming to Jerusalem in 597 B.C. where he took the top of the cedar, i.e. young king Jehoiachin.

4. He broke off from the Davidic cedar young king Jehoiachin (2 Kg. 24.10–12, 15). The word for **trade** is *Canaan*. The Canaanites were great traders and the word 'Canaan' eventually came to be used to denote trade. The land is Babylonia; the city, Babylon, known as a great commercial centre.

5. Though Zedekiah was also a member of the Davidic house, the figure used to denote him is the vine, intentionally chosen since he was only a regent (cf. on 1.2). Strong emphasis is placed on the good care lavished on the regent by Nebuchadrezzar. The word for **like a willow twig** occurs only here and is completely unknown. RSV is based on Rashi, but is likely incorrect. The word 'like' is not in the Hebrew, and even a teller of fables would not mix vines with willows. G. may well be closer with its *epiblepomenon*. It read only *sph*, a root meaning 'to look out, keep watch'. MT has *spsph*, a partial dittograph of some noun like *ṣāpeh*, probably meaning 'something watched or cared for'.

6. The first two verbs should be read as short form imperfects rather than as *waw* consecutives to express purpose; thus: 'that it might sprout and become'. Zedekiah was to remain humble, **a low spreading vine,** dependent on Babylon (branches turning towards Nebuchadrezzar). **and its roots remained where it stood** incorrectly renders MT. The verb is imperfect and the Hebrew says 'and that its roots might be under him', i.e. under Nebuchadrezzar, who was to be his only support. The remainder of the verse is in past tense and probably represents an accretion.

7. The second great eagle, not described in such fulsome terms as the first, was Hophra of the 26th Dynasty in Egypt (588–569 B.C.); cf. Jer. 37.5 for his belated help to the besieged city shortly after becoming Pharaoh. RSV follows G. in reading **another** for MT 'one' correctly. **its branches** in MT refers wrongly to the eagle, rather than to the vine. **bed** is plural in MT as in verse 10, but this need not be changed. Its use is like the English 'terrace' or 'terraces', either being possible. **bent** occurs only here as a verb, though as a noun it is known with the meaning 'hunger'; thus to 'hunger towards', 'yearn'. The reference is to Zedekiah's seeking Egyptian help and revolting against Babylon. The actual ruler of Egypt appealed to may have been Psammetichus II, but he died, and Hophra, his successor, responded belatedly. **he** in **he might water it** (i.e. the vine) is the eagle. The figure is somewhat bizarre.

8. Together with the last part of verse 7 (from **from**) is an expansion. For **he transplanted it,** MT with better sense has 'it was transplanted'. It was Nebuchadrezzar who had set out the vine; it was not later transplanted by the Pharaoh.

9. This presents the divine question **Will it thrive?**, which is better than the statement of MT. MT's text is the result of haplography. Of doubtful originality is **say,** which both here and in verse 12*b* crept in under the influence of verse 3. MT's *tybš*, 'it will dry up', is correctly omitted by RSV as a gloss. **It will not take ... people** is an interpretative accretion. MT has no verb here, simply 'neither by a large arm nor by many people'. The rest may be a still later accretion to give an unnecessary predicate to the tradition.

10. The traditionist misunderstood the transplanting in verse 8.

(b) THE INTERPRETATIONS 17.11–24

The paragraphing in RSV shows two distinct layers of interpretations, verses 11–21 and verses 22–24. The second is much further removed from the original fable, interpreting it in complete disregard of details as referring to Yahweh's restoration of the Davidic dynasty. This is a late tradition, at the earliest late exilic, but more likely post-exilic.

The earlier interpretation is itself the result of a tradition history. The fable must date from 588 or 587 B.C., well before the fall of Jerusalem in 586. But parts of the interpretation presuppose knowledge (cf. the expansions in 12.1–16) of the events of 586. Verses 20–21 represent the same tradition as 12.13–14 and presuppose knowledge of Zedekiah's fate, and are a post-586 expansion. The original oracle ending the interpretation is in the oath formula of verse 19. The original interpretation has also been expanded. Verses 12–15 are written in a rather poor poetic prose, but verses 16–18 are simply prose. These prose verses are precisely the ones which have knowledge of Zedekiah's fate. Thus the original account is contained in verses 11–15, 19.

12. rebellious house is here the exilic audience as representative of Israel. G. adds 'son of man' at the beginning. The verse reflects the events of 2 Kg. 24.10–16, and interprets verses 3–4.

13 interprets verses 5–6*a*; cf. 2 Kg. 24.17. The last clause is an expansion of the statement in verse 12 that he brought 'her princes' to Babylon. The verse refers to the oath of fealty which Nebuchadrezzar imposed on Zedekiah.

14. The terms of the covenant imposed are complete submission, **kingdom . . . humble,** and loyalty, **not lift itself up,** i.e. rebel, interpreting verse 6*a*. **that . . . it might stand** refers to the kingdom. A variant Hebrew text has 'to serve him', i.e. 'to keep his covenant to serve him', but MT may be preferable here suggesting the other part of the covenant, viz. Nebuchadrezzar's promise that the kingdom will last as long as Zedekiah submits.

15 interprets verse 7; cf. 2 Kg. 24.20*b*. Zedekiah broke the covenant, something which Yahweh cannot allow since Zedekiah, as his change of name by Nebuchadrezzar to a throne name with the theophoric element of *Yah* implies, broke the oath of the covenant sworn in Yahweh's name. Cf. verse 19, where the covenant is called 'my covenant'.

16. For **Lord GOD,** as in verses 19, 22, cf. on 2.4. The expansion is introduced by an oath formula. **who made him king** indicates this as an accretion. Ezekiel never calls Zedekiah a king. MT punctuates its text to place 'with him' with the final phrase, i.e. 'with him in Babylon he shall die', which seems unlikely. For Zedekiah dying in Babylon, cf. 12.13.

17. For Hophra's belated aid, cf. Jer. 37.5. **company** means 'military company'; it is also used in 16.40 as 'host', but in a different sense. **will** (not) **help him** is based on reading *yśyʻ* for MT *yʻśh*. MT means 'will (not) act for him'.

18. For **gave his hand** as a symbol of co-operation (cf. 2 Kg. 10.15), or as a sign for sealing a treaty (Lam. 5.6). Here it was a sign of submission as in 1 Chr. 29.24; 2 Chr. 30.8.

19. my (oath) and **my covenant,** cf. on verse 15. Zedekiah's breaking of the covenant brought dishonour on Yahweh, whose name he had invoked. Appropriately the divine oath will effect the results on Zedekiah himself. MT has 'requite it', but this is wrong.

20. For verse 20*a*, cf. 12.13. G. omits verse 20*b* as well as the first three words of verse 21: **And all the pick of.** This is a still later accretion to the text. Actually Zedekiah was judged in Riblah rather than Babylon (2 Kg. 25.6).

21. RSV makes the best of a peculiar Hebrew sentence by emending the text. MT has 'and as for all his fugitives with his troops, they shall fall by the sword.' RSV changed 'and as . . . with' to 'and all the pick of'. The words are a late gloss and MT in turn is certainly corrupt. On the basis of 12.14 it is possible to reconstruct the original text; for **troops,** cf. on 12.14.

22–24 present a messianic promise under the guise of interpreting the fable. But Yahweh, not the eagle, effects the restoration.

22. G. omits **lofty** as a late gloss on **cedar** and **and (I) will set it out,** a gloss on **(I) will plant it.** The details of verse 4 now become the vehicles of salvation. The tender twig is the promised Messiah of the Davidic line. For the Messiah as 'branch', cf. Isa. 11.1; Jer. 23.5; 33.15; Zech. 3.8; 6.12. The **mountain** is Jerusalem, to which the exiled scion will return.

23. The verb **will I plant it** is the same as 'transplant' in verses 8, 10, which would be more appropriate here. The Messiah's establishment in Jerusalem will effect the general well-being and good fortune (cf. 34.25–31; 37.24–28; Jer. 17.25–26; 33.14–16; Mic. 5.2–3(MT 4–5)). G. has **all kinds of beasts** instead of MT's 'all birds', and RSV rightly follows G.

24. The recognition formula is given cosmic scope. This theme of complete sovereignty became even more pronounced in apocalyptic writing, e.g. Dan. 4.25, 32.

Q. The Righteous and the Wicked: A Disputation 18.1–32

This passage is formally introduced as a disputation (cf. 12.21–25) where a proverb is cited and answered. The objections are cited, verses 19, 25, 29, and each is answered in turn. Finally an oracle of judgment leaves no more room for dispute. The passage has only a few formulae, as might be expected from its formal character as a disputation (for prophetic disputation, cf. especially Malachi). The oracle conclusion formula occurs in verses 9, 23, 30, 32, and in verse 3 together with the oath formula.

Zimmerli has made an interesting suggestion concerning the origin of the literary type represented in verses 5–18. He believes this to be rooted in a cultic encounter: a list of laws rooted in indigenous apodictic law as a kind of confessional, a priestly declaration that such an individual is righteous (verse 9) or wicked, and finally a declaration of cultic life or death. Von Reventlow adds a fourth stage between the first and second, a general judgment on the relations of the cultic participant (i.e. observe statutes and judgments, since these are not apodictic), but this is dubious since neither is cited in verses 10–13.

An examination of the first list shows a list of fifteen laws whose observance characterizes the righteous. All but nos. 4 and 13 are given in verses 14–17 with some change in order after no. 9, viz. 12, 10, 11, 15, and 14. This might support the notion of a standard list testing the fitness of a cult participant. The second list, verses 10–13, however, plays havoc with the list. Only eight of the list occur; a new one is added in seventh place, and the order is 1, 3, 5, 7, 6, 2, (16), 10, 11. The conclusion is obvious: the list of laws is not a well-known one such as the Decalogue.

That the declaration 'he is righteous' is formulaic is possible in view of the priestly formulae found by Rendtorff (*FRLANT*, N.F. 44, 1954) in the H Code, but that the formula is priestly is not assured. The priestly formulae concern purification, but Ezekiel is dealing with sin and his topic is individual responsibility for one's sinful acts. It is a formula that goes back to the recitation of apodictic law rather than a liturgy of entrance, cf. Ps. 15 and 24, and might rather be part of a feast of covenant renewal in which the demands of the covenant were recited and vocally accepted by the participants. Possibly some declaration of fitness for such participation may have been made. A blessing, a declaration of cultic life(?), would have sealed the covenant renewal.

But regardless of the origins of the literary form, Ezekiel makes use of it as an argument for individual responsibility for his exilic audience. The exiles constituted the hope for the future. Jeremiah had characterized them as the good figs in contrast to the ones remaining in Jerusalem as bad figs (Jer 24.5–10). And yet it was they who were exiled. The inference was clear; they must be suffering for the guilt of the fathers. It is this conception with which he struggles. Yahweh's justice cannot permit this. Every man suffers for his own sin. Past records do not count, only the present state of one's heart. Yahweh desires that the wicked turn to him and the righteous remain constant. He does not punish good and bad indiscriminately.

Clear as Ezekiel is here, and in the related passage in 33.10–20, he is not always fully consistent. The exiles do take corporate responsibility as is indicated by his use elsewhere of the term 'rebellious house', e.g. 17.12. Jerusalem will be completely destroyed and no regard for the righteous in it (such as Jeremiah) will save it (cf. Gen. 18.22–33). Usually no provision is made for their escape in the general destruction, though in the vision of the departing glory the scribal messenger does mark the righteous, 9.4–6. None the less Ezekiel here makes his most valuable contribution, viz. that man is not bound by laws of generation to a fate; rather each man individually faces God and is judged on his own merits.

The text is remarkably free from later expansions, except for minor ones which will be pointed out below, with one exception. Verses 26–29 is an expansion which repeats the argument of verses 21–25. A traditionist noted that the oracle of verse 30 is addressed to the house of Israel and thus added a parallel section to the preceding reversing the two cases considered and placed the words of the objector in the 3rd person. This may have been a 'second edition' by Ezekiel himself.

2. G. has 'son of man' at the beginning. But the address is throughout in the plural. If G. represents the original text it must have been with an imperative such as 'son of man, say to the house of Israel' as at 33.10. The plural address without such an imperative does not occur elsewhere and the suggested insertion was probably original. **set on edge** means 'to be blunt' (as of an axe edge). Why eating sour grapes should blunt teeth is not clear; it was probably an old wives' tale. The point of the proverb is none the less clear. The children suffer the consequences of the father's actions. The proverb is also quoted in Jer. 31.29–30 with a rebuttal similar to verse 4*b*. It applies the words of the Decalogue: visiting the iniquity of the fathers upon the children to the third and fourth generation of them that hate me (Exod. 20.5) to the contemporary situation, i.e. concerning the land of Israel. This does not necessarily presuppose the defeat of 586 B.C., but rather the 597 B.C. deportation. The proverb is general; no specific fathers are intended but the exiles were well acquainted with the traditions of the sins of the fathers.

3. For **Lord GOD,** as in verses 9, 23, 30, 32, cf. on 2.4. The proverb will fall into disuse because its falseness will be exposed.

4. soul means the self as the life principle and is not used in the modern sense of soul as the immaterial *v.* the material body. It might better be rendered as 'individual'. The second clause may represent a variant tradition to the first clause, one being a later accretion. The refutation of the proverb is enunciated in the last clause: whoever sins, he shall die.

5–17. A series of three sample cases stated in the form of casuistic law. They reflect three generations: a righteous man, his wicked son, and the son's righteous son. The proverb could hardly apply in the first case since the parentage is not stated, but it is necessary to explicate the **father.** In form the three cases are parallel, except that the second and third are somewhat shorter and omit the declaration of verse 9*ba*. The passage is a direct challenge to a generation theory of guilt by inheritance.

5. The sentence is typical of casuistic law especially common in the H and P Codes. The two terms **what is lawful and right** are words regularly rendered by 'justice and righteousness' in RSV. The presupposition is that this is a case of a righteous man, and the declaration in verse 9 simply declares what is set out as given.

6–8 list some characteristics of the righteous which reflect apodictic laws, i.e. of the 'you shall not' or 'do not' type, to which verse 9 adds two general terms.

6. eat on the mountains: a reference to partaking of sacrifices on the high places which had been declared illegal by the D reform (cf. on 6.3 and 16.16). Each of these characteristics can easily be reconstructed as a law, e.g. 'You shall not sacrifice on the high places.' Partaking of food refers to the sacrificial meal in which the worshipper takes part in eating the dedicated food (cf. 1 Sam. 9.12–13). The second law observed is that against idolatry. For **idols** as dung-idols, cf. on 6.4. **lift up . . . eyes** is here used in sense of observe and thus seek help from; cf. Ps. 121.1, so worship; cf. also 23.27, 33.25. The first two are a pair corresponding to the first part of the Decalogue, dealing with cult. The next pair deals with sexual mores. Adultery was condemned from earliest times (cf. Gen. 26.6–11), and strictly forbidden in the codes (cf. Exod. 20.14; Dt. 22.22; Lev. 18.20; 20.10), whereas taboos concerning relations with a woman in her menses were imposed in H (Lev. 18.19; 20.18) and in P (Lev. 15.19–24).

7. RSV rightly changes 'his pledge, debt' to **to the debtor his pledge** (*ḥwb* to *ḥyb*). The first three deal with property. Oppression in a society where men were intended as social equals was already forbidden in the Covenant Code (Exod. 22.21(MT 20)) regarding strangers, but especially by H (cf. Lev. 19.13, 33; 25.14, 17). The restoration of pledge is demanded by the Covenant Code in Exod. 22.26–27 (MT 25–26) as a rule of ordinary humanity (cf. also Dt. 24.10–13). Robbery is a term implying violence. Laws against violent seizure are found in H (Lev. 19.13) and P (Lev. 6.2–4(MT 5.21–23)). The last pair cannot be exactly paralleled in the laws, though laws for helping the needy abound in D, e.g. Dt. 15.7–11, and also H, e.g. Lev. 19.9–10; cf. also Jesus' parable of the sheep and the goats (Mt. 25.31–46).

8. The first pair concerns money-lending. The taking of interest on a loan was strictly forbidden (Exod. 22.25(MT 24), Dt. 23.19(MT 20)), and in H (Lev. 25.36), where **increase** is also prohibited. Increase probably refers to capital increases in contrast to interest in which capital remains the same until repaid. The last pair concerns morality in legal action. To withhold the hand from iniquity is a reflection of the law in H (Lev. 19.15, 35), i.e. not doing injustice in judgment, which has its positive counterpart in the second of the pair.

9. The second verb, **is careful,** is by scribal error in the perfect. All other verbs in verses 7–9 are in the imperfect. RSV apparently presupposes G.'s 'to do them' (after **ordinances**) for MT 'to do truly'. For the general summary pair of laws typical of D, and found also in H, cf. Dt. 7.11; 11.32; Lev. 25.18, 26.3. The term **live** as the reward for personal righteousness has been variously interpreted. Some have thought Ezekiel to mean a long life as over against premature death. Others have interpreted life eschatologically, as a promise of participation in a blissful messianic age. Neither fully expresses Ezekiel's intent. Life is not just animation, but involves true communion with God; cf. Ps. 73.27–28, where in contrast to perishing the writer revels in nearness to God. Such life means wholeness or peace, i.e. a complete existence as person in which personal integrity, corporate involvement in society, and communion with God constitute the promised life. Part of the mystery of the promise is that in the exile cult in any Palestinian sense was impossible, but this in turn gave greater emphasis to the individual's relation to God.

10. MT has a partial dittograph which reads 'and a brother does none of these'. This verse introduces the first generation, a wicked son of a righteous man. Such a son is doubly characterized as a **robber** (7.22, Jer. 7.11, lit. 'one who breaks up, is violent') and a **shedder of blood,** lit. 'one who pours out blood', probably a term for murderer.

11. Verse 11*a* is a doublet of verse 10*b* (omitted by RSV); only one is likely to be original. The list of sins in verses 11*b*–13*a* is shorter and scrambled; cf. discussion above.

12. Unique in the lists of laws is the last one; **abomination** is a favourite of Ezekiel and refers to idolatry (cf. 5.9).

13. For **shall he then live . . . live** read 'he shall surely not live (*hyw* for *why*)', the negative equivalent of the formula in verse 9. Death is a breaking of the bond between God, the source of life, and man (cf. Gen. 3.3–4). RSV changes 'he shall surely be put to death' to a Qal construction (**he shall surely die**), as throughout the chapter. The last clause is a gloss on this (cf. the legal formula recurring throughout Lev. 20.11–27).

14. and fears (*wyr*'), for MT *wyr'h* 'and sees'.

17. from iniquity is doubtless right, cf. verse 8, rather than MT 'from the poor'.

18. MT *gzl'ḥ* is an error of auditory transmission for *gzlh*. Thus for **robbed his brother,** render 'committed robbery'. For '*myw*, **his people,** 'my people' is preferable. The last letter is a dittograph; Ezekiel always uses the singular for fellow citizens. 'My people' then refers to Yahweh's people. This verse recapitulates the judgment for the second case, verses 10–13.

19–20. A summary statement of the principle that underlies the judgments in the three particular cases cited, viz. that retribution is not communicated by generation but is borne only by the individual concerned.

19. The spelling *wayya'ᵃśeh* is a conflate of two readings; *wayya'aś* ('and observed') and *wᵉya'ᵃśeh*. The latter, **to observe** or 'to do', is preferable. Righteousness results in life.

20. And iniquity inevitably issues in death (cf. Ps. 1).

21–25. A corollary to the above argument. A father's wickedness is no nemesis overtaking the fate of the son, and neither is one's own past such a nemesis. If a wicked man repents and his repentance issues in a righteous life, he lives. And conversely a righteous man loses life by becoming wicked. Man is not judged quantitatively but rather by what he becomes. Yahweh desires lives that issue in righteous lives; not by past history but in present action is a man judged.

23. Cf. Lk. 15.7; 1 Tim. 2.4; 2 Pet. 3.9. Yahweh's real desire is not death but life.

24. The reverse of the case in verses 21–22. Past righteous deeds will not avail; only the present counts. The righteous man turned wicked dies. **and does . . . live** probably represents a later explanation of **commits iniquity.** G. omits the verbs showing an earlier shorter version of the accretion, viz. 'according to all the lawless acts which the lawless one did.'

25. Many suggest reading 'Yahweh' for **the Lord** here and in verse 29, but MT is probably original. The point made by the disputant is precisely that the one who dominates is not just. The rebuttal places the blame properly. The exile is not evidence of divine injustice but rather of the wickedness of the exiles. In the original account the oracle of verse 30 followed verse 25.

26–29. A doublet version of verses 21–25. The cases of verses 21–22 and 24 are reversed.

26. for it: an attempt to render '*lyhm*, 'for them', omitted by G. as a late gloss. The plural (acts of wickedness?) shows that it is secondary.

28. Because he considered and turned away: read 'when he turns away', i.e. *bšwbw* for *wyšwb*. The first word, *wyr'h*, 'because he considered', is a copyist error which somehow crept in from verse 14*b*. G. does not have it.

30. The oracle is not introduced with the usual introductory formula, but simply by **Therefore.** Every man will be individually judged. The verb **turn** is transitive with the modifier 'your faces' understood (cf. 14.6). 'stumbling block of iniquity' occurs at 7.19; 14.3, 4, 7, and 44.12 as well, and here characterizes **your transgressions.** The phrase should be rendered 'and you will have no more stumbling block of iniquity', i.e. iniquitous stumbling block, for **lest iniquity be your ruin.**

31. transgressions involves the idea of revolt and rebellion, a conscious breaking of law. **against me** follows G. rather than MT ('against them') correctly. The rebellion of the wicked is against God. Usually it is Yahweh who gives a new heart and spirit in the O.T. (e.g. 11.19, 36.26; Ps. 51.10 (MT 12); Jer. 31.33), but here it is part of the call upon man to repent.

32. Cf. verse 23. **so turn and live** is a late gloss, not in G. It was probably a marginal note summarizing the theme of this section.

R. A POLITICAL LAMENT **19.1-14**

This chapter contains two nationalistic poems, the second of which, verses 10–14, is clearly dependent on and later than the first. Both are dirges, i.e. poems in which the second hemistich is usually shorter than the first. This halting or limping rhythm is called *kinah* or lament metre, and is the dominant pattern in many of the laments in Lamentations; cf. also Am. 5.1–3, Isa. 14.4–21. The Hebrew dirge is largely political in content, a poem chanted on the death of some leader (2 Sam. 1.17–27; 3.33–34). Such lamentation was often exercised by professional mourners (Jer. 9.17 (MT 16)), and taught in turn to their daughters (Jer. 9.20 (MT 19)). A number of the oracles against the nations are called lamentations, 26.17; 27.2, 28.12; 32.2. It has been suggested that the dirge had its origin in the cult, i.e. in the lament for the dying vegetation god, but in the Israelite form it had no such connotation even in its earliest example, 2 Sam. 1.17–27, which is a political dirge.

Both dirges here are in allegorical form. In the first a lioness produced whelps. One of these grew up under its mother's direction, but when it performed its leonine functions it was caught and brought to Egypt. A second was then substituted, but it too was captured and transported to Babylon. The allegory refers to the two young kings, Jehoahaz and Jehoiachin. Both reigned for three months, and were taken captive, the former by Necho to Egypt, the latter by Nebuchadrezzar to Babylon. The poem was composed at some time during Zedekiah's reign. The text of the poem has suffered somewhat and a few accretions obtain. Verse 7*a* is such an accretion as can be seen by its failure to continue the figure. Lions do not lay waste cities or ravage fortresses. It was a later attempt to enhance the prowess of Jehoiachin. In verse 9 **With hooks** is a late gloss based on verse 4*b*, as is seen from its absence in S. The clause **they brought him into custody** is a later comment on the preceding clause.

The second dirge is even in its original form considerably later than the first and is the product of later traditionists. The theme of the earliest layer in the poem is the destruction and exile of the dynasty rather than of individual members. The fruitful vine produced stems which became rulers' sceptres. But the vine was plucked up and cast aside. Later traditionists added references to a single ruler, viz. to Zedekiah in verse 11*aβ*, *b*. For later glosses in verses 12–13, cf. below. Verse 14 is a still later attempt to put the blame for the destruction of the royal house on Zedekiah. For original remnants in the verse, cf. below.

1. the princes: G. has the singular, but this is an attempt to harmonize with the singular **your** (mother) of verse 2. The poem deals with princes, not with one. Strangely the chapter does not begin with the usual 'and the word of Yahweh came to me', showing that at one time this must have been attached to another section, probably either to chapter 15 or 17.

2. MT punctuates incorrectly as: 'She crouched among lions; she reared her whelps in the midst of young lions.' The use of the singular 'your' in **your mother** is poetic licence as is well understood by V. but not by G. The lioness could not be the queen of the good Josiah, Hamutal, daughter of Jeremiah of Libnah (2 Kg. 23.31), as most scholars maintain. Hamutal was the mother of Jehoahaz and Zedekiah (cf. 2 Kg. 24.18). Jehoiakim was also a son of Josiah but a half-brother (2 Kg. 23.36), and his son, Jehoiachin, was of course unrelated to Hamutal. The mother must be Judah. For Judah as a lion, cf. Gen. 49.9.

3. The first whelp to be reared for kingship was Jehoahaz. He reigned for only three months and nothing is known of his rule. He was put in bonds at Riblah by Pharaoh Neco, taken as a captive to Egypt where he died (2 Kg. 23.31–34). The attributes of young lions (catching prey, devouring men) should not be pressed for his reign.

4. The first sentence in RSV is based on an unnecessary emendation of MT, which reads, 'Nations heard about him.' For the idiom 'to hear about', cf. 2 Kg. 19.9 (an exact parallel); Gen. 41.15; Isa. 37.9. **with hooks** may be intended literally. Captives were often brutally treated. The passage in 2 Kg. 23 refers only to his being bound. For another poem bewailing Jehoahaz's fate, see Jer. 22.10–12.

5. she was baffled: based on Cooke's guess on the basis of G. Admittedly MT's *nwḥlh* 'had waited' is difficult and various attempts to improve the text have been made. It is best to follow MT in the sense 'was made to wait' (hence 'was postponed') with 'her hope' as the subject. Thus 'when she saw that her hope was postponed, had perished'. **another** follows G. rather than MT's 'one'. The second whelp must be Jehoiachin or Zedekiah, who were both taken to Babylon. That it referred to the former is likely. Ezekiel recognized Jehoiachin as king (cf. on 1.2), but Zedekiah only as regent. To have bypassed the former for the latter would seem unlikely. It is suggested above that the poem was composed before Zedekiah's capture and exile. What might seem odd is the fact that Jehoiakim who reigned for eleven years between Jehoahaz and Jehoiachin should have been bypassed. But the poem deals only with exiled princes and princes who are presumably still alive, whereas Jehoiakim was dead and never exiled.

7. The first clause is corrupt in MT, which has 'and he knew its widows'. **The**

RSV reading is based on a slight change of MT, viz. *wyr' 'rmnwtm* for *wyd 'lmnwtyw*. Since the 3rd plural suffix of the second word as well as of **their cities** has no antecedent it is better to omit **their** throughout. Verse 7*a* abandons the figure of the lion and is secondary. The hyperbole of verse 7*b* is not to be pressed; it simply carries out the figure of the fear-inspiring character of the lion.

8. The first sentence is mistranslated in RSV. In Ezekiel the verb *ytnw* normally takes an object. The plural is simply the indefinite. **snares,** based on an unnecessary emendation of MT's 'from the provinces'. Verse 8*a* should be rendered: 'Then nations were set against him, from provinces round about.'

9. G. omits *'wd*, 'still' (with the negative, **no more**), probably a late gloss. For a discussion of the original form of this verse, cf. above. The word *swgr* occurs only here. It probably represents a neck stock made out of wood rather than a **cage.** (Cf. E. I. Gordon, *Sumer* 12, 80ff.) **into custody:** based on *bmṣrwt* for MT *bmṣdwt* 'with nets'. The original verse might be rendered: 'They put him into a neck stock and brought him to the king of Babylon so that his voice . . .'. Jehoiachin's deportation in 597 B.C. remained a sad reminder to the exiles of their subject condition.

10. For **in a vineyard** MT has 'in your blood', which must be a corruption; a minority reading has 'of your vineyard'. For the figure of the vine, cf. on chapter 17. For **transplanted,** see on 17.8. The mother is still Judah as in verse 2.

11. RSV has smoothed out the difficulties. The first sentence should be rendered: 'Its strong stems became rulers' sceptres.' Judah produced numerous kings. The remainder of the verse is in the singular and represents a later traditionist's attempt to apply the poem to Zedekiah pictured here as the chief stem on the vine.

12b. The first two words are plural verbs—'they are broken off and dried up' with no subjects expressed, and represent later accretions to the text. The verb 'dried up' has as its object 'its fruit'. Render: 'the east wind dried up its fruit (they are broken off and dried up); as for its strong stem, fire has devoured it.' The strong stem is probably the royal house. The east wind is Nebuchadrezzar. For a commentary on the last line, see 2 Kg. 25.7.

13. and thirsty is a late gloss not present in G. The transplanted vine refers to Judah's existence in exile after its destruction in 586 B.C.

14. and fruit (lit. its fruit) is a late gloss on **its branches,** not found in G. The reference to fire coming out of the royal house to consume Judah's branches is a later traditionist's reference to Zedekiah's revolt against Babylon (2 Kg. 24.20*b*), with its destructive results. The remainder of the poem may be part of the original as a reference to the weakness of the royal house in exile. For the prose colophon, cf. 32.16. Unusual is **has become.** It may testify to its popularity as a nationalist lament used by the exiles.

S. RECITAL OF JUDGMENT 20.1–44

That verse 45 introduces a new section is clear from the section introduction formula. Verses 45–49 are the first five verses of chapter 21 in MT. Verses 1–44 are introduced as at 14.1 with elders coming for instruction, followed by the standard introduction to prophetic account in verse 2.

The section has been understood in many different ways. Thus May and Hölscher attribute all of it to later editors, but Fohrer attributes all of it to Ezekiel, and Zimmerli most of it (except verses 27–29). Matthews, Bertholet, and Herrmann attribute it to Ezekiel, but to two distinct periods in his life, verses 33–44 dating from the later restoration period. Herntrich takes verses 1–32 as Ezekiel, but verses 33–44 as secondary. Irwin finds an original oracle only in verse 3.

As in the case of the rest of the book, so here the present text is the product of a long history of oral and written tradition. An original prophecy was constantly being brought up to date by accretions to the text by members of the Ezekiel school. Such accretions were usually made not only within the text itself but also by expansions at the end, postscripts to reflect later situations.

With this in mind it becomes clear that verse 31 represents the conclusive answer to the question posited in the introductory question in verse 3, and is thus the end of the original account. Certainly verses 33–44 presuppose a situation quite foreign to a pre-586 date, as verse 1 demands. The nation is exiled and God is now going to purge the exiles and the purged will return to the land of Israel. This section will be dealt with separately below. Verse 32 presents difficulties since it has no close connection either with what precedes or follows. It seems best to understand it as a reflection by a later traditionist on verses 30–31, objecting to a view that the exilic community by its idols will be assimilated into its pagan environment and consequently lose all identity in the future.

The original account must then be found in verses 1–31. Formally it is a recital of the abominations of the fathers (verse 4), in three stages: the stay in Egypt (verses 5–9), the first generation in the wilderness (verses 10–17), and the next generation in the wilderness (verses 18–26), with two concluding oracles both introduced by the formula 'Therefore say to the house of Israel, Thus says Yahweh', viz. verses 27–29 and 30–31. The recital warrants only one conclusion and only the second fits the account (cf. verse 31b). Verses 27–29 are thus a later accretion. A traditionist noted that Ezekiel had overlooked in his recital the entire period of the settlement in Canaan and added his judgment on this period. It introduces a completely different form from the three stages which are parallel (cf. the three cases in 18.5–17). Verse 29 possibly represents a separate addition with its artificial play on the word *bāmāh*.

Ezekiel presents in this account the pre-Canaan history of Israel's sin. In direct contrast to some of the earlier prophets, particularly Hosea, Israel's tendency to sin was not due to the influence of the Canaanites. The period of the wilderness journey was not an idyllic period of the good old days, but one of rebellion. Israel's sinfulness was not due merely to outside influences, but from the time of their origin as a nation in Egypt rooted in their sinful nature.

The recital is in the form of a prophetic invective patterned on a schematized historical framework paralleling some of the central affirmations of faith in Yahweh's acts of salvation, viz. Israel's choice as Yahweh's nation, the promise of a land flowing with milk and honey, the Exodus from Egypt, the giving of statutes and ordinances, the safe-keeping during the wilderness journey. The recital of Israel's sinfulness is given contemporary significance by attributing the divine intention to exile his people among the nations already to the wilderness period (cf. verse 23).

As a historical recital of Israel's early days it has no obvious relation to any of the early histories. Major happenings are telescoped in order to fit the framework, viz. demands for obedience, rebellion, resolve to punish, and a relenting at the end for his name's sake. Details will be discussed in the commentary below.

(a) THE ABOMINATION OF THE FATHERS 20.1–32

1. The date given is August 591 or 590, probably the former; cf. on 1.2. For the verse, cf. on 14.1.

3. For **Lord GOD**, as in verses 5, 27, 30, 31, cf. on 2.4. For the question directed to the elders, cf. the parallel question in 14.3.

4. The double question implies a command, as is clear from the **then** clause. G. understood this partially in its free rendering, 'I will judge them with a judgment.' The recital of the abominations is Yahweh's judgment, not Ezekiel's.

The first stage: Israel in Egypt 5–9

5. **I swore,** lit. 'I raised my hand', a gesture still used today in taking an oath. The expression occurs twice here without giving the content of the oath, whereas in verse 6a it is given. Both clauses are amplifications of the text in verse 5. The oracle originally probably read: 'On the day when I chose Israel I made myself known to them in the land of Egypt, saying, I am Yahweh your God.' Yahweh first revealed himself by name to Moses and then promised to bring the people out of Egypt to Canaan. This is Ezekiel's only reference to Israel's election as the people of Yahweh, a notion common in D. The concept is however fully developed as the elements of self-revelation, promise, giving of laws, enumerated in the recital show. The time of the choice is not given as in the Pentateuchal Codes as being in the patriarchal age, but rather in the Egyptian period. Ezekiel shows no interest in Israel's pre-Egyptian traditions. For the formula of self-revelation, cf. the introduction to the Decalogue for the full formula (Exod. 20.2; Dt. 5.6). Election could hardly be earlier because Yahweh had not revealed his name before the time of Moses (Exod. 3.13–15 for E and Exod. 6.2–8 for P, but not in J.). Ezekiel's affinities with the later P tradition are clear from the reiterated 'I am Yahweh' in Exod. 6.2, 6, 7, 8.

6. The idiom 'I raised my hand' occurs throughout this section rather than the verb 'I swore' (characteristic of D). Involved in election is the oath-directed promise of deliverance from Egypt and the gift of the promised land. Yahweh himself has investigated, **searched out** this land. The verb really means 'to spy out' as in Num. 13–14. G. avoids the anthropomorphism by using the verb 'I prepared'. **flowing . . . honey** occurs often in the Pentateuch, but elsewhere only in this

section and in Jos. 5.6; Jer. 11.5; 32.22. **the most glorious** was later common in
Daniel as a term for the land of Palestine (cf. also Jer. 3.19).

7. Yahweh's demands are those of sole worship. Since Yahweh is their God, all
the detestable things, i.e. idols in general as objects of scorn, as well as **idols,**
i.e. dung-idols (cf. on 6.4), are to be abandoned. The command is put in legal
(casuistic) form common in H: **every one,** verb modifier, and plural imperative
(cf. on 14.1–11). Ezekiel's telescoping of history is evident here. The giving of the
law in Egypt is not attested in the Pentateuch; but it must be employed here to fit
his general theme.

8. G. omits **every man,** a late gloss from verse 7. The only rebellion in Egypt
described in Exodus is their castigation of Moses in 5.21 (J), but this is hardly
idolatry. The erection and worship of the Golden Calf in Exod. 32 is sometimes
ascribed to Egyptian influence, however (cf. Jos. 24.14). Israel's rebellion stimulates
Yahweh's resolve to punish them in Egypt. The intent is stated in general terms.
Note that in the next two stages the resolve to punish becomes increasingly specific.

9. Yahweh acted redemptively in the Exodus for his name's sake, i.e. for his
reputation. His name was by his self-revelation to Israel inextricably bound to
their fortunes. Yahweh's reputation would be rendered common if his people had
been left in Egyptian bondage. Yahweh's character would necessitate punishment,
but his reputation demands that he put off the evil day.

The second stage: the first generation in the wilderness **10–17**

11. Ezekiel's close relations with H appear from a comparison with Lev. 18.5, in
which this verse is found in legal form together with the identification formula of
verse 7b. The giving of statutes and ordinances refers to the giving of the law on
Sinai in general rather than to a specific prohibition against idolatry. For life as the
reward for keeping the law, cf. on 18.9.

12. The institution of the Sabbath as a day in which no work is done had its
origins in an agricultural society; gradually it evolved from a taboo-day to a day
of worship, a transformation which the exile undoubtedly hastened. In the exile the
Sabbath was one of the few cultic practices which could be observed without the
paraphernalia of the Jerusalem Temple, and so its observance became the distinctive badge of the exiled patriot. There is no good reason for considering
references to the Sabbath in this chapter (cf. also verses 13, 16, 20, 21, 24) as
necessarily later additions to the account. For a later (P) commentary on this verse,
cf. Exod. 31.12–17, where profanation of the Sabbath is regarded as a capital crime.
The Sabbath is a sign or pledge by which the peoples will receive continual
assurance that Yahweh sanctifies them, rendering them a holy people. Ezekiel's
close relations with H (cf. Lev. 19.2) are again evident, as are his priestly origins
and interests.

13. The reference to Yahweh's sabbaths is tacked loosely on to the stylized legal
phrase **by whose . . . live** and is an accretion to the text as it is in verse 21. The
verse is modelled on verse 8, expressing the same recital themes of rebellion and
resolve to punish.

14. Cf. on verse 9.

15. (given) **them,** a minority reading (and G.S.V.) not found in MT. Yahweh's resolve to punish is now specific, i.e. not to redeem his promise of the good land. This is probably a reflection of the tradition of the older generation dying in the wilderness as punishment for rebellion (cf. Dt. 1.34–38; Num. 14.28–30 (P)).

17. Yahweh spared those not over twenty years of age (Dt. 1.39, Num. 14.31).

The third stage: the second generation in the wilderness **18–26**

18. The word for **statutes** is, as in verse 25, unusually masculine. For **idols,** cf. on 6.4.

21. they profaned my sabbaths: cf. on verse 13.

22. But I withheld my hand: not attested in G.S., nor is it found in verses 9, 14; it is probably a late gloss supplying the obvious but unstated adversative 'but I did not'.

23. As D had warned from the standpoint of the wilderness of possible exile for sins (Dt. 4.26–27, 28.63–64), so Ezekiel takes the viewpoint that the exile was already determined by a divine oath before Israel entered Canaan (cf. Ps. 106.26–27).

24. The resolve is morally conditioned. The exile is the result of Israel's sin. A strong exilic priestly note is evident from the elevation of the Sabbath requirement to the same level as the divine ordinances and statutes. For **idols,** cf. on 6.4.

25. Not only exile but also evil statutes and ordinances which issue in death constitute the punishment for disobedience. For **statutes,** cf. on verse 18. That Yahweh might at times mislead people is clear from 2 Sam. 24.1 and the story of Micaiah (1 Kg. 22.17–23). But Ezekiel goes further by maintaining that the law itself, otherwise good and leading to life (Pss. 19, 119), could mysteriously become **not good** and leading to death.

26. I did . . . LORD: not in G., a late gloss added to avoid the notion that Yahweh did such things simply to horrify people. That Yahweh should have ordered the sacrifice of the firstborn by fire is a misunderstanding of what Yahweh did say in his law. In Exod. 22.29*b* (MT 28*b*) the apodictic law reads: 'The firstborn of your sons you shall give to me' (cf. Exod. 13.12). The law is good but it becomes a statute 'not good' when people's minds are wilfully darkened so that it is misinterpreted to mean child sacrifice. For actual child sacrifice in Israel, cf. 2 Kg. 16.3; 21.6.

27. The traditionist introduces this accretion incongruously with introductory formulae from verse 30 where they are appropriate. The initial verb is also unusual, i.e. **speak** rather than 'say'; but cf. 14.4. The secondary character of the verse is also apparent from the opening words of the oracle **In this again.** In contrast to the 'abominations' (verse 4), rebellion (verses 8, 13, 21), profanation (verses 9, 14, 16, 22, 24), Israel's sins are characterized as blasphemy and treachery.

28. and presented . . . offering: a late gloss not in G. Possibly the next two clauses also represent later layers of tradition. For **high hill, leafy tree,** and **soothing odours,** cf. 6.13, a verse which probably represents the same layer of tradition.

29. A further expansion, a fanciful word play on the word *bāmāh*—'high place', thus later than verses 27–28 on whose diatribe against worship on the high places this is based. Since *māh* means 'what' and *bā* means 'going', *bāmāh* is punned on by 'what is the *bāmāh* to which you go?' The etymology is pure fancy.

30–31. Originally after verse 26. The 'therefore' oracle applies the recital to the exiles themselves. Will the exiles continue as the fourth stage? Defilement reflects verse 26 and the detestable things are mentioned in verses 7–8. Verse 31 has received some later expansions, the latest of which is **and sacrifice your sons by fire,** which is not in G. The exile did not engage in child sacrifice as far as is known. It is probable that the entire first sentence represents a later expansion. The original oracle contained thus the question of verse 30, the question in verse 31, and the negative oath in answer to that question, recapitulating the opening question in verse 3. Yahweh will not permit himself to be inquired of by those who continue in idolatry (cf. 14.1–11).

32. The traditionist here wants to correct any misapprehension which verses 30–31 might give. Since Ezekiel is condemning the present Israel for idolatry, it might be thought that the exiled community would become non-Yahwists, worshippers of wood and stone, and thus become like the pagans around them. He gives assurance that this lurking suspicion is unfounded. There will always be an Israel distinct and serving Yahweh.

(b) YAHWEH WILL PURGE AND RESTORE ISRAEL **20.33–44**

As was suggested in the introduction to this chapter, this section is not part of the original recital of judgment. The situation presupposed is the full exile. Jerusalem and Judah are destroyed. And yet this section is closely related to the recital and reflects on it. Verse 36 speaks of the judgment in the wilderness; verse 39 refers to idols and to profanation; gifts, offerings, and pleasing odours in verses 40–41 reflect the recital, and so do references to pollution or defilement in verse 43, and Yahweh's actions **for my name's sake** in verse 44. The passage reflects later expansions of the original recital.

The first expansion begins with the oath formula in verse 33 and ends with the recognition formula in verse 38. It is perfectly possible that this represents Ezekiel's own postscript since there is nothing inherently inconsistent with verses 1–31. It is however post-586 B.C. Since a conclusion formula occurs in verse 36*b*, verses 37–38 may be a later accretion explaining the judgment of verse 36.

Verses 39–44 contain two recognition formulae, verses 42*a* and 44*a*. The introductory oracle formula occurs in verse 39 and the conclusion formulae in verses 40 and 44. Since the text of verse 39 is somewhat in disarray it is uncertain what is intended by it. It must have served to introduce verse 40. Verses 43–44 are a second conclusion and are probably subsequent to the preceding.

33. For **Lord God,** as in verses 36, 39, 40, 44, cf. on 2.4. G. somewhat inappropriately has 'therefore' at the beginning, thereby connecting it with verse 32. G. probably understood verses 33–38 as an oracle in response to the **thought** in verse 32. The double phrase **with a mighty hand and an outstretched arm** is a double phrase typical of D (cf. Dt. 4.34; 5.15; 7.19; 11.2; 26.8); the third is a typical Ezekiel phrase **wrath poured out**, e.g. verses 8, 13, 21 from the recital. In D the hand and arm are instruments of divine redemption, but here they are symbols of judgment. Yahweh will exercise his kingship over them both as leader and as judge.

34. The scattered exiles, not just the Judeans in Babylon but probably also those exiled to Assyria (2 Kg. 17.6) and Egypt (2 Kg. 25.26; Jer. 44) as well, are to be gathered together in a second exodus.

35. But this second exodus is not intended as an act of redemption but one of judgment. The first exodus had been into the wilderness of the land of Egypt. Since this one is an exodus from lands and peoples it can only be into a **wilderness of the peoples.** No specific place is intended by it.

36. The judgment **with your fathers** probably reflects the recital, especially verses 10–17. The designation of the wilderness of the first exodus as **of the land of Egypt** is unique, but intentionally used to contrast with wilderness of the peoples in verse 35.

37. by number (as in G.): MT has 'in the bond of the covenant'. 'The covenant' is a partial dittography of the next word (*hbryt wbrwty*), and 'in the bond of', *bmsrt*, is an error for *bmspr* 'by number'. To **pass under the rod** is a figure taken from shepherd's life. The sheep are allowed to pass under the shepherd's rod into the door of the shelter and thus be counted and sorted.

38. For **they** (shall not enter) MT has 'he'. Read *yb'w* for *ybw'*. G. has misread the first word *wbrwty*—'and **I will purge out**' as *wbhrty*, 'and I will choose'; cf. on verse 5. Yahweh will purify, cleanse ('purge out') his people. Just what is to happen to the rebels and transgressors is left unstated. They will be brought out of exile presumably into the wilderness of peoples but not for restoration. It is implied but not stated that those who are not rebels and transgressors will be restored. The recognition formula concludes the expansion.

39. The text is peculiar. Literally the oracle in MT may be rendered: 'Each man, his idols go serve; and afterwards if you do not listen to me! But my holy name no longer profane by your gifts and your idols.' RSV has simply tried to make sense out of it, but MT hardly permits this translation. On the basis of verse 7 and G., Zimmerli suggests a corruption in the first line of 'go serve' from 'cast out', i.e. *hšlykw* for *lkw 'bdw*, which would make sense ('let each man cast forth his idols'). The phrase 'and afterwards if you do not listen to me' is also corrupt. Possibly it represents a corruption of a 1st singular verb for 'and afterwards', something like *w'hrh*, 'and I shall be angered', for *w'hr*, 'and afterwards'. It would then represent a marginal addition 'and I shall be angered if you do not listen to me' later inserted between the two parallel clauses. The verse is then clear; it is a warning against idolatry and profanation.

The counterpart to the purging of verse 38 **40–42**

Those who remain will be restored to Israel, and the new cult in Jerusalem (foreshadowing chapters 40–48) will be fully acceptable to Yahweh.

40. in the land: a late gloss not in G. This verse shows two layers of interpretation. The first is the oracle referring to Israel in the 3rd plural. It simply states that
Israel will once again serve Yahweh on his holy mountain and be received of him.
With **and there I will require** begins another layer which addresses in the 2nd
plural. Thus the list of acceptable things is a different tradition explaining what is
meant by **I will accept them. my holy mountain** occurs only here in Ezekiel.
For the explanatory **mountain height of Israel,** cf. on 17.23. The emphasis
intended by **all of them** is probably on a reunited Israel, not just Judah. In the
secondary expansion three things are mentioned as being required in the new cult
(the word **require** is the same as 'inquire' in verses 3, 31 but in quite a different
sense). The first, **contributions,** is common in Ezek. 40–48 and in P. It is variously
used but is always some kind of contribution, usually for cultic use, here possibly
of the products of the land. The **gifts** are designated as **choicest,** which is the word
for first or 'beginning' and could mean first fruits. Gifts are voluntary, possibly the
contributions were assessed. The last one, **sacred offerings,** literally means 'holy
things'. It probably refers to gifts and offerings which had been dedicated in some
way such as by vows to cultic use and were thus by the worshipper's action or word
taken out of the realm of the profane. Once set aside, such offerings were
mandatory and could never again enter into common use.

41. As, based on an emendation for which there is no evidence. Rather 'By
(a soothing odour)'. What the traditionist is saying is that by means of sacrifice
Yahweh accepts his people; the author speaks from a purely priestly point of view.
manifest my holiness among you, renders a Ni. verb in MT; it also occurs at
28.25; 36.23; 38.16; 39.27. In all these passages except 28.25 it is rendered 'vindicate
my holiness'. What is meant is that 'my deity will become evident among you',
thus a variant of the recognition formula.

43. that you have committed is a late addition unattested by G. The emphasis
of this tradition is on the repentant state of mind which Israel will show after they
are restored to favour.

44. The references to **for my name's sake** and **deal with** reflect verses 9, 14, 22.

T.   SWORD ORACLES 20.45–21.32 (MT 21.1–37)

(a) THE SWORD OF YAHWEH 20.45–21.7 (MT 21.1–12)

In MT verses 45–49 occur as the first five verses of chapter 21, where they actually
belong. This section, like chapter 17, contains an allegory proclaimed as an oracle,
verses 47–48, and its interpretation, verses 3–7 (cf. 17.3–10 and 12–21). The allegory
presents the prophet proclaiming an oracle to the south stating that Yahweh will
kindle a fire which will completely burn up all trees. As in 17.11 the interpretation
is fully introduced by the standard Ezekiel introduction to a new section. The three
words for **south** in verse 46 are now interpreted as **Jerusalem,** the **sanctuaries,**
and the **land of Israel.** The fire kindled by Yahweh becomes the divinely
unsheathed sword. The universal recognition formula of verse 48 is restated in

verse 5. Quite at variance with this highly stylized form are verses 6–7, which abandon the interpretation of the allegory to bid the prophet to show great agitation as a prophetic symbol (cf. 12.17–20 and 24.15–27). These represent a later expansion to the text more in the spirit of Jeremiah than of Ezekiel, probably by a traditionist wanting to apply the situation in a personal way to the exilic audience. Also somewhat unusual in the context is verse 4, which is put in the form of a demonstration oracle. In the usual demonstration oracle the 'because' clause is a prophetic invective. In verse 4, however, a traditionist has repeated verse 3b for the 'because' clause and verse 3aβ for the 'therefore' clause, thereby making the reason for the divine action the divine intent, a fairly obvious conclusion.

Whether the original account is actually Ezekiel is uncertain; many have denied the passage to him. The allegory and its interpretation is highly stylized, each element in the former recurring in the latter. The recognition formula uses the verb 'see' rather than 'know'. Vocabulary items occur not usually found elsewhere. The notion that the righteous and the wicked shall perish alike contradicts chapter 18 and 33.10–20, but, on this, cf. on verse 3 below. On the other hand the prophecy lies at the heart of Ezekiel's message, viz. that Yahweh is fully determined to destroy Jerusalem and nothing can dissuade him.

46. forest land in the Negeb: an unusual construction in MT: lit. 'forest of the field south (Negeb)'. 'the field' is probably a gloss explaining 'forest'; read 'forest of the south (Negeb)' as in verse 47. The three parts of the tristich are completely parallel. **the Negeb** does not mean the dry steppe land in the southern part of Judah, but is here a general term for south. All three words for south are taken as place names in G.: *Thaiman, Darom*, and *Nageb*. The first recurs in 47.19; 48.28; the second is used repeatedly in chapters 40–42; the last is the term for south most frequently found in chapters 40–48 and never in the sense of Negeb in Ezekiel. The verbs, **set your face, preach, prophesy,** are also parallel, recurring in the same order in verse 2. That the land of Judah should be called south from Babylon which was east of Judah is not strange. Babylon, as all enemies from the Tigris–Euphrates, came from the north along the Fertile Crescent southwards from Upper Syria.

47. As in verse 46 change **Negeb** to 'south'. For **Lord God,** as in verses 49, 7; cf. on 2.4. **blazing flame** is an attempt to render two words for flame, *lhbt, šlhbt,* which occur side by side. The second is a rare word, a Shaphel form which is unusual in Hebrew, and the former is an explanatory gloss. Fire as a symbol for destruction is Ezekiel's most common figure. For **green tree** and **dry tree,** cf. 17.24. Such a co-ordination of opposites as green and dry, good and evil, righteous and wicked, represents a Hebrew idiom denoting an entire range from one extreme to the other. The entire forest will be burned to the ground; so intense will be its heat that all those watching will have their faces scorched. An important element in the allegory is that the fire is out of control; i.e. **shall not be quenched.**

48. G. under influence of the usual formula has 'know' for **see,** but the unusual word is doubtless original. Since this is an allegory the unusual **see** is also part of what must be interpreted, and in verse 5 it is duly interpreted as **know.** Universal recognition of Yahweh as actor occurs only in this section; it is more common in Deutero-Isaiah (cf. Isa. 40.5; 49.26).

49. The bridge between the allegory and the interpretation. For **allegories,** cf. on chapter 17.

21.2. G. adds 'Therefore prophesy' at the beginning, which can hardly be original. G. correctly attests 'their sanctuaries' for MT **the sanctuaries,** in which one letter has fallen out (i.e. *mkdšyhm* for *mkdšym*). The first 'south' is interpreted as **Jerusalem**; the second as (their) **sanctuaries** (with indefinite antecedent), and the third as the **land of Israel.** Though only one legitimate sanctuary obtained, the Jerusalem Temple, Ezekiel often refers to the various shrines which are to be destroyed, e.g. 16.16. The three, capital, cultic centres, and land, are intended to include everything.

3. In strict parallel to the allegory, verse 47, the third as the most inclusive is addressed. Omitted however is the phrase 'hear the word of Yahweh'. The interpretative oracle identifies the divinely kindled fire as the divinely unsheathed sword. That it was actually the sword of the Babylonians which was being unsheathed is irrelevant. They are only instruments acting under Yahweh's direction. The devouring of all trees (every green tree and every dry tree) means that the sword will cut down every man (**both righteous and wicked**). G. misunderstood the Hebrew idiom here and in verse 4 and avoided doctrinal error by rendering the phrase by 'unjust and lawless'.

5. The unquenchability of the fire (verse 48) means that Yahweh will under no conditions sheathe his drawn sword again.

6–7. A member of the Ezekiel school felt that such an awful message of inescapable judgment should evoke some emotional response. The command to show such reaction is probably based on 12.17–20. The prophetic action of grief in public (contrast 24.15–18) will then be explained as due to the report; for **tidings,** cf. on 'byword' 16.56. **When . . . water** does not fit into its context. Originally the **behold** clause immediately followed 'tidings' which is the subject of its two verbs. The sentences would then mean: 'Then you shall say concerning the report: Behold it has come and is being fulfilled.' A secondary tradition misunderstood this, as the insertion shows.

(b) THE SWORD SONG **21.8–17** (MT 13–22)
The text of this song of the sword is extremely difficult and any reconstruction can only be tentative. It consists of two strophes; most lines seem to have five beats, three in the first hemistich, and two in the second. Since little is known about Hebrew metre, this should simply be treated as a general observation. In the commentary below an attempt will be made to restore each line with as little change as possible to the text. Some expansions to the text can be identified. If the restoration of verse 10b below is correct it was probably original. Most of verse 13 is secondary; it reflects on and contradicts verse 10b. Verse 12 is prosaic and is commentary from the post-586 B.C. period. It also does not fit in the context of

this poem. The last part of verse 11 **to be given . . . slayer,** is outside the poetic line and is an expanding gloss.

The two strophes are similarly introduced by a call to prophesy. The first describes the sharpness and burnish of the sword, unsheathed, held and ready. The second describes the sword at work slaughtering and terrifying, restless in all directions. Only the final line, verse 17, adapts the song to a prophetic word. It is Yahweh who is behind it all exulting in the work of the sword.

9. **Lord:** the *Qerê* has completely displaced the original 'Yahweh'; cf. on 2.4. The next word **Say** is a gloss. This never occurs after the introductory oracle formula. MT *mrwṭh* is a participle, but a passive verb is expected, i.e. *mwrṭh*, 'it is polished'.

10a. The second hemistich is corrupt. The line is a three-three stich and can be rendered: 'Sharpened for slaughter, polished to become a lightning flash.' The figure refers to the extremely bright burnishing of the sword.

10b. Totally corrupt; no satisfactory reconstruction of the original has ever been made. MT has: 'Or shall we exult? The staff of my son; she despises all wood.' G. simply guessed; it has, 'For destruction, slay, annihilate, destroy every tree.' Only the last two words are recognizable. A possible reconstruction as follows at least makes some sense. 'Or shall we exult' (*'w nśyś*) may be a corruption of 'and a man' (*w'nwš*); 'my son' (*bny*) may be a corruption of *bnh*, here intended in the sense of Gen. 2.22 as 'fashion, form'. The line then can be rendered: 'When a man fashions a staff, it (the sword) despises any wood.' In other words, there is no defence that man can make against this sharp, glistening sword; it will demolish any weapon made of wood.

11. The word *lmrṭh*, 'to be polished', should be vocalized as a bound verbal noun with 3rd fem. singular suffix, *leʿmorṭāh*, 'to polish it'.

12. Yahweh is here the speaker and bids the prophet wail because of the slaughter. It is quite contrary to the exultant, almost bloodthirsty character of the original poem. **they are delivered over** is a somewhat anaemic rendering of the Hebrew, which has 'they have been thrown down (to the sword)'. The verse reflects the anguish suffered by the exiles when princes and people were killed and exiled in 586 B.C. For smiting the thigh as a sign of grief, cf. Jer. 31.19.

13. Obscure. It is certainly secondary since it is partly dependent on verse 10b. RSV is based on an emended text, but some sense can be wrung out of MT, though it is hardly poetry. It can be rendered: 'Surely it (my people) has been tested. What if there be a staff, it (the sword) despises (it); shall it not be? says Yahweh.' The first sentence is a comment on the grievous lot of the exiled peoples. The next is an expanded version of verse 10b and is quite out of place here.

14. The last stich needs minor revision. The verse then can be rendered: 'And you, son of man, prophesy. Clap your hands. Let the sword work doubly, even triply; it is the sword for the slain, the great sword for the slain terrifying (as G.) them.' The prophet is called on to exult in the slaughter, which can only make sense when it is recalled that the work of the sword is here the execution of justice.

15. For **fall** MT vocalizes *hmkšlym* as 'the stumbling blocks' which must be wrong. The word *'bḥt* is completely obscure; RSV renders 'glistening'; G. must have read *ṭbḥt*, 'slaughter', which may be original. The word *'ḥ*, 'brother' (emended to read 'aḥ' in RSV, but actually auditory error for *ḥ* prefix), must be omitted as at 18.10. The verse can now be rendered: 'that their hearts may melt and the fallen be multiplied; at all their gates have I given slaughter (?); O sword made for flashing, grasped for slaughter.' RSV is based on an emended text reading **polished** for 'grasped', but this is unnecessary; cf. the word in Isa. 22.17.

16. RSV probably represents the original text. The sword is addressed and told to slash indiscriminately to all sides.

17. Many scholars consider this verse secondary, because it brings Yahweh in as responsible for the ecstatic fury of the sword at work. But this is precisely the point. It is Yahweh who claps his hands and executes his fury over Jerusalem, and the sword is but the instrument in his hands. If this verse is secondary all that is left is a secular poem with little relevance to the prophetic message. If Ezekiel is called on to prophesy he must proclaim a divine word, one in which he obediently claps his hands to incite the sword to double, even triple fury; now Yahweh shows that he himself is manipulating the work of the sword.

(c) THE SWORD OF NEBUCHADREZZAR 21.18–27 (MT 23–32)

This section is formally placed within this chapter because of its allusion to the sword of the king of Babylon, but has further no connection with the sword song. The prophet is told to engage in prophetic symbolism (cf. commentary on 4.1–5.17) by drawing a main exit road from a country and at the fork in the road to put up a road-sign pointing in the two directions, one labelled 'Rabbah of the Ammonites' and the other 'Judah fortified in Jerusalem'; cf. on verse 20. Nebuchadrezzar is depicted as consulting the diviners at the junction point and on divine instruction proceeding to Jerusalem to invest it. The oracle then explains all this as due to Jerusalem being legally convicted of sin; this is the divine sentence being carried out.

The literary form is rendered somewhat obscure by another oracle against Zedekiah tacked on at the end. It is undoubtedly Ezekiel but is not germane to verses 18–24, which precede it. This is clear from the oracle of verse 24, which interprets verse 23*b*, whereas verses 25–27 are addressed solely to the wicked prince. Note that verse 24 is 2nd plural but verse 25 is in 2nd singular. The editor placed it here because of the reference to the **time of . . . final punishment,** verse 25 (cf. verse 29). Since verses 28–32 obviously relate to the sword song and belong to this chapter, the Zedekiah oracle too finds its place here.

19. MT has 'from a land of one', which RSV rightly changes to **from the same land.** A number of copyist dittographs have crept into verse 19*b* and verse 20*a*. By eliminating these the text may be rendered: 'And set a sign at the head of the way to a city: "Rabbah of the Ammonites" and "Judah, fortified in Jerusalem".' How the prophet was to indicate this map, whether in the sand or on a builder's tile (cf. 4.1), is not indicated.

20. It is also idle to speculate on where in Syria or Lebanon this parting of the ways in which the road to the left led to Rabbah, and the one to the right, to Jerusalem, was located, whether at Riblah (Nebuchadrezzar's camp), Damascus (the great trade route), or near the Jordan below the Sea of Galilee. It is a prophetic symbol, not a geography lesson. Rabbah (i.e. 'the great city') was later Philadelphia of Hellenistic-Roman times, and today 'Amman, the capital city of Jordan, 23 miles east of the Jordan, bordering on the River Jabbok (Wadi-z-Zerqa). 'Fortified in Jerusalem' is what MT says rather than **and to Jerusalem the fortified.** The sign is not a double one, i.e. Judah and Jerusalem, but rather indicates that Judah's strength lay in Jerusalem. The Ammonites and their neighbours had made a covenant of revolt against Nebuchadrezzar and he was going west to break up the insurrection. This must have been in 588 B.C. (cf. Jer. 27.1−3).

21. The king must decide which to attack first, and so, as Assyrian and Babylonian kings from time immemorial, consults the diviners before embarking on a military venture. The technical term for a fork in the road is lit. 'mother of the way', to which has been added the explanation **at the head of the two ways.** The three forms of divination used are arrow, teraphim, and liver divination. The first is best known from pre-Islamic Arabia and apparently was a bedouin form of obtaining an answer from the gods. Marked arrows were placed in a quiver, here apparently one marked 'Rabbah' and another 'Jerusalem'. One would then be extracted and whatever it said was the answer. The second form is completely unknown; cf. Zech. 10.2 where teraphim is used in parallelism to diviners and dreamers. They appear to be some type of oracle, but elsewhere in the O.T. they are idols. In Gen. 31.19, 32, 34−35 they were small household gods which could be hidden in a saddle, but in 1 Sam. 19.13, 16 they are a human-sized image placed in a bed, of such a size that a casual glance convinced Saul's servants that it was David. In any event, the consulting of teraphim appears to have been an illegitimate Israelite custom. Liver divination was typically Babylonian and many clay livers have been found in Tigris−Euphrates sites, models originally used for study and teaching by diviners (cf. *ANEP* 594 for a picture of one such). An animal was sacrificed, and its liver examined for the blood vessels, all of which were supposed to mean something.

22. By a copyist's error 'to set battering rams' was repeated in MT from verse 22*b* after **Jerusalem** in *a*. By metathesis the original **cry** occurs as 'murder' in MT. **lot** probably refers to the outcome of the arrow divination. The answer is Jerusalem. The siege attack is to consist of a **cry, shouting, battering rams, mounds, siege towers.** The first is the bitter 'sound' of the day of Yahweh in Zeph. 1.14, apparently some kind of battle-shout (cf. Isa. 42.13). 'Shouting' originally referred to some kind of cultic shout used by the Israelites in the holy wars. For the remaining three, cf. on 4.2.

23. they have sworn solemn oaths: a late gloss based on 17.13−14 unattested by G.S. Jerusalem dwells in a false security, not believing the report of Nebuchadrezzar's approach. Verse 23*b* uses terms taken from law. To bring **guilt to remembrance** is the office of the prosecutor in court. The subject here is

Nebuchadrezzar. **that they may be captured** means 'to be arrested' or even 'caught in the act' (Num. 5.13).

24. For **Lord God**, as in verse 26, cf. on 2.4. **because you have come to remembrance:** a dittograph from verse 24*a*. **in them** is based on G., whereas MT has 'with the hand'. MT is original and **taken in them** should be rendered 'forcibly seized' or 'arrested'. The oracle applies verse 23*b* to Jerusalem's situation. Jerusalem stands self-condemned. She is her own prosecutor and her sinfulness is exposed, and now sentence is being passed: forcible arrest by the Babylonian forces now approaching.

25. The word *ḥll*, 'unhallowed', should be vocalized as a bound form, i.e. 'unhallowed among the wicked' (collective). The reference is to Zedekiah. Zedekiah is the profane one among the wicked because he has broken his sacred oath of vassalage in which he swore fealty in Yahweh's name to Nebuchadrezzar; cf. on 17.13–19. For **prince**, cf. on 7.27, 12.10. **final punishment** is probably what MT's 'iniquity of the end' means, since '*wn* can mean 'iniquity' or its 'punishment'. For **time** or 'day' has come, cf. on 7.12. Zedekiah will not escape.

26. The perfect verbs in the oracle of MT must all be revocalized as imperfect as RSV. The turban is attested in P as part of the high priest's dress (Exod. 28.4), but it was originally a royal headdress; cf. Isa. 62.3, 'diadem'. **things . . . they are,** lit. 'this will not be this'. Everything will be turned upside down.

27. trace: based on an unnecessary change of *z't* 'this' to '*wt*. The clause should read 'not even this shall remain until'. **ruin** actually means distortion, a twisting. **whose right it is:** many think, as did G., that this is a reflection of Gen. 49.10, 'until he comes to whom it belongs', and interpret this messianically. This would seem peculiar in an oracle of judgment. The noun elsewhere in Ezekiel means 'judgment', e.g. 23.24. The one who has the judgment is Nebuchadrezzar. The ruin will not take place until he arrives. Yahweh has given him the judgment over Zedekiah.

(d) SWORD AGAINST THE AMMONITES 21.28–32 (MT 33–37)

This section is the product of the Ezekiel school and not of Ezekiel. It uses the sword song, but not accurately. It is a reflection on the malice and exaltation of the Ammonites on the occasion of Jerusalem's fall in 586 (cf. 25.1–7). It is also subsequent to verses 18–24 (cf. verse 29*a* with verse 23*a*) and to verses 25–27; cf. the use of 'unhallowed wicked' in a different sense from verse 25 and cf. verse 29*b* with verse 25*b*. For the secondary verse 30*aa*, cf. commentary below.

28. say (A sword): a copyist's error; cf. on verse 9. The **reproach** of the Ammonites is defined in 25.3, 6. For **Lord God**, cf. on 2.4. **to glitter,** based on an emendation of MT 'to contain'. Versions seem to favour the change of *lhkyl*, 'to contain', to *lklh*, 'for destruction', which is a good parallel to 'for slaughter'. The last phrase is probably a later correction to bring the verse in line somewhat with verse 10*a* which verse 28*b* quotes rather poorly.

29. RSV wrongly changed a 2nd singular suffix to a 3rd fem. singular, thereby altering the sense. The verse should be rendered: 'to put you—since they see false visions about you and divine lies about you—on the necks . . .'. It is the sword which is being addressed. In the preceding verse too 'A sword, a sword' should be rendered 'O sword, sword'. The sword is to slaughter the Ammonites because they prophesy falsely about it, probably that it was only intended for Jerusalem. **unhallowed wicked** is here simply a term of reproach, though based on its use in verse 25a. For the last phrase, cf. on verse 25b.

30. A later traditionist addresses Nebuchadrezzar in the opening sentence, which is foreign to the context. The remainder of the verse is in 2nd fem. singular, however, and is addressed to Rabbah. **place where you were created** means 'your native land', as the parallel **land of your origin** (cf. on 16.3) shows. Though technically Rabbah is addressed, the addressees intended are its inhabitants, the Ammonites.

31. blow is unusual in this context, since it is also used in the sense of puffing out evil incantations (Ps. 10.5; 12.5(MT 6)). **brutal men,** neatly rendered 'barbarians' in G., were probably the people of the east mentioned in 25.4; cf. commentary *ad hoc.* The last phrase is literally 'forgers of destruction'. For 'destruction', cf. on 5.16.

32. The first sentence is probably a late accretion as its loose syntactic construction and its 2nd masc. singular verb in MT shows. The greatest of all punishments is to be no more remembered (cf. Ps. 109.13–15).

U. JERUSALEM CONDEMNED 22.1–31

The editor has put together, as in 20.45–21.32 (MT 21.1–37), three oracles with a common theme. The theme is the condemnation of Jerusalem's sins.

(a) THE BLOODY CITY 22.1–16

This section is introduced in a way similar to chapter 20 (cf. verse 2 with 20.4), but after that the similarity no longer obtains. It is a straightforward invective against Jerusalem society. Formally the oracle begins with the vocative in verse 3, followed by an invective in verse 4 with the 'therefore' clause of judgment in verses 4b, 5. The main invective is, however, found in verses 6–12, beginning with 'behold' and ending with the oracle conclusion formula. Verses 13–16 present a special problem since it again begins with 'behold' (there is no **therefore** in MT) and has two conclusions, the affirmation formula in verse 14 and the recognition formula at verse 16. Verse 13 is a later accretion commenting on **make gain** in verse 12, an attempt along with verse 14 to provide a divine judgment at the end. Verses 15–16 are a second judgment by another traditionist who felt the first to be insufficiently specific.

The indictment in verses 6–12 is stylistically divided into three parts, each introduced with a clause ending in **to shed blood.** Most of the section is in 3rd plural plus **in you**, but verse 8 and verse 12b are in 2nd fem. singular, which is not an indication of a later accretion, at least not in verse 12b, since this would leave no list of sins in the third section. The first part is headed 'princes of Israel each according to his power'; the second 'slanderers'; and the last 'takers of bribes'. For details, cf. below.

2. As in 20.4, verse 2b is a command to proclaim a prophetic invective. The invective is, however, not about the sins of the fathers but about Jerusalem's abominations (cf. on 20.4).

3. For **Lord God**, as in verse 12, cf. on 2.4. The oracle should be read as address: 'O city.' Her crime is classified as twofold: bloodshed and idolatry. The first term is generic for any form of violence and is explicated by the list of crimes in verses 6–12. For the second, which is not explained further, cf. on 6.4. The prophet adds a purpose clause to each which is factually the result of the respective crimes. Bloodshed brings on the day of judgment; idolatry, defilement.

4. the appointed time . . . come: better, 'and brought in the appointed time of your years'. The invective in the verse explicates each of the four elements in the description of the city in verse 3 and represents an interpretative accretion to the text. The traditionist then had to make the original text **I have made . . .** a 'therefore' element. The original oracle in verses 3–5 is the vocative of verse 3, and the judgment in verses 4 and 5. RSV incorrectly follows an emendation based on T. of 'your days' to **your day.** This is unnecessary as 12.23 shows and unoriginal as its parallel to **years** proves.

5. G. has 'near to you' for **near**; MT is a case of hendiadys. The vocative at the end is peculiar in view of the long vocative in verse 3 and may be a marginal gloss giving the theme of the passage in general. Once it became part of the text it could only be interpreted as a vocative. **you infamous one** is an over-free rendering for 'by reputation (or name) unclean'. For **tumult,** cf. on 7.7.

6–8. The first interpretation of 'shedding blood' deals with social relations. To this a later traditionist has added verse 8 in 2nd fem. singular concerning holy things and sabbaths, neither of which have anything to do with violence. The original list had no cultic sins, which omission the Ezekiel school rectified by this addition. The original list probably contained a decalogue of sins, three in the first part, four in the second (for the secondary character of verse 11, cf. below), and three in the last.

6. The first group concerns the royal house as leaders in Israel. Their sins are ones of violence; **power** is an interpretation of MT's 'arm'. The outstretched arm is the symbol of power. For Yahweh's arm, cf. 20.33–34; the arm is here used for oppression rather than for deliverance. The phrase 'for shedding blood' recurs in verses 9, 12, 27.

7. The three sins of the princes (and by extension of Jerusalem) are disrespect for parents, extortion of the sojourner, and oppression of the helpless. The verb in the first means 'to make light of'. Respect for parents was a basic tenet of Israelite law (cf. Exod. 20.12; Dt. 5.16; Lev. 19.3); disrespect for parents was a capital crime in D and H (cf. Dt. 27.16, Lev. 20.9). For the sojourner and his rights, cf. Exod. 22.21(MT 20); 23.9. Protecting the sojourner was actually invoking the laws of hospitality, since the sojourner was a resident alien, a non-Israelite who lived in Israel and abided by its laws. The orphan and the widow are the standard symbols in the O.T. for the helpless (cf. Exod. 22.22–24 (MT 21–23)).

8. This is a direct reflection of the H command in Lev. 19.30 but with 'holy things' identified as 'sanctuaries'.

9–11. The second group concerns slanderers and theirs are sins of impurity. Verse 11 lists three sexual sins, but in an individual form which stylistically betrays their secondary character.

9. Why the second group should be called 'slanderers' (slander is forbidden in Lev. 19.16) is not clear. For eating on the mountains, cf. on 18.6. Lewdness (cf. 16.27) is a term occurring more frequently in Ezekiel than in the rest of the O.T., especially in chapter 23 of gross sexual immorality. It is often used as a symbol for idolatry. In Lev. 18.17 and 20.14 it is descriptive of particular forms of incest punishable by death.

10. uncover is singular in MT, but Versions rightly read the plural. Coitus with one's mother or stepmother was forbidden by Lev. 18.7, 8; 20.11, and a capital crime (cf. Dt. 27.20). For verse 10*b*, cf. on 18.6.

11. Three specific sexual taboos. For the first, cf. on 18.6. Incest with one's daughter-in-law was forbidden by Lev. 18.15 and branded a capital crime for both in Lev. 20.12; with one's sister, similarly, Lev. 18.9, and involves excommunication from the community (Lev. 20.17).

12. The third group concerns those who take bribes and are sins of commerce. Bribery was a disease indigenous to the Near East and is denounced already in the Covenant Code (Exod. 23.8; cf. Dt. 16.19—bribery 'blinds the eyes of the wise and subverts the causes of the righteous'). For **interest** and **increase,** cf. on 18.8. The sin of 'making gain' is alluded to in Exod. 18.21 as 'bribe', but is rather profit made by violent and oppressive means. The notion recurs in 33.31, but the sin is not reflected in any specific prohibition. All such sins are rooted in forgetting Yahweh.

13. For striking the hands, cf. also on 21.14(MT 19). Here it is used as a sign of extreme displeasure. The distinction between **dishonest gain** and **the blood** shows that the traditionist did not fully understand the original oracle.

14. Rhetorical questions. In the time of judgment hearts (**courage**) will quake and hands will be slackened for the terror of those days, cf. 7.17; 21.7(MT 12).

15. For the first two clauses, cf. on 12.14. To consume the filthiness here means to put an end to the situation of defilement by means of the dispersal of the people from the land.

16. The first verb is 2nd fem. singular still addressing the city and not 1st singular as RSV. It is the people who are profaned since they are forcibly absent from their country. The confusion is brought about through the gloss **through you,** probably a copyist's variant for **out of you** at the end of verse 15. The section ends with the recognition formula.

(b) THE CITY IN THE SMELTING FURNACE **22.17–22**

The figure of smelting impurities out of silver as a symbol for a promised purification of Israel is a common one, first found in Isa. 1.22, 25 (cf. also Isa. 48.10; Jer. 9.7 [MT 6]; Zech. 13.9; Mal. 3.2–3; cf. also Jer. 6.27–30). The purpose in smelting was to retain the silver, whereas the slag would be discarded. The figure employed by Ezekiel refers only to the first stage in refining where silver ore with all the other minerals still present is melted, the heat being intensified by the use of bellows. But Ezekiel uses the figure only partially (cf. also on chapter 15). Israel is the slag; nothing is said of the silver. Later traditionists had trouble with the figure of smelting as one signifying judgment. Verse 22 is such an attempt to reinterpret the fire of smelting silver rather than of dross. Verse 21 is probably also an accretion explaining **to blow the fire** of verse 20. Verse 19 is now a demonstration oracle, but it can hardly be original in its present form. The 'because' clause is an accretion on the basis of verse 18 by a traditionist who wanted to have all elements in verse 18 repeated in the oracle, but by putting it into a demonstration oracle form created confusion. The original oracle began with **behold** and ended with verse 20.

18. MT has the word **silver** at the end where it belongs. The silver is not part of the dross. 'Dross silver' probably means 'dross from silver (ore)'. Silver ore is placed in the smelting furnace and when melted the silver, being lighter, floats, and the bronze, tin, iron, and lead sulphides constitute the slag. Israel is this slag.

19. For **Lord God**, cf. on 2.4. No one would put slag into the smelting furnace; slag is discarded. Originally Ezekiel simply said **Behold, I will gather you into the midst of Jerusalem.** The figure is changed in the oracle; it refers to the original unrefined silver ore.

20. As, not in MT, but Versions all read it and it is mandatory. G. rightly attests neither **and in my wrath** nor **and I will put you in.** Originally it was a single accretion *whmty hnhty*, i.e. 'and I caused my wrath to rest' but due to the preceding *b'py*, 'in my anger', the first word was copied as *wbhmty* by a copyist under influence of the common phrase 'in my anger and in my wrath', and eventually a conjunction was added to the verb to produce MT. In the comparison all the metals are listed co-ordinately because it is the raw ore which is put into the furnace and then the bellows are worked to produce enough heat to melt it.

21. This again states that Israel will be melted in the process.

22. Again Israel is melted, but now as silver.

(c) NONE RIGHTEOUS IN THE LAND 22.23–31

This section presupposes the fall of Jerusalem and is a defence of Yahweh's actions in destroying Judah. The failure of each of the social classes to fulfil their duties made the destruction (verses 24, 31) inevitable. The passage is based on and is an amplification of Zeph. 3.1–4, 8; since the literary dependence is clear, the entire section probably comes from the school of Ezekiel rather than from the prophet himself. The formal elements are few. Outside the usual introduction only a 'therefore' clause and an oracle conclusion formula obtain. The language of the passage is also highly unusual, verses 25–28 being a series of inclusive clauses modifying **a land** in verse 24. For the introductory word **her** in these verses 'whose' should be substituted.

Zeph. 3.3–4 speaks of four classes of officials of the rebellious city, officials, judges, prophets, and priests, whereas this list has princes, priests, officials, and prophets, with the people of the land somewhat lamely tacked on at the end. Even the particular comparisons are similar. Thus officials are roaring lions, and judges evening wolves (cf. verses 25, 27); the priests profane the sacred and do violence to the law (cf. verse 26). Furthermore, verse 31 is an adaptation of Zeph. 3.8, which refers to the pouring out of indignation, the heat of anger, and the fire of jealous wrath. The traditionist was, however, fully schooled in the thought of Ezekiel, as the amplifications on the Zephaniah passage show. For details, cf. the cross-references below. There is little evidence for later accretions to the text, though the change in construction in verse 29 might indicate its secondary character; nor are **the people of the land** a class of officials as are those in verses 25–28.

24. Usually the cross-reference of a pronoun is antecedent, but here **land** comes after **her.** G. has 'watered' for **cleansed,** which is probably original since it makes a perfect parallel for **rained upon. day of indignation** refers to Judah's destruction in 586 B.C. Now it is a desert bereft of life.

25. G. has 'whose leaders' for MT's 'a conspiracy of her prophets', which RSV rightly follows with *BH*[3]. Throughout this entire passage the perfect aspect is employed with one exception, which anomaly RSV rightly corrected. The **princes** are members of the royal house (cf. 17.12). The comparison to a roaring lion is taken from Zeph. 3.3. The Davidic house was responsible for law and order but instead engaged in murder and robbery in their desire for wealth. For murder as common in Jerusalem, cf. 11.6.

26. The first two accusations are taken from Zeph. 3.4. The priests were responsible for instruction in the law (Jer. 18.18); doing violence to the law may mean teaching it for money (Mic. 3.11). Profaning holy things involves the entire realm of priestly duty to guard the realm of the holy. It was the priest who was responsible for keeping clear the distinction between the holy and profane and between clean and unclean (cf. Lev. 10.10; 11.47 and 20.25). In fact P legislation is largely the priestly attempt to keep the distinction clear in all realms of life. The disregard for the sabbath was to the Ezekiel school a prime example of profaning the holy (cf. 20.12, 13, 16, 20, 21, 24). By this neglect of priestly duty Yahweh himself is rendered profane.

27. destroying lives: a late gloss absent in G. **princes,** Zeph. 3.3 renders 'officials'. 'Nobles' is probably a better rendering. The comparison to wolves is based on Zeph. 3.3. Like the princes the noble class should be models of morality. For **dishonest gain,** cf. on verse 12.

28. For **Lord GOD,** as in verse 31, cf. on 2.4. The castigation of Judah's prophets is based on 13.3–16.

29. The people of the land can hardly refer to the peasants who were left in Judah after 586 B.C. (cf. 7.27). Rather it referred to the ordinary citizen before the catastrophe. They are condemned in terms of extortion, 18.18, robbery, 18.7, 12, 16, oppression of the poor and needy, 18.12, and mistreating the sojourner, verse 7.

30. For **build . . . breach,** cf. on 13.5, where this is said to be the duty of the prophet. Yahweh himself looked for a righteous man in the land that for his sake he might spare it, but found none (cf. Gen. 18.23–33). This is in direct contrast with 14.12–20.

31. This is an amplification of Zeph. 3.8. Therefore he destroyed Judah. To 'requite the way on the head' is a common phrase in Ezekiel (cf. 9.10; 11.21; 16.43).

V. OHOLAH AND OHOLIBAH 23.1–49

This chapter constitutes a single section. The section introduction formula occurs only at verse 1 and the theme of the idolatrous sisters holds it together. The allegory of the two kingdoms as harlots may be compared to chapter 16, where harlotry is also used as a symbol for Jerusalem. Because of the common figure the text of this chapter has been strongly influenced by that of chapter 16. The two do have quite different themes: chapter 16 is a condemnation of Jerusalem's cultic aberrations while this is a condemnation of Israel's political alliances. Like Isaiah, Ezekiel defended political isolationism as evidence of national dependence on Yahweh.

Like chapter 16 this chapter has been subjected to a great deal of expansion by later traditionists. The most obvious expansion is verses 36–49, which abandon the intent of the allegory, viz. a condemnation of political pacts, for a series of reinterpretations, mainly judgments on immorality, idolatry, and cultic sins. It will be analysed separately.

a) THE ALLEGORY AND ITS INTERPRETATION 23.1–35

Ezekiel throughout has used various literary devices to analyse the sins of the peoples, which are usually followed by short but telling judgments based on the figure employed. This section contains four such judgments (note the introductory formulae), only one of which is original. The first is verses 22–27. It takes the figure of the lovers from the allegory and makes them the instrument of destruction, exactly as expected (cf. the original judgments in chapters 12, 16, 21.2–7 (MT 7–12)); this undoubtedly represents the original end of the account. A second judgment has been added in verses 28–30 which is a parallel to the first but takes verse 17*b* as its point of departure. It does not fit the allegory as well since it introduces idolatry as the form of pollution. The next addition, verses 31–34, is a short poem on the cup of wrath which Jerusalem must drink, introduced by a prose introduction and the introductory formula. The last addition, verse 35, is in the form of a demonstration oracle. It is the shortest of the four and actually adds little. For later accretions within expansions, cf. below.

The original allegory and its interpretation is then in verses 1–27. This too has received numerous expansions, some on the basis of chapter 16, others based on a misunderstanding of the original point of comparison. The account divides into four parts: the childhood of the sisters in Egypt, verses 2–4; the story of the elder sister, verses 5–10; that of the younger, verses 11–21; and the judgment, verses 22–27. The first section was expanded by the identification of the sisters as Samaria and Jerusalem in verse 4*b*, which is extraneous to the allegory itself. The second part deals with the northern kingdom's relations with Assyria. A later traditionist added a cultic interpretation by the tradition of verse 7*b*. Verse 8 is an accretion repeating much of verse 3 and is not germane to the original account. The next part begins by stating that Oholibah was more corrupt than her sister, but this greater corruption is not explained until verse 14*b*. The intervening section, verses 12–14*a*, is an expansion based on verses 5*b*–6. Verse 13 applies the alliances with Assyria to both sisters, and also introduces 1st singular discourse which is foreign to the allegory. Verse 14*a* restates verse 11*a* in order to reintroduce the greater corruption of the younger sister. Verse 18 can also be identified as secondary since this changes the 3rd fem. singular to 1st singular discourse again to show Yahweh's disgust. Verse 21 represents another expansion in 2nd fem. singular based on verse 3, probably from the same traditionist responsible for verse 8. The original judgment has also received commentary. Verse 23*b* is based on verses 5–6 where reference to the Assyrians is appropriate; here they are alien. Verses 24*b*–25*aα* introduce a 1st singular discourse in the middle of a 3rd plural judgment. Only at the end should direct discourse be introduced, i.e. at verse 27. Verse 26 introduces clothes and fine jewels which is introduced from 16.39, its proper context, and is a direct quotation by a later traditionist.

The original account is thus found in verses 1–4*a*, 5–7*a*, 9–10*a*, 11, 14*b*–17, 19–20, 22–23*a*, 24*a*, 25*aβ*, *b*, and 27. The two sisters in their youth had illicit relations with Egypt, but Yahweh eventually took them as brides and children were born to both. The elder Oholah (the northern kingdom) had relations with the Assyrians, and so Yahweh gave her into their hands and they killed her and took her children captive, an allusion to the history of that kingdom from 735 to 722 B.C., when Samaria was finally taken by Sargon. Her sister was also harlotrous, first seeking relations with the Babylonians; when these revolted her she turned to the Egyptians. Because of this Yahweh will give her into the hands of the former, who will come with a large army and wreak their wrath on them. This is Yahweh's way of putting an end to Judah's relations with and dependence on Egypt.

2. For **daughters of one mother,** cf. 16.45–46.

3. played the harlot: used in the account for political alliances. Ezekiel believed Israel to have been sinful from earliest times. What he means by such relations with Egypt in the time of her youth is not clear. It may be a reference to Solomon's marriage alliance with Egypt (cf. 1 Kg. 3.1); then the time of her youth would be the period before the kingdoms parted after Solomon's death. Or the reference could be a general reference to the Israelite sojourn in Egypt (cf. 20.5–9). On the whole the former fits more smoothly into the allegory. The last clause is neatly rendered by G. as 'there they were deflowered'.

4. The allegorical names given the sisters remain obscure. They were probably names intentionally sounding alike, like the modern Western custom in the case of twins. Here the names highlight the similarity between the sisters in their tendencies and actions. Both names seem to be puns on the word for 'tent', '*ōhel*. It is likely that the names were intended in a bad sense, as in the case of Israel the 'faithless' and Judah the 'false' one in Jer. 3.6–14, a passage which may have given Ezekiel the impulse to this allegory; cf. e.g. verse 11 with Jer. 3.11. The traditional explanation of the names Oholah as 'her tent' and Oholibah as 'my tent is in her' cannot be based on MT, and are not over lucid. The basic element of 'ōhel occurs occasionally in Phoenician names, in the Hebrew name Oholiab (Exod. 31.6), and in the Edomite feminine name, Oholibamah, in Gen. 36.2, 5, but these are no help. Nor is reference to the tent of meeting at all likely.

5. while she was mine: lit. 'under me' or 'in my place'. If the latter is intended the meaning would be 'instead of relations with me', a zeugma suiting the context. For the northern kingdom's relations with Assyrian, cf. 2 Kg. 15.19-20, 29.

6. Four classes of Assyrians are listed, warriors, governors, commanders, and horsemen. **warriors** more commonly means 'neighbours', which is geographically impossible. The word is undoubtedly related to the word *ḳrb*, an old Hebrew word (northern dialect?) meaning 'war'; thus the meaning 'warriors' is correct. **governors** is probably an Assyrian loanword referring to the ruler of a particular district. **commanders** is also an Assyrian loanword referring to higher administrative officials not always clearly distinct from 'governors'. The first and last are military, whereas the second and third are administrative.

7b. A secondary reference to idolatry; for **idols,** cf. on 6.4.

9. The judgment, as in 16.37, 39, and in verse 22, is appropriately deliverance into the power of the lovers. Verse 9*b* may be an explanatory accretion identifying the lovers, though this is not certain. In any event it is already obvious.

10. For **uncovered her nakedness,** cf. on 16.8. The capture of Oholah's sons and daughters is a reference to the Assyrian exile of the northern inhabitants (2 Kg. 17.6), and the slaying of Oholah with the sword refers to the fall of Samaria and to the end of the kingdom in 722 B.C. Verse 10*b* introduces an alien element into the narrative, viz. that Oholah became a terrible example for women, which is more in kind with verses 36-49 and may be a reflection of 16.41.

11. This seems based on Jer. 3.7*b*. In spite of the example of her sister Judah enters on even more alliances, i.e. both with the Babylonians and the Egyptians.

12. This expansion along with verse 13 is the product of a later traditionist who wanted to add the note that in the time of Ahaz Judah also made alliances with Assyria; it is a repetition of verses 5*b*-6 with the four classes in a somewhat more logical order.

14. For **men portrayed upon the wall,** cf. on 8.10. Possibly Ezekiel is referring to decorations in Babylonian buildings known to him personally. It is of course not germane to ask how Judah could have seen such since the account is an allegory. The use of vermilion for painted reliefs is known for Assyria, and probably was also common in Babylon. For the palace in Jerusalem having rooms painted in red, cf. Jer. 22.14. Since Ezekiel distinguishes carefully in verse 23 between Babylonians and Chaldeans it is unlikely that he should confuse the two in verses 14-17. Undoubtedly the distinction was later lost and **Chaldean** became the general term. Ezekiel clearly means Babylonian (see verse 15); thus **the images of the Chaldeans** must be secondary, probably a later summary on the margin, afterwards incorporated into the text.

15. The inclusive phrase at the end designating Chaldea as homeland is probably secondary, based on the occurrence of Babylonians in verse 15 but **in Chaldea** in verse 16. For the warrior's belt, or better 'loin cloth', cf. the description of the Assyrian soldier in Isa. 5.27. **officers,** lit. 'third men'. Probably their original function was that of third man on the war chariot, but its use in the O.T. seems to be less specific; cf. 'captain', 2 Kg. 7.2, 19; 15.25. The word may simply mean an officer of the third rank.

16. What Ezekiel had in mind is not fully clear. It may have been the election of Jehoahaz after Josiah's death. Or is it a reference to Jehoiakim's submission to Nebuchadrezzar referred to in 2 Kg. 24.1? Actually Josiah's attempt to stop Egypt at Megiddo from going to the help of Assyria was aid to Babylon, and this may be what sending messengers may refer to.

17. Babylon was the great world power and Judah's alliance with Babylon was imposed on her by Nebuchadrezzar (cf. 2 Kg. 24.1). That this submission was 'disgusting' to Judah was natural, but 'turning from them' was suicidal.

18. flaunted her nakedness is the same phrase as that used in verse 10a, but here with herself as subject which is unusual. The verse is a secondary comment on **disgust** in verse 17.

19. The disgust of verse 17 did not lead to isolationism but to a recollection of the good old days of youth, the days of Egyptian alliances.

20. paramours elsewhere means 'concubines'; this is the only exception. Emphasis on the size of Egyptian male organs and seminal ejections shows Ezekiel's general attitude towards Egypt. Egypt was for him the symbol of depravity and of undependability, whereas Babylon was simply the pagan instrument in Yahweh's hands for punishing Judah. For overtures to Egypt for help in the revolt against the Babylonians, cf. 17.15 (cf. also Jer. 37.5, 7).

21. RSV rightly restores **pressed** for the meaningless *lm'n* ('because of') of MT; cf. verse 3. The direct address as well as the reliance on verse 3 show the secondary character of this verse. **longed for** would better be rendered 'sought after'.

22. The judgment is properly introduced as an oracle. For **Lord GOD** as in verses 28, 32, 34, 35, cf. on 2.4. The Babylonians against whom Judah had revolted Yahweh will now stir up to attack her.

23. The list of tribes is connected with conjunctions, except for **all the Assyrians with them.** The words introduce a secondary expansion based on verses 5b–6 (cf. verse 12). Babylonians here probably refer to the earlier inhabitants in contrast to the Aramaic-speaking Chaldeans; whereas the term 'Chaldea' referred to the entire land. The next three names explicate **Chaldeans. Pekod** was an Aramaean tribe of farmers living on the east bank of the Lower Tigris. They are mentioned in the annals of the Assyrian kings and were finally subdued by Sargon II. **Shoa** is often identified with the Sutu, a nomadic Aramaean tribe which eventually settled east of the Tigris but the identification is tenuous. The identification of **Koa** as the Guti is even more uncertain. In any event, it must represent some Chaldean tribe.

24. from the north: based on G. MT has *ḥṣn* which is completely unknown.

Possibly the original text had *ḥṣpn*, 'the north'. This certainly was the direction from which invaders from the east always came into Palestine (cf. Jer. 4.6). The Babylonians will come with the full panoply prepared for war; cf. the more detailed account in 26.7–11. For **chariots, wagons, buckler, shield, helmet,** cf. *IDB*, *s.vv.* Wagons (lit. 'wheels') were mainly used for transport of materials. The terms 'buckler' and 'shield' are not consistently rendered in RSV. The buckler is the small round shield, *mgn*, whereas the shield was the large body shield, *ṣnh*. They are reversed in MT.

25. Barbaric treatment of captives was accepted practice among Semitic peoples of ancient times, but especially of the Assyrians; for the Babylonians, cf. 2 Kg. 25.7. Verse 25*b* consists of two clauses; the first reflects verse 10*a* and the second is a variant of **and your survivors . . . sword.** Ezekiel seldom thinks in terms of survivors remaining in the coming destruction of Jerusalem.

27. Here Yahweh shows himself as the director behind the scenes. The judgment clearly shows Ezekiel's anti-Egyptian bias; the purpose of the judgment is to put an end to Egyptian alliances.

A second judgment 28–30

That this is an expansion on verses 1–27 is clear from the use of the same figure of harlotry. Probably secondary to it is the reference to pollution by idols in verse 30 which shows cultic interest foreign to the judgment.

28. The Babylonians are now defined as **those whom you hate** rather than 'your lovers' as in verse 22, on which this verse is a further comment; this is clear from verse 28*b*, which reflects verse 22.

29. The first clause is a variant on verse 25*aα*, itself secondary. The remainder of the verse reflects some of the language of chapter 16; cf. **naked and bare** with 16.7, and the last clause with 16.37.

30. The last two nouns in verse 29 are correctly taken as the subject of the main verb by RSV, which must be changed to plural in MT. The traditionist in summary puts the blame for Judah's predicament on her own shoulders. The expansion probably dates from after 586 B.C.

A third expansion 31–34

After a prose introduction which introduces the idea of a cup of judgment the third expansion consists of a short poem whose text has been corrupted and expanded.

31. The cup as a symbol of divine wrath is common in the prophets; cf. Jer. 25.15–28 for an extended use of the figure.

32. RSV has mistranslated the verb *thyh* as 2nd fem. singular instead of 3rd fem. singular thereby hiding the secondary character of 'she shall be laughed at and held in derision' which is a late gloss not present in G.

33. and desolation: rightly absent in G. **Samaria** is probably an explanatory gloss to identify the sister; cf. the secondary character of verse 4*b*. The word **drunkenness** is often criticized as not fitting the context and a slight change to make 'breaking' suggested. But the figure of being drunk from the cup of God's wrath is fitting; cf. also the 'cup of staggering' in Isa. 51.17, 22. Its co-ordination with **sorrow** is simply a zeugmatic construction meaning 'producing sorrow'.

34. G. omits **and tear your breasts** which is a late gloss. **and pluck out your hair** is based on S. and is probably not correct. MT has 'and you shall break up its sherds', which is usually given up as completely corrupt. Sherds do represent the broken cup, however, and would seem a fitting end to the judgment. JV renders the verb by 'craunch', i.e. chew the sherds in order to get every last drop, which is possible. The verb is *tgrmy* and it is possible that MT is a corruption of *tmgry* 'to throw down'. That would make fine sense. Judah will drain the cup completely dry and then throw down its broken pieces as a symbol that the judgment is complete.

The last conclusion **35**

harlotry is here defined as forgetting Yahweh and as rejection.

(b) REINTERPRETATIONS OF THE ALLEGORY 23.36–49

This section is a later expansion to verses 1–35 reinterpreting the sins of the sisters first as cultic (verses 36–40a), then apparently again as engaging in foreign alliances (verses 40b–44), and finally they are punished as adulteresses (verses 45–49). That the section is secondary is clear from the fact that the two sisters are described, judged, and sentenced together in contrast to verses 1–27. MT is badly corrupted and at times completely untranslatable. RSV has smoothed the text. References in verses 36–37 are all 3rd fem. plural, but in verse 39 they are 3rd masc. plural. In verse 40 they are again 3rd fem. plural, but beginning with the second sentence through verse 41 are 2nd fem. singular thus secondary to its context. Verse 42a is in 3rd fem. singular, but b is again 3rd fem. plural. Verse 43 is untranslatable but the references are in 3rd fem. singular again along with verse 44a, whereas b is again plural. **them** verse 45a is masculine but **their** in b is feminine. In verses 46–48a the verbs and pronominal suffixes are completely mixed up between 3rd masculine and feminine. Verse 48b introduces 2nd fem. plural which continues through verse 49a. Verse 49b is quite properly 2nd mas. plural since at least in theory some audience is intended.

The state of the text is obviously so confused that there is little purpose served in an attempt to recover its literary history beyond a general outline. It seems that the original nucleus must have been the 3rd fem. plural account, but even this is confused. The traditionist represented by the masculine references in verse 39 seems to think of the people rather than the sisters. Verses 40b–41 are syntactically awkward and do not fit into the context; these are a separate tradition. Verse 43 appears to represent yet another addition. As for the judgment in verses 45–49a, all is confusion.

36. For similar introductions, cf. 20.4, 22.2.

37. For the double crime of adultery and bloodshed, see 16.38; for adultery with idols, cf. 16.17; for child sacrifice, cf. on 16.20–21.

38. For a parallel, cf. on 22.8, and cf. the law in Lev. 19.30. G. omits **on the same day** here and in verse 39; they are late glosses.

39. The change to the masculine marks this as an explanatory addition to verses 37–38. **to profane** it hardly represents the purpose of entering the sanctuary. Rather their entrance entailed profanation.

40a. A reflection of verse 16; cf. also verse 42. Apparently foreign entanglements are meant here.

40b–41 applies details of 16.9–13 to the toilet of the one sister, presumably the younger, preparatory for entertaining her foreign paramours. **painted** means to paint with *kohl*, a black pigment still used by women in the Near East today. Verse 41*b* is based on 16.18.

42. drunkards is a dittograph of the word **brought**. The first letter of *mwb'ym*, 'brought', is a dittograph as well. For **drunkards were brought**, read 'coming in'. The remainder is also obscure. Verse 42*a* may originally have been a judgment on the adulterous woman of verses 40*b*–41, and could be rendered, 'But with the noise of the crowd she was cast out (*šlwkh* for *šlw bh*) to men of the common herd coming from the desert.' She is abandoned to the life of a common prostitute. Verse 42*b* is unrelated to *a*, resuming 3rd fem. plural discourse. The verb is plural indefinite, and the line should be rendered, 'bracelets were put on their hands and beautiful crowns on their heads'. This is a gloss on the basis of 16.11, 12.

43. MT is untranslatable. Verse 43*a* on the basis of G. may be rendered: 'Then I said, have they not committed adultery with these?' In *b* for '*t yznh*, read *m'šy znh*, for *tznwth, tznh*, and for *why', hy'*. This can now be rendered by, 'The works of a harlot she practices, even she.' Along with verse 44*a* the verse refers to the one sister.

44. RSV rightly adopts the plural 'they' of a minority reading. Verse 44*b* again refers to both women.

45. righteous men: judges who will give proper sentence. The double crime reflects verse 37 and 16.38.

46. For **Lord God**, as in verse 49, cf. on 2.4. **For,** delete with minority reading. The **host** here probably means the community.

47. the host: a copyist's gloss from verse 46. The first two verbs should be read as imperatives: 'stone them and despatch them'. **with their swords** should be taken with the next clause (which is masculine and probably a gloss based on verse 25). For **burn . . . houses,** cf. 16.41.

48. Verse 48*a* is based on verse 27. The fate of the sisters will serve as a warning to women against lewdness (cf. verse 10).

49. Verse 49*a* is based on ideas in 16.52, 54, 58. Verse 49*b* is addressed not to the women (feminine), but to the audience (masculine).

W. The Boiling-Pot 24.1–14

This section presents another allegory and its interpretation, but has mixed in with it another related figure and its interpretation. Because of this the resultant text being imperfectly understood received accretions which were intended to explain but have rather added to the difficulty.

The allegory is a short secular poem about preparing a meal of mutton. It is fully possible that this little poem, verses 3b–5, was well known to Ezekiel's audience. It simply calls on the cook to fill a pot with water, set it on the fire, put in all the pieces of meat, stoke up the fire, and let the meat boil.

But to the prophet this needs interpretation; it was an allegory. The impetus to the use of the figure in applying the figure of a pot and its meat to Jerusalem and its inhabitants was probably its earlier use in 11.3–12. Formally there appear to be two interpretative oracles beginning at verse 6 and verse 9 respectively, both introduced by **Therefore thus says the Lord GOD**. The first one, verses 6–8, however, has no relation to the allegory at all but compares the bloody city to a rusty pot. The second, verses 9–14, does apply to the oracle in verses 9–10, but verses 11–13 again deal with the rusty pot. The original interpretation of verses 3b–5 is to be found only in verses 9–10.

Verses 6–8, 11–14 are then a separate account, which because they too referred to a pot were tied to this allegory. In fact if verse 11 is read after verses 6–8 it will be seen to make fairly consistent sense. The bloody city is likened to a badly corroded pot. The bloodshed is the rust; the blood was spilt on bare rock and being uncovered continued to cry for redress. So put the pot on the coals and make it so hot that the rust will be burned out. This second figure was heavily commented on because it had no separate interpretative oracle. Verse 8 is told in the 1st person; it interprets verse 7 by making Yahweh responsible for seeing to it that innocent blood would not be covered up. Another traditionist added verse 12, a comment that the thick encrustation would not be removed by the fire. Verse 13 is false commentary since lewdness rather than bloodshed is the interpretation of the rust. The general 1st person statement in verse 14 is an expansion of the last clause in verse 13 and may well be part of the same accretion.

It now becomes clear how the two original traditions, both from Ezekiel, became intertwined due to some later traditionist. The verbs in verse 10 represent verbal nouns which continue the finite inflection of verse 9b. But since these verbal nouns are homonyms for imperatives, the traditionist made the action ordered for the rusty pot the continuation of the seething-pot actions, joining verse 11 to verse 10. This left the earlier part to be added between the allegory and its interpretation. There is no reason why both accounts should not come from about the same period.

1. The date, January 588 B.C., was probably added later. **tenth** (month) differs in form from the usual pattern in Ezekiel and is here based on 2 Kg. 25.1. Later the date of the beginning of the siege became celebrated as a fast day, cf. Zech. 8.19, and because of verse 2 was appended to the usual formula introducing a section.

2. this very day in verse 2a is probably based on b and added to explain the unusual **the name of this day.** The question often posed is how Ezekiel could know at a distance the exact time when the siege of Jerusalem began, in other words, did Ezekiel have second sight? Cases of second sight are not well authenticated and there is no need to invoke it here. Since the date in verse 1 was added later (cf. on verse 1), this is not second sight but simply another case of prophetic inspiration. Furthermore **has laid siege** lit. means 'leaned' (on, against) (cf. Am. 5.19), and may not necessarily have meant the beginning of the siege originally. Later, when the date in verse 1 was added, it was of course understood in that way.

3. For **Lord GOD**, as in verses 6, 9, 14, cf. on 2.4. The suffix of *bw* ('in it', masc.) must be changed to read *bh* ('in it', fem., as in verse 4). For **allegory**, cf. on chapter 17. For **rebellious house**, cf. on 17.12.

4. the pieces of flesh: rightly with G.S. for 'its pieces of flesh'. G. does not have the late gloss **fill it. all the good pieces:** lit. 'every good piece', may well be an accretion in view of **choice** in the last phrase.

5. RSV has made a number of changes all of which are necessary: 'the bones' to **the logs**; 'its boilings' to **its pieces,** and 'seethed' to **seethe.** The superlative **choicest** is however unwarranted. The same word occurs in verse 4, and it should be rendered 'a choice one'. **pile** means to 'put things around', here of arranging the pieces of wood for the fire.

6. Verse 6b belongs with verses 3b–5 rather than with *a*. It is an expansion on verse 5 by a traditionist who wanted to emphasize that everyone in Jerusalem was caught up in the conflagration indiscriminately. In verse 6a **whose rust is in it** should be changed to 'on which there is rust'. Exactly what is meant by rust is not clear. Verse 11 shows that a copper pot is intended, and copper may blister but does not rust. **rust** occurs only in this passage; it is a derivative of a root involving disease or sickness. Some kind of encrustation is meant.

7. RSV correctly paraphrases the first clause of MT: 'For her blood was in the midst of her.' It relates 'bloody city' to 'rust'. Uncovered blood calls for vengeance (cf. Gen. 4.10; 9.5–6; Job 16.18; Isa. 26.21). Jerusalem callously sheds innocent blood not even covering it, but puts it on a bare rock leaving it completely exposed.

8. my wrath: wrongly for 'wrath'. Yahweh himself sees to it that the shed blood remains exposed, since that will arouse wrath and promote vengeance in the natural course of events. Exposed blood must be avenged; that is a law of nature.

9. G. omits **Woe to the bloody city!** The allegory has nothing to do with bloodshed and the phrase is an accretion taken over from verse 6. The interpretation is that Yahweh himself will be the cook and stoke the fire.

10. The Hebrew verbs can be interpreted as imperatives, but in this verse they are not so intended. Rather the original meant: '(I) will heap on the logs, kindle the fire . . .'. **and let . . . up** is a late gloss not found in G. It was added to make clear that the inhabitants of the city would be killed. RSV rightly follows G. in **and empty out the broth.** A copyist's error created MT's meaningless 'and mix the spices'. Neither the allegory nor its interpretation speak of Jerusalem's sin. It is too late for that. Judgment is here, with Yahweh himself seeing to it that it will be carried out.

11. G. rightly does not have **empty.** This gloss only becomes necessary once the verse is in its new context. To clean the pot of encrustations it had to be made very hot before these would disappear. The point of the comparison is clear. The Jerusalemites are these encrustations and only the fire of warfare can do away with them.

12. In vain . . . myself: RSV has attempted to make something of the first two words, but they are simply a copyist's partial dittograph for the last two words in verse 11. All the traditionist is saying is that the rust is so bad that fire will not touch it, which was not the point of the comparison at all.

13. Because . . . filthiness: a late gloss omitted by G. RSV has taken the last word of verse 12, 'its rust', itself a copyist's dittograph, and joined it as subject of the first two words in verse 13. The original verse should be rendered: 'By reason of your filthy lewdness, you shall not be cleansed . . .'. The time for repentance is past; Yahweh will now vent his fury on the bloody city.

14. I will not repent: a gloss, not in G. **I will judge you:** rightly with Versions for MT, 'they have judged you'.

X. THE DEATH OF EZEKIEL'S WIFE 24.15–27

This section falls into two parts, the second being an editorial adaptation of the language of the first, but in content unrelated to the first.

(a) NO MOURNING FOR THE DEAD 24.15–24

Ezekiel is warned that his wife is to die suddenly, but he is not to engage in the usual mourning rites for the dead. When his wife dies and he acts in this unusual way he is asked to explain and an oracle applies this action to contemporary events. The Temple is about to be destroyed and the Jerusalemites put to the sword.

A number of scholars have suggested that the reference to the death of Ezekiel's wife is secondary and that the oracle in verses 16–17 pertains only to Jerusalem, as **the delight of your eyes.** It is difficult, however, to imagine why later traditionists would have introduced the reference to the death of his wife. Nor is there any textual reason for considering **at a stroke** as secondary.

As the text stands the passage presents another symbolic action; cf. on 4.1–5.17 and 12.1–16. The passage has received some accretions however. The first clause in verse 18 seems out of place since the communication with the people is unexpected before the death of his wife and his failure to observe mourning rites. It is probably a variant on the last clause in the verse, introducing the discourse with the people in verse 19. The explanatory oracle in verses 21–24 also contains expansions of the original oracle. Verses 22–23 are clearly an insertion since Ezekiel here personally addresses the exiles whereas the context is an oracle in which Yahweh is speaker. The insertion repeats details of verses 16–17 more or less reversing the pairs. Verse 23*b* is a separate tradition with its reference to iniquities. The original oracle is contained in verses 21, 24. The section could only have originated in Babylon shortly before the fall of Jerusalem (cf. verse 21*b*).

16. nor shall your tears run down: absent in G. and secondary. It is also absent from the recapitulation in verses 22–23. **delight of your eyes** is a reference to

Ezekiel's wife, who is to be removed by a sudden plague or stroke (Exod. 9.14; Num. 14.37). The theme of failure to observe usual mourning rites as a sign of a great national calamity is also found in Jer. 16.5–9.

17. Sigh . . . dead does not recur in verses 22–23 and may represent a late tradition. The passage presents a problem of translation however. The word for **dead** occurs immediately after *dm*, meaning silence, and before **mourning.** Thus RSV has disregarded the word-order of the Hebrew in order to make sense. If the word for 'dead' be taken as a gloss incorporated from the margin the passage is clear: 'Sigh in silence; make no mourning.' RSV substitutes **mourners** for 'men' as V. *lugentium* here and in verse 22 (cf. Hos. 9.4), but this is not necessary. 'Bread of men' probably refers to ordinary food eaten after the interment provided by neighbours, as still customary in old Jerusalem today. The usual mourning rites include removal of headdress (cf. baldness in Jer. 16.6), going barefooted and covering the face.

18. The blow strikes that evening, and **on the next morning,** which would be the time of interment, Ezekiel observed no mourning rites.

19. G. omits the gloss **for us.**

20. Unusual is the use of the section introduction formula.

21. For **Lord God,** as in verse 24, cf. on 2.4. **desire** occurs only here; in the parallel passage in verse 25, the word *mś'*, 'burden, lifting', occurs. The word comes from a root meaning 'to carry', not from the homonym 'to have compassion'. The phrase means 'the lifting of your persons', i.e. that which bears one up. Yahweh states that he will profane, i.e. destroy, through Babylonian hands, the Temple, and the families of the exiles still in Jerusalem will be killed. The exile of 597 B.C. must have created many breaks in family life.

22. For **mourners,** cf. on verse 17.

23. The positive prediction in verse 23*b* introduces an alien element. The point of not observing mourning rites is that the calamity is too great, not that the exiles will be too busy pining away in iniquities. For 'groaning' as a sign of suffering, cf. Prov. 5.11.

24. Mention of the prophet's name only here and at 1.1, and only possible since it is part of the oracle. For the prophet as a sign to Israel, cf. on 12.6.

(b) THE PROPHET FREED FROM RESTRICTIONS **24.25–27**

As in the case of 3.24–27, this section represents a literary creation of a later member of the Ezekiel school. The next eight chapters were collected by an editor and inserted between the collection of oracles from before the fall of Jerusalem in 586 B.C. (chapters 1–24) and those after that event (chapters 33–48). At some earlier stage, chapter 33 must have followed chapter 24. The passage in 33.21–22 speaks of news of Jerusalem's fall reaching the prophet and of his mouth being opened. A later traditionist interpreted 33.22 as representing a period of dumbness (cf. also on 3.24–27), and attempted to bridge 24.15–24 and 33.21–22 with a prediction paralleling the latter passage. Verse 25 adapts the language of verse 21, whereas verses 26–27 use that of 33.21–22. Verse 26 is often described as secondary to the passage and in its present form must be. But its content is a necessary parallel to 33.21. **on that day** was carelessly copied from verse 27 by an early copyist, thereby creating the difficulty.

25. their joy and glory: lit. 'the object of their beautiful joy'; the reference is to the Temple.

26. It would be quite impossible for an escapee to notify Ezekiel in Babylon of Jerusalem's fall **on that day** (cf. note above).

27. MT does not have **to** (the fugitive). It is likely that **the fugitive** was merely a marginal notation indicating the theme of the passage, and should be omitted. For **sign,** cf. verse 24. There is no oracle, so the recognition formula is in 3rd plural.

SECOND SECTION **25.1–32.32** JUDGMENT AGAINST NATIONS

A. MALICE OF NEIGHBOURS DENOUNCED **25.1–17**

With chapter 25 begins a collection of oracles against foreign nations which the editor of the book has inserted here for reasons of his own (cf. Introduction). This chapter contains five short doom oracles: two against Ammon, and one each against Moab, Edom, and Philistia. Formally they constitute a single section, since the section introduction formula occurs only at verse 1 with each oracle introduced by the introductory oracle formula, and concluded with a recognition formula. The oracles themselves are demonstration oracles, with an invective in the 'because' clause and the doom oracle in the 'therefore' clauses. In theme they are also similar; all are condemned for their malice shown at the time of Judah's defeat in 586 B.C. The second Ammon oracle appears to be dependent on the first since its introductory formula is preceded by a causal particle. It is also not the product of the same writer. Both oracles are in direct address in contrast to the other three, but the first is in 2nd fem. singular whereas the second is 2nd masc. singular. The recognition formula ends all five oracles, but the first is 2nd masc. plural and the second 2nd masc. singular, whereas the last three are all 3rd plural.

The oracle against Moab is also dependent on the first oracle, as is clear from verse 10, in which the judgment of verse 4 is cited. In view of the impersonal 3rd fem. singular of the oracle it may be the work of another writer. The last two oracles are parallel oracles (cf. Am. 1–2.5). Both have 'vengeance' as a theme throughout, even in the recognition formula; both use the stylized judgment form: '(Behold) I will stretch out my hand . . . and will cut.' In both the 3rd plural predominates. The two are probably from the same traditionist.

These oracles all come from the period after the fall of Jerusalem and originate with the Ezekiel school. The earliest of these is the first oracle against Ammon in verses 3b–5, but even this is not from Ezekiel himself, as the reference to the house of Judah in verse 3 shows. Ezekiel's term is 'Israel' rather than 'Judah'.

(a) AGAINST AMMON **25.1–7**

The Ammonites had for centuries occupied the area in Transjordan south-east of

Gilead centred about its capital Rabbah. In 599 B.C. they had, together with Aramaeans and Moabites, co-operated with Babylon against Judah (2 Kg. 24.1–2). Later, in 593, they joined a conspiracy to revolt against Babylon (Jer. 27.3) together with Judah, Edom, Moab, Tyre, and Sidon. Though Ammon remained a rebel (cf. on 21.20(MT 25)), Jerusalem was destroyed first and Ammon continued for some time. It was, however, completely destroyed in the latter years of Nebuchadrezzar's reign. After 550 settled town culture came to an end in the area and it became completely nomadic for about four hundred years, the Ammonites probably being replaced by the **people of the East** (verse 4).

3. For **Lord God**, as in verse 6, cf. on 2.4. Ammon is condemned because it exulted when Temple, land, and people were devastated.

4. the people of the East: the nomads of the desert. Their nomadism is apparent from their circular **encampments,** temporary enclosures for their animals around which they put a stone wall. Their **dwellings** were tents. **fruit** and **milk** were the products of plant and animal husbandry.

5. Rabbah (cf. on 21.20(MT 25)) was their capital. **cities . . . Ammonites,** for MT 'Ammonites', but this is often used to signify their land.

6. This introduces the second oracle, which is much less specific than the first, both in invective and judgment.

7. G. lacks **behold,** which is a late gloss, and should not occur with perfect verb. Also secondary is **I will destroy you,** the asyndetous character of which is also apparent in RSV.

(b) AGAINST MOAB 25.8–11

Moab traditionally occupied the area between the Wadi-l-Ḥesā (Brook Zered) and the Wadi-l-Mōjib (River Arnon), but often pressed northward into Reubenite territory, and for most of its existence occupied areas to the north. The cities mentioned in verse 9 are all north of Wadi-l-Ḥesā. For Moab's relations with Babylon, cf. on verses 1–7. Its fortunes and the end of its settled existence paralleled that of the Ammonites.

8. For **Lord God**, cf. on 2.4. RSV follows G. in omitting 'and Seir' after **Moab,** which cannot be original since Seir was in Edom. Moab's malice is shown in its statement that Judah has become identical in its fate with other nations.

9. RSV rightly follows G. in omitting the dittograph 'from its cities' after **cities.** Moab's flank is the high tableland to the north which could be seen from the Jericho plain. **Beth-jeshimoth** is modern Tell el-'Azeimeh, about 3 miles NE. of the junction of the Jordan and the Dead Sea. **Baal-meon,** modern Ma'ūn, to the south-east, is c. 9 miles E. of the Dead Sea and 5 miles SW. of Madebah. **Kiriathaim,** possibly modern al-Qureiyāt, 5 miles NW. of Dibon and c. 10 miles S. of Ma'īn. Thus the three are on a line of retreat from the north-west corner back towards the Arnon.

10. MT has the awkward gloss, 'Ammonites', copied from verse 10a after **remembered.** It cannot be original since the verb is 3rd fem. singular. The similar fate to that of the Ammonites is historically accurate.

(c) AGAINST EDOM 25.12–14

Edom was Moab's neighbour to the south. Edom joined in the revolt of 593 B.C. against Babylon, but due to its greater inaccessibility and mobility was not wiped out along with the Ammonites and Moabites as the author seems to realize. With the weakening and eventual destruction of Judah, Edom began pressing northward from the extreme south of Judah and occupied the Negeb areas. It, more than any other neighbour, was hated by the Judeans, and is castigated repeatedly (Ob.; Ps. 137.7; Lam. 4.21–22; Isa. 34.5–17; Jer. 49.7–22; Mal. 1.2–5).

12. For **Lord GOD,** as in verses 13, 14, cf. on 2.4. The theme of vengeance both in this oracle and in verses 15–17 of which the respective nations are accused may refer to incursions on the desolated land of Judah when Judah was helpless.

13. **cut off . . . man and beast** means complete slaughter. **Teman** has been identified as modern Ṭawīlān, north-east of El-ji, near Petra. **Dedan** has not been identified as a place name except as Daidan, which is in NW. Arabia near the oasis of el-'Ula, far outside Edomite territory. If this is intended, which is most unlikely, it would be an inexact designation, whereas the author seems to refer to known cities in Edom.

14. For Edom a special judgment is given. The hated enemies were to be dealt with by Israel itself, a notion otherwise completely foreign to the book of Ezekiel. If, however, **by the hand . . . Israel** is a late gloss, it is at least pre-G.

(d) AGAINST PHILISTIA 25.15–17

The Philistines occupied the Pentapolis to the south-west from the twelfth century and were early enemies of Israel until they were effectively subdued by David. Their revolt against Babylon was effectively quelled in 605 B.C. by Nebuchadrezzar, who deported the leaders of Gaza, Ashdod, and Ashkelon. Some kind of Philistine civilization remained, however, as this oracle and Jer. 47 show. Later the Philistine cities became cities of mixed populations (cf. Zech. 9.6).

15. For **Lord GOD,** as in verse 16, cf. on 2.4. In 35.5 it is Edom who is accused of undying enmity. The Philistines had been traditional enemies from early times, a position later transferred to Edom.

16. **cut-off:** MT *krt,* making an intentional word play with **Cherethites,** a synonym for Philistines. The name means Cretans and shows the Aegean origin of a Philistine tribe. They, together with the Pelethites, another Philistine clan, formed David's personal bodyguard. **rest of the sea-coast** refers to what remained of the Philistine cities.

17. **with wrathful chastisements,** not in G., and may be a late gloss. MT does seem over-repetitive.

B. ORACLES AGAINST TYRE 26.1–28.19

Tyre was for centuries the chief city of Phoenicia. Its location on a rocky isle unconnected with the mainland made it peculiarly impregnable, and its fame as a commercial centre dependent on its navigational supremacy was international. A marriage alliance with the Omrid dynasty made Tyre influential in Israelite affairs. Jezebel, daughter of Ethbaal of Tyre, attempted to impose the Tyrian cult of Baal on the northern kingdom, and though she remained unsuccessful because of prophetic opposition, Baalism remained influential on Israel's, and to a lesser extent on Judah's, cult. Prophetic opposition to Baalism must have included a hatred for its strongest centre, Tyre.

Tyre, in spite of its attractive geographical position, was also caught in the international politics of the times. It was forced to pay heavy tribute to the Assyrians during their empire period and naturally rejoiced in their downfall. But their Babylonian successors were no better, and eventually Tyre joined a conspiracy with Sidon, Judah, Edom, Moab, and Ammon in 593 B.C. to revolt against Nebuchadrezzar. Meanwhile Egypt got into the act in 588 by attacking Tyre and Sidon to secure their help against Babylon. Nebuchadrezzar first dealt with Jerusalem, which was destroyed in 586, and then began a thirteen-year siege against Tyre (586–573) according to Josephus (*Antiq.* X. xi. 1; *Contra Apionem* i, 21), with inconclusive results, 29.18.

No prophetic cycle has more to say against Tyre than Ezekiel. Ezekiel believed that Nebuchadrezzar was Yahweh's instrument for punishing the entire Mediterranean world, in which Tyre and Egypt appeared as the strongest forces. All those who had been involved in Judah's fortunes, Ammon, Moab, Edom, Philistia, Tyre and Egypt, were to be subjected to Babylonian rule.

(a) TYRE SHALL BE DESTROYED **26.1–21**

Chapter 26 is an amalgam of four oracles introduced by a single dated section introductory formula on the pattern of chapter 25. Each oracle has its own introductory formula; with the second and fourth a causal particle precedes. The first ends uniquely with the recognition formula; the second with an affirmation formula; the third ends without a formula; and the last ends with an oracle conclusion formula (also found in the first in verse 5*a*).

The literary history of this set of oracles is complicated by the fact that the first and second are doublet versions. The first is patterned on the oracles of chapter 25 as a demonstration oracle but materially based on the second, which is far more detailed. The first one is apparently the product of the same traditionists responsible for chapter 25, but is subsequent to the second. The date of verse 1 (cf. commentary below) is then applicable not to the first but to the second. The causal particle introducing the oracle is then the product of the editor of the chapter, who thereby made the second dependent on the first.

The originality of the third oracle is rendered suspect by its lack of a conclusion formula. This is further substantiated by a comparison of this oracle with 27.32–36. The two are obviously related, but in the latter context must be original, whereas in chapter 26 it can be considered an expansion. The last oracle is also an expansion by a traditionist applying the theme of Egypt's descent into Hades of 32.17–32, particularly in the light of 32.30, to Tyre, which is not mentioned there although its neighbours, the Sidonians, are. The original oracle is thus to be found in verses 7–14. The hand of the editor is apparent in the manner in which the four oracles are strung along in the same way as in chapter 25. The later oracles probably all date from the period 586–573 B.C.

Tyre judged for her malice 1–6

1. The date given as the eleventh year is often said to be too early. At 33.21 the date of the news of the fall of Jerusalem is given as the twelfth year, whereas verse 2 presupposes news of Jerusalem's fall. But as has been argued above, verses 2–6 are not the original oracle for which the date was intended, and the argument against its correctness is irrelevant. The year is 587/6 B.C., but because the month is not given it is impossible to be more specific.

2. RSV has unnecessarily changed MT 'gates' to the singular in view of the singular verb. This lack of number agreement is probably due to the occurrence of Jerusalem which is feminine singular. G.T. read 'the fulness' for **I shall be replenished,** which may be preferable. Read: '(Its) fulness has been laid waste.' The invective accuses Tyre of being shamelessly happy at Jerusalem's fall, since this will mean no competition. The 'gates of the peoples' may refer to the city as an important centre politically (cf. Jer. 27.3), as well as a commercial rival to Tyre.

3. For **Lord GOD,** as in verse 5, cf. on 2.4. **many nations** is indefinite and not fully appropriate to Nebuchadrezzar. For the island fortress the figure of the sea bringing up waves is most appropriate however.

4. Tyre was not destroyed until Alexander the Great attacked it by building a causeway from the mainland in 332 B.C. For **bare rock,** cf. 24.7, 8.

5. a place for the spreading of nets: an isolated place. Tyre will be so devastated that only fishermen will use it.

6. Tyre ruled Phoenicia by reason of her commercial and political prominence. **daughters . . . mainland** (lit. 'in the field') are the Phoenician cities under Tyrian hegemony.

Nebuchadrezzar will destroy the city 7–14

7. For **Lord GOD,** as in verse 14, cf. on 2.4. The name of the famous Babylonian is spelled correctly in Ezekiel and usually so in Jeremiah. The name in Babylonian is a sentence: *Nabu-kuddurri-uṣur,* 'may Nabu protect my boundary stone' (or 'my eldest son'). That he will come from the north is traditional language. People from the Tigris-Euphrates valley always came along the Fertile Crescent into Syria. **king of kings** is not as yet attested as a title ever used by Nebuchadrezzar, but it was known in Assyrian times as well as to the Persians. Some have argued that the use of the term mitigates against Ezekiel authorship, but the term was well known. As a designation for the conqueror it is certainly appropriate. For **a host of many soldiers** MT has 'a host and numerous people'.

8. The first stage in the campaign will be to isolate Tyre by capturing the cities in the provinces (cf. on verse 6). The description of the siege itself is in conventional terms which in Tyre's insular situation would not actually apply. MT lacks **roof of**

but the picture is vivid. The **shields** are the large body shields (cf. on 23.24), which will be raised as a shield from behind which the archers will attack.

9. shock and **battering rams** occur only here and the sense is inferred from the context. The first word apparently comes from a root meaning 'to strike', and the second is not known at all in Hebrew. Some kind of siege-engine or war machine must be meant. **axes** is too specific, since the usual meaning is 'swords'. A general term such as 'weapons' would be preferable.

10–11. *The violent fall of the city.* **as one enters** is plural in MT and should be rendered 'as at the entrances of'. The figure is a mixed one. The point is that the Babylonians will pour into the city through various breaches; so overwhelming is the defeat. Whether **mighty pillars** refer to something specific, as the two famous pillars of the temple to Melkart seen by Herodotus (II, 44), or to general strength of the city as typified by pillars is not certain.

12. waters. Better 'sea' with G.S. Tyre will not only be ravaged for plunder, but even her ruined defences will be uprooted and thrown into the sea. For a similar picture, cf. Mic. 3.12.

14. For **bare rock**, cf. 24.7, 8. For **spreading of nets**, cf. on verse 5.

A lament over Tyre's fall 15–18

15. For **Lord God**, cf. on 2.4. The oracle as well as the lament is in direct address. MT has **the coastlands shake** at the end of the verse, which shows the awkward construction of the intervening words. **when the wounded . . . you** is probably secondary. The language is reminiscent of 31.16*a*.

16. A picture of princes engaged in mourning rites: descent from their thrones, removal of rich robes, sitting on the ground (cf. Job 2.13), and being appalled. More commonly robes would be rent, but because of the royal estate of their wearers they are 'stripped off'. The removal of the robes is repeated. **tremble every moment** recurs in 32.10. **princes of the sea** refers to those rulers of distant places with whom Tyre engaged in naval trade.

17. G. omits **to you** rightly, and has for the first line of the lament 'how you have been destroyed from the sea'. **vanished** was an explanatory gloss on *nšbt* 'you have been destroyed' (instead of MT *nwšbt*, 'O inhabited one') and **sea** was read as singular as in 17*b*. **that was . . . inhabitants:** G. omits possibly by parablepsis. The text is quite corrupt, and the subject is 3rd fem. singular, showing its secondary character. But the remainder is in turn also secondary, it being in 3rd plural and again mentioning 'its inhabitants', thus a doublet version. The original lament in the verse was probably 'how you have been destroyed from the seas, O city renowned'.

18. G. omits verse 18*b*, which is a late gloss, as can also be seen by the different spelling for the word for **isles.**

Tyre's descent into Hades 19–21

This oracle is an amalgam of phrases from chapters 30–32. It is again told in direct discourse. Tyre's ruin will be Yahweh's own doing. For the oracle in general, cf. on 32.17–32.

19. For **Lord GOD**, as in verse 21, cf. on 2.4. For **city laid waste**, cf. 30.7. **deep** and **great waters** are synonyms for the abyss, chaos, the underworld. The language is borrowed from mythology and is symbolic for death.

20. have a place: rightly with G. for 'I will give beauty'. The error arose through faulty word division. Tyre is here personified as going down to Hades, there to stay with other peoples no longer living, and never again to be rebuilt, i.e. take her place in the land of the living.

21. G. omits the late gloss **though you be sought for, you will** (not) **be found.** The words **never again** are an adaptation to the gloss from an original 'for ever' (cf. 27.36; 28.19). The death of Tyre will be an end of terrors, a true judgment of Yahweh.

(b) A LAMENT OVER THE SHIP OF TYRE 27.1–36

This section is comprised of a poem in the form of a lament in two parts separated by a long prose expansion. In the first part the construction of the ship of state and its company is described, after the usual section introduction in verses 1–3a, in verses 3b–9a. Verse 9b in its present form has been expanded to refer to ships of the sea as though the reference is to the Tyrian harbour rather than to a ship. A reference to its sailors all being on board to engage in trade must have been part of the poem. It was some such reference as this that gave rise to the long addition of verses 12–25a.

Verses 10–11 constitute a separate expansion which abandons the figure of the ship and prosaically describes the manning of the defences of the city. It is based on verses 8–9, which deal with the ship's company. That it is not part of the original poem is clear both from its prose character and its reference to the Arvadites as watchmen protecting the walls of the city, whereas in the poem they are rowers of the ship of state. Verses 12–25a are a late adaptation of a rather fulsome trade list which has been added at the end of the first part of the poem taking its cue from verse 9b. The expansion of verses 10–11 must in turn be subsequent to it, since those are inserted between verses 9b and 12. The section is purely prose and various commercial idioms recur with each item. The names of cities or areas are given together with their specialities and joined with recurring idioms such as 'trafficked with you', 'exchanged for your merchandise', 'traded with you', 'because of your abundant goods', 'because of your great wealth'. As a sixth-century document on trade this is a valuable source for the early history of commerce. It is, however, not part of Ezekiel's work.

The second part of the poem is found in verses 25b–36 and describes the wreck of the heavily laden ship of Tyre in a storm at sea and the resultant lament over this disaster by the inhabitants of the coastlands. This part has also been somewhat expanded by the accretion of verse 27, which repeats the list of the crew as going down with the ship, anticipating verse 34, and possibly by verse 33, which emphasizes the former wealth of Tyre and seems somewhat discordant between verse 32*b* and verses 34–36. The poem as a whole was probably written at some time early in the siege of Tyre, but there is no further indication of the date of its composition, except that it could not have been composed after the siege was lifted in 573 B.C. The original prose list of Tyrian trade must have been earlier than the poem since Judah (and Edom) is listed as one of the traders, verse 17. Its adaptation to this poem is of course much later.

2. Cf. 19.1 and 32.2 for parallels.

3. RSV rightly changes 'entrances of a sea' to **entrance to the sea,** a reference to its position. **merchant . . . coastlands** is an editorial description which is commented on in detail in the prose expansion. For **Lord GOD,** cf. on 2.4. **I am** read 'a ship'. Because '*ny* was misunderstood the gloss **you have said** was added to make sense. The oracle begins: 'Tyre is a ship, perfect in beauty.'

4. beauty is used for Tyre in 28.12, 17 as leading to the sinful pride of its king.

5. planks: uniquely dual in MT, and RSV is correct in correcting to **your planks. Senir** was an old Amorite name for Mount Hermon (Dt. 3.9), but probably referred to the general area of the Anti-Lebanon in contrast to Lebanon in verse 5*b*. **for you,** '*lyk*, is a corruption for '*lyny* and belongs with the next verse.

6. Read 'Of the highest **oaks**'. **inlaid with ivory** represents a copyist's error in MT. RSV rightly makes one word out of the two 'daughter of Asherim' of MT to read **of pines.** This meaning is not certain; it may refer to a species of cedar or cypress. **Bashan,** the wooded area north of the Yarmuk and south of Mount Hermon, was noted for its fine oak (cf. Isa. 2.13). The Hebrew name for Cyprus, *ktym,* is based on the name Kition, modern Larnaka, in southern Cyprus, which was colonized by the Phoenicians and extensively used as a harbour by the Tyrians.

7. serving as your ensign: secondary and outside the parallelism between verse 7*a* and *b*. **your awning** represents a revocalization of MT 'the one covering you'. Possibly **and purple** is secondary. Tyre itself was famous for its purple, but the common phrase 'blue and purple' easily created MT. For **fine . . . linen,** lit. 'linen with embroidery'; cf. on 16.10. **sail** elsewhere means 'a spreading out'. **awning** is simply a covering, as in Gen. 8.13 for the deck roof of the Ark, and in P of the skins covering the tent of meeting. Here probably it refers to the covering of the cabin to the rear of the mast. **Elishah** is ancient Alashia, the oldest known name for Cyprus, possibly more specifically Enkomi on the east coast.

8a. For **inhabitants** read 'nobles' with G. For **Sidon,** cf. on 28.21. **Arvad,** modern *Ruad,* was another island city 40 miles N. of Tripoli. It was defeated by Nebuchadrezzar and its king deported to Babylon.

8b. MT has 'your skilled men, O Tyre were . . .'. If this is original it is secondary to the poem. But the change adopted is probably correct. **Zemer,** modern *Sumra,* lay between Arvad and Tripoli. The Zemarites are mentioned in Gen. 10.18 as brothers of the Arvadites.

9. and her skilled men: an expansion as the parallel stichs in verse 8 show. **caulking your seams** is lit. 'strengthening your breaches' and it is likely that ship's carpenters are meant. Verse 9*b* has been expanded by **the ships of the sea** by a traditionist who misunderstood the line. The original for **with their mariners**

was then probably 'your mariners'. Tyrian sailors took their part in the ship's crew as merchants, thereby giving a *raison d'être* to the ship.

10. The three names give some difficulty because of their geographical location. Persian mercenaries in Tyre seems absurd. **Lud** refers to the Lydians of western Asia Minor, whereas **Put** is an old name for Libya, as G. realized. The Libyans were well-known mercenaries in the Egyptian army from early times. The conjunction of Lud and Put as a rhyming pair occurs also in 30.5; for others cf. 25.16, 23.23, as well as Gog and Magog in chapters 38–39. For the hanging of shield (the small round shield; cf. on 23.24), cf. Ca. 4.4

11. Helech is also Hebrew for 'your army', but a proper noun seems preferable. It may refer to Cilicia in Asia Minor which was known as *Hilakku*. The first **round about** is not present in G.S. and is probably a copyist's dittograph based on verse 11*b*. **men of Gamad** are not certainly identified; possibly the Kumidi known from the Amarna Letters are meant. But possibly 'Gomer' should be read in which case it means the Cimmerians, a warlike Indo-European tribe which invaded Asia Minor in the eighth century. It is quite doubtful, however, that the Cimmerians, nomadic by nature, would have served as mercenaries. For **beauty**, cf. verse 3*a*.

12. Tarshish: probably Tartessus, a Phoenician port in southern Spain. The name became a symbol for a distant place reached by water. For the metals, cf. 22.18. **exchanged** is 'gave' in Hebrew, and indicates a barter system of commerce.

13. Javan became the Hebrew word for Greeks in general, but more specifically refers to Ionia. **Tubal** and **Meshech** are both in Asia Minor. Tubal lay somewhere in Cappadocia and with Meshech was famous for its metallurgy. It was regularly associated with Meshech in the Assyrian inscriptions (*Tabal* and *Mushku*), as well as in Herodotus (*Tibarēnoi* and *Moschoi*). Meshech designates Phrygia, whose capital, Gordion, was sacked by the Cimmerians; cf. on Gamad, verse 11. Their wares were slaves and bronze vessels.

14. Beth-togarmah, in Asia Minor, called *Til-garimmu* by the Assyrians and reflected in modern Gürün, east of the southern end of the Halys. It is commonly identified as Armenia. Asia Minor was known for its horses; cf. 1 Kg. 10.28–29, reading 'Egypt' as *Musri*.

15. Rhodes (with G. for MT Dedan), a large island in the Aegean, was a commercial centre on the maritime trade route from the East. **your own special markets** (similarly in verse 21) is an attempt to render MT: 'trade of your side'. Rhodians could hardly have produced ivory and ebony which came from Africa, but they were themselves mariners and probably middlemen. *hwbnym*, **ebony,** is an Egyptian loanword.

16. MT has 'Syria' for **Edom,** but both G. 'men' and S. 'Edom' presuppose *'dm*, which must be right, cf. verse 18. For Edom, cf. on 25.12–14. The list of wares is a peculiar amalgam of textiles and precious stones, but since very little is known of Edom's place in ancient commerce it is best to accept the role of Edomites as middlemen for such wares. **emeralds** is mentioned as a stone in the High Priest's breastplate and was probably a garnet rather than an emerald. **coral** is a conjectural rendering based on an early Rabbinic tradition, whereas **agate** also occurs in Isa. 54.12 as comprising the pinnacles of redeemed Jerusalem. It was probably red in colour, but its identification as agate is insecure.

17. and the land of Israel: probably an accretion. Israel had not existed politically since the fall of Damascus in 722 B.C. **wheat, olives** for MT 'wheat of Minnith', probably correctly. MT has an obscure *png* for **early figs,** which is based on a change to *pgym,* occurring in Ca. 2.13. It has been suggested that it represents a loanword from Akkadian *pannigu,* some kind of baked product. **balm** was some kind of aromatic gum, possibly of the mastic tree; it was commonly associated with Gilead (cf. Jer. 46.11; see also Gen. 37.25).

18. for your abundant goods: a doublet for the next phrase, and omitted by G. **Helbon** still exists today north-west of Damascus as a centre of grape culture. Its wine is listed by Nebuchadrezzar as brought to Babylon. The word for **white** is *ṣḥr* and may well be a place-name 'Sahar', modern Ṣaḥra, the desert area north-west of Damascus where grazing is still common today.

19. The first two words in MT are *wdn wywn,* 'Both Dan and Javan', which makes no sense. The change of *ywn* to *yyn* yields **wine.** A. Millard (*JSS* 7, 201ff.) suggests reading *wdny,* 'and casks of', for the first word, which makes fine sense but the meaning is not attested in Hebrew. **Uzal** is probably *Izalla* between Haran and the Tigris known in antiquity for its wine. Unfortunately the place-name for the set of wares in verse 19*b* (*a* is still part of Damascus trade notice) has fallen out and there is no evidence of any kind to give a hint. **cassia** is an aromatic resin which might point to S. Arabia, and **calamus,** some kind of sweet-scented spice made from reeds, points in the same direction, but **wrought iron** is then out of place.

20. For **Dedan,** cf. on 25.13. 'Saddle' in **saddle-cloths** occurs only here and is inferred from the context.

21. Arabia and **Kedar:** general designations for the bedouin in the desert extending from the Syrian desert southward to N. Arabia. These semi-nomads were sheep- and goat-herders and Damascus was their trading centre, as it still is for many such today.

22. The traders of is unique in designating the traders in this list and may be secondary. **Sheba** is well known as the ancient kingdom of the Sabaeans in S. Arabia. **Raamah** was a city near Ma'in in S. Arabia. In Gen. 10.7 it is listed as the father of Sheba and Dedan and anachronistically as brother of Seba (another spelling of Sheba). The S. Arabian kingdoms for centuries held a monopoly on the spice routes to India.

23. After **Eden** MT has 'the traders of Sheba', a copyist's dittograph from verse 22. The remainder of the verse is a further expansion. **Chilmad** is a corruption of an original 'all Media'. **Haran** was a famous centre of trade and centre of Sin worship in ancient times. It still exists under the same name *c.* 60 miles E. of Carchemish. **Canneh** must also have been in Mesopotamia, but though known in Assyrian sources is not yet identified. It is often equated with Calneh (Am. 6.2,

Isa. 10.9), but this is unnecessary. **Eden,** also known as Beth-eden in Am. 1.5, and as *bit Adini* in the Assyrian inscriptions, was also occupied by Aramaeans, and was a district south of Haran.

24. RSV rightly divides the last word in MT 'in your market' to make **in these . . . you.** This verse contains five hapax legomena, but RSV is probably correct throughout. For **choice garments,** cf. the cognate word in 23.12. **clothes** in Aramaic means 'mantle'. **carpets** is thus rendered on the basis of T. in Est. 1.3, whereas the word for **coloured stuff** is known in Akkadian and Arabic as 'multi-coloured'. The word for **made secure** in Arabic means 'make firm', hence 'tied', possibly here a technical term used in carpet weaving.

25a. It is unnecessary to change MT 'were your caravans' to **travelled for you. ships of Tarshish** is a general term for large ships (cf. on verse 12).

25b. This resumes the poem with the figure of Tyre as a heavily laden ship.

26. *The ship founders.* **high seas** is lit. 'many waters', a phrase commonly used for the deep. It has no mythological implications here, but is parallel to **heart of the seas.** The **east wind** is still known as a destructive force in Palestine today (cf. Ps. 48.7 (MT 8)). It is not to be taken as an allusion to Nebuchadrezzar, who came from the north, 26.7.

27. For **with all** read 'and all' as G. For **caulkers,** cf. on verse 9. That this verse is secondary is apparent from the references to **men of war** which are referred to in the expansion in verses 10–11, but not as part of the ship's company in verses 8–9.

28. countryside: uncertain. The word is used in 45.2; 48.17 of the open land immediately outside the sanctuary and city, but here it occurs in the plural as commonly of grazing land. Thus it refers to the shoreland hearing the outcries of the crew.

29. The mariners, etc., are not of course those on the sinking ship, but other sailors.

30. For throwing dust and ashes as a sign of sadness, cf. Job 42.6. For scattering dust, cf. Job 2.12; for 'wallowing in ashes' as mourning rite, cf. Jer. 6.26; 25.34.

31. For the signs of mourning here, cf. on 7.18.

32. In their wailing: probably secondary. For **Who . . . Tyre** MT has, 'Who like Tyre like silence.' Possibly *kdmh* is a corruption of *ndmh*, 'be destroyed'. This is the basis for RSV. On the other hand *ndmh* also means 'to be like', which would make excellent sense. Render 'Who can be likened (to) Tyre.'

33. MT incorrectly reads **wealth** in the plural.

34. Now you are wrecked: with G. for MT's 'At the time of being broken'. If MT were original it would mean that verse 33 was secondary, since the phrase would have to modify Tyre in verse 32.

35. convulsed usually means 'thundered' but in 1 Sam. 1.6 the troublesome 'to irritate her' probably means 'to humble her'; so here better 'downcast'.

36. Almost an exact duplicate of the end verse of an oracle against Tyre in 28.19, with the substitution of **merchants** for 'all who know you' and **hiss** for 'are appalled'. Furthermore, the last two sentences also occur in the concluding verse at 26.21, which is later than Ezekiel. The conclusion that this is an editorial expansion is unavoidable.

(c) THE PROUD KING OF TYRE SHALL DIE 28.1–10

Though verses 1–10 may be related to the lament that follows in verses 11–19, it is an independent oracle, as the separate section introduction formulae in verses 1 and 11 show. In form the oracle is a demonstration oracle with the 'because' clause in verse 2 and the 'therefore' clause in verses 7–10. The original oracle has been expanded considerably. The most obvious accretion is verses 3–5, which separates the two parts of the oracle by a prosaic explanation of how the Tyrian king attained such an exalted position that he could think in terms of self-deification. RSV shows its intrusive character by separating it by dashes. But the oracle itself has also been expanded. Due to the expansion preceding the 'therefore' clause it became necessary again to summarize the 'because' clause by repeating its last clause, verse 2*bβ*. The clause **Because . . . therefore** in verses 6–7 is thus secondary. In the oracle of judgment the actual judgment is found in verses 7–8, but a later traditionist added verses 9–10*a* almost as a taunt repeating phrases from the original invective of verse 2.

The oracle is best understood as a judgment against the city as personified under the figure of its king, a classical case of hybris, of man forgetting that he is mere man in the pattern of the J story of Gen. 3. The original oracle must have been composed along with chapter 27 at approximately the same time as 26.7–14 (cf. on 26.1). In contrast to the oracle that follows, this section is almost wholly free of mythological overtones (with the possible exception of **seat of the gods** in verse 2).

2. For **Lord GOD**, as in verses 6, 10, cf. on 2.4. The term *ngyd*, **prince**, is used only here in Ezekiel. A. Alt (*Kleine Schr*. II, 23, n. 2) suggests as a possible meaning for the term 'one who is told', which is suggestive here. If the prince is the 'informed one' then the hybris of his self-deification is set in even clearer light. The term was commonly used of a charismatic leader, thus of Saul, David, Jeroboam, *et al*. Only later, especially in Chronicles, is the term adapted to rulers in various capacities. As applied to a king it is limited to Israel and Judah outside this passage, though cf. Dan. 9.25, 26. The content of Tyre's pride is defined by the parallel claim to being God. That the term *El* is used for God has no special significance. El was the head of the Canaanite pantheon, but this is irrelevant, and the rendering **a god** is correct. Actually the chief deity of Tyre was Melkart. The point is that Tyre usurps a title proper only to Yahweh.

In Canaanite mythology the usual designation for the divine dwelling-place was the mountain in the north; cf. Ps. 48.2(MT 3), Isa. 14.13, and cf. verses 14, 16. In verse 13 the garden of God is referred to. Here the seat of the gods is set on the rocky isle of Tyre, a notion not otherwise attested. For **man, and no god** as applied to Egypt, cf. Isa. 31.3.

3. For **Daniel** (Hebrew *Danel*), cf. on 14.14. Verse 3*b* is difficult in MT. The verb '*mmwk* means 'they grow dark, dim' but has a 2nd singular suffix, and 'every secret' is singular and cannot be the subject. The verb should probably be vocalized as a Pi'el, which then is doubly modified and has a plural indefinite subject, i.e. 'they do not darken (puzzle) you with any secret'.

4–5. Tyre's wisdom was clearly commercial.

6b. Lit. (as in verse 2bβ) 'because you have set your heart as the heart of God'. Since heart is the intelligence in Hebrew the RSV rendering (as in verse 2b) is more or less adequate.

7. strangers. the most . . **nations** recurs in 31.12, and cf. 30.10, 11; 'the most . . . nations' is identified as that of Nebuchadrezzar. **beauty** is used in the oracles against Tyre as a term of pride in physical wealth. **beauty of your wisdom** here means the prosperity attained through wisdom. The Babylonians will use their weapons against the splendour of Tyre.

8. The seat of the gods (**heart of the seas**) will become the grave of Tyre. The divine Tyre is human after all; it will die. For going down to the Pit, cf. 32.17–32.

9. those who slay you: rightly for MT singular. The parallel phrase is vocalized as 'those who defile you' in MT, but RSV corrects. The expansion makes explicit the message of the oracle.

10. uncircumcised: a term of contempt especially applied to Philistines. The rite was practised by Egyptians and most Semites, though not by Assyrians and Babylonians (cf. Jer. 9.25, 26).

(d) LAMENT OVER THE KING OF TYRE **28.11–19**

In this lament the king of Tyre is compared in a sustained figure to Primeval Man of a Paradise myth. The myth has some parallels to the J story of Adam and Eve of Gen. 2 and 3. In both a primeval state of perfection obtained; in both a garden of God is a setting; in both Primeval Man sinned and was ejected to die; in both a cherub is involved. But the Ezekiel myth has numerous elements which are at variance with the J story. Only one individual is involved. Though Eden is mentioned, the dominant setting is the mountain of God. The description of primeval bliss is one of adornment, whereas in J the first pair were naked; fiery stones were present on the mountain of God; only one cherub is present who takes part in the ejection, and the final punishment was not only ejection but consumption by fire.

The text of the lament is full of uncertainties and has been expanded considerably. Later traditionists added on the basis of the poem in verses 1–10 references to the wisdom of the king, viz. in verse 12 **full of wisdom,** and for verse 17a, cf. verses 2, 7. In verse 13 a list of nine gems taken from the list of stones in the High Priest's breastplate in Exod. 28.17–20 was added to explain the reference to **precious stone.** In verse 16a **In . . . violence** is an accretion explaining the iniquity of verse 15 as commercial in character. The divine judgment begins at verse 16b in the 1st person, and expansions are easily identified since they are in the 2nd person. Verse 18a interrupts the 1st person discourse and represents a later comment. Verse 19 is an editorial conclusion which the editor added as in the case of 26.21, 27.36, thereby joining these chapters into a larger unit. For smaller expansions and glosses, see below.

In contrast to the original poem in verses 1-10 this poem probably deals with the person of the king rather than as personification of the city. When Nebuchadrezzar lifted the thirteen-year siege on Tyre in 573 B.C. the Tyrian king accompanied him as captive; thus the reference may well be to Ittobaal. Since the judgment in verses 16*b*-18 is told in past tense the poem may have been composed shortly after Ittobaal's exile.

12. For **Lord GOD,** cf. on 2.4. For **raise a lamentation,** cf. 19.1; 27.2. RSV rightly vocalizes *ḥwtm* as **signet,** instead of participle 'sealing'. In Hag. 2.23 the Messianic king, Zerubbabel, is called a signet ring. According to 1 Kg. 21.8 the king's signet was used to authenticate written orders. **of perfection** is probably incorrect. Seals were commonly used to ensure that a particular document was genuine. The word *tknyt* occurs only here and in 43.10 and is usually derived from the root *tkn*, meaning 'to regulate or measure', thus 'proportion', hence a 'model signet'. But if the word is derived from the root *knh*, 'betitle, give a name', the meaning is clear; it means authentication, a seal which assures genuineness. Why the king of Tyre should be called a signet at all is obscure, since the term never occurs elsewhere as part of Paradise stories.

13. Eden, the garden of God seems to be at variance with the **mountain of God** in verses 14, 16, but the garden may be visualized as on the mountain. **covering** is not certain. It probably is related to the root *swk*, 'to fence in, close in', and so 'that which surrounds', such as a garment or belt. The list of nine stones is a much later insertion taken from the list of Exod. 28.17-20. G. has all twelve. The order in MT is somewhat different, possibly, according to Cooke, due to a dissatisfaction with the colour arrangement. The order here is 1-2, 6, 10-12, 5, 4, 3. The translations are by no means certain. **carnelian** is a red stone, as the name *'dm* implies. The word for **jasper** is rendered as 'diamond' in Exod. 28.20. **chrysolite** and **topaz** are related, but the difference is not clear. **beryl** is a greenish stone, but the Hebrew word is sometimes rendered by onyx, whereas in Exod. 28.20 the word for **onyx** is rendered by 'jasper'. **sapphire** is a doubtful rendering; it should be 'lapis lazuli'. **carbuncle** is probably a garnet. **emerald** was not known until considerably later and 'green feldspar' is probably meant. **your settings** and **your engravings** are unknown words; they were probably technical terms used by goldsmiths, and so RSV has interpreted. **they were prepared** is a late gloss unattested in G. **On the day . . . created** originally modified the preceding descriptive clauses. The picture presented is of Primeval Man present in the garden of God, bedecked with jewels and gold ornaments at the time when he was created. As in Gen. 2, so this Paradise myth is connected with creation.

14. With rightly with G.S. for MT 'you were'. **With . . . cherub** must be connected with verse 13. The reference to the cherub is peculiar. The word for **guardian** is *hswkk*, 'the one covering'. But another word similar to it means 'to anoint'. The word 'anointed' is a later commentary on the word, but an incorrect one. The article is not present for 'cherub', which normally makes the phrase a bound structure in Hebrew, i.e. 'the cherub of the hovering one'. But possibly the article is here deictic, i.e. 'that cherub which hovers'. For the sense of *swkk*, cf.

1 Chr. 28.18. **guardian** is over influenced by the Gen. 2 story. Since **I placed you** is preceded by a conjunction in MT it must go with the next phrase. G. does not attest **you walked** which may be secondary. The verse then would originally be: 'together with that cherub which hovers. I placed you on the (**holy**—also secondary?) mountain of God; you were in the midst of stones of fire.' The stones of fire may be a reference to sparkling jewels. The mountain of God reflects the same motif as the mountain where the gods dwelt, a Canaanite Mount Olympus. The notion was widespread throughout the Near East, and is attested both in Ugaritic and in Akkadian literature (cf. Isa. 14.13).

15. Primeval Man was created without blot, but then he sinned.

16. What that sin was is not told in the original poem, which simply used the term **iniquity** in verse 15 and **sinned** here. A later commentator identified the sin as violence (cf. 7.23) exercised in trade. MT *mlw twkk*, 'they filled your midst', is the result of haplography from *mlyt twkk*, 'you filled your midst' (with violence). The judgment begins with verse 16*b*. The verb 'and I profaned you (from)' is a hendiadys for 'profaned and cast out', as RSV understood. Similarly the next verb, which MT wrongly points as 1st singular. MT has lit. 'made you to perish from'. The role of the cherub is similar to that of Yahweh himself in contrast to the role in Gen. 3.24.

17. Verse 17*a* reflects the language of verse 2*aβ* and verse 7*b*. This comes from another tradition which interpreted the iniquity of verse 15 as pride, in line with verses 1–10. The mountain of God extends above the earth and ejection means being cast down to earth (**ground**).

18. Again in verse 18*a* a traditionist expanded on the identification of the sin of the Tyrian king, but now leaves the figure of Primeval Man entirely. Added is the cultic sin of profanation of the sanctuaries. Verse 18*b* does continue the judgment, but this is more applicable to the city. It refers to warfare and the consequent destruction of the conquered city. This is probably a late expansion on the judgment, which in the original myth was expulsion from the mountain of God (cf. Gen. 3.24).

19. For the editorial character of this verse, cf. on 27.36.

C. CONCLUDING ORACLES TO CHAPTERS 25–28 **28.20-26**

The recurrence of the recognition formula at verses 22, 23, 24, and 26 shows the composite nature of this section. The first section is an oracle against Sidon, but without the invective usual for Ezekiel in small oracles against the nations (cf. 25.3, 6, 8, 12, 15; 26.2; 28.2). The oracle is only one distich in length in direct address, plus the recognition formula. To have these have been added accretions which can easily be identified since these are in 3rd fem. singular. The accretions of verses 22*bβ*–23 are composed of typical Ezekiel phrases and again end with the recognition formula. Verse 24 is an expansion which no longer applies specifically to the Sidon oracle but is a conclusion to the set of oracles in chapters 25–28, applying the oracles against neighbouring nations to Israel. A final and late oracle based mainly on excerpts from chapters 34–39 concludes the section with Israel regathered in Palestine, prosperous and secure over against the neighbours now under judgment.

21. For the formula, cf. 6.2; 21.2; 25.2; 29.2. Sidon is otherwise mentioned together with Tyre in prophetic writings. It lies 25 miles N. of Tyre with an excellent harbour on two sides. Until the time of David it was more prominent than Tyre (cf. Gen. 10.15). Sidon took part in the conspiracy against Babylon mentioned in Jer. 27.3 and suffered a fate similar to Tyre. Its king was exiled to Babylon, though when this occurred is not known.

22. For **Lord GOD**, as in verses 24, 25, cf. on 2.4. The judgment aside from the stereotyped phrase beginning an oracle of judgment is that Yahweh will be glorified in Sidon, a phrase which in the context must mean that Yahweh will be honoured through judging the city. For **execute judgments,** cf. 5.10. The concluding clause is an expansion on the verb 'be glorified'.

23. G. does not attest **for I will send** and **into her.** If this is a late gloss, the first line would simply have been: 'pestilence and blood will be in her streets', but G. probably has omitted by parablepsis. For **pestilence,** cf. on 5.12; for **blood,** 5.17; for **sword,** 5.1 .

24. For the figure of thorns as representing hateful neighbouring nations, cf. Num. 33.55, Jos. 23.13. The neighbouring nations, Ammon, Moab, Edom, Philistia, Tyre, and Sidon, have all been judged, and so Israel is left in peace.

25. This oracle of restoration was adapted as a conclusion after verse 24 as verse 26ba shows. For **gather . . . scattered,** cf. on 11.17. **manifest my holiness** is based on and subsequent to verse 22bβ. Verse 25b is borrowed from 37.25.

26. For **shall dwell securely,** cf. 34.25–28. **they shall build . . . vineyards** is not an Ezekiel expression but rather Trito-Isaiah (Isa. 65.21 and cf. Jer. 29.5, 28).

D. ORACLES AGAINST EGYPT 29.1–32.32

The editor has gathered together seven oracles against Egypt, all but one, 30.1–19, being dated and one, 29.17–21, completely out of chronological sequence. As in the case of Jeremiah, Ezekiel devoted more oracles to Egypt than to any other foreign nation, probably because Egypt remained Nebuchadrezzar's most powerful enemy, and Nebuchadrezzar was Yahweh's instrument of judgment not only for his own people but also for Israel's neighbours. Furthermore Egypt had for long been involved in Judah's affairs, inciting her to revolt with promises of support but only seldom actually coming to her aid in a crisis.

The contemporary dynasty in power was the Saite house, 663–525 B.C. It was Neco, the second ruler, 609–594 B.C., whose army slew Josiah at Megiddo in the first year of his reign and later deposed his son Jehoahaz and took him captive to Egypt (cf. 19.4). In 605, however, Neco was crushingly defeated by Nebuchadrezzar at Carchemish (Jer. 46.2), and retreated to Egypt. Four years later the two fought again on the borders of Egypt, but with inconclusive results. His grandson, Hophra, 588–569 B.C., had incited Judah to revolt, and briefly came to Jerusalem's aid, causing a temporary raising of the siege probably early in 587 (Jer. 37.5–7).

Jeremiah predicted for him a fate similar to that of Zedekiah (Jer. 44.30), a prediction which finally was fulfilled in 566 when he was killed by Amasis, his successor. Hophra was thus the Pharaoh of Ezekiel's oracles.

(a) A JUDGMENT ON PHARAOH AND EGYPT 29.1–16

As in the case of chapters 25 and 26, this section represents a collection of four related oracles, for only one of which the introductory date in verse 1 is applicable. The first oracle, verses 3–6a, is a short allegory in poetic form. The original poem may well have been shorter; in any event, the present poem seems to have been prosaically expanded by references to the fish of the rivers. Pharaoh is the great crocodile who arrogantly thinks himself master and creator of the Nile. For this Yahweh will drag him out with hooks from the Nile, throw him into the desert where he will die unburied, a dishonoured corpse. The expansions are a later attempt to include the Egyptians in the judgment on their king. The date of verse 1 is intended for this oracle.

The second oracle, verses 6b–9a, is a demonstration oracle against the land of Egypt. It is undated and is without formulaic introduction, but it must be later than the date of verse 1 since it condemns Egypt for its lack of support for Israel in the crisis of 586 B.C. There is nothing in the oracle to preclude Ezekiel's authorship. Like the first (and the last) oracle it ends with the recognition formula.

The third oracle, verses 9b–12, is formally not a separate oracle since no formulae accompany it, but in content and construction it must be. It is a demonstration oracle, with the 'because' clause in verse 9 based on verse 3b, and the 'therefore' clause in verses 10–12. It is subsequent to verses 1–9a since its language is based on them. It is a later accretion from the Ezekiel school. This is also true of verses 13–16, which are an expansion on verses 9b–12. By this time the traditionist has completely abandoned the figure and language of the first oracle. The oracle involves a mitigation of the punishment. The only allusion in this oracle, which is properly introduced by an introductory oracle formula, is to the second oracle in verse 16a (cf. verses 6b, 7).

1. This is the earliest of the oracles against Egypt, being dated January 587 B.C., thus about a year before Jerusalem's fall. The date in 26.1 is later, but the oracles against Egypt were grouped together by the editor.

2. For the formula, cf. 6.2; 21.2; 25.2; 28.21. For **Lord GOD,** as in verses 8, 13, and 16, cf. on 2.4. The original oracle was probably only against Pharaoh, as 32.2–8; the words **and against all Egypt** are an accretion by the traditionist responsible for the widening of the terms of reference of the poem.

3. speak: absent in G., probably a late gloss. So is **king of Egypt,** which may have been copied by error from verse 2. The word for **dragon** is anomalously *htnym* for *htnyn*, but it also occurs at 32.2. *htnym* means 'jackals'. The term is often used in a mythological sense as representing the principle of primeval chaos in the O.T., but here it is to be taken literally as the Nile dragon or crocodile. **streams** is plural of *y'r*, the Egyptian word for 'Nile', and refers to the Nile streams. Probably the singular should be read throughout (cf. verse 9). **lies** usually means 'crouches';

possibly 'lurks' would give the sense. MT has 'myself' for it in **I made it,** which is an impossible form. Pharaoh's sin is arrogance.

4. Both references to fish of the streams sticking to scales are secondary. The latest accretion, **which stick to your scales,** is absent in G. These accretions reinterpreted the original oracle to include all the people of Egypt along with Pharaoh. But a divine fisherman catching all the fish in the Nile is somewhat bizarre. Yahweh will hook the Pharaoh and draw him out of his Nile (for **streams,** cf. on verse 3; the plural was introduced by the traditionists). **your streams** (Nile) is an ironic reflection on Pharaoh's boast in verse 3.

5. Secondary is **you and all the fish of your streams. and buried** follows a minority reading for MT 'and collected', which can be interpreted in much the same sense; cf. the similar idiom 'and was gathered to his people' (Gen. 25.8). Pharaoh's corpse will be thrown out on the adjoining desert, there to be food for wild animals and birds. Such a fate was particularly horrible to an Egyptian king, who believed that his immortal well-being was conditional on proper burial in a sumptuous royal tomb.

6b. The second oracle condemns Egypt for its treachery in times of crisis. RSV rightly restores **you (have been)** with G.S. for MT 'they', which is a careless attempt to connect verse 6b with a. The figure of a reed staff is appropriate since it is easily broken. The prophet, however, uses another characteristic of the reed as well, viz. its splinter-like nature.

7. For **shoulders** G. rightly has 'hand'; the reed only affected the hand which grasped it. **with the hand** (for MT 'with your hand') is a copyist's dittograph. For the figure of a crumpled reed which pierces the hand of a man leaning on it, cf. 2 Kg. 18.21, which also applies the figure to Egypt. The original verse 7a may be rendered 'when they grasped you, you crumpled and broke open (lit., split) their whole hand'. **shake** is a correction of MT's 'stand' (cf. Ps. 69.23(MT 24)). Egypt cannot be relied on; she is treacherous.

8. The judgment oracle is an amalgam of stereotyped phrases. For **I . . . upon you,** cf. on 5.17; for **cut off . . . beast,** 14.13; for **desolation . . . waste,** 12.20.

9b. you said: with Versions. MT has 'he said', an attempt to link this oracle to the preceding. The traditionist reflects Pharaoh's saying in verse 3b.

10. utter waste: an attempt to render MT *lḥrbwt ḥrb,* a bound verbal noun with cognate modifier. Since this is a reflection on verse 8, MT may be the result of dittography and the original be *lḥrbh,* 'waste'. The location of **Migdol** (the Hebrew word for 'tower') is unknown, but it must be one of the frontier fortresses on the eastern Delta, since **Syene** is Aswan near the first cataract of the Nile, thus the southern border. The idiom **from Migdol to Syene** means 'from north to south'; cf. 'from Dan to Beersheba'. **Ethiopia** lay south of Aswan, but exactly where its northern borders were during the Saite period is not certain.

11. A predicted total devastation and depopulation of Egypt for forty years is envisaged. The notion of a forty-year punishment for Judah occurred in 4.6, and the same traditionist may be responsible for its application to Egypt.

12a. Almost the same words occur in 30.7, which is, however, in the passive, with the exception of the reference to forty years. In verse 12*b* the language of 12.15; 22.15 is applied to Egypt. She is to be exiled, a prophecy (cf. also Isa. 20) which was never fulfilled.

13. G.S.T. rightly omit **For.** Though this oracle is an expansion on the preceding it is hardly the basis for it. The repopulation of Egypt after a period of punishment must have been a popular prophetic notion at this time (cf. Jer. 46.26). Possibly in view of Egypt's role in salvation history, a restored Israel without an Egypt to the south was unthinkable.

14. For **restore the fortunes,** cf. on 16.53. **Pathros** is the Egyptian word *pa-to-resi*, 'the south land', referring to Upper Egypt, which is designated as **the land of their origin** (cf. on 16.3). The Saites ruled from the Delta in the north, but the writer maintains that the Egyptians originally came from Upper Egypt. Does this reflect an awareness of an earlier Theban rule in Egypt? The restored Egypt will be a small kingdom occupying Upper Egypt only. This will leave Lower Egypt unpopulated, a security against Egypt's ever becoming strong again.

16. it: the Versions all attest 'they', which seems original in view of the plural in the rest of the verse. The promise makes the situation described in verses 6*b*-7 impossible for the future. Israel's sin in the past had been turning to Egypt instead of to Yahweh for aid (cf. on 17.7). Egypt will be so humble a nation in the future that Israel will not be tempted as in the past. For **recalling their iniquity,** cf. 21.23-24(MT 28-29).

(b) NEBUCHADREZZAR'S COMPENSATION 29.17-21

This section is the latest dated oracle, April 571 B.C., after Nebuchadrezzar had lifted his thirteen-year siege against Tyre. Tyre had not been destroyed as Ezekiel had confidently expected, 26.7-14. None the less Nebuchadrezzar had been acting as the unconscious instrument of Yahweh's judgment. As payment for his work he is to receive Egypt as plunder.

The section contains both an oracle conclusion formula, verse 20, and a recognition formula, verse 21. Verse 21 is a later expansion interpreting Egypt's ruin as the time of restoration for Israel and of full recognition of the prophetic office. The original oracle in verses 18-20 was itself expanded by a late theologian by **because they worked for me** in verse 20, which is absent in G. and S.

18. For the spelling of **Nebuchadrezzar,** cf. on 26.7. **made bald, rubbed bare** reflect the result of carrying loads on head and shoulders. Precisely what kind of work was involved against the island fortress is not clear. Alexander the Great built a causeway from the mainland; did the Babylonians make an original attempt in this direction? In any event, the attempt failed.

19. For **Lord GOD,** as in verse 20, cf. on 2.4. G. omits **and he shall carry off its wealth,** which may be an expansion to make clear what the payment is to be. But the army's wages would be plunder, and the expansion is unnecessary. Nebuchadrezzar did invade Egypt in 568-567, claiming a victory, but how extensive the victory was is not known.

20. Clear from this is the fact that Yahweh is the ultimate arbiter of historical movement. Yahweh is giving to Nebuchadrezzar his wages which, since he had been sent against Tyre (26.7), he had coming to him.

21. horn is a symbol of strength (Ps. 92.10(MT 11)). **to spring forth** is lit. 'to sprout forth', a mixed figure. The promise has it that when Egypt is given to Nebuchadrezzar, Israel will receive new vigour. For the 'sprouting horn', cf. Ps. 132.17 where it refers to a descendant of David. The second promise is the opening of the prophet's lips; this has no connection with the sealing of his lips, 3.26–27 (cf. 24.27; 33.22), but rather to the authentication of the prophetic office through the fulfilment of prophecy (cf. Jer. 28.8–9).

(c) YAHWEH'S DAY FOR EGYPT 30.1–19

The oracles of Ezekiel against Egypt are all dated oracles except for this one, though the section introduction formula does occur. The oracle introduction formula occurs four times, verses 2, 6, 10, and 13. Conclusion formulae occur at verses 6, 8, 12, and 19. Since G. does not attest the introductory formula at verse 6, its secondary character might be suspected. Verse 5 is a prose catalogue identifying **Those who support Egypt** in verse 6 and is a later accretion. The formula at the beginning of verse 6 then became necessary. The excision of verse 5 and the formula presents a logical consecution. The first oracle is thus in verses 2–9. Verse 9 comes after the recognition formula in verse 8, is introduced by **On that day** (cf. 29.21), and is a later prose commentary on the helpers of verse 8. The first oracle is then left with two concluding formulae. Since verse 7 is a variant form of 29.12 it would seem that verses 7–8 come from the same traditionist. This leaves the original oracle to be found in verses 2–4, 6. Whether this is from Ezekiel or from his followers is uncertain.

The second oracle, verses 10–12, seems to be an elaboration based largely on chapter 29, especially added to show how Yahweh was to effect his day for Egypt. The mention of Nebuchadrezzar reflects the oracle of 29.17–21, whereas the drying up of the Nile reflects 29.9*b*–12 and thus reflects the school of Ezekiel. In view of the prediction of verse 10, the oracle must have been composed before Nebuchadrezzar's attack on Egypt in 568 B.C.

The last oracle, verses 13–19, is a learned but confused catalogue of various cities in Egypt which are judged in stylized phrases; cf. a similar list in Mic. 1.10–15. The order in which the list is given is in complete geographical disarray and betrays only a distant knowledge of Egypt. The particular judgments are unspecific as well, and betray the same kind of expansion as the list of verse 5

1. The fact that no date is given has led some scholars to deny any of verses 1–19 to Ezekiel. This by itself is hardly compelling.

2. For **Lord GOD**, as in verses 6, 10, 13, cf. on 2.4. G. omits **Wail**, but as an imperative it gives point to the next phrase, which is the content of the wailing.

3. is near, the day: a dittograph. RSV interprets 'the time' as **a time of doom.** It is in the light of 7.12 a good parallel for the day of Yahweh, and should not be changed to 'the end'; cf. G. For **the day of the LORD,** cf. chapter 7. Here it is interpreted as effecting the nations. For a **day of clouds,** cf. Jl 2.2; Zeph. 1.15.

4. G. omits the expansion **and her wealth is carried away.** This verse renders 'the day' more specific. Ethiopia is often paralleled with Egypt since, near the end of the eighth century, the Ethiopians consolidated their rule over Egypt and retained it until 663 B.C. (cf. Isa. 20.3–5).

5. Arabia is based on a revocalization of MT's 'mixed people', referring to people of mixed origins. Since it is preceded by **all,** MT is probably correct. **Libya** is based on a change of MT 'Kub' to 'Lub' supposedly on the basis of G. But G: *Libues* is the regular rendering of 'Put'. In fact, G. has a different list of four: Persians, Cretans, Lydians, and Libyans, the last two representing Lud and Put; cf. on 27.10, to which G. is closer than to MT here. What people 'Kub' represents is unknown. **people . . . league** is an attempt to interpret MT, but misses the meaning. MT has 'sons of the people of the covenant', which can only mean Israelites, probably those who had at various times settled in Egypt. **them** refers to the people of Egypt.

6. For **proud might,** cf. 7.24. For **from . . . Syene,** cf. on 29.10.

7. she, a correction with G. of MT 'they'. **her cities** must be correct for MT's inexplicable 'his cities'. For the verse, cf. 29.12.

8. set fire to: submitted to the ravages of warfare; cf. e.g. Am. 1.4. For **helpers broken,** cf. verse 6.

9. swift: based on G.S.; but MT has 'in ships' which is fully possible in view of Isa. 18.2; then the ships would be heading up the Nile. **from me** is a theological accretion lacking in G. G. also omits **unsuspecting,** which may be correct. There is no textual basis for **doom**; MT has 'on the day of Egypt'; cf. 'the day of Midian' in Isa. 9.4(MT 3) for a parallel. The subject of **it comes** is indefinite and not 'day', as RSV might imply. The Ethiopians will, because of their close association with Egypt, share in the terrors of the day of judgment.

10. For the spelling of **Nebuchadrezzar,** cf. on 26.7. Cf. commentary on 29.19 for the verse.

11. For **the most terrible of the nations,** cf. 28.7, where Babylon is also thus described but without being identified. The verse is an adaptation of 28.7; only the conclusion **fill . . . slain** is new, for which cf. 9.7; 35.8.

12. the Nile is plural in MT and should be rendered 'Nile streams'. G. omits **and will . . . men**; the clause is a doublet of the next sentence. This verse insists on Yahweh being the actual subject of the judgment, whereas the Babylonians (**foreigners**) are his instrument.

13. It is doubtful whether this verse originally intended any reference to idols. G. has 'great men', *'ylym*, for **images,** *'lylym,* and the plural for **prince** in the next line. This makes an excellent parallel. The other lines of the oracle in the verse are an accretion. The original read: 'I will put an end to the chieftains of Memphis and there shall be no more princes in the land of Egypt.' Memphis lies 16 miles S. of Cairo. It was the capital of united Egypt during the Old Kingdom, but was afterwards eclipsed, though it remained an important centre. For most of dynastic history Memphis remained Egypt's largest city. For anarchy as a form of judgment, cf. Isa. 3.1–5.

14. G.S.V. have 'land of Pathros'; cf. on 29.14, where the full expression also occurs. **Zoan** is probably better known as Avaris, the capital of the Hyksos, and known in Greek as Tanis. It lay in the eastern part of the Delta and may be the same as the Raamses of Exod. 1.11; modern *Ṣān el-Hajar*. **Thebes** was undoubtedly Egypt's most important city for most of Egypt's dynastic history after *c.* 2000 B.C. until its destruction by the Assyrians *c.* 662 B.C. It was in Upper Egypt, the political capital during the Middle Kingdom and Empire Periods and the centre of Amon worship. G. rendered it as 'city of Zeus' due to Greek equation of Amon and Zeus (cf. Nah. 3.8).

15. For **Thebes** G. has 'Memphis', i.e. *np* for *n'*. **Pelusium** was an old fortress in the north-east corner of the Delta, modern *el-Faramā*, 1 mile from the Mediter- ranean and less than 20 miles from Suez. G. simply transliterates Hebrew *syn* by *sain*. Its designation as Egypt's stronghold may be due to its location.

16. Here Hebrew *syn* does not stand for **Pelusium,** but, as G. well understood, is 'Syene', i.e. Aswan, on the extreme southern border of Upper Egypt above Thebes (cf. on 29.10). A third mention of Thebes is monotonous. G. must have been right in verse 15, cf. *ad loc.* **and its . . . down** is based on an unsupported emendation proposed by Cornill. MT has 'and as for Memphis distresses daily (to her)', which is no clearer in Hebrew than in English. MT has *wnp ṣry ywmm*. G. has 'and waters will be spread about', i.e. *wnprṣw mym*, but this makes no sense at Thebes, which is far up the Nile. Could *ywmm* be a corruption of *mwsd* or *yswd* and the original have been 'and the foundation breached' (*nprṣ*)?

17. On (not 'iniquity' as vocalized by Masoretes) was Heliopolis, 6 miles NE. of Cairo near modern *Maṭariyah*. It was the centre of sun worship, as its Greek name implies. It was more important as a religious than as a political centre. The city was destroyed by Cambyses. **Pibeseth** is better known by its Greek name Bubastos, modern *Tell Basta*, about 40 miles NE. of Cairo. It was the capital of the 22nd and 23rd Dynasties (cf. Herodotus, II, 60). The last clause can hardly be original in the text. MT does not have **the women** but 'they', feminine without antecedent. This must be a variant text based on the last clause in verse 18.

18. shall be dark is based on the Versions, but MT points as 'shall withhold'. **dominion** is based on a revocalization of MT 'yoke bars', which is unnecessary. **Tehaphnehes,** or Tahpanhes, was the place to which Johanan ben Kareah and other rebels along with the unwilling Jeremiah fled after the murder of Gedaliah (Jer. 43.7). It is to be identified with modern *Tell Defneh* on the Suez in northern Egypt. The site became important in the seventh century and remained such as a frontier station on the route from Syria. The geographical knowledge of the writer is obviously not profound. Though the important cities are in the main mentioned some were already destroyed; a few were in the south, and most, as would be expected, were in the Delta. But the list is in complete disarray, flitting from Upper Egypt to Tanis, and from Pelusium to Thebes.

(d) THE BROKEN ARM OF PHARAOH 30.20-26

This section is dated almost three months later than the first. It is constructed somewhat like 29.17–21, but in unusual fashion. Instead of the common imperative after the term of address, Ezekiel is informed of what Yahweh has done to Pharaoh. The oracle that follows is introduced with **Therefore** and the introductory formula, but no 'because' clause precedes it. The oracle that follows has two formal conclusions, both recognition formulae, verses 25, 26, as well as numerous doublets. Verse 23 is repeated in verse 26; 24aα equals verse 25aα; verse 22aγ finds its parallel in verse 24bα; quite similar are verses 22b and 25aβ. It would appear that an originally short account has been successively expanded.

Clearly verse 21 must be tied to the original date. It mentions a specific action on Yahweh's part, probably the defeat of Hophra when he proceeded against the Babylonians who were besieging Jerusalem (Jer. 37.5). The oracle in verses 22–26 is in the form of a judgment oracle, but was it originally related to verse 21? Verse 22 can hardly be an application of verse 21, since Yahweh says that he will break the arms of Pharaoh, but in verse 21 the arm has already been broken. Verse 23 interrupts the argument and is an expansion subsequent to verse 22. Verse 24 does follow verse 22, continuing the theme of the broken arms and the arming of Nebuchadrezzar. Verse 25 is a doublet expansion except for the recognition formula, whereas verse 26 introduces the dispersion of the Egyptians, which is, as in verse 23, quite foreign to the oracle as a whole.

To reconstruct, verses 20–21 constitute a single oracle. What was probably a completely separate oracle from Ezekiel but related in theme is embedded in verses 22 and 24, possibly ending in a recognition formula, though this is pure surmise. Verse 23 is a later expansion, and so are respectively verses 25 and 26. The editor was then responsible for joining the two because of the recurrence of the same figures, and made the dated oracle the basis of the judgment oracle by adding 'therefore' at the beginning of verse 22.

20. The oracle is dated April 587 B.C.

21. G. omits the late gloss **by binding it.** Verse 21b might then be rendered: 'And lo, it has not been tied up to promote healing, with a bandage to keep it firm so that he may hold on to the sword.' Hophra was badly defeated in his attempt to push back the Babylonians in 588 B.C. and his military wounds are such that he is not able to come to Jerusalem's aid once again. The utterance is a warning to the exiles against any false hopes.

22. For **Lord GOD,** cf. on 2.4. **both . . . broken** is a secondary expansion attempting to link this oracle with the preceding. Originally this oracle simply referred to Pharaoh's arms. The date of this oracle may be much later than that of verse 21, possibly as late as that of 29.17–20. To make the sword fall means to render militarily impotent.

23. For the stereotyped clauses, cf. 20.23; 29.12b.

24. For verse 24b G. has: 'and he will bring it against Egypt and plunder it and despoil it', based on 29.8–9, 19, showing a different stage in the tradition. The king of Babylon will be Yahweh's instrument for war against Pharaoh, wielding Yahweh's sword.

25. A doublet of verse 24; cf. on verse 23.

(e) THE DOWNFALL OF THE COSMIC TREE **31.1–18**

This chapter contains a poem, verses 2b–9, and two prose interpretations, verses 10–14 and 15–18. The poem may well in its original form have been an independent one which began in verse 3, the form of which has received some accretions. In view of such an independent poem about a cosmic tree being taken over by the prophet the usual introductory oracle formula would not be employed, but simply a question, **Whom are you like in your greatness?**, attached to the beginning, which line is then the only one of the poem originally by Ezekiel. The interpretations are, however, oracles, and accordingly formulae do occur at verses 10 and 15.

The poem began simply, 'Lo, a pine tree with beautiful branches and of great height with its top in the clouds.' For the text of verse 3, cf. below. Probably secondary is verse 5, which begins with 'therefore' which seems odd in a purely descriptive poem. The verse also contains two Aramaic words in a poem which is otherwise good Hebrew, both of which occur in their Hebrew equivalents in the original poem. Most of verse 9 is also later. The final clause **that . . . God** may be an explanatory gloss, stating the obvious. **I made it beautiful** is a theological adaptation added late in the text history, since G. does not yet have it. **in the mass of its branches** is a variant text to verse 7aβ copied into the text at the wrong place.

The myth of the cosmic tree was widespread throughout antiquity; cf. 17.23; 19.11 for possible allusions to it. It stood in the centre of the earth with its top in the heavens and its roots watered by the primeval waters below the earth. It towered above all other trees. All birds nested in its foliage; animals were sheltered by it as well as all mankind. The myth is clearly related to that of the tree of life in the garden of Eden (Gen. 3.22–24). The poem compares other trees, cedars, firs, and plane trees, in the divine garden with it to its favour.

The poem is only germane in the context of an oracle against Pharaoh and his multitude by the addition of verse 2b and some kind of interpretation. Of the two formally introduced interpretations, only the first, verses 10–14, comes into question. The second is much more distant from the poem with its introduction of Sheol and its inhabitants, a theme based on 32.17–32. The mixture of figures—the trees of Eden go down to the nether world—betrays a much later stage in tradition history than verses 10–14 which takes the poem and applies it to the Egypt situation. Within this section verse 14, with its peculiar syntax and its introduction of the theme of universal mortality, is an expansion. Verse 11b is also secondary, the last verb probably being a marginal word summary. The 'because' clause in verse 10 and verse 11 begins the judgment. The original oracle is then to be found in verses 10, 11a, 12–13.

Like Isa. 14 the poem as well as the oracles are in past tense. RSV's attempt to render the tense of the oracles as prophetic future is based on a faulty understanding of the literary form. These are written in the lament rather than the judgment oracle form, and the verbs in verses 11–13, 15–17 should all be rendered in past tense.

1. The date is June 587.

2. multitude also occurs in the final statement in verse 18. The question is closely tied to the interpretation in verse 10: **your greatness** is there judged as **its heart was proud of its height.**

3. MT has 'Assyria' for **I will liken you to,** which can hardly be right. Read 'pine' as in 27.6, i.e. *t'šwr* for *'šwr.* **a cedar in Lebanon** was then a secondary explanation of the word. G. does not have **and forest shade,** a late addition. '*bwtym* **(clouds),** also in verses 10, 14; elsewhere it means 'boughs', but here must mean 'clouds'. Usually the plural is simply '*bwt,* but to the feminine plural suffix a further masculine plural suffix is added.

4. MT has 'going' for **making flow,** which in view of the *'t* construction after it is impossible. The verb must be transitive as G. *mt'h* **(its planting)** must be vocalized with a 3rd masc. singular suffix; otherwise 'its' will refer to **deep. waters** and **deep** refer to the cosmic subterranean waters. The 'its' in **its streams** as in **its rivers** refers to the 'deep'. **streams** usually means 'channels' and some have tried to interpret the poem as directly alluding to the Nile streams, but this is to misunderstand the nature of the original poem which merely describes the cosmic tree. The waters of chaos, 'surging deep', 'many waters', 'the abyss', 'the Sea', were the waters below, which could issue earthward through fountains; cf. Gen. 7.11, where these are contrasted with the windows of heaven.

5. its boughs grew large, in its shoots may be late glosses; both are absent from G. **boughs** and **towered** are Aramaic in MT. The verse adds nothing new though it renders explicit what is clearly implicit in the poem. **in its shoots** is based on a correction of MT's *bšlḥw,* 'when it sends forth', to *bšlḥyw.*

6. dwelt, correction of MT: 'will dwell'. S. does not render the impossible **all** after 'dwelt'. RSV has tried to make sense by interpreting 'many nations' as **great nations,** but this is not what *gwym rbym* means. The verse extends the description of the protection offered by the tree in 17.23 to include under its shade many nations. This is also illustrated by its use as a place for animals producing offspring. The description of the tree strongly influenced Dan. 4.10–12(MT 7–9).

7. abundant waters: subterranean waters; cf. on verse 4. The poem insists that the chaotic deep, otherwise often a symbol of evil in the world, is here harnessed to good ends producing the tree of great beauty and size.

8. The tree is incomparable, which reflects ironically on the preposed question in verse 2b. For **garden of God,** cf. on 28.13. In Gen. 3 Eden is also filled with trees, but for food, not for stateliness.

9. For the text, cf. above. The original poem ended with a reference to the jealousy of the trees in Eden. It emphasized the water as responsible for the beauty of the tree. A later traditionist corrected this pagan thought by adding Yahweh as creator of the tree's beauty. A 1st person reference was not part of the poem.

10. For **Lord GOD,** as in verses 15, 18, cf. on 2.4. The poem by itself would be meaningless as applied to Pharaoh, and scholars who find Ezekiel's words only in the poetic part of this chapter have tried to find some poetic original in verses 10–18 recounting the fall of the tree. When it is seen that the original oracle is not the poem itself, but is rather in the interpreting oracles, there is no need to look for poetry at all. This verse is introduced by **Therefore** since the point of the comparison (verse 2b) now needs explication. The oracle is all in the 3rd person, except for verse 10a, which is anomalously in direct address; this must be an error and RSV rightly follows S.V. The interpretation is, perforce, not always fully clear, because the poem used by Ezekiel was not an allegorical composition. Thus Pharaoh is judged because of his height—this uses the imagery of the poem. But the real accusation lies in the last clause, i.e. his **proud heart,** something which the prophet had to drag in from outside the poem. For pride of a foreign ruler as the reason for judgment, cf. 28.17; Isa. 14.13–14.

11. Render 'I gave it . . .'. The oracle uses the past tense of the lament. Verse 11b is in the imperfect aspect, which shows its secondary character. The addition was made in order to castigate the Pharaoh more severely as getting his just deserts; he was wicked. **a mighty one** is lit. 'a ram', then by extension 'chieftain, leader, mighty one'; cf. on 'images' at 30.13. The reference is to Nebuchadrezzar.

12. Read past tense here and in verse 13. **go from** does not render *yrdw*, but rather *yddw*. RSV follows MT punctuation, but it is better to take **on the mountains** with the preceding verb. For **Foreigners . . . nations,** cf. on 28.7; cf. also 30.10–11. Throughout the oracles against the nations these terms refer to the Babylonians. Destruction on mountains, valleys, watercourses recurs together with hills at 6.3; 35.8, 36.4, 6, and means 'everywhere'. The abandonment of the tree is reflected in this verse, and verse 13 reflects verse 6 of the poem.

14. *'sy mym,* **trees by the waters,** reflects a corruption by dittography. It was originally *'sym,* 'trees'. RSV correctly interprets *'lyhm* as **to them,** whereas MT vocalizes as 'their gods'. The expansion of verse 14a is a parenetic application showing that the fall of the cosmic tree will serve as an example to all other trees not to grow to such heights. Verse 14b is a later accretion based on verses 15–18. All are mortal; cf. on verses 17–18.

15. RSV rightly follows G. in omitting 'I have covered' and reading the last word as **shall faint.** The verbs are all past in this oracle until verse 18b. For the descent to Sheol, cf. on 32.17–32. Sheol is the place of the dead. The fall of the tree is now changed to that of descent into the grave. The deep and its streams as representing the evil powers naturally grieve at the death of Egypt. The fall of Egypt also creates gloom in Lebanon, the house of great trees. Throughout Yahweh is the agent of both the fall and of the universal distress caused by it.

16. and best: a late gloss omitted by G. Verse 16a speaks of the fear engendered in the nations by the fall, whereas the scene in b is laid in the nether world, to which the trees of Eden have gone. Possibly G. shows an earlier version by omitting **nether,** in which case the apparent inconsistency is removed. On the other hand, verse 17 locates all these in Sheol as well. In any event, here the trees are comforted by the fall of Egypt, whereas in verse 15 they are in gloom. Verse 16*b* seems to represent a further accretion to the text.

17. Verse 17*b* represents a corrupt text. MT has 'its arm they dwelt in its shadow among the nations'. The corruption was early and the Versions are no help. The corruption lies in *zr'w yšbw*, 'its arm they dwelt'. If this be read as *gd'w* (Pu'al) *yšby* good sense is obtained. Render: 'Those who dwelt in its shadow were hewn down among the nations.' In other words, all men including those who sat in Egypt's shadow (cf. verse 6) are designated for Sheol.

18. thus is a copyist's error. Delete, with G. and a minority reading. Verse 18*a* reflects the introductory question in verse 2*b*, but now the comparison is to the trees of Eden. For the **uncircumcised** and the **slain by the sword** as inhabitants of Sheol, Eissfeldt suggests reasonably the meaning of the young and the slain (in *Studies in O.T. Prophecy presented to Prof. T. H. Robinson*, 71–81). The subscription reflects the imperative of the introduction in verse 2*a* and applies the chapter to Pharaoh and his people, something not at all evident from the composition itself.

(f) A LAMENT OVER PHARAOH 32.1–16

This section is formally a collection of six parts, as the occurrence of the introductory oracle formulae in verses 3, 11, and of oracle conclusion formulae at verses 8, 14, and 16 as well as the recognition formula in verse 15 shows. These are then verses 2, 3–8, 9–10, 11–14, 15, and 16. The section is introduced as a dated section, cf. 29.1, 17; 31.1 and 32.17, and orders the prophet to raise a lament, as 27.1; 28.11. But the actual lament form continues only through verse 2, which is characterized formally by the use of the past tense and a certain type of metre; cf. on chapter 19 for characteristics of the dirge. But the lament commemorates some calamity, whereas verse 2 simply describes the action of the dragon.

The second part is an oracle of judgment on the dragon, but clearly connects with the lament fragment in verse 2. Characteristic of both parts is the use of mythological concepts and language. The word for **dragon** is the same as that of 29.3, and some of the idioms are similar; but it is not now the crocodile of the Nile but rather the dragon of the seas, i.e. the mythological symbol for primeval chaos which rules in the primeval waters. The judgment, too, is in cosmic terms. The carcass will be fed upon by all the beasts of the earth; valleys will be filled with its outflow, land drenched with its blood, etc. Its defeat will be accompanied by supernatural darkness, a phenomenon usually descriptive of the day of Yahweh.

The original section is to be found in these first two parts and may be interpreted as the fragment of a lament with an oracle of judgment accompanying it as a commentary, thereby giving point to the lament. For small accretions to the text, cf. below.

The third part, verses 9–10, abandons the figure of the dragon completely; it is a prosaic commentary on the reaction of nations to Egypt's exile. Its lack of connection and change of style identify it as a later accretion. Verses 11–14 are presented formally as an oracle but are also an expansion. It introduces Nebuchadrezzar as the instrument of Yahweh's judgment on Egypt (cf. 29.19–20; 30.24). Its addition here is conditioned both by the mention of **sword** in verse 10 and the original section. Mention is made of **many waters,** not in a mythological sense as in verse 2 but now as referring to **their waters,** i.e. the waters of Egypt, the Nile. The Nile will be stilled, though not because of the destruction of the dragon, but rather by the destruction of the cattle of the Egyptians, who will thus be unable to muddy its water any more. Verse 15 is a tradition subsequent to verses 10–14 since it presupposes the desolation caused by Yahweh's judgment through the Babylonians. The traditionist ties this judgment to the recognition formula. The subscription in verse 16 is particularly verbose and incorrectly identifies all of the preceding as a lament. Subscriptions also occur in Ezek. 19.14 and 31.18; this one is editorial, recapitulating the original injunction to the prophet in the introduction to the section, verse 2a.

1. The date is given as March 585 B.C., whereas the next section is earlier. A minority reading followed by G.S. reads 'eleventh' for **twelfth** year and is probably original. Thus the lament would date March 586.

2. On **dragon,** cf. commentary on 29.3. **you consider yourself** renders *ndmyt,* which never occurs as Ni. elsewhere. It is rather the homonym: 'you are destroyed'. This rendering is also made more likely by the fact that this is a lament. **lion** is then vocative. The reference to lion is anomalous and RSV has introduced a contrast with the next line which is unjustified. Ezekiel is fond of animal symbols for royalty: lions, chapter 19; eagles, chapter 17; crocodile, chapter 29. **seas** are the primeval waters of chaos. **you burst forth in your rivers** equals MT. By the change of *bnhrwtyk* to *bnḥryk* the sense is much improved; the clause then reads 'you snorted with your nostrils', as in Job 41.20(MT 12). The last two verbs in RSV must be in past tense as in MT. The cosmic dragon has muddied the primeval waters.

3. For **Lord GOD,** as in verses 8, 11, 14, and 16, cf. on 2.4. **with . . . peoples** is a secondary accretion which reinterprets the divine net as the Babylonians, which is not the point here at all. After the addition of the phrase, MT further adapted the text to the accretion by changing **And I** (as still in G.V.) to 'and they', thus referring this to the **many peoples.** The subject throughout the oracle of judgment is 1st person. In 12.13; 17.20, the divine net is to catch Zedekiah, but here in a mixed figure the dragon. In the *Enuma elish* Marduk also catches Tiamat in a net; thus the figure is well established in the language of myth. **dragnet** is used in Ezek. 26.5, 14; 47.10, of the fisherman's net only.

4. beasts of the whole earth: better is the minority reading followed by G.S. 'all the beasts of the earth'. Verse 4a is reminiscent of 29.5, and verse 4b of 31.13. The dragon at home in the waters will lie as an abandoned carcass on the dry ground where its carrion will feed the wild animals.

5. your carcass is an attempt to make sense out of the obscure *rmwtk* which occurs only here. The root 'to be high' is well known. Sym. has 'your worms', based on the same Hebrew consonants, as S.V., which by a dubious extension might produce RSV. It might be better to emend the word to *mmwt(y)k,* 'your slain (body, or members)'; cf. 2 Kg. 11.2 and also 28.8. For **mountains, valleys,**

and **watercourses** (verse 6), cf. on 31.12. The extravagant language of this and the next verse shows an intense bitterness against Egypt.

6. flowing is a noun, and **blood** is an explanatory gloss on the unusual word. The word in Hebrew means 'your outflow'; of course, blood is meant. **even . . . mountains** is probably an accretion. If the figure of the overflow of the Nile is at all in mind, the accretion is inappropriate, but probably only the terrible end of the dragon is meant. It is obvious that no ordinary dragon is intended!

7. The Hebrew expresses no 'I' in **when I blot you out**; the subject is impersonal and it would be more correctly rendered by a passive construction. The verb means 'to quench', usually of fire, but in Isa. 43.17 also of the death of army personnel, i.e. extinction of life. The figures employed here and in verse 8 are more typical of apocalyptic writings. Supernatural darkness was the next to the last plague in Egypt (Exod. 10.21–23), and this might seem appropriate here in a judgment on Egypt. Though not mentioned, it does reflect the description of the day of Yahweh (cf. Am. 5.18, 20; Zeph. 1.15; Jl 2.2, 10).

8. A summary of verse 7. **bright lights** is lit. 'the luminaries of light', which in spite of P's restrictive use in Gen. 1.14–16 to sun and moon here includes also the stars.

9. captive follows G. for MT 'destruction', i.e. šbyk for šbrk, lit. '(when I bring) your captivity'. The reference here is to Egypt as a whole, not to Pharaoh. For **trouble** in its more usual meaning 'provoke to anger', cf. 8.17. For Egypt going into exile, cf. 29.12.

10. For the reaction of peoples at the fall of a nation, cf. 26.15–18; 27.28–32; 28.19. **brandish** lit. 'make fly back and forth'. For **every moment**, cf. 26.16.

11. king of Babylon: Nebuchadrezzar. The tradition is thus prior to 568 B.C.; cf. on 29.19.

12. mighty ones is lit. 'warriors', and **most terrible among the nations** is a favoured description in the oracles against the nations for the Babylonian army, 28.7; 30.11; 31.12. The **pride of Egypt** lay in its strength, cf. 30.6, 18, represented by its **multitude**, verses 16, 18, 20; 30.10, 15; 31.2, 18.

13. many waters must mean the Nile. Egypt will be completely desolated; all its people exiled and its cattle (rather than **beasts**) destroyed, cf. 29.11–12.

14. With no cattle to disturb it the Nile will settle so that its waters are clear. The antecedent of **their rivers** is 'many waters' of verse 13; the rivers must then be the Nile streams.

15. A theologically oriented conclusion with the recognition formula is the end purpose of the judgment. For **desolate,** cf. 29.10, 12; 30.7, 12. **is stripped** should be 'is made desolate', intentionally used to echo the first clause.

16. To 'chant' is a denominative verb from 'a lament', and should be rendered 'lament'. **daughters** are mentioned since women usually performed the role of mourning (Jer. 9.17–18(MT 16–17)). The subscription comes from a traditionist who no longer used 'lament' as a technical word.

(g) EGYPT'S DESCENT INTO HADES 32.17-32

This final oracle against Egypt is unique in the book of Ezekiel in that it is called a 'wailing'. Unfortunately this is the only clearly attested illustration of such a mourning song in O.T. The word occurs in 2.10 along with two synonyms filling the scroll, front and back, which the prophet in his commission was commanded to eat. The mourning song is not to be confused with the lament, for which cf. on 19.1. The lament has a clearly defined form quite different from that which is found in this section. The section contains, apart from the usual introduction, two oracle conclusion formulae, verses 31, 32, which, however, are apparently part of expansions to the original text. The only formal characteristic which this mourning song betrays is the fact that the song as a whole is told in the 3rd person with a concluding application in direct address, verse 28.

The text of the song is extremely corrupt and has been heavily commented on by later traditionists. The original ending of the song must have been verse 28. Three nations of antiquity are portrayed as being at rest in Sheol. A similar end is depicted for Egypt. A later traditionist has added a similar reference for certain contemporary groups, viz. Edom, the princes of the north, and the Sidonians. Their later character is betrayed by their departure from the terms used in the original song. Accordingly Edom is blamed for her **might,** and the Phoenicians have **gone down in shame with the slain.** Verse 31 represents a still later accretion with its reference to Pharaoh. The original song refers only to the **multitude of Egypt.** Verse 32 betrays its secondary character by its 1st person reference. MT has, 'For I spread his terror . . .'. The traditionist was attempting to assure Yahweh's role as ultimate actor in world events. For accretions within the song itself, cf. below.

If the detailed commentary below is correct, this section is a primary document for understanding the Israelite conception of Sheol. Sheol is portrayed as in charge of the 'mighty heroes', verse 21. These mighty heroes apparently have helpers; their function is not stated. Possibly the positions of the various nations in Sheol is under their control.

The three nations listed as resident in Sheol are Assyria, Elam, and Meshech/Tubal. These are said to be among the **uncircumcised** and the **slain by the sword,** i.e. the dishonoured. Lods (*Comptes Rendus*, 1943, 271-83) has shown that 'uncircumcised' is probably a technical term for infants who have died prematurely, and thus barred from burial in the family tomb by reason of lack of circumcision, whereas the term 'those slain by the sword' is a technical term for all those who have been killed by violence (cf. on 31.18). The nations listed are thus united in their being interred among the dishonourably dead.

That this interpretation is correct is apparent from the contrast between the position of those buried in the midst of the uncircumcised and those slain by the sword, and that of the ancient heroes, verse 27, with whom these nations do not lie. The heroes' interment is described as being an honourable warrior's burial, i.e. with their weapons and shields. In contrast to the theme of Job 3.13-19, distinctions do apply in the grave. This is a common Israelite conception implied in such phrases as 'go down in peace to Sheol', or 'being gathered up to one's fathers'.

17. MT lacks **in the first month,** which is based on G. The date is April 586 B.C.

18. The verse makes little sense and represents a corrupt text. MT has 'make him bring her down', with no antecedent for 'him'. And who can the 'daughters of nations' be? **daughters of** is probably a copyist's error which crept in on the basis of verse 16, where it makes good sense. By a simple change of *whwrdhw* to *whwrdw* the verse becomes sensible. The relevant part can then be rendered: 'Majestic nations have brought her down to the nether world.' The mourning song thus begins with a dirge over Egypt's fate. Her nationhood is at an end; like other ancient peoples she now lies dead in the regions of Sheol. **to (those)** is based on a minority reading; MT has 'with', which also makes good sense.

19. The first three words of verse 20 in MT must be added to verse 19, i.e. 'among those slain by the sword'. The words are directly addressed to the multitude of Egypt. G. has changed the verse order, placing verse 19 in the middle of verse 21. This, though unnecessary, is based on the proper intuition that the content of the verb **speak** is found in that verse. Like the concluding oracle formula, the content precedes the statement that it is spoken. The first line is ironic—Egypt is no better than others; she too must lie in a dishonourable grave.

20. This is almost completely corrupt. Once 'among those slain by the sword' was removed from verse 19, it needed something to modify and a scribe added the verb **they shall fall.** The remainder of the verse is also later. **sword** is a dittograph; the remainder is a corruption of 'and they made a bed with her and all her multitude', a doublet text to part of verse 25a, badly copied and by error inserted here.

21. That this verse gives the source of the words of verse 19 is still clear from the first word 'they shall speak', which must not be changed to 'and they shall speak'. **mighty chiefs** is the plural of the Messianic title 'Mighty God' given the child in Isa. 9.6 (MT 5), and could be rendered 'mighty gods' just as correctly. The term may well have originated in a much earlier time as a reference to the gods, but in Israelite monotheism such a reference was impossible and the position of such 'lesser gods' had to be downgraded. Thus *bny 'lhym*, 'the gods', was reinterpreted to mean 'angels'. The 'mighty gods' were demoted as well to a position in Hades where they might hold at least in popular thought limited sway. These rulers in the nether world apparently also had assistants. The antecedent of **them** is the multitude of Egypt. Verse 21b is really a thematic statement of the song, almost a title. It was probably originally a marginal aid showing the theme of the song which was later copied into the text. As a theme it is well stated; it says, 'The uncircumcised, those slain by the sword have come down, have laid down.'

22. their graves round about her: MT has 'around it its graves', which should be read as in verses 23 and 24 as 'is round about her grave'. **fallen:** rightly with a minority reading for MT 'those fallen'. Assyria is mentioned first since it represents most vividly that ancient nation who lived by violence. The memory of her terror spread among the nations was still alive in the prophetic writings, especially in Isaiah.

23. and her company . . . sword is a dittograph from verse 22, with *wyhy* added to make sense. Specifically of Assyria is it said that her graves are in the **uttermost parts,** i.e. the position of greatest dishonour (cf. Isa. 14.15).

24. Elam lay to the east of Babylon, with its capital at Susa. It was subdued by Ashurbanipal *c.* 650 B.C., and though Jer. 49.35–39 still speaks of Elam as a great power to be destroyed, for all practical purposes as an independent power she could rightly be described as dead. Secondary to the original song are the words **who went . . . world,** as can be seen both from its syntactic position (two relative clauses juxtaposed) and its reinterpretation of the term **uncircumcised** not in the technical sense employed throughout but in a literal sense.

25. G. has omitted all but **they are placed among the slain** because of parablepsis. The verse is largely repetitious and parts are probably secondary. Phrases based on verse 24 must be secondary, i.e. **with all her multitude, their graves round about her, for terror of them was spread in the land of the living, and they bear their shame . . . Pit.** Probably only **They have made her a bed among the slain, all of them uncircumcised, slain by the sword** is original.

26. RSV has added **and** between **Meshech** and **Tubal,** but this is wrong since the pronominal suffixes in the verse are in the singular. Tubal is probably secondary and should be omitted. For Meshech, cf. on 27.13. For **their graves round about them,** cf. on verse 22. In contrast to chapters 38–39, Meshech is here defined as a 'dead' nation, probably because in contrast to the past they no longer gave trouble.

27. of old rightly with G. for MT 'from the uncircumcised'. **shields** is based on an emendation proposed by Cornill reading *ṣntm* for MT '*wntm*, 'their iniquities', which must be corrupt. The Consonantal Text for **fallen** might better be read as 'Nephilim' (cf. Gen. 6.4), who were known as 'mighty men that were of old'. Verse 27a could then be rendered: 'And they do not lie with mighty men, (the) Nephilim of old.' These were the renowned heroes of antiquity who were, in contrast to Assyria, Elam, and Meshech, buried in honour. Such honourable interment accorded the ancient worthies involved burial with the panoply of the warrior. Secondary to the verse is the last clause **for . . . living,** which was thoughtlessly added by a traditionist who brought the lot of the ancient heroes into line with the others. Because of this expansion G. misunderstood the verse and omitted the negative, which upsets the whole point being made.

28. G. rightly omits **you shall be broken and** as a doublet on 'you shall lie'. The mourning song is now applied to Egypt. She too will be buried in dishonour.

29. For **Edom,** cf. on 25.12–14. **with those** rightly following a minority reading for MT 'and with those'. The traditionist who added Edom to the list uses the traditional refrains, but his hand is betrayed by his substitution of **princes** for 'multitude', and **might** for 'terror', as well as by a different spelling of the Hebrew word for **there** (as verse 30). The doublet **her kings** is probably secondary to the tradition. Hatred for Edom undoubtedly inspired the addition.

30. MT has 'every Sidonian' instead of the minority reading of the plural, which is to be preferred. In view of its conjunction with the Sidonians **The princes of**

the north must refer to the Phoenician regents in general, possibly those of Tyre in particular. For **uncircumcised** read 'with the uncircumcised'; the word *'t* must have fallen out; Phoenicians were circumcised, and the reference here is to dishonourable burial. As in the case of Edom these are not nations of antiquity but contemporary states which are pictured as already in Sheol.

31. G. omits the late explanatory gloss **Pharaoh and . . . sword.** For **Lord GOD**, as in verse 32, cf. on 2.4. The notion that Pharaoh will comfort himself when he sees his companions in Sheol is paralleled somewhat in 31.16. The consolation apparently consists of noting that he is not the only one suffering this fate.

32. A second conclusion by a traditionist who did not wish to have the mourning song ending with Pharaoh comforting himself. MT has the first verb in the 1st person; the author insists that Yahweh is the director of history even though that history be one of Egyptian terror. Literally MT has, 'For I have set his terror in the land of the living.' The 'his' refers to Pharaoh. The next clause is a simple result clause.

THIRD SECTION **33.1-39.29** PROPHECIES OF RESTORATION

A. THE PROPHET AS WATCHMAN **33.1-20**

Chapter 33 begins another major section of the book, a section comprising oracles of hope to the disconsolate exiles. Jerusalem has fallen; the predictions of chapters 1–24 have all taken place. At the end of the first book the editor collected and placed the oracles against the nations, chapters 25–32. The last book also is a distinct unit, and the editor has intentionally introduced it by a delineation of the prophetic office under the figure of a watchman. The section has close parallels in 3.16–21; 14.12–23; and chapter 18. The first of these was an editorial extraction based almost literally on verses 7–9. That it is purely secondary at 3.16–21 was argued *ad loc*, whereas here it is germane to the argument. The second is related only in that it deals with the individual and his lot, whereas chapter 18 has many points of contact with this section, since the theme of verses 10–20 is identical with that of chapter 18. In fact, it seems likely that verses 10–20 are literally based on chapter 18, and may simply be the editor's extraction from that chapter here as a fitting conclusion to the description of the prophetic office. Thus verse 15 lists only two of the details descriptive of the life of the repentant wicked in 18.14–18 (cf. on chapter 18).

The section consists of five parts, the first four being introduced by the vocative 'Son of man', verses 2, 7, 10, 12, and the last a reflection on the people's objections to Yahweh's ways, verses 17–20. The first two, verses 2–9, constitute a larger whole, since verses 2–6 reflect on the responsibility of a watchman to warn a city in times of danger, and verses 7–9 apply this general observation to Ezekiel as the prophetic watchman for the house of Israel. If part of this section is original it must be these verses.

The remainder of the section is probably based on chapter 18. It abandons the figure of the watchman and is a disputation on individual responsibility. A comparison of this section with 18.21–32 makes the relationship between the two passages obvious. Verse 11 is related to 18.23, 32; verse 12 is based on 18.26–27; verse 13 on 18.24; verses 14, 16 on 18.21–22; and for verse 15, cf. 18.14–18, especially verses 16–17. The last section, verses 17–20, is clearly based on 18.25–27, 30. The materials of 18.21–32 have been restructured, but in a less coherent order, and the reworking is probably the work of the editor. The reason for the insertion is probably found in verses 8–9, where reference to warning the wicked gave the impulse to the editor to add these remarks. It is given an occasion in the present disconsolate situation by verse 10, which is original to the editor.

2. In contrast to the application in verses 7–9, verses 2–6 are to be addressed to **your people,** thus identifying the prophet with the exiles who stand over against Yahweh who may attack them with the sword. The watchman is a figure taken from military life; a guard is set to alert a camp in the event of attack. So in ancient times a watchman on a city tower kept constant guard for the populace; cf. 2 Sam. 18.24–27, where the watchman is on the roof of the gate, and 2 Kg. 9.17–20, where the watchman reports from a tower in Jezreel.

3. The duty of the watchman is to warn of approaching attack by blowing the trumpet (cf. Am. 3.6; Hos. 5.8; Jer. 4.19). The blowing of the trumpet was also used to signalize the advent of cultic feasts such as the new moon or the full moon (Ps. 81.3(MT 4)).

4. Failure to heed the warning meant that the watchman was absolved of guilt should the consequences be disastrous. For **his blood . . . head,** cf. 17.19.

5. The last sentence is peculiar since it appears as an afterthought. Many wish to emend *nzhr* to *hzhyr*, i.e. 'but he has given warning and has saved his life', but this is based on misunderstanding the reference of *hw'*, 'he', as being the watchman rather than the inhabitant. The sentence is probably a secondary accretion intended to spell out all the possibilities.

6. The watchman is responsible for sounding the alarm. Failure to do so means that the death of the inhabitants will be on his head, i.e. the *lex talionis* will be invoked on the watchman who has by his neglect become guilty of murder. Since it is Yahweh who brings the sword, the death of citizens is, however, perfectly justified; they die in their **iniquity.**

7. Cf. 3.17. As prophetic watchman Ezekiel does not use his own powers of observation but serves as medium for the divine word of warning. He is to pass on God's warning. Yahweh does not as at Sinai speak directly to the people, but only through the watchman-prophet.

8. Cf. 3.18. **O wicked man** is a dittograph and is to be omitted with 3.18, G. and S. **you shall surely die** seems to be a formula; cf. Gen. 2.17; 20.7, and often. It is an apodictic judgment pronounced on the disobedient, e.g. 1 Sam. 14.44; 1 Kg. 2.37. The prophetic office is thus one of warning against disobedience, since disobedience entails capital judgment.

9. Cf. 3.19. **to turn from his way** is secondary; it is absent from 3.19.

10. The editor's setting for a recapitulation of 18.21–32. The exiles are in despair.

We are suffering for our sins, and the judgment for sin is death. The exile sees no hope for life; cf. on 18.9. The passage to follow is then intended to show the pathway to life for those under the sentence of death.

11. For **Lord God**, cf. on 2.4. For the verse, cf. on 18.23, 32. Here the rhetorical questions of 18.23, 32 are a positive asseveration, to which is added a passionate call to repentance. For the final question, cf. 18.31*b*.

12. Cf. on 18.26, 27. Verse 12*b* is peculiar in that MT 'by it' (RSV interprets as **by his righteousness**) has no immediate reference. It is probably secondary, an intrusion from the margin where the theme of the passage was noted. The lack of antecedent would be no problem since on the margin it would naturally be **righteousness** of verse 12*a*. **shall not fall** is lit. 'shall not come to stumbling'.

13. Cf. on 18.24. Verse 13*a* is formulated rather differently, however. As in verse 8 a formulaic judgment is expressed, **he shall surely live**; cf. on 18.9 (there is no **that** in MT) concerning a righteous man. The formula, as in 18.9, is in the 3rd person. Reliance on such an acquittal formula is of no help in the future, however, since future iniquity cancels out all past performance. There is no storehouse of good to neutralize later wickedness. G. omits **but** in verse 13*b*, probably rightly (cf. 18.26).

14. Cf. on 18.21. As in verse 13 the editor changes the condition in terms of a formulaic judgment (cf. on verse 8). It is to be noted that the judgment is always in the 2nd person, but the acquittal formula (verse 13; 18.9) is in the 3rd person.

15. **the wicked** is a copyist's error and is absent in G.S. Only two of the characteristics of the righteous life listed in 18.5–17 are given here, viz. restoration of the pledge and return of that taken by robbery (cf. on 18.7). Such a repentant life is aptly described as walking in **the statutes of life,** i.e. statutes leading to life as the reiterated acquittal formula notes both positively and negatively.

16. Cf. on 18.22.

17. For **Lord** instead of the minority reading 'Lord', as in verse 20, cf. on 18.25. For the verse, cf. on 18.25.

18. A shorter version of 18.26. **for it** is an attempt to render *bhm* 'for them'. The word is probably not original.

19. An abbreviation of 18.27. Again **by it** is for a plural '*lyhm*, 'because of them', which is probably secondary.

20. Verse 20*a* reflects 18.29*a*, whereas *b* is paralleled in 18.30*a*.

B. News of Jerusalem's Fall 33.21–22

For the relation of this account to 24.25–27, cf. commentary *ad loc*. This small section is unique in that it simply details a happening rather than some prophetic word. The account is dated and speaks of a fugitive arriving with news that Jerusalem is fallen. The prophet had been in a state of ecstatic dumbness the preceding night, but this had passed by the time the fugitive had arrived. A misunderstanding of verse 22 led later members of the Ezekiel school to speculate on a long period of dumbness (cf. 3.25–27 and 24.25–27). Why the editor placed this account here is hard to see. It has no relation to its context.

21. The date given when compared with the actual date of the fall of the city given in Jer. 39.2; 52.6–7 (9.4.11) and of its destruction in Jer. 52.12 (10.5.11) seems to be much too late (5.10.12), i.e. a span of almost seventeen months between the destruction of the city and the arrival of the news. But since Ezekiel is based on the Babylonian calendar in which the year began in the spring, whereas Jeremiah and Kings are based on the Palestinian reckoning (autumn to autumn), the interval is only five (or six) months. The date is thus January 585 B.C. It is not fully clear what is meant by one **who had escaped**. Possibly it simply means 'one who had escaped death' and was therefore one of the deportees. Refugees would hardly escape to Babylon but rather to Egypt.

22. For **the hand of the LORD** as referring to the ecstatic state, cf. on 1.3*b*. The opening of the mouth may only refer to the prophet's reception of an oracle, though the content of the oracle is not given; no actual ecstatic dumbness would then be involved. But possibly it does refer simply to the ability to speak. **the man came** is based on a metathesis of *bw'* (i.e. as *b'w*), and is probably correct.

C. Two Unrelated Oracles 33.23-33

This section includes two oracles which the editor has put together under one section introduction formula, probably because both end with a recognition formula in 3rd plural.

(a) Judgment on those still in Judah 33.23-29

This section is formally a disputation, verse 24 citing a proverbial saying (cf. 18.2), and verses 25–29 the oracle. The oracle is in turn doubly introduced with the oracle introductory formulae, verses 25, 27, the first introducing the prophetic invective; the second, the judgment. The people under judgment are the **inhabitants of these waste places in the land of Israel,** i.e. those who were left in Judah by Nebuchadrezzar in 586 B.C. How Ezekiel knew of the conditions in Judah is not known, but apparently some communication must still have existed. It is also possible that the oracle of verses 25–29 was the original reply to 11.15 where the survivors of the earlier exile of 597 similarly laid claim to the land involuntarily abandoned by its owners. Note that 11.16–21 do not really constitute a judgment on the rapacious Judeans as might be expected, whereas verses 25–29 would serve admirably. The new setting, i.e. verse 24 with its reference to Judeans after 586, is then the creation of the editor who wanted to apply the oracle to those not exiled. This will then also give meaning to verses 28, 29*b* which promise desolation of the land, a prediction with little meaning after the total destruction of 586.

24. The reference to Abraham is unique in Ezekiel, but cf. Isa. 51.2. Recourse to the patriarchal promises is rare in the prophets. Here it is used to press a specious claim to right of possession.

25. G. has omitted all but the introductory imperative sentence along with verse 26 by parablepsis. For **Lord GOD,** as in verse 27, cf. on 2.4. **your eyes** rightly for MT singular. The first accusation is peculiar and many have suggested changing *hdm*, 'the blood', to *hhrym*, i.e. '(you eat upon) the mountains' (cf. 18.6), which is probably correct. MT literally says 'you eat upon the blood', which RSV has interpreted. Thus the three accusations are all marks of the wicked man; for the first two, cf. on 18.6; for the last, cf. on 18.10. Possession of the land is conditional on a righteous life. The Judeans, however, engage in wicked practices which will entail judgment.

26. you commit is incorrectly feminine. The first accusation is literally 'reliance on the sword', not otherwise mentioned in Ezekiel, but its reference is to violence, e.g. commit robbery, oppress the poor and needy (cf. 18.12). For the second, cf. on 18.12, and for the last, cf. on 18.6.

27. to be devoured: read 'for food' with a minority reading, G.S.V. The reference to **waste places** probably led the editor to reapply the oracle to a post-586 situation. Here it simply contrasts graphically with **open field, strongholds,** and **caves** all of which are more or less desolate. Furthermore, use of the word allowed alliteration with the following word: *bḥrbwt bḥrb*. For a threefold destruction, cf. 5.12, where, however, wild beasts are not mentioned, but cf. 5.17.

28. For **a desolation and a waste,** cf. 6.14. For **her proud might,** cf. 7.24; 30.18. For **mountains of Israel,** cf. 6.2; and for the last phrase, cf. 14.15. The land was eventually desolated in 586 by the Babylonians.

(b) POPULAR MISUSE OF THE PROPHETIC OFFICE **33.30–33**

This section is addressed directly to the prophet. Yahweh is aware that people enjoy listening to prophetic oracles, but unfortunately they do not change their lives as a result. When the prophet's predictions are fulfilled the people will suddenly realize that a true prophet has spoken. Unusual is the recognition formula in verse 33. The section is throughout unusual in that the prophet is not ordered but is simply himself encouraged in his prophetic office. This is probably the reason for its placement immediately before chapters 34–37.

The passage has received some accretions from later hands, particularly in verse 31 which as a result is somewhat obscure. Verse 31*b* is a comment on the word **love** in verse 32, intending to emphasize the wickedness of the people. But this is not what the passage intended; rather it intended to emphasize the captiousness of the people's attention. The preceding clause, **and they hear . . . do it,** is a doublet of verse 32*b*, and the phrase **as my people** is a copyist's error. In verse 30 **to one another** is absent in G. and is a doublet to the next phrase.

30. The exiles live in a city; they talk in alleys and doorways. Listening to the prophet is the latest craze.

31. as people come might be paraphrased 'in crowds'. For **sit before you** as disciples before and around a teacher, cf. 8.1; 14.1.

32. MT '(like a love) song' is corrected to **like one who sings love songs,** i.e. to *šayyār* or *šār*. Prophecy is simply regarded as entertainment by the exiles rather than as a call to action. The verse may give some information on the manner of the prophet's recitation of an oracle. Was it possibly chanted?

33. There is no antecedent for **this** or **it,** but from the context the meaning is clear. When the prophetic oracle is fulfilled the prophet's office will be recognized. For a parallel statement, cf. Jer. 28.9 and also Dt. 18.21–22. A prophet is thus by definition one who faithfully mediates the divine word which he has received to the people (cf. Exod. 7.1–2).

D. Israel's Shepherds and the Sheep 34.1–31

Though this chapter is placed in a single section, and has by means of an editorial application at the end, verse 31, been given a spurious semblance of unity, it actually is comprised of two distinct sections with different themes. The first section is verses 1–16 and deals with wicked shepherds whom Yahweh will judge. After the judgment Yahweh himself will play the part of the shepherd. Verses 17–31 deal first with the division between good and bad sheep, then with the Messianic age in which the Messianic prince will rule and the Edenic conditions which will then obtain. It does appear, however, that the second section is based on the first and that it is the product of later traditionists.

(a) the shepherds of israel 34.1–16

The designation of shepherd for ruler was widespread and a favourite throughout the ancient Near East; the title is well-attested from Sumerian to Neo-Babylonian times. So too among the Hebrews. David, the ideal king of the Golden Age, was according to an old tradition a shepherd in his youth. Jeremiah in particular used the term to designate Judah's rulers (Jer. 2.8; 3.15; 10.21; 22.22; 23.1–4; 25.34–37; 50.6). For a later usage of the term dependent on this passage, cf. Zech. 11.4–17. The N.T. makes use of the same figure (Mt. 9.36; Mk 6.34; 14.27; and especially Jn 10.1–18).

The section has two oracle conclusion formulae, verses 8, 15, and three introductory formulae, verses 2, 10, 11, and two imperatives demanding attention to a divine oracle, verses 7, 9. Thus the section divides formally into five parts: verses 2–6, 7–8, 9–10, 11–15, 16.

Verses 2–6 are a woe oracle, a form of prophetic invective as at 13.3–7. The expected 'therefore' clause follows, but in two forms, only one of which can be original. Verse 10 gives the expected judgment in the standard Ezekiel form: 'Behold I am against . . .', and is the original judgment. Furthermore, verses 7–8, though introduced by 'therefore', are not a judgment at all, but a recapitulation of the invective in the form of a 'because' clause introduced by an oath formula. Verse 7 is an exact copy of verse 9, and the conclusion that verses 7–8 are secondary is unavoidable. Verse 10 is, however, not the end of the original account, which is to be found in verse 15. Verses 11–15 are the positive counterpart to the judgment in verse 10; this is clear from the causal particle introducing the introductory formula. Yahweh will rescue his sheep from the evil shepherds by himself taking over the shepherd function. Verse 16 is an editorial appendix which serves to summarize the work of Yahweh, the good shepherd, based on verse 4 and at the same time to introduce the notion of justice which is thematic in the first part of the next section. It is the work of the traditionist responsible for verses 17–19.

2. to them: a late gloss absent in G.V. For **Lord GOD,** as in verses 8, 10, 11, 15, cf. on 2.4. The oracle against the evil shepherds is based on the pattern of Jer. 23.1–2. There too a woe oracle against the shepherds (who destroy and scatter the sheep) is followed by a judgment oracle. Ezekiel's oracle is, however, much more detailed. The invective charges the shepherds with neglect of the sheep. The office of shepherd means complete devotion to the needs of the flock; for the work of the ideal shepherd, cf. Ps. 23; Jn 10.1–18. There is no point in attempting to identify the shepherds since Ezekiel simply had the class of rulers in mind.

3. G. understood *ḥḥlb* as 'milk' rather than **fat,** probably correctly. It probably refers to the curds or cheese made from milk, as at 1 Sam. 17.18. The shepherd naturally used the the products of the flock for his needs, and it is not this to which objection is made. The objection is that he usurps the privileges of the shepherd without taking on the responsibilities.

4. them: probably a copyist's error by partial dittography. An earlier doublet attested by the Versions is **and harshness** added under the influence of the idiom 'to rule with harshness' (Lev. 25.43, 46, 53). The word for **weak** is the passive for 'sick', but Ezekiel often uses two forms of one root co-ordinately. The verse gives an excellent summary of the shepherd's duties. The opposite of 'force' is gentleness. The shepherd must rule gently.

5. For **they (were scattered)** G.S.V. have 'my sheep'. The sheep had no true shepherd and thus were scattered among the nations, prey for invading peoples.

6. were scattered is actually the last word in verse 5 of MT. **they wandered,** a late gloss absent in G., which became necessary when the verses were incorrectly divided. **My sheep were scattered** was originally a marginal note indicating the theme of this section. Originally the verse read: 'Over all the mountains and on every high hill and over the face of all (as G.) the earth were my sheep scattered. . . .' This is a reference not only to the Babylonian exile but to dispersion in general.

8. For **my shepherds** G.S. read 'the shepherds'. The traditionist insists that though the shepherds neglected their duty, yet they rule by Yahweh's sanction. The verse adds nothing to verses 2–6, except to single out feeding the sheep and searching for the lost as the principal tasks of the shepherd.

10. G. has 'my sheep' for **the sheep,** but this may be smoothing out the text. In the judgment he will **require,** i.e. demand an accounting for the shepherd's charge. Yahweh will remove his sheep from danger, since the wicked shepherds do not simply neglect the sheep but actually attack them.

11. Yahweh himself will become their good shepherd. The lost he will **search for,** the same verb as **require** in verse 10, but now in a somewhat different sense. In that ideal kingdom no human shepherd is necessary, a theme which is presupposed in verses 25–31 as well.

12. MT has 'when he is in the midst of his sheep', which can hardly be intended. By omitting *btwk*, 'in the midst of ', and the suffix on the verbal noun as well as the repointing of 'made distinct' as **scattered abroad,** good sense is obtained: 'When his sheep have been scattered abroad.' There is no basis for RSV's **some of. day of . . . darkness** is descriptive of the day of Yahweh; here the destruction of Jerusalem in 586 B.C. is meant. **all places** is not just Babylon, but Egypt to which many exiles fled (cf. Jer. 43:5–7) as well.

13. Yahweh will collect his peoples together no matter where they are. Ezekiel probably had in mind the earlier exiles of the northern tribes in the eighth century as well. For the divine ingathering, cf. also Isa. 43.5–6; 49.12, 22; Jer. 23.3; 31.8; 32.37; Mic. 2.12; 4.6–7; Zeph. 3.19–20; Zech. 8.7–8; 10.8–11. **fountains** is misleading; rather the stream beds, wadis, are meant.

14. The Palestine to which scattered Israel is restored will be excellent grazing land. Yahweh 'will make them lie down in green pastures' (Ps. 23.2).

15. G. follows another tradition in concluding this section with the recognition formula, instead of the oracle conclusion formula, and introducing verse 16 with the introductory formula.

16. and the fat, not in G.; possibly a traditionist's gloss on **and the strong** in terms of the figure of sheep. MT has 'annihilate' for **watch over** (*'šmyd* instead of *'šmr* which G.S.V. read), and may be original. The antecedent of **them** is **the strong** in MT. The shepherd cares for the needy and destroys the strong who would attack the helpless sheep and feed them with (not **in**) justice. For the shepherd as protector, cf. 1 Sam. 17.34–35.

(b) YAHWEH'S CARE FOR HIS SHEEP 34.17–31

This section is a series of at least six accretions, the limits of all but one being formally marked by the use of formulae. The first expansion is verses 17–19, introduced by an introductory formula, as is the next. The figure of the sheep is retained, but that of the shepherd is abandoned. Here it is not shepherd *v.* sheep but sheep *v.* sheep, and Yahweh promises judgment between sheep and sheep. The passage is undoubtedly the pattern for the N.T. parable of the sheep and the goats (Mt. 25.31–33). The second section, verses 20–22, is a loosely tied parallel to the first by an introductory **Therefore.** The traditionist is explicating verses 18–19 by distinguishing between strong and weak sheep; presumably it is the strong sheep who are responsible not only for the scattering of the sheep, verse 21, but also for trampling pastures and muddying waters, verse 18.

That verses 23–24 constitute a separate tradition is not formally marked but is clear from the content. The theme of judgment is dropped and the appointment of the Messianic prince is introduced. The passage presupposes 37.15–28, where it is a secondary accretion but at least in a restoration context, whereas here it is at odds with verses 11–15. It also marks an abrupt change from verse 22, which ends with Yahweh's threat of judgment between sheep and sheep whereas verse 23 promises a human shepherd who will feed the sheep, reverting to the theme of verses 2–10. The accretion ends formally with an affirmation formula.

Verses 25–27 are still another expansion without any formal introduction but ending with a recognition formula. The figure of the sheep is now completely abandoned and the traditionist describes the Edenic conditions of the Messianic age in terms reminiscent of Lev. 26.3–13. The following tradition, verses 28–30, simply expands on the security and prosperity of that age of restoration, though still reflecting the language of H. It too ends with a recognition formula, but expanded in terms of the covenant formula and concluded with an oracle conclusion formula. Verse 31 is an editorial adaptation rather loosely reintroducing the figure of sheep in terms of a covenant formula and ending with the conclusion formula.

17. For **Lord GOD**, as in verses 20, 30, 31, cf. on 2.4. **rams and he-goats** probably refers to the people in power in the community.

18–19. So callous are the people that they not only rush in to feed themselves with the choice grass, but after satisfaction selfishly trample what they no longer need so as to make it unfit for others still hungry. Apparently only these are addressed, since verse 19 refers to my sheep; on the other hand it is **my flock** in verse 17. The text is not precise.

20. to them: a late gloss not in G. The judgment here is between the fat and lean sheep, presumably between the powerful oppressor and the poor afflicted.

21. The invective charges the powerful with ruthless butting aside the **weak,** lit. the 'sickly'. The reference to scattering simply continues the figure of sheep without a shepherd rather than being a hidden allusion to exilic conditions. Even in the exile the strong oppressed the weak.

22. Though this is the judgment there is no introductory 'therefore', which in view of the 'because' of verse 21 would be expected. The judgment is soteriological, i.e. the flock will be saved, an uncommon notion in Ezekiel, but cf. 36.29; 37.23. Judgment is here a proclamation of redemption from oppression; the judge between sheep shows his positive side as saviour. This salvation means being no longer helpless over against the oppressor.

23. he shall feed them (2°) is a doublet omitted by G. **over them** may also be secondary. If so, the original pronominal references in the verse were all feminine, whereas in verse 24 the figure of shepherding the flock being abandoned the references are all masculine. Yahweh will raise up a single shepherd, i.e. there will not be two kingdoms in the coming age, but one united kingdom as in the time of David and Solomon; this promise is parallel to 37.15–28. Over this united fold David will serve as shepherd in contrast to verses 11–15, where Yahweh himself serves as shepherd. David is, however, not a ruler but Yahweh's servant. As servant he is not only faithful to Yahweh's demands, but also takes a lower rank under Yahweh. A servant does not impose his will, but rather the will of his master. It is Yahweh's will that the flock be cared for (cf. verse 16a), and this will David is to carry out. That the Messiah is named David does not involve a *David redivivus*, but simply one in the Davidic line. The Messiah must be of the royal house, since Yahweh had promised David that his throne would be established for ever, 2 Sam. 7.16. Not that the Messiah was to be the agent for bringing in the coming age— this was Yahweh's prerogative. That the Messiah is actually named David (cf.

37.24) represents a future recapitulation of the idyllic golden days of long ago. David was the ancestral hero of the kingdom and it was fitting that those days should return.

24. In Hos. 3.5 and Jer. 30.9 David is called 'their king', but here in accordance with the usage of the Ezekiel school the indigenous term **prince** is intentionally used. The term implies subordination since it literally means 'one who has been raised'. A prince (or 'chieftain') is one who has been raised either by Yahweh or by his fellows to a position of leadership. This proper station is emphasized by placing David's position as prince in second place to Yahweh as their God, as well as by **among them** (lit. 'in their midst'). **my servant** was mistakenly copied from the preceding, as its absence in G. shows. The divine actor is again emphasized by a concluding affirmation formula.

25. The promises of this verse and verses 26–28 closely resemble Lev. 26.4–6. Yahweh will establish a **covenant of peace** with his people in that Paradisiac age. What **peace** involves is then explained in the remainder of the passage. Wild beasts will be banished (cf. Lev. 26.6b); places that would normally be dangerous because of beasts of prey, i.e. wilderness and woods, will then be perfectly safe.

26. Verse 26a in MT is difficult. G. omits **a blessing** as well as the conjunction after **them,** thus 'And I will set them around my hill', which would mean that Yahweh will restore his people to the mountains of Israel; but hill is unusual as a general designation for the land. Another aspect of the covenant of peace is sufficient rainfall (cf. Lev. 26.4a). Without regular and sufficient showers during the rainy season famine results; showers are truly 'of blessing'.

27. For the first two clauses, cf. Lev. 26.4b for the same language. 'To dwell securely' is the mark of the coming age in all its aspects, i.e. freedom from fear, verse 25, freedom from hunger, verses 26–27, and from slavery, verse 27b. For verse 27b, cf. Lev. 26.13.

28. This partly reflects Lev. 26.5, but in the main simply recapitulates what has already been said in verses 25–27.

29. prosperous plantations: MT has 'planting place for renown' ('plantations' is misleading; MT means a field for planting, i.e. arable land). G. is original in presupposing *šlm*, **prosperous**, for *lšm*, 'for renown'. It means 'fertile, productive fields'. Israel will suffer neither famine nor international shame.

30. with them: omit with minority reading and G.S. The recognition formula then consists of the usual covenant formula showing the two partners, Yahweh and Israel, in their covenantal relations, God and people, appropriately concluding the section on the covenant of peace, though this was not exactly what the traditionist of verses 25–27 had intended. None the less these terms are also valid for the covenant of bliss for the future age.

31. RSV rightly omits with G. 'and you' and the incomprehensible 'man' (after **my pasture**). The word *'dm*, 'man', is probably but a partial dittograph of the following *'tm*, making 'you are man'. Then another 2nd plural pronoun was necessary for the subject, which was made feminine (*'tn*) to agree with **sheep**. For **sheep of my pasture**, cf. Jer. 23.1.

E. EDOM AND ISRAEL 35.1–36.15

The editor has placed together two disparate sections, 35.1–15 and 36.1–15, probably because both are addressed to mountains. Furthermore Edom is dealt with throughout chapter 35 but is also mentioned in 36.5. Though the editor considered this as a single unit, no purpose is served in trying to treat it as one.

(a) VARIOUS ORACLES AGAINST EDOM 35.1–15

It is surprising to find in this division of restoration prophecy oracles against Edom which might more logically have been added to the earlier oracle against Edom, 25.12–14, in the division on foreign nations. It was obviously the editor who placed these here, probably to set the promises of restoration to 'the mountains of Israel' in clearer perspective. These oracles are also against Mount Seir rather than Edom, which is mentioned only at the end in verse 15. That oracles against Edom should be popular during the days of the exile and even later is comprehensible in view of the growing hatred for a people who not only gave aid to the attacking enemy but gradually encroached on its southern borders, eventually settling the entire Negeb area.

The chapter is a series of four separate though related oracles, all in direct address to Mount Seir in 2nd masc. singular. Each ends with the recognition formula, verses 4, 9, 12, 15, but only the first and third in 2nd singular, the second being in 2nd plural, and the fourth in 3rd plural. The first and fourth are also formally introduced with an introductory formula, verses 3, 14. The second and third are parallel in form, beginning with a 'because' invective, and issuing in a 'therefore' clause introduced with an oath formula.

There is no way of determining whether these oracles are from Ezekiel or from his followers, but the latter is much more likely. The oracles have received some expansions from later traditionists. In the second oracle (verses 5–9) verses 7–8 are secondary, as can be seen from the 3rd masc. singular references. RSV has glossed over this by changing 3rd singular pronouns in verse 8 to 2nd person, but cf. commentary below. In the third oracle, verses 10–12, verse 10b is an addition by a traditionist who wanted to make Edom's voraciousness even more appalling by pointing out that this was land belonging to Yahweh. The reference is hardly original to a 1st person oracle. Verse 13 is also secondary, as its plural reference indicates. It is an expansion on **heard** of verse 12. Formally the verse is neither part of the third nor of the fourth oracle, since it follows the end of the recognition formula of verse 12 and precedes the introductory formula of the last oracle. The latter has also been expanded by an explanatory doublet, verse 15a, an attempt by a late traditionist (subsequent to G.) to explain what verse 14b was all about. Since verse 14b is badly corrupt and the text of MT makes little sense, it needed explanation. The doublet probably gives a correct explanation.

2. For **set your face . . . and prophesy,** cf. 6.2. **Mount Seir,** modern *Jebel esh-Shera*, is the mountain range which covers most of Edom from the Wadi-l-Ḥesā southward to the Wadi-l-Hismeh and from the Arabah eastward to the desert. Here, as in Num. 24.18, the term is an equivalent for Edom. Cf. also on 25.8.

3. For **Lord GOD**, as in verses 6, 11, 14, cf. on 2.4. The judgment in verses 3–4 is in stereotyped phrases. For **desolation and waste,** cf. 6.4.

5. Perpetual enmity was descriptive of the Philistines in 25.15; for a commentary on the perpetual feud between Edom and Israel, cf. Obadiah. This enmity went back for centuries, to the days of David who enslaved all of Edom (2 Sam. 8.13–14), and Solomon who used Edomite territory for his own commercial interests (1 Kg. 9.26–28). Tradition rooted the enmity in ancestral rivalry and hatred (Gen. 25.27–34; 27.41–45). Historically the hatred was given fresh impetus at the time of Jerusalem's destruction in which they may have given aid to the enemy. The 'final punishment', cf. 21.25(MT 30), was the fall of Jerusalem in 586 B.C.

6. G. omits **I will prepare you for blood and blood shall pursue you,** a doublet to verse 6b. RSV follows G. in reading '*šmt*, **are guilty of,** for MT's *śn't*, 'hated' (cf. 22.4 and 25.12). To be guilty of blood means guilty of bloodshed. Shed blood had to be avenged (cf. on 24.7–8). Here the blood is personified as the *gō'ēl* who demands full retribution (cf. Gen. 9.6).

7. a waste and a desolation: RSV rightly follows a minority reading instead of MT 'a waste and a waste'; cf. verse 3. The verse is in 3rd singular and is an expansion. Verse 7a is a variant of the last clause in verse 3; b is a stereotyped idiom for complete destruction. The last clause is lit. 'who pass by and return'.

8. MT has 'And I will fill its mountains with its slain' in verse 8a, continuing the 3rd singular of the expansion. A later hand added in explanation 'your hills and your valleys and all your ravines'; it can be identified as later by the 2nd singular pronouns. Verse 8b originally read 'those slain by the sword shall fall on them'. The gloss was probably added under the influence of 6.3. For the slain on the mountains, cf. 6.7.

10. MT has 'and we will take possession of it', but the Versions attest 'and I will take possession of them', which must be correct; cf. *BH³*. The two nations are the northern and southern kingdoms of Israel and Judah (cf. 37.22). Edom insultingly laid claim to Israelite territory after the 586 destruction. Historically Edom only pressed into Judean territory, but geographical considerations should not be pressed, since to the Ezekiel school the land was now a single unit (cf. 37.15–23).

11. according . . . showed: G. omitted by parablepsis. **among you** rightly with G. for MT's 'among them', a copyist's error. **I will deal with you** is absolute in MT and should be rendered 'I will act'. For the anger, envy, and hatred of the Edomites at the time of Jerusalem's fall, cf. Ob. 10–14. For Yahweh making himself known among nations by his judgment, cf. 38.23.

12. G. attests the text of MT by an auditory error ('the voice of' for **all**). The recognition formula attendant on the judgment of Edom entails Yahweh's having noted Edom's revilings. When Yahweh takes note, he acts. For **mountains of Israel,** cf. 6.1–7; 36.1–15.

13. G. omits **and multiplied . . . against me** by parablepsis. The verb is apparently a Hebraized form of an Aramaic word meaning 'to multiply'. A noun based on this root occurs at Jer. 33.6.

14b. Obscure. Literally, MT has 'according to the rejoicing of all the earth, a desolation will I make for you'. A somewhat longer doublet occurs in verse 15a, which was added after G., which does not have it; this was added to explain the cryptic line. The occurrence of 'all' after 'rejoicing' shows that **As you rejoiced** is a correct interpretation. The next two words, 'earth, desolation', probably refer to the land which was desolated, i.e. Judah. The last words 'I will do to you' are then the subject. The line originally may have read 'I will do to you according to your rejoicing over the land which was a desolation'; for Edomite gloating, cf. Ob. 12–13.

15b. Mount Seir is apparently taken as feminine here, as appears from *klh*, 'all of it (feminine)', and the verse should read, 'Mount Seir shall be a desolation, and all Edom, all of it. . . .'

(b) THE MOUNTAINS OF ISRAEL 36.1–15

This section is the restoration counterpart of chapter 6, where the mountains of Israel are condemned. Unfortunately the literary history of the section is incredibly complicated. If the original oracle was straightforward and more or less consistent, as one surely must presuppose, the oracle received many accretions to the text resulting in a hodge-podge of materials. Thus oracles are introduced seven times and there are three formal conclusions in this section. Introductory formulae occur in verses 2, 3, 4, 5, 6, 7, 13; the command to **prophesy and say** occurs three times, verses 1, 3, 6, and a demand for attention to the oracle together with the vocative occurs both in verses 1 and 4.

As for concluding formulae, verse 11 has the recognition formula in 2nd masc. plural, since the mountains are addressed. But verses 14 and 15 have oracle conclusion formulae. Since an oracle normally begins and ends but once, it is clear that later traditionists have expanded the text considerably.

To begin with the conclusions, it is obvious that verse 15 is not the original conclusion. It repeats part of verse 14 and is an accretion subsequent to it. Verses 13–14 formally constitute an oracle of the 'because-therefore' type. Its theme deals with the mountains being accused of bereaving the nations and the promise is given that this will no longer be true. This is, however, in turn an expansion of the last clause of verse 12, which verse 14 in part repeats. Since this is subsequent to verse 12, only the conclusion in verse 11 can be considered as original. The recognition formula in verse 11 concludes the promise of a re-peopling of the mountains and of their fertility, a theme developed in verses 8–11 fairly consistently, the only inconsistent clause being verse 10b, which abandons the theme of mountains for cities and waste places, whereas a is a doublet to verse 11a. Verse 12 is not part of the original oracle, but an expansion summarizing the intent of verses 8–11.

Verses 8–11 are, however, not the complete oracle. The promise of Paradise regained needs an introduction contrasting the promised state with the former. The present state of verses 2–7 shows two 'because' clauses and four 'therefore' clauses, to all of which verse 1 must be the introduction. The unscrambling of the original introduction can be approached in two ways, both of which lead to the same conclusion. If verse 1 is the proper introduction then verse 3 cannot be original since it repeats the call to prophesy. This leaves verse 2 as the original 'because' clause. For similar reasons verses 4 and 6 are shown to be secondary, since verse 4 repeats the call to attend on the oracle and verse 6 the command to prophesy. Which leaves either verse 5 or verse 7 as the original 'therefore' clause.

An examination of the content of the verses leads to the same conclusion. Verses 8–11 speak of re-peopling of the mountains by restored Israel. Though both verses 3 and 4 speak in terms of others possessing the mountains, only verse 2 actually refers to the mountains, **The ancient heights.** Verse 4 is the counterpart to verse 3 and probably part of the same tradition; i.e. **derision** in verse 4 parallels the **talk and evil gossip** of verse 3. Verse 7 is an oracle against nations, but its language is reminiscent of verse 15, which may come from the same traditionist. This leaves verses 5–6. Of the two, verse 5 best fits verse 2 since reference is made to giving the land to themselves. Verse 6 in its first clause is a doublet of part of verse 5 and in its second is like verse 7 reminiscent of verse 15. Verse 5 in its present form may be expanded somewhat; **and against all Edom,** with its Aramaic spelling of 'all', is an accretion.

1. The attachment of this section to the preceding is enhanced by **mountains of Israel** (cf. 35.12).

2. For **Lord GOD,** as in verses 3–7, 13–15, cf. on 2.4. For the word of glee on the part of the enemy at Israel's misfortune, cf. 25.3 of Ammon, and 26.2 of Tyre. **heights** is the same as 'high places', but in restored Israel the word is again used without evil connotations, as in Mic. 3.12; Num. 21.28; Dt. 32.13. **ancient heights** is a poetic designation for the mountains. Since Israel is dispossessed its land is now ours, the enemy says.

3. For the repeated **because,** cf. 13.10. **crushed** may better be rendered by 'trampled', as at Am. 2.7; 8.4. **rest of the nations** reflects verse 5. Not only are Israel's mountains possessed by others but they are mocked as well, probably as an example of a land deserted by its God.

4. A 'therefore' clause related to verse 3, but the judgment is left unexpressed. **rest of the nations** again occurs showing its relation to both the original verse 5 and to verse 3. The traditionist was dissatisfied with **mountains** and defines it by a series of six geographical designations. **a prey** is also dependent on the original oracle (rendered **and plunder it** in verse 5).

5. Yahweh's **hot jealousy** refers to his zeal for his honour. The enemy claiming the ancient heights of the land of promise as theirs is an infringement on his name. Since he had promised the land to Israel, its possession by others was an insult; it temporarily voided his word. It was not theirs to claim, certainly not with glee and contempt. The word for **contempt** occurs only in Ezekiel, 16.57; 25.6, 15; 28.24, 26. **that . . . plunder it** is obscure, and RSV renders freely, changing *mgršh* to *mwršh*, 'to inherit it'. The word *mgrš* occurs in chapters 40–48 of the open land around the holy city and Temple (cf. on 27.28), and it is unlikely that it is here an Aramaic verbal noun meaning 'to drive out'. The suffix refers to **my land** and the clause should be rendered 'for the sake of its open area—for prey'. What it means is 'to plunder the open stretches', i.e. the fields and vineyards.

6. Verse 6a repeats part of verse 1; ba, verse 4ba. For the oracle itself, cf. above.

7. I swear is lit. 'I raise my hand'; cf. on 20.5. The oracle invokes the *lex talionis*; retribution will consist in bearing their own reproach, i.e. that which they had poured out on Israel.

8. In contrast to Mount Seir, 35.3, Israel's mountains will again be productive. For **branches** as a sign of productivity together with bearing fruit, cf. 17.8. The verb in the last clause is Pi. 'bring near' with indefinite plural subject, thus '(the time) is brought near for entering'. Israel is on the eve of the return. Possibly this came from the time of Jehoiachin's release in 561 B.C. (cf. 2 Kg. 25.27–30), when expectations for speedy return must have been high among the exiles.

9. (behold I am) for you, in a favourable sense; elsewhere it is always to be rendered 'against you'. This is proved by the co-ordinate **turn to you,** also in Lev. 26.9.

10. The traditionalist emphasizes that the productivity of man and beast (verse 11) is particularly true of Israel; note the repetitive **the whole house of Israel, all of it** (cf. 37.11), emphasizing reunited Israel.

11. G. omits **and they shall increase and be fruitful,** originally a marginal notation showing the theme. Its intrusive character is clear from the 3rd plural reference. The time of restoration will not only be a restoration to former prosperity, but will surpass it.

12. The secondary character of this verse is clear from the change to the 2nd singular. The mountains are personified in the last clause as rendering the Israelites childless. The verb recurs in verses 13, 14, and 15 as a thematic word.

13. The 'you' in **to you** is plural with the mountains in mind, but the 2nd person subject of the next two verbs is feminine singular, as though 'land' were the reference. Since verse 14 continues in 2nd fem. singular this must be simply *ad sensum*.

14. RSV follows the Hebrew margin and the Versions in reading **bereave.** The Consonantal Text has by metathesis 'cause to stumble' as in verse 15, but there without Masoretic correction.

15. and no longer . . . stumble (error for 'bereave') is a dittograph from verse 14 and is omitted by G. The reproach and disgrace is probably the traditionist's reflection on the barrenness of Israel's mountains referred to in verses 13–14.

F. THE DIVINE BASIS FOR RESTORATION 36.16–38

Formally this section divides into five parts: verses 17–21, 22–23, 24–32, 33–36, and 37–38. The first section is introductory and is addressed to the prophet. The second is introduced with an introductory formula and ends with a recognition formula, to which is attached an oracle conclusion formula; cf. on verse 23. The third section has no formal introduction, but ends with a conclusion formula plus an exhortation to humility. Verses 33–36 are formally introduced, as is the last oracle, and end with an affirmation formula. The last part concludes with a recognition formula.

The literary history of the section may be traced in four stages. That the first two parts, verses 17–23, represent the original section is easily demonstrated. Thematically it deals with Yahweh's reason for embarking on the return of Israel to the promised land. The introductory part presents in the form of a divine recital the reasons for the exile and its repercussions on the divine honour. The oracle which follows is introduced with 'therefore' and is to be proclaimed to Israel. The oracle states bluntly that it is not for Israel's sake but in order to vindicate Yahweh's reputation among the nations that he is about to restore the people. The next part describes the changed state both of the returned people and of the land, both of which were involved in the dishonour to God's name. That it was added by another traditionist is clear from the somewhat lame recapitulation of the theme of the original oracle in verse 32.

Verses 33–36 are a description of the restoration in stereotyped phrases. That it was added by another traditionist is clear from the opening phrase **On the day that,** i.e. referring to the preceding oracle, specifically to verse 29. The final oracle betrays its accretionary character as well by its opening words **This also.**

It is doubtful whether even the original section is from Ezekiel. Its theme is particularly relevant to the late exile with its background of an imminent return. Its similarity to some of the leading ideas of the exilic Isaiah also makes it probable that it is somewhat later than Ezekiel, though Ezekiel's authorship of the original section is not necessarily excluded. Certainly the remainder, with its mixture of the ceremonial and the moral, is from the school of Ezekiel. Bertholet[2] calls this section a complete compendium of Ezekiel's theology; it would be more accurate to describe it as a compendium of the theology of the Book of Ezekiel.

16–23. The present exile was made necessary by the uncleanness of the people, but this has created an even greater problem for Yahweh, since by the exile his holy name is rendered profane. In the eyes of the nations the ancient triad of God, people, and land has been broken. The Israelites are known as Yahweh's people, and the land of Israel as his land, and now the nations are pointing to the fact that Yahweh's people are exiled from his land. Moses argued similarly when Yahweh wanted to destroy the rebellious people in the wilderness (Num. 14.13–19). And so Yahweh is resolved to act quickly to clear up this blot on his reputation. His deity (holiness) has been called into question and the people must be restored, not because Yahweh is kind or loving, merciful or forgiving, but because he is God. The recognition formula is here the key to the passage. His identity will be recognized by the nations in the act of restoration since he is the actor, the Israelites those acted upon, and the nations the viewers of the action, verse 23b. The assurance of an end to their exile rests thus not on the exiles' deserts or on the historically questionable love of God, but on a divine necessity, that of Yahweh's own being.

17. The reason for the exile was the fact that Israel rendered the land ritually unclean, which fact is the burden of chapters 1–24; cf. especially chapters 8, 14, 16, 20, 22, and 23. The priestly interest of the Ezekiel school is illustrated by verse 17b. For the impurity of the woman in menses, cf. Lev. 15.19–30.

18. G. omits **for the blood . . . defiled it,** which may be a late expansion explaining the impurity in terms typical of Ezekiel, viz. social violence and idolatry, cf. 22.4. Its secondary character is also shown by its re-use of **poured out** and **defiled**. For **idols**, cf. on 6.4.

19. and they . . . countries is in 3rd plural, though the rest of the verse is in 1st singular and may be secondary, possibly a marginal theme. On the other hand, the parallelism **nations–countries** is common in Ezekiel. G. gets rid of the difficulty by changing the verb to 1st singular. In spite of how the nations interpreted the exile it was God's doing, a judgment on Israel's actions.

20. RSV follows a minority reading and the Versions with the first verb as plural. It is Israel which is responsible for the profanation of Yahweh's name among the nations. For the distinction between holy and profane, cf. on 22.26. Yahweh's **holy name** is here personified as something apart from Yahweh himself. The **name** has been attached to both people and land, so that they are people and land of the name of Yahweh. **holy** refers not to a moral attribute but to an essential one; people and land had been separated, put into the realm of the divine. Yahweh's punishment was being misunderstood as divine impotence, a failure to protect what was his.

21. I had concern for is lit. 'I pitied'. There is no valid reason for rendering 'profaned' here by **caused to be profaned**; it is the same verb as in verse 20.

22. Cf. on verse 32. For **Lord God**, as in verse 23, cf. on 2.4. For acting 'for the name's sake', cf. on 20.9.

23. G. omits **says the Lord God,** which is peculiar after the recognition formula. But why would it be added by a traditionist? Possibly it was incorporated to make this key verse even more impressive. G.Pap. 967 omits from the end of the recognition formula to the end of verse 38 by parablepsis, both parts ending in 'know that I am Yahweh'. **vindicate the holiness of** is lit. 'render holy'. The profanation of Yahweh's holy name will be removed and Yahweh will be recognized throughout the world as the God who acts for his people.

The conditions which will obtain in the restoration (i.e. the new state of the people)
24–32

In view of their unclean condition they will be outwardly cleansed, verse 25; inwardly renewed, verse 26; and divinely empowered to obedience, verse 27; and so will live properly in the promised land in the covenant relation, verse 28. Verse 29*a* summarizes all this as salvation from uncleanness. Verses 29*b*–30 are loosely attached to the preceding and introduce the divine promise of fertility of the land. It does, however, explicate how the holy name as attached to the land will react in the future age. Verses 24–30 thus come from a traditionist who interprets in the spirit of verses 17–23 what the vindication of the holy name involves for people and land. Verse 31 is a variant of 20.43, showing the reaction of shame for former sin on the part of the people. Verse 32*a* links the passage to the preceding by repeating the opening words of the oracle in verse 22.

24. A 2nd plural variant of 34.13*a*. The first stage in Yahweh's vindication of his name is his gathering of the exiles and bringing them back to their land.

Throughout this section (except for verse 31, which may well be a pious accretion) it is Yahweh who acts independently.

25. Sprinkling with clean water is the symbol of cleansing. The language is figurative, and borrowed from the cult. Similarly in Ps. 51.7(MT 9) the petitioner asks that God should purge him with hyssop that he may be clean. That the outward cleansing is symbolic of divine pardon for the past is clear from verse 25*b*. (RSV does not follow the accentuation of MT. The verse should be rendered: 'I will sprinkle . . . and you shall be clean; from all your uncleannesses and . . .'.) The uncleannesses and idols represent the past which must first be forgiven, i.e. cleansed, before the new estate can take effect.

26. Cf. Ps. 51.10(MT 12). The verse is also cited in 11.19. For the restoration to be a meaningful vindication the people must be changed. For **heart** and **spirit,** cf. on 11.19. The heart of stone represents the inward impulse to disobedience which characterized Israel before and during the exile. **flesh** is not here opposed to **spirit,** but to **stone.**

27. The new spirit of verse 26 is here defined as Yahweh's own spirit. As the principle of divine life it can only enliven obedience to Yahweh's will (cf. Jer. 31.33). For the work of the divine spirit as giving life, cf. 37.14. The gift of the divine spirit was a characteristic of apocalyptic notions of the age to come (cf. 39.29; Jl 2.28, 29(MT 3.1, 2); cf. Ac. 2.4–21, 33; 10.44–47; 15.8; 19.2–7).

28. With the divinely inspired new obedience the people can dwell in the promised land. For the covenant formula, cf. on 11.20.

29. For **deliver,** cf. 'save' in 34.22; salvation is by the removal of uncleannesses, since defilement involves separation from the holy, from Yahweh. In the new estate Yahweh will also cause productivity of the land (cf. Hos. 2.21–23(MT 23–25)). Famine was common in Palestine and this was well known among the nations. But Yahweh will give perpetual productivity to the land.

31. Cf. on 20.43.

32. The return is not based on the people's deserts; Yahweh acts in spite of them. The return is not an occasion for jubilation but rather for shame and humiliation. For **Lord God,** cf. on 2.4.

33–36. The nations round about will take note of the new conditions in rebuilt Palestine. The traditionist is concerned to emphasize that what has been promised will have the desired effect when it is realized.

33. For **Lord God,** cf. on 2.4. For verse 33*b*, cf. verse 10*b*.

34. For the land being tilled again, cf. verse 9*b*.

35. For **garden of Eden,** cf. Isa. 51.3 and on 28.13. The testimony of the nations to the changed conditions in Palestine, involving both the fertility of the once barren land and the well-built cities formerly ruined, vindicates the once violated honour of Yahweh. The fortification of the rebuilt cities contrasts with 38.11, where all cities and villages remain unwalled.

36. Reference to **nations . . . about you** shows that the oracles against neighbouring tribes in chapter 25 have been fulfilled. Cf. on chapter 25. **I will do** has no object in MT and should be rendered 'and I will act', or 'take action'.

The repopulation of Israel in the future age **37–38**

37. let . . . ask me is lit. 'I will allow myself to be inquired of'; cf. 14.3; 20.3, where search for an oracle was denied; here Yahweh permits it. 'To be inquired of' involves more than simply a divine oracle since the divine oracle involves action. Yahweh will grant Israel's request for numerous offspring, which normally was considered a sign of divine favour, but particularly so in the new age.

38. Two figures are employed for large numbers; the first is lit. 'flock of holiness' (cf. 'holy offerings' in Num. 18.19), i.e. flocks set aside from common use for a sacred purpose, viz. sacrifice. These probably recall the daily sacrifices of the Jerusalem Temple. The second comparison is in apposition to the first and refers to the flocks sacrificed at the designated feasts, a reference to the great cultic festivals. **flock** or **flocks** is a collective and should be rendered consistently as 'flocks'.

G. THE VALLEY OF THE DRY BONES **37.1–14**

This most dramatic and best-known passage in Ezekiel is a description of an ecstatic experience in the same setting as the inaugural vision. The prophet is on the plain (cf. on 3.22) when he experiences the 'hand of Yahweh on him' (cf. on 1.3). With ecstatic eyes he sees the plain covered with dry human bones, bleached by the sun, a symbol of death. He is commanded to prophesy to the bones and predict their resurrection. Immediately skeletons were properly assembled and bodies formed. Again he is called on to prophesy and order the winds to breathe on the bodies, whereupon the bodies lived and rose.

This account, verses 1–10, is followed by an interpretation in verses 11–14. The occasion for the vision is the hopeless despair of the exiles, verse 11. As a nation Israel is dead. From the human point of view the nation is a graveyard of bones, very dry bones. But with Yahweh all things are possible; He will cause these bones to rise and live.

Formally the interpretation has two conclusions, only one of which is original to Ezekiel. Verse 13*a* and verse 14*b* contain recognition formulae addressed to Israel, the latter ending with the conclusion formula. Verse 11 is unquestioned since it is pivotal to the entire section. Verse 12*aα* introduces the interpreting oracle both with the command to prophesy, as in verses 4, 9, and the introductory oracular formula. But the remainder of verse 12, together with verse 13, introduces a new figure, that of the grave, whereas verse 14 properly applies the vision to the exilic situation as a prediction of divinely given life issuing in a return to the land. Verse 14 is thus the original interpreting oracle, whereas verses 12*aβ*, *b*, 13 are a doublet accretion from a later traditionist.

As a literary unit this passage is unique in the book. An ecstatic experience is described and is then used to make vivid an oracle which makes good sense without the bizarre figure of the vision. But as a whole the passage is far more telling than the isolated oracle would have been, as its use in liturgy and art throughout the ages demonstrates. The passage is unfortunately undated, but must come from the period after 586 but considerably before chapter 36.

1. The verse begins abruptly with *hyth* (**was**), which elsewhere follows normally on a date. It has often been suggested that an original date has fallen out, which seems likely but there is no evidence for what it might have been. **he brought me out by the spirit of the LORD** is peculiar since Yahweh is the subject of the verb. Either 'by the spirit of Yahweh' is a technical term for prophetic ecstasy and the inconsistency was therefore not noted, or the verb has an indefinite subject, i.e. 'one brought me'. If the latter, it would be preferable to render 'I was brought out'. **set me down** revocalizes MT's 'caused me to rest', but the verb occurs in a similar context in 40.2 and the emendation is unnecessary. In any event, it is not necessary to think of ecstatic transport as at 8.3; 11.24, since the prophet is already in Babylonia. **valley,** or better 'plain' (cf. on 3.22), is probably the physical scene for the vision. What is visionary is the bone-strewn surface.

2. RSV to avoid monotony translates *whnh* variously as **and behold** and **and lo,** thereby missing the literary power by repetition intended as a device used throughout the passage. **bones** (verse 1) creates a problem since its gender changes bewilderingly throughout the vision; no satisfactory solution has yet been proposed. Two things about the bones are stressed, their number and their aridity. The second shows that they have been dead for a long time; the first emphasizes the satiety of death.

3. For **Lord GOD,** as in verses 5, 9, 12, cf. on 2.4. Yahweh's question to the prophet points out the seeming hopelessness of the situation. From a human point of view the question is purely rhetorical: the dead are dead, and that is the end of it. The prophet's answer shows no hint of a belief in a resurrection, but he realizes that Yahweh is the author of life. The divine possibility is left open.

4. For prophecy to inanimate objects, cf. 6.2–3; 20.46–47(MT 21.2–3); 36.1, 4. But an oracle to the dead is certainly unusual.

5. For **breath, and you shall live** G. has 'breath of life', but in view of verses 6, 9, 10, 14, MT is preferable. **breath** renders *rwḥ*, a word difficult to render. It means 'spirit' in verse 14, 'wind' in verse 9, but here 'breath' is probably what is meant. In any event, it is the animate principle in man. The impossible is promised; these bones will live.

6. This explicates the promise of verse 5 in accordance with the J creation story in Gen. 2.7. The resurrection will be in two stages; first complete bodies are formed (**sinews, flesh,** and **skin**), and then the bodies are to be animated with breath. It has often been suggested that Ezekiel, probably because of his priestly background, shows intimate anatomical knowledge in the series: sinews, flesh, and skin, but the series is fairly obvious to the observant.

7. G. omits **a noise** which may be a late gloss on **a rattling.** The assemblage of skeletons begins the transformation.

8. had covered is vocalized as a transitive verb apparently, as in verse 6. But the Qal may be both stative and transitive. The Ni. is usually suggested as the correct form. The first stage is now complete, i.e. the parallel to 'forming man out of dust' in Gen. 2.7.

9. In contrast to Gen. 2 the source of the breath of life is the **four winds**; these signify the four directions, thus the ends of the earth, 42.20; cf. also Jer. 49.36; 52.23, and the post-exilic use of the idiom in Zech. 2.16; 6.5; 1 Chr. 9.24; Dan. 8.8; 11.4. The corpses are called the **slain**, appropriately in view of the nation's destruction.

11. A minority reading and G. rightly omit **and**. The clue to the interpretation lies in what the exiles are saying about their situation. The three expressions all signify the death of the nation. The first undoubtedly gave rise to the vision itself. The second is lit. 'our hope has perished'; cf. 19.5 for the same expression. The third is well illustrated in Isa. 53.8, 'cut off out of the land of the living', which is what is meant here. The vision is interpreted as pertaining not simply to the Babylonian exiles, but to the **whole house of Israel**, cf. 36.10.

12. The secondary oracle applies the vision in terms of a resurrection, not of the unburied slain, but of the dead from their graves. The reference is, of course, not to a physical resurrection, but to a restoration to political existence, as the last clause intimates. The oracle is a doublet version of verse 14 and adds nothing new to the original oracle. **O my people** is a late gloss absent in G.S. here as well as in verse 13 (lacking in S.).

13. Even the recognition formula is a doublet, though a weaker one, to verse 14.

14. 'Breath' is here interpreted as Yahweh's **Spirit**, which alone is the source of life (cf. Gen. 2.7). But Israel's new life can only be rendered concrete by a visible expression, by a return to its own land.

H. THE TWO STICKS 37.15–28

This section orders another symbolic action (cf. 4.1–3; 5.1–2; 12.3–6; 12.17; 24.16–17), and gives an interpretation. Like most symbolic actions it has been heavily commented on by later traditionists of the Ezekiel school. After the usual section introductory formula the prophet is commanded to take two sticks, label them respectively with the names of the northern and southern kingdoms, and then join them in his hand as though they were one stick, verses 16–17.

The passage in its present form has two interpretative oracles, both introduced by an introductory formula, verses 19, 21. The second, verses 21–28, ends with a recognition formula as well, and is a verbose amalgam of restoration hopes representing the later hopes of the Ezekiel school. The earliest part is that which properly interprets the original interpretative oracle of verses 19–20, viz. verses 21–22, which states that the two kingdoms will be united into one and be returned to the land of Israel. Another traditionist added the references to the **king** in verse 22 as well as in verse 24. Verse 23 represents a covenant tradition in which Yahweh will keep his people from idols and make them ritually clean. Verse 25 gives assurance of perpetual restoration, but represents a differing tradition from verse 24 in that the Messiah is called **prince** (cf. on 34.24) rather than **king**. The remainder, verses 26–28, probably represents a single tradition with its theme of the indwelling God, a restored sanctuary and an everlasting covenant of peace. The stress here falls on the promise of a sanctuary in Israel's midst as a token of God's presence and symbol of the reality of the covenant formula of verse 27.

The original interpretative oracle is thus to be found in verses 19–20. But both the description of the action and the interpretation have been expanded as well. The words to be written on the sticks were originally only **For Judah** and **For Joseph** respectively. The term **Israel** is never used by Ezekiel for the northern kingdom. But a later traditionist, fearful that Joseph might not be understood, added **the stick of Ephraim** and **which . . . Ephraim** in verses 16, 19 respectively. Still another traditionist added the references to all the associates to avoid any misunderstanding of the terms as single tribes rather than as kingdoms. Verse 20 is also secondary, intended to round out the abruptness of the oracle; it is not part of the interpretation but a variant to verse 17. The original passage beginning with verse 16 may be rendered: 'Son of man, take one stick and write on it: Judah's; and take another stick and write on it: Joseph's; then join them together into one stick. And when your people say to you: Will you not explain to us what these things of yours mean?, say to them, Thus says Yahweh. Behold I am about to take the staff of Joseph and put it on the staff of Judah that they shall be one in my hand.'

16. then take: rightly with G. as an imperative rather than *wlkḥ* of MT, which presupposes 'and he shall take'. A better possibility is *wlkḥt*, 'and you shall take'.

17. that they may . . . hand: a copyist's error based on verse 19. The word for **one** is in the plural, which in spite of its occurrence in Gen. 11.1 is here impossible. The intent of the symbolic action is clear, even though the manner in which two sticks could become one stick is not. Presumably they were simply tied together and held as a single unit.

18. For your people, cf. 3.11.

19. For Lord God, as in verse 21, cf. on 2.4. MT is corrupt in verse 19*b*. Literally it has 'and I will put them on it with the stick of Joseph . . .'. 'With' is a variant of 'upon', and 'them' is a later gloss than its antecedent **tribes.** The unification of the whole house of Israel is a recurrent theme in the restoration prophecy of Ezekiel (cf. verse 11; 36.10). The original text must have had the synonym *šbṭ* for '*ṣ*, 'stick'. The word *šbṭ* can mean either 'staff' or 'tribe'; G.'s mistranslation 'tribe' shows the original play on words intended in the oracle.

20. Read: 'The sticks on which you shall write shall be in your hand before their eyes.'

21. Behold . . . take is identical to the phrase in verse 19 and should also be rendered, 'Behold I am about to take.' The verse is applying the interpretation to the exiles. The Diaspora is about to end (cf. verses 12, 14; 11.17; 20.41; 34.13; 36.8–11, 24).

22. G.S. rightly omit the late gloss 'king' in **shall be king.** *lmlk*, **king,** may be a copyist's dittograph of *lklm*, 'for all of them', in scramble. **and one king . . . all** is not part of the interpretation and is secondary. The awkward apposition of **upon the mountains of Israel** betrays its probable secondary nature. For **king** in Ezekiel, cf. on 1.2. The hopes of Ezekiel and his school was a fully reunited Israel as in the days of David and Solomon (cf. 34.23–24).

23. and their detestable things, or with any of their transgressions is a late amplification of **idols,** as its absence in G. shows. **backslidings** with Sym. corrects MT 'dwellings', which corruption is the result of metathesis. For **idols,** cf. on 6.4. **save** occurs elsewhere in Ezekiel only at 34.22; 36.29; restoration, not salvation, was the hope of the Ezekiel school. In the covenant state of the restoration the people will remain clean; this again reflects the strong priestly element of the school.

24. For verse 24*a*, cf. on 34.24; for *b*, cf. 18.9*a*.

25. RSV glosses over the awkwardness of the double relative clause; the second one, **where your fathers dwelt,** is an expansion on **land, that I gave . . . Jacob.** G.S. have 'their' for **your (fathers),** which is more likely to be original. For **gave . . . Jacob,** cf. 28.25. The emphasis is on the perpetuity of the age of restoration. **David** is not a reference to a particular prince but to the Davidic dynasty. There is no thought of a Messiah living for ever.

26. and I will bless them is based on T. for MT's corrupt 'and I will give them'. It, together with **and multiply them,** is a late expansion unattested in G. For **covenant of peace,** cf. on 34.25. For **everlasting covenant,** cf. on 16.60. The sign of the eternal presence of Yahweh in the midst of his people is, however, his sanctuary, which is to be detailed in the final section of the book, chapters 40–48, especially 40–42. For the sanctuary in the middle of the land, cf. 48.8, 10, 21.

27. with them incorrectly renders '*lyhm,* which may mean, 'upon, above, or on behalf of them'; probably 'above' is meant since the Temple stands on a hill. That it does not mean 'heaven' is clear from its being **in the midst of them** in verses 26, 28 (**sanctuary** and **dwelling place** are synonyms). According to this tradition its presence assures the reality of the covenant formula.

28. The recognition formula involves Yahweh rendering Israel holy, i.e. a people separate from the common (cf. 22.26). This is especially relevant because of the presence of the sanctuary which involves the details of the cult for which holiness is the prerequisite.

I. Oracles Against God and Magog 38.1–39.29

These two chapters are formally a unit, as the single section introduction formula of 38.1 shows. Earlier prophets had made predictions about a great enemy which was vaguely identified as coming from the north. This evil from the north (Jer. 4.6–17) is a destroyer of nations, a lion coming out from his lair. Its coming is like clouds; they are besiegers from some far-off country. Again in Jer. 6, evil, even a great destruction, looms from the north and devises a sudden attack. This people is called 'a great nation arousing itself from the farthest parts of the earth'. Their cruelty is proverbial and when rumour of their approach circulates 'our hands fall helpless', 'terror is on every side' (cf. also Jer. 1.13–15). Other prophets had referred in awesome terms to the terror of the day of Yahweh (Zeph. 1.14–18) as a day when all the land will be devoured and all its inhabitants come to a complete end; cf. also Jl 2.20, which is related to this passage.

Chapters 38–39 deal with these as yet unfulfilled prophecies and in their present form have taken on an eschatological form. The enemy from the north is still coming to an Israel now restored. But in view of the restoration promises of chapters 34, 36–37 their doom is sealed. They will be completely destroyed in a terrible conflict. Yahweh will himself order the elements against the enemy and the result will be complete annihilation. The corpses will be so numerous that it will take seven months to bury them. Their now useless weapons will serve as fuel for fire sufficient for seven years. Even the birds and beasts are invited to partake of the flesh and blood resulting from the immense slaughter. From these details it will be clear that we have here left Ezekiel's world for a later one; for an original Ezekiel oracle without these eschatological overtones see below.

The oracles deal with Gog and Magog. Magog also occurs in the table of nations in Gen. 10.2 as one of the sons of Japheth together with Gomer, Madai, Javan, Tubal, Meshech, and Tiras, three of which (Gomer, Tubal, and Meshech) occur in this section, 38.3, 6; 39.1. Madai refers to the Medes; for Javan, cf. on 27.13; Tiras is not yet certainly identified. Magog is unfortunately not identified, though Josephus (Antiq. I. VI. 1) identifies the term as referring to Scythians. This cannot be correct for Gen. 10, where Scythians are referred to as Ashkenaz, a branch of Gomer. In fact, the Scythians did follow the Cimmerians somewhat later in coming from south Russia southward, the Scythians occupying areas to the south and east of the Black Sea, an area which to Ezekiel would be the extreme north. Even more problematic is the term Gog. It probably was not an actual historical figure but was formed on the basis of Magog, which was taken to mean 'place of Gog'. Many have attempted to identify Gog; thus the following suggestions have all been made: an apocalyptic pseudonym for the Babylonians; the Scythians; an O.T. Antichrist; a mythological figure based on the Sumerian word *gug* meaning 'darkness' (thus a kind of principle of evil, a Tiamat); Gyges the Lydian king, *c.* 660 B.C.; Gagaia (mentioned in the Amarna Letters as barbarians), one of Cyrus's generals; Alexander the Great; Antiochus Eupator; Mithridates VI; Artaxerxes Ochus; and even by peculiar and faulty mathematics a hidden allusion to 666, the number of the beast in Rev. 13.18. The fact is: no one really knows. It was probably simply used as a rhyming pair (cf. on 27.10). What is clear is that the feared but vague enemy from the north, allied somehow with Meshech and Tubal (cf. on 27.13), as well as with Beth-togarmah (cf. on 27.14) and Gomer (cf. on 'Gamad', 27.11), was meant.

That the chapters are composite is clear. 38.1–9 refer to Gog being directed by Yahweh to assemble and advance for conquest. Verses 10–14 show a different point of view. Gog himself devises the evil scheme to attack defenceless people to amass spoil. Verses 14–16 predict that Gog will come up against Israel. Verse 17 speaks of Gog as the one predicted by former prophets as attacking Israel. Verses 18–23 show Yahweh aroused to wrath by Gog's dastardly attack and by earthquake, pestilence, bloodshed, rain, hail, fire, and brimstone killing off the hordes of Gog. In 39.1–8, Gog is again roused up against Israel but will be stricken and killed. Verses 9–10 describe the abandoned weapons as enormous in quantity; verses 11–16 speak of the seven-month burial of the corpses in a specially devoted cemetery east of the Dead Sea. Verses 17–20, however, find the corpses newly slain with birds and beasts invited to take part in the gruesome banquet. Verses 21–29 have nothing to do with Gog and Magog but recapitulate some of the ideas of the restoration prophecies as a postscript.

The apparent contradictions which appear in these chapters have led a number of scholars to assume two parallel recensions which have been interwoven, presumably by the editor, to make one section. Thus Bertholet finds 38.1–9, 16*b*–17; 39.1–7, 17–22 as one recension in which Yahweh stirs up Gog; at the end the birds and beasts devour them. In the second recension, 38.10–16*a*, 18–23; 39.8–16, Gog devises his own plan of attack, is supernaturally overthrown, and is buried by Israel. But this kind of analysis raises more problems than it solves. If the difficulties which Bertholet makes much of actually exist, why would an editor emphasize these by putting them side by side, e.g. 38.1–9 and 38.10–16*a*? Furthermore, the difficulties are not really insurmountable and are better dealt with as traditions expanding an original text. What does remain as a real possibility is the preservation of more than one original oracle.

Formally these chapters are extraordinarily complex. There are three commands **son of man, prophesy,** 38.2, 14; 39.1. The introductory oracle formula occurs seven times, 38.3, 10, 14, 17; 39.1, 17, 25. Oracle conclusion formulae eight times, 38.18, 21; 39.5, 8, 10, 13, 20, 29, and there are six recognition formulae, 38.16, 23; 39.6, 7, 22, 28, i.e. a total of fourteen conclusions. If the introductory formulae are taken into consideration, seven separate traditions emerge, 38.3–9, 10–13, 14–16, 17–23; 39.1–16, 17–24, 25–29. But the situation is more complex. The first section, 38.3–9, has no conclusion, and neither has the second, though these are separate traditions, as the contents show. The third, 38.14–16, ends with a recognition formula. The fourth, 38.17–23, is more involved. Verse 18 begins with **on that day,** which often marks a new section, and materially as well is quite separate from verse 17. The oracle concludes three times, the last time (verse 23) with the recognition formula. The other conclusions are not genuine conclusions in the literary history at all and their relevance is questionable. 39.1–16 is particularly complex. Oracle conclusion formulae occur in verses 5, 8, 10, 13, but not at verse 16. Verses 14–16 may simply be an expansion on verses 11–13, which in turn are quite separate as a tradition with its initial **On that day.** Verses 9–10 constitute a separate unit as well, as its theme of weapons for fuel shows. This still leaves the passage with four endings, verses 5, 6, 7, 8. Verse 5 is probably secondary, explaining how the 'beasts of the field' of verse 4 (not **wild beasts**) could devour the fallen of Gog who were fallen **upon the mountains of Israel.** For the original ending, cf. below.

Verses 17–24 are also not a unity; they have a concluding formula at verse 20, a recognition formula at verse 22, but no formal conclusion at verse 24. The tradition actually ends with verse 20, and verses 21–22 and 23–24 are separate. Only the former could be conceived as an expansion on the Gog materials; the latter is part of the restoration teaching. Since the recognition formula of verse 22 has

The house of Israel as subject it seems clear that this too is separate from the Gog materials. This is also the case with verses 25–29 with the two conclusions in verses 28 and 29, the former being a recognition formula with Israel as subject. Possibly the editor placed these here as restoration materials to bring chapters 32–39 to a close on a restoration theme.

Though Magog is not as clearly identified as the nations in chapters 25–32, none the less the original impetus must be that of an oracle against the nations. In that complex every original oracle was characterized in one of two ways. Either the oracle began directly with a judgment (26.7; 29.18; 30.21), or the prophet is commanded to speak against the nation or ruler in question (27.2; 28.2, 12; 29.2; 30.2; 31.2; 32.2, 18). The latter is the favoured type. In the oracles against Gog three such commands occur, 38.1, 14; 39.1. Since 38.14 begins with **Therefore** and the oracle begins with **On that day when,** it is dependent on prior materials and can hardly be considered the original oracle. This leaves 38.2–9 and 39.1–8 as possibly original. Of the two only 39.1–8 present a complete oracle of judgment. 38.2–9 are in oracular form beginning with **Behold I am against you,** but it is not a judgment at all. The passage simply predicts Gog's approaching campaign against Israel, but expresses no condemnation except in the initial formulaic expression. 39.1–8 are, on the other hand, an oracle of judgment complete in itself. It too begins with the formulaic **Behold I am against you.** The entire oracle is in 1st person addressed to Gog. Yahweh will bring Gog from its distant home in the north against Israel, but then he will strike the weapons from its hands and Gog will be completely destroyed. Problematic is the identity of the original ending. Verse 8 can be excluded since *a* (even including the formula) is a copy of 21.7 (MT 12). Verse 5 is secondary, and verses 6, 7 remain as possible conclusions. Both would be fitting, but verse 7 contains the phrase **the Holy One in Israel,** the common appellative for Yahweh in the Isaiah cycle but never in Ezekiel. Furthermore, the profanation of the holy name was more properly thematic in 36.17–23, on which it is apparently based. Verse 6 is thus the original conclusion. For its text, cf. below.

The original oracle may well come from Ezekiel, but it was extensively commented on by later members of the Ezekiel school. Because many of these expansions were eschatological in nature the section was not placed by the editor with the oracles against the nations (cf. also chapter 35), but at the end of the restoration section.

One further problem needs attention: the relation of the expansions to the original oracle. The larger expansions can be understood as expansions on segments of the original oracle in 39.1–4, 6. Thus 38.2–9 are an expansion on verses 1 and 2, whereas 38.10–13 amplify verse 2 from a different point of view, attributing Gog's invasion of restored Israel to its own godless machinations. 38.14–16 are a commentary on verse 2*b*, whereas verses 18–23 expand verse 3. Verse 17 is a general comment by a traditionist explaining the relevance of the oracle in the first place. 39.9–10 are an expansion on **I will send fire** in verse 6, though hardly in the spirit of the original comment. 39.11–13 are a detailed commentary on verse 4*a*, and verses 14–16 are expansions in turn on the preceding verses. 39.17–20 are an expansion on verse 4*b*. Eventually the materials were collected more or less in the order of the expansions, but because 38.2–9 began with the same formula as the original oracle, it was placed first. Why the original oracle occupies the middle place is puzzling. The appendix in 39.21–29 will be treated separately.

(a) THE DESTRUCTION OF GOG AND MAGOG 38.1–39.20

38.2. MT has 'land of the Magog'; the words are incorrectly divided and should be 'to' **the land of Magog**. The words are probably secondary in the text. **chief prince** does not adequately represent MT, where **prince** is a bound form. The phrase also occurs in verse 3 and 39.1. The Hebrew means 'prince of the head of ', which is peculiar. Possibly the original text simply had the unusual 'head of ', and 'prince' was added to interpret it. The word for 'head' is *r'š* and was misunderstood by G. as a proper name, 'Ros', leading to bizarre identification by the misinformed with Russia! For **Meshech** and **Tubal**, cf. on 27.13.

3. For **Lord GOD** as in verses 10, 14, 17, 18, 21, cf. on 2.4.

4. G. omits **and I will turn . . . jaws**, a late expansion based on the oracle against Pharaoh, 29.4. **all of them with . . . swords** is an accretion on **armour**. The verse explains that Yahweh is bringing out Gog fully armed.

5. That this is secondary is obvious from the 3rd plural reference in **with them**, which in the original oracle would be 2nd singular. Nor does the list make good sense. **Persia** might be possible as taking part, but **Cush** (Ethiopia) and **Put** (cf. on 27.10) could hardly accompany the northern hordes. The accretion comes from a traditionist amplifying the list of mercenaries in verse 6, but without full geographical comprehension.

6. For **Gomer**, cf. on 27.11, and for **Beth-Togarmah**, on 27.14. **uttermost parts of the north** is a term for vague and unknown but feared area from which the enemy is to come (cf. Jer. 4.6; 6.1); it is also the place where God was mythologically thought to dwell (Isa. 14.13; Ps. 48.2(MT 3)).

7. G. has 'for me' instead of **for them**. Gog and his hordes are commanded to be in Yahweh's service ready for the call to action.

8. upon the mountains . . . waste is an expansion more closely identifying the location of restored Israel. Verse 8*b* is a further expansion on *a*. The oracle dealt with Gog, not with Israel. The land against which they will go is, of course, Israel, now restored from exile. The order from Yahweh to march comes after a long interval. **latter years** is unusual; normally 'latter days' occurs as an apocalyptic term for the end time, verse 16. The passage presupposes Israel already restored.

9. Either **coming on** or **you will be** is secondary; S.V. have the former only. Render: 'You will advance like a storm; you will come like a cloud covering the land.' The remainder of the verse is secondary, a dittograph from verse 6*b*. For the storm as figure for war, cf. Isa. 10.3; the second figure occurs in the same context of the coming of the enemy from the north in Jer. 4.13.

10. On that day shows the secondary nature of the oracle. In contrast to verses 1–9 Gog itself devises the evil plan to attack defenceless people. To the Ezekiel school this was not contradictory; Yahweh was the ultimate arbiter of historical movement, but peoples themselves are responsible movers within that orbit.

11. RSV follows Versions rightly in reading '*l* (**upon**) before **the quiet people.** In contrast to 36.35 the Israelite cities are unfortified and thus easily attacked by a ruthless invader. The time presupposed is the early post-exilic period. Having no walls the towns obviously have no gates or drawbars for the gates.

12. assail is lit. 'bring back my (with G. for MT "your") hand on'. The purpose of the invasion is plunder. Israel is at the centre of the earth, a notion common to various peoples. This primitive notion of tribal arrogance was given a theological basis in Israel's faith (cf. on 5.5).

13. its villages with G. for MT 'its young lions'; instead 'its traders' a word which looks somewhat like 'its villages' has been conjectured, but there is no proof for it. That ancient Tartessus (cf. on 'Tarshish' 27.12) may have had suburbs also engaging in trade is quite likely though not otherwise known. For **Sheba,** cf. on 27.22; for **Dedan,** on 25.13. For **and the merchants of,** many prefer to read 'and its merchants and', which does make sense, but since this is hardly poetry parallelism is no criterion. The great traders of the East eagerly gather like vultures hoping that Gog's acquisition of spoil will give them economic advantage.

14. you . . . yourself. Rightly with G. reading *t'r* for MT *td'*, 'will you (not) know?'

15. Largely an amalgam of phrases from verses 4, 5.

16. For verse 16*a*, cf. on verse 9. For **In the latter days,** cf. on verse 8. For **vindicate my holiness,** cf. on 36.23. This is the first indication that judgment on Gog is coming.

17. Both G.V. read the oracle as a declarative sentence. The interrogative prefix in MT is a dittograph. Gog had not been mentioned by name by earlier prophets, but they did speak of a terrible invasion by some unnamed enemy (Jer. 4.5–6.26; cf. also Zeph. 1.14–18). The tradition is considerably later than Ezekiel, who was Jeremiah's younger contemporary. **for years** is a possible translation, though unlikely to be correct. It is probably an interpretative gloss meaning 'a long time ago'. Those prophecies had not yet been fulfilled and the traditionist points out that Gog is now their fulfilment.

18. For **on that day,** cf. on verse 10. **my wrath will be roused** is lit. 'my wrath will come up in my nostrils', i.e. 'I will snort in my wrath', a strong anthropomorphism avoided in G., which omits 'in my nostrils'.

19. The divine anger (**jealousy** here is but a synonym) will be roused against the infidel hordes and it will create an earthquake, often predicted as part of the eschatological end time (Isa. 24.17–20; Jl 3.16; Hag. 2.6–7; Zech. 14.4–5).

20. When Yahweh personally appears the world of nature is in turmoil; for theophanies, cf. Exod. 19.16, 18; 20.18; 1 Kg. 19.11–12; Ps. 18.7–15(MT 8–16); Hab. 3.3–15. For the division of organic life into four as typical of P, cf. Gen. 9.2, also Gen. 1.26, 28, 30. The earthquake will even make mountains fall. **cliffs** occurs elsewhere only in Ca. 2.14.

21. MT has 'And I will summon him a sword for all my mountains' for the first sentence; the last two words 'my mountains, a sword' may be a corruption of the word for 'terror', as G. shows. On the other hand verse 21*b* presupposes the word 'sword' in *a*. Possibly MT means 'And I will give the name: Sword, to all my mountains against him', i.e. God will summon the falling mountains to act as swords, i.e. destroy Gog. There is no need for changing MT 'him' to Gog; this is obvious from the context. Verse 21*b* describes the panic which will overtake the terrorized hordes.

22. For **pestilence and bloodshed,** cf. 5.17. Verse 22*b* is not typical of Ezekiel at all; the complete defeat of Gog will be at the hands of nature under divine mandate to summon all its destructive forces against the invader.

23. That it is Yahweh at work is clear from the three reflexive verbs: exalt myself, show myself holy, reveal myself.

39.1. Cf. on 38.1–2. For **Lord God,** as in verses 5, 8, 10, 13, 17, 20, cf. on 2.4.

2. In the original oracle the emphasis is throughout on Yahweh directing affairs. It is he who brings Gog from his northern homeland against the mountains of Israel (cf. 36.4).

3. But Yahweh brings Gog only to destroy him. As in the earlier reference (Jer. 6.23) the northern invader is armed with the bow, but before he can attack he is smitten, though in what way is not said.

4. **birds . . . sort** is lit. 'vultures, birds of every wing'. 'Birds of every wing' may be a secondary explanation of the more unfamiliar word. Appropriately the enemy will fall precisely on the mountains which they intended to attack. **hordes** and **peoples** promoted the identifications in 38.6. **wild beasts** is lit. 'beasts of the field'. For 'food for birds and beasts', cf. 29.5.

5. For its secondary character, cf. above. **open field** is the same word as 'field' in verse 4.

6. The inclusion of the coastal peoples in the judgment seems inconsistent with the judgment. Verse 6*a* originally meant 'And I will send fire on Magog and the coastlands shall dwell in safety'. Magog is pictured as spreading widespread terror and its defeat will give far-off peoples peace. The subject of the recognition formula is the coastlands. **send fire on** was common among eighth-century prophets for violent destruction; cf. e.g. Am. 1.4; Hos. 8.14 for the complete idiom.

7. The theme of the holy name and its sacredness is based on 36.20–23 (cf. on 20.9). A minority reading followed by V. has 'the Holy One of Israel', but the more unusual text of MT (as RSV) is to be preferred. The purpose of the divine judgment on Gog is given by this tradition as the revelation of Yahweh's holy name in Israel.

9. **and burn them** is a late gloss unattested in G. added to explain the rare word **make fires** (Ps. 78.21; Isa. 44.15). For **shields and bucklers,** cf. on 23.24. For **shields** G.S.V. have 'poles'. In any event the pair seems to be secondary in Hebrew as the absence of the preposition with these shows. The Israelites will be able to use the weapons of the slain as fuel for seven years. The number **seven** became a favourite in apocalyptic writing.

10. Israel will take its revenge and pillage the pillagers, a case of *lex talionis*.

11. Travellers is probably better taken as a proper name 'Abarim'. Abarim was the name of the mountains in northern Moab overlooking the Dead Sea (Num. 33.47–48), and by extension the name is here applied to the valley below on the east side of the Dead Sea, thus appropriately outside the Holy Land itself. For **On that day,** cf. on 38.10. After **place** MT has 'there', which G.V. point as 'name', hence 'memorial', thus 'a memorial place as a burial', which is probably correct. That the place was **in Israel** would not be correct in post-exilic times, but it had been so historically. **it will block the travellers** represents a corrupt text. G. has 'and they shall enclose the mouth of the valley'. **the travellers** is secondary, probably a dittograph. **the Valley** presupposes *gy'* for *hy'*, 'it'. Read 'they shall block up the valley'. It will be unclean ground since the infidels are buried there, and this action will keep the holy people from inadvertently straying in. **Hamon** means 'multitude', often used of non-Israelite multitudes in the oracles against nations.

12. The slaughter was so great that it took Israel seven (cf. on verse 9) months to bury the slain. Corpses defiled the land as long as they were unburied, and their burial outside the land kept the land holy.

13. The burial is done by **the people of the land,** i.e. the common people, not the priests. The eschatological predictions are evident in the references to the day when Yahweh reveals His glory.

14. After **bury** MT has 'the travellers', a copyist's error, as its absence in G.S. shows. Bertholet plausibly suggests the change of 'bury' to 'search out', i.e. *mkbrym* to *mbkrym* which makes good sense since the buriers do not perform until verse 15*b*. **continually** modifies **men** rather than the verb in MT. They are permanent inspectors who must look for dead bodies which defile the land. They only begin their work after the seven-month mass burial is finished.

15. sign means 'cairn' or 'gravemarker'. Such a marker would keep people from inadvertently defiling themselves by touching the bones.

16. The pedantic parenthetical remark is probably secondary. No such city is known.

17. S. more logically has the introductory formula after **field.** Verse 17*b* is a condensed doublet of verse 18*a* and probably secondary. This section is logically prior to the preceding, since here the slain are still unburied. Yahweh has prepared a sacrificial meal for birds and beasts on the mountains of Israel.

18. The meal consists of the flesh and blood of the slain; the sacrificial character is clear from verse 18*b*, where they are described as proper animals for sacrifice— the height of sarcasm. **mighty,** as in verse 20, refers to warriors.

19. Even more revolting is the animals gorging themselves on fat and blood, which were not eaten in sacrifice proper but were offered to God, 44.15. From the earliest legislation (Covenant Code) these were set apart (Exod. 23.18). The fat was not to be eaten (Lev. 3.17; 7.23–25), nor was the blood (Lev. 7.26–27). The blood was usually sprinkled (Lev. 5.9; 16.19) or poured out (Exod. 29.12; Lev. 4.7), or even burned (Num. 19.5).

20. MT vocalizes **riders** as 'chariots', which can hardly be correct.

(b) AN APPENDIX OF RESTORATION ORACLES **39.21–29**

This mosaic of restoration oracles was collected by the editor to conclude the section between the oracles against the nations, chapters 25–32, and that on the new cultic order, chapters 40–48. The oracles are general restoration themes from the Ezekiel school. The first, verses 21–22, ends in a recognition formula; the second, without any formulae, verses 23–24, is a justification for the Exile. The promise of full restoration in verses 25–29 begins with an introductory formula but is subsequent to the preceding as **Therefore** indicates. It has two formal conclusions: a recognition formula based on a summary of verses 21–27 in verse 28 and a conclusion formula in verse 29 after a promise to pour out the divine spirit on the restored house of Israel.

21. The judgments on nations is a manifestation of the divine glory. 'To lay the hand on' means to execute judgment.

22. that day is probably the day of Israel's restoration since this is part of the judgment on the nations. Israel's release must involve their captor's judgment.

23. Verse 23*b* logically succeeds verse 24. In view of the fact that **I hid my face from them** ends verse 24 as well, it may have been copied into the wrong place. That the Exile was due to Israel's sin was basic to Ezekiel's thought.

25. For **Lord GOD**, as in verse 29, cf. on 2.4. In contrast to much of 38.1–39.20 the return from exile is still future. **fortunes** is lit. the 'exile'. Yahweh promises an end to the captivity. The designation **Jacob** is rare in Ezekiel; cf. 20.5, where 'house of Jacob' occurs in an unusual election theme. **jealous** here means 'zealous' in contrast to its more common use of 'angry', cf. on 38.19.

26. forget: MT points as 'bear', which the Versions follow. That the exiles would 'bear their shame' means that they will remember their sins also during the coming age as a perpetual warning on the one hand and recognition of God's mercy on the other.

27. many nations represents an impossible Hebrew construction: *hgwym rbym*. G. shows that 'many' is a late gloss. For verse 27*b*, cf. on 36.23.

28. G. omits **and then gathered . . .**, but this can hardly be original since recognition of Yahweh by the nations is based in this context on the full cycle of action: exile and restoral. Verse 28*b* is part of the supplement to the oracle continued in verse 29.

29. God reveals himself to Israel by pouring out his spirit (cf. on 36.27).

FOURTH SECTION **40–48** THE NEW TEMPLE AND CULT

A. THE VISION OF THE NEW TEMPLE **40.1–42.20**

With 40.1 begins the last major section of the book, the vision of the new Temple, its cult, its personnel, and its setting in the restored community.

Stylistically it is completely different from the rest of the book. This has led many scholars to deny any of it to Ezekiel. The entire section is presented as a vision of the restored community in which a purified cult stands at the centre of a purified community. As in the remainder of the book, however, it will be seen that a process of accretions to an original Ezekiel core has taken place. The glory of Yahweh which had departed from the Temple, 11.23, because of the cultic abominations in the holy city (cf. on chapter 8), must return to the Temple of the restored community, 43.4–5, a community where the presence of God is assured by a pure cult.

Chapters 40–42 describe the Temple complex, and more particularly its various dimensions. The section opens with the usual dated introduction formula indicating a vision experience, intended by the editor to introduce the entire section but relevant chiefly to chapters 40–42, as appears from the description of the visionary guide's equipment.

The text of these chapters, particularly of chapters 41 and 42, has suffered greatly at the hands of copyists; even with the help of the versions only a tentative reconstruction is possible. RSV is one such reconstruction and only in those passages where comment or clarification of the RSV is necessary will textual discussion take place.

The literary history of these chapters has been complicated by a series of accretions of a descriptive nature. The introduction to the vision, 40.1–4, details ecstatic transport of the prophet to a high mountain in Israel on which the Temple complex was centred. A man appears in the vision to serve as guide to the prophet and to measure the various parts of the complex. The complex is approached from the outside, and the outer wall is first examined, though its overall measurements are not detailed until the summation in 42.15–20.

The guide begins detailed measurements at the outer east gate, 40.6–19. This section, together with verses 20–37, is clearly a literary unity. The structure is largely based on Ezekiel's memory of the Solomonic Temple together with visionary projections of ideal relationships. Thus the three gateways were all of the same size, and there was a progression of higher levels as one approached the nave: the gateways had seven steps (cf. on 40.6); the outer court, eight steps, verses 31, 34, 37; and the Temple itself was reached by ten steps, verse 49. It is useless to attempt to find archaeological parallels to such an ideal construction.

The remaining outer gates, the north and the south, are then measured, 40.20–23 and 24–27. The same visionary style found in verses 5–19 is followed in these passages. The guide leads the prophet to the area to be measured and then proceeds to measure it in detail. These are part of the original narrative.

This also applies to the measurements of the inner gates: south, verses 28–31, east, verses 32–34, and north, verses 35–37.

With verse 38 the style of the vision is abandoned. The guide does not bring the prophet forward nor does he measure anything. Verses 38–43 describe a chamber in the vestibule—presumably in the north gate, though this is not stated—intended for the washing of the burnt offering, as well as eight tables all for sacrificial use. Emphasis on the use to which parts of the complex were intended is alien to the nature of the original narrative, which simply details the measurements. The accretion is due to interest in particular details of the performance of the cult in the Temple, as in 46.21–24.

Verses 44–46 are also secondary. The vision style is absent (verse 44*aa* in RSV is based on G.; MT has 'And on the outside of the inner gates were chambers for singers in the inner court'). Explanations concerning the use to which the chambers were to be put are made by the guide, including a statement that only Zadokite priests were allowed to perform sacrificial duties. This passage is one of the latest layers of tradition in this section.

With verse 47 the original narrative resumes. The outer and inner gates have now been measured, and progressing towards the centre the guide now determines the dimensions of the court. There is no need for the guide to bring the prophet to it since he is actually already at the inner north gate (verses 35–37).

There still remains to be measured the actual Temple itself, 40.48–41.4. The prophet is brought first to the vestibule, and then to the nave, both of which are measured. Finally, the visionary guide appropriately enters the adytum alone and measures it. Throughout the passage the visionary style is used, with the possible exception of verse 4*b*, where the guide identifies the inner room as the adytum.

One might expect the description to end with some kind of summary statement such as that of 42.15–20, but instead a series of detailed descriptions follow. The first accretion is 41.5–15*a*. That it is secondary is clear from its style as well as its content. The prophet is not led about, so presumably is still in the nave. But from that vantage-point it would be impossible to see either the side-chambers of the Temple or the building at the west end. Furthermore, the passage is an architectural description in part based on the account in 1 Kg. 6.5–10 rather than a continuation of the measurements of the complex. In verses 13–15*a* measurements are taken by the guide but these are based on the secondary materials of verses 6–12 in imitation of the original vision. The original narrative had thus no account of the three-storeyed side-chambers nor of the west building behind the adytum.

Verses 15*b*–26 return to a description of the Temple itself, but are independent of the original narrative. The guide's only function is to identify the **table which is before the LORD,** verse 22. He neither measures nor leads. The passage is a purely descriptive piece detailing the decoration of the interior of the Temple in part reminiscent of the decoration of the Solomonic Temple (1 Kg. 6.14–36).

The last major accretion is 42.1–14. The text is so corrupt that very little can be made of it. It is clear, however, that the west building is presupposed, so the tradition must be later than that of 41.5–15*a*. It is not completely clear what is being described, but apparently it concerns side-chambers adjoining the west building on the north and south sides. The guide is finally depicted as stating the priestly uses to which these chambers were to be put, probably based on such traditions as 44.17–19, 28–30, and 46.19–20.

The section concludes with the guide bringing the prophet outside the complex, and measuring the large wall enclosing the complex. The present form of the

Hebrew text (the use of the perfect throughout instead of the waw consecutive characteristic of the original narrative) indicates a late version of a statement of similar content which must have concluded the original narrative. The symmetry of the various parts of the complex in the vision is also apparent here. This complex is a perfect square.

The original vision is thus to be found in 40.1–37, 48–41.4, and 42.15–20.

(a) THE INTRODUCTION 40.1–4

1. The date of the vision is given as April 573 B.C. The usual calendric system based on the year of Jehoiachin's captivity is employed as well as a second based on the fall of Jerusalem eleven years later. The latter may have been added by the editor to tie the vision of the restored Temple from which the divine glory returns in with that of the now destroyed Temple from which the glory departed; cf. on chapters 8–11. **beginning of the year** occurs only here; it is appropriate as marking the new beginning envisaged by the vision. For **hand . . . me,** cf. on 1.3.

2. Mount Zion is idealized as a **very high mountain.** That the Temple complex looked like a city was owing to its wall enclosure. **opposite me** represents a correction of MT 'towards the south', which is probably a gloss based on a mis-understanding of **city** as referring to Jerusalem. The city was south of the Temple area.

3. Though the guide in the vision is simply called **a man,** his appearance **like bronze** shows his celestial character. The man has two measures in his hand, the **reed** for shorter, the **line** (or 'rope') for longer measurements.

4. That the guide is a heavenly ministrant is clear from his commission to the prophet (otherwise usually given by Yahweh himself). For a similar instruction, cf. 43.10.

(b) THE OUTER EAST GATE 40.5–16

5. Galling maintains that this verse is secondary since the measurement of the outer wall would hardly precede that of the gateways, but the starting-place is from the outside. Only the thickness and height are measured. Most of the measurements that follow are two-dimensional only, i.e. length and breadth. These terms are relative; when the dimensions differ, length is always the longer regardless of direction. The long cubit is approximately 21 in. (exactly 20·67 in.), thus the reed is *c.* 10½ ft. The height of the wall is surprisingly low (only 10½ ft); an actual wall would be much higher than its width. In the vision, however, symmetry is more important than realism.

6. G. has for **its steps** 'by seven steps', which is preferable, cf. verses 22, 26, **eight** steps in verses 31, 34, 37, and **ten** steps in verses 49. The east gate is first measured since east was the usual orientation and thus the most important one, cf. 44.1–3. The guide mounted the steps to the threshold, which was 10½ ft long.

7. The corridor of the gateway is flanked by three chambers on either side, 10½ ft square, separated by a space 8 ft 9 in. wide, probably intended for the Temple guard, 44.11. The threshold at the far (west) end was the same length as the outer one.

8. Proceeding inward the vestibule measured 14 ft (east to west), and 35 ft across.

9. The jambs were 3½ ft thick; the jambs were the inner walls of the outer gate on which the roof of the gateway must have rested.

11. The difference in width between the door of the gate (17½ ft) and the gateway itself (22 ft 9 in.) is probably to be accounted for by the stone door-sockets on which the doors were hung.

12. barrier: lit. 'border', of 21 in. in front of the side-chambers; possibly a projecting railing is intended.

13. from door to door: rather 'door over against door'; the side-chambers were directly opposite one another. Overall measurement from the rear wall of a side-chamber to the opposite rear wall was 43 ft 9 in., i.e. the width of two opposite chambers (21 ft) plus that of the gateway (22 ft 9 in.).

14. The text of MT is impossible and that of G. not much better. Symmetry would suggest 25 rather than 20 cubits for the north–south dimensions of the vestibule, thus 43 ft 9 in. (cf. on verse 13).

15. The overall dimensions of the gateway from east to west are 87½ ft, i.e. the sum of two thresholds, three side-rooms, two intervening spaces, the vestibule, and the jamb, cf. verses 6–9.

16. windows, narrowing: probably better 'windows recessed' (cf. 1 Kg. 6.4). The verse can be rendered: 'The side-rooms had recessed windows, and so did their jambs inward toward the gate round about . . . and the jambs had palm-tree decorations.'

(c) THE OUTER COURT **40.17–19**

17. Thirty chambers were built against the inside of the outer wall of the complex, and fronted on a pavement which served as the outer rim of the outer court.

18. The width of the pavement corresponded to the length of the gates, i.e. 87½ ft. Its identification as **the lower pavement** is probably secondary, based on a comparison with the 'raised platform' of 41.8–11.

19. From the edge of the pavement, i.e. from the inner side of the outer gates, to the other side of the outer court, i.e. the outer side of the inner gate, was 175 ft.

(d) THE NORTH AND SOUTH OUTER GATES **40.20–27**

These gates are replicas of the east outer gate as detailed in verses 6–16, and are symmetrically located, i.e. the distance from the inner side of the outer gates to the outer side of the inner gates respectively was 175 ft (cf. on verse 19). The account is a summary rather than a detailed repetition of measurements.

(e) THE INNER GATES **40.28–37**

The prophet is successively led to and witnesses the measurements of the south (coming from the south outer gate), east, and north inner gates. In contrast to the pre-exilic Temple, Ezekiel's had both an outer court for lay worshippers and an inner court for priestly use only. The overall dimensions were again identical with those of the east outer gate, but the internal arrangement of the gates was reversed, i.e. the vestibule was near the outer end rather than towards the inner court. In contrast to the rise of seven steps leading to the outer gates, the inner were on a rise of eight steps.

30. This is a doublet of verse 29. Its omission by G. shows its secondary character. The gate had but one vestibule.

(f) ARRANGEMENTS FOR SACRIFICES IN THE INNER GATE 40.38–43

Presumably the north inner gate is intended here.

38. A room in the vestibule was designated for rinsing the burnt offering (cf. Lev. 1.9). Whether some laver was present (cf. 2 Chr. 4.6) is not recorded. In any event it could not be large.

39. G. omits **the burnt offering and** since it was already mentioned in verse 38. But the sacrifice was slaughtered before it was washed. The **sin offering** was a sacrifice intended to restore the worshipper to a cultically pure condition, whereas the **guilt offering** was rather a fine which had to be paid for damage.

40. Since the vestibule of the inner gate was near the outer end of the gate, **outside** must refer to the outer court next to the steps leading up to the gate.

41. *Summary of verses 39–40.* **of the side of the gate** may have been a theme incorporated from the margin.

42. Presumably near the tables for slaughter (verses 39–41) were four small stone tables, each 21 in. high and 31 in. square, intended for holding the tools for sacrifice.

43. hooks: a dubious rendering for an obscure Hebrew word, based on T. Possibly it should read 'rims' (as G.), though how they were to be fastened to a stone surface is not clear. G. has 'hewn' instead of fastened, which would make better sense. Verse 43*b* can hardly apply to the tables of verse 42, but rather to those of verse 41. It may have been a comment on the entire section.

(g) CHAMBERS FOR THE PRIESTS 40.44–46

44. Read 'And outside the inner gate were two chambers. . . .' The point of view is now from the inner court.

45–46. The distinction between two ranks in the priesthood may have originated with the Deuteronomic reform in 622 B.C., whereby non-Jerusalem priests became priests of second rank (cf. 2 Kg. 23.9). The identification of these as Levites as opposed to the privileged Zadokites in verse 46*b* is probably an accretion based on the tradition of 44.15.

(h) THE DIMENSIONS OF THE INNER COURT AND THE TEMPLE 40.47–41.4

47. The vantage-point of verses 35–37, i.e. the north inner gate, continues here with the measurement of the inner court (175 ft square). Since the original section was only concerned with dimensions, the reference to the altar in verse 47*b* may be a secondary accretion based on 43.13–17.

48. The vestibule is measured first. The depth of its jambs were 8 ft 9 in. Measured across the doorway to the vestibule it was 24½ ft wide, and the side-walls 5 ft 3 in. on either side.

49. The total width (**length,** i.e. north–south) of the vestibule was thus 35 ft; in depth it was 21 ft (differing from the Solomonic Temple, which was 17½ ft deep, 1 Kg. 6.3). The pillars are based on the two pillars in 1 Kg. 7.15–22. The Temple itself stood on an elevated platform (ten steps upward).

1–2. *The nave.* The wall between vestibule and nave (**jambs**) was 10½ ft and jutted inward 8 ft 9 in. to make the entrance only 17½ ft wide. The nave itself was 35 ft broad and 70 ft deep.

3. Only the heavenly guide entered the adytum since it was tabu for the prophet. The thickness of the wall between nave and adytum was only 3½ ft. The width of the entrance was 10½ ft, thus each of the jambs extended inward 12 ft 3 in.

4. The dimensions of the adytum itself were 35 ft square. Since in the original account there is no other reference to the heavenly guide speaking after the introductory injunction of 40.4, it is doubtful whether verse 4*b* is original.

(i) THE SIDE-CHAMBERS 41.5–11

5. Two measurements are given, that of the Temple wall as 10½ ft and that of the side-chambers as 7 ft.

The construction of the side-chambers **6–11**

The architectural details are so obscure and the text so corrupt that only a vague general picture can be reconstructed. The use to which these cells were to be put is not given. The passage is apparently based on the account of the Solomonic Temple in 1 Kg. 6.5–6, 8, 10. The chambers were three-tiered, ninety cells in all, probably around three sides (all but the east) of the Temple. In some way the structure was independent of the Temple structurally. As in 1 Kg. 6 the base storey was the narrowest and the top broadest. This simply means that the walls became thinner since the outer face must have been perpendicular. Ascent to the upper floors was by steps of some kind, whether by ladder or stairway is not clear.

8. raised platform is a doublet rendering of MT 'height' and G. 'platform'. What seems to be meant is the elevation on which the Temple itself stood, i.e. ten steps (40.49) equalling 10½ ft. The rendering of verse 8*b* can only be approximate since the last word in MT is completely unknown.

9. The elevation on which the Temple stood extended outward beyond the outer walls of the side-chambers for 8 ft 9 in., the walls themselves also being 8 ft 9 in. thick.

9b–10. An open space 35 ft in width surrounded the Temple elevation apparently. MT is unintelligible.

11. Entrance to the side-chambers was from the outer side, i.e. **the part, left free,** cf. on verse 9.

(j) VARIOUS MEASUREMENTS 41.12–15a

What the building to the west, i.e. behind the Temple, was for is nowhere detailed, unless it was the 'parbar' of 1 Chr. 26.18. It is simply called **the building.** Its measurements are given in verses 12, 13*b*, and 15, whereas verses 13*a*–14 give those of the Temple. The inner measurements of the building from north to south were 157½ ft; the outer, 175 ft. From east to west the inner measurements were 122½ ft; the outer, 140 ft. Between the east face of the building and the rear of the adytum a yard of 35 ft obtained to make overall symmetrical dimensions 175 ft square.

The same overall dimensions are obtained for the Temple, i.e. 175 ft square. By adding to the east–west dimensions of the Temple itself in 40.48–41.4, the Temple wall and side-chambers of verse 5 and the outer wall of the side-chambers of verse 9, 175 ft is obtained. Similarly, by adding a 35-ft yard to the north and south of the Temple elevation (adding up to 105 ft), a dimension of 175 ft is also obtained.

(k) ORNAMENTATION OF THE TEMPLE INTERIOR 41.15b–26

15b. **The nave . . . room** wrongly follows G. for MT's 'the inner nave'. The section does not describe the interior decoration of the adytum at all. Possibly what was originally intended may have been 'the nave towards the inside'.

16–17. Completely obscure; apparently much wood panelling was used both in the vestibule and the nave.

18. Decorative cherubim and palm motifs were characteristic of Solomon's Temple (cf. 1 Kg. 6.29), which is probably the basis for this passage. Since the cherubim are two-dimensional they are only two-faced in contrast to the four in 10.14, and cf. 'the living creatures' of 1.10.

19. Only human and lion faces obtain.

21b–22. *The table of showbread.* It looked like an altar of wood and its dimensions were 5 ft 3 in. high and 3½ ft square. For the considerably smaller table in P, cf. Exod. 25.23. The significance of the showbread for the Hebrew cult is not clear; in H (Lev. 24.7–9) it is called a 'memorial portion' and 'a most holy portion out of the offerings by fire' (cf. also 1 Sam. 21.3–6).

23–25a. *The double doors of nave and adytum.* Cf. 1 Kg. 6.34–35. They were decorated in the same fashion as the walls of the nave.

25. Lit. 'And there were wrought on them, on the doors of the nave. . . .' 'On the doors of the nave' is a gloss explaining 'on them'.

25b. canopy. Completely unknown; some have suggested 'railing'; others, 'cornice'.

26. The verse is unintelligible. Windows and palm trees on the sides can hardly be correct, and verse 26*b* is completely rewritten by RSV to make sense

(l) THE CHAMBERS OPPOSITE THE YARD 42.1–14

The text of this section is extremely corrupt and one can only attempt a possible reconstruction. The best reconstruction of the text is that of K. Elliger (*Beitr. z. hist. Theologie* 16 (1953), 79ff.), with which RSV agrees in part. Apparently these chambers flanked the west building and were 175 ft long and 87½ ft wide, there being one to the north and one to the south of the building.

3. Obscure architectural details. **gallery** is an unknown word. G. renders verse 3*b* 'pillars opposite each other arranged in triple rows', which is also a guess.

4. For **and a hundred cubits long** read 'and a wall of one cubit' (reading *gdr* for *drk*). This is the wall referred to in verse 7.

5–6. Also obscure. There seem to be three storeys, the upper ones being narrower, but it is not clear why this was so. Why absence of pillars should make this necessary or what and where the pillars of the courts (thus MT for **outer court**) were is unknown.

8. It seems that flanking the chambers were still other chambers only half (i.e. 87½ ft) as long as the chambers of verses 1–6.

9. The door to these smaller chambers was to the east, at the place where the wall of the court (for **the outside wall**—verse 10*a*) begins. This is the wall referred to in verses 4 and 7.

10–12. A summary statement showing a mirror image construction of the building to the south.

13–14. The use of the chambers is given by the guide as sacristies for the priests. These sacristies are at variance with 40.44–46 and represent a separate tradition. Beside the sin and guilt offerings (cf. on 40.39) the **cereal offering** is also mentioned. These three were reserved for the priests, 44.29.

14. For the strict tabu regulations concerning holy *v.* profane garments, cf. 44.19.

(m) OVERALL TEMPLE MEASUREMENTS 42.15–20

The style of the original vision, the guide conducting the prophet and measuring, is resumed. Verse 15 originally must have followed 41.4.

15. The prophet is led out from the nave to the outer east gate to watch the measuring of the outer wall. Though it is not stated, he presumably followed the guide on the tour since at 43.1 he is again brought to the east gate.

16–19. Successively the east, north, south, and west walls are measured, i.e. the same succession followed in 40.6–37 with the addition of the rear or west wall. The entire complex is a square of 875 ft. The measurement across would be the total of four gateways (350 ft), the inner court (175 ft), and twice the space (outer court) from outer to inner gates (350 ft). In length the same dimensions are obtained by two gateways (175 ft), two courts (350 ft), the Temple (175 ft), and the space of 175 ft from the rear of the Temple to the west wall which in the later accretions is occupied by the west building.

20. four sides: lit. 'four winds'; cf. on 37.9. The purpose of the outer wall is to guard the sacral area.

B. THE CONSECRATION OF THE NEW TEMPLE 43.1–12

Once the dimensions of the ideal Temple have been measured the stage is set for the re-entry of the glory of God. It had left (11.23) as a symbol of judgment; it now is to return as a sign of restoration. Appropriately the guide again brings the prophet to the east gate (cf. on 42.15) through which the divine glory was to come. As in the inaugural vision the prophet is overwhelmed (cf. 1.28). As in 8.3 he is raised and ecstatically transported by the spirit (not led by the guide any more, who is, however, still with him), this time to the inner court. Verse 3a represents an expansion of the text similar to those in 8.4; 10.15, 22.

As in the inaugural vision, the prophet hears a voice speaking (cf. 2.2), obviously of Yahweh himself, who assures him that he will remain here in the midst of Israel for ever. The remainder, verses 7b–12, is a series of accretions. Verse 7b represents a later priestly tradition concerning the defilement of corpses. Proximity of the royal cemetery to the Temple renders the Temple profane. This is a defilement of the holy name. This same tradition occurs in 9.7, for which cf. commentary there. Verse 8a is dependent on the preceding and is an explanation by a later traditionist of how the defilement obtained. Verse 9 is dependent on verse 7b and repeats its substance as a warning. Verse 8b is a statement of judgment quite at variance with its context of restoration.

Verses 10–12 are also secondary, but their relation to the context is not clear. Verses 10–11 are a new command to the prophet to delineate in writing all the details of the Temple architecture and ordinances. As such it is an elaboration of 40.4, but now near the end of the vision rather than at the beginning where it belongs. The verses are probably an editorial summary. Verse 12 may be taken either as a subscription to all the foregoing or as a superscription to the remainder of the book. It is clearly a later tradition in any event. Its reference to the holy character of the Temple complex shows that it is probably no earlier than the traditions in verses 7b–9.

1. G. omits the dittograph **the gate.** The prophet had been outside the complex, presumably following the guide measuring the outer wall.

2. The glory had departed through the east gate (cf. 11.23) and now returns from that direction. For **sound of many waters,** cf. 1.24 where the simile is applied to the movement of the living creatures.

3. Only **and I fell upon my face** is original to the vision. The analogy with the visions in chapter 1 and chapters 8–11 is obvious. MT 'when I came' is an error for the minority reading **when he came.** For verse 3b, cf. on 1.28.

5. That the Spirit should now transport the prophet is appropriate since the climax of the vision is approaching, viz. the vision of the glory of Yahweh filling the Temple (cf. 1 Kg. 8.10–11). Transport is of course only to the inner court; the Temple itself is too holy, and is to be entered by priests only.

6. the man: rightly with Versions for MT 'a man'; the reference is to the angelic guide of the vision, who no longer serves any purpose in the vision; **While . . . beside me** may well be secondary. As a literary device the angelic guide is retained in later chapters (cf. 44.1, 4; 46.19). For **one speaking,** cf. on 1.28. The speaker, i.e. Yahweh, is heard (not seen) speaking from within the Temple.

7. MT does not have **this is.** G. has 'you have seen', which is possible (r'yt 't for '*t*). For Jerusalem as the throne of God, cf. Jer. 3.17; 17.12. The combination of throne and footstool both referring to the Temple is unusual and betrays the solemnity of Yahweh's transfer to the Temple of the future. The last word in the verse is 'their high places', which is probably an explanatory word for **dead bodies,** intending thereby to call attention to the royal tombs. RSV rightly omits it. Defilement of the divine name according to the traditionist can occur either through idolatry (**harlotry**) or through the presence of corpses.

8a. This explains the danger of defilement. In the Solomonic Temple the palace was part of the overall complex, the palace conclave being part of the great court, with only the inner court actually part of the Temple itself (cf. 1 Kg. 7.2–12). The holiness of the Temple complex was not only guarded by the outer wall, 42.15–20, but was also to have nothing profane adjacent to it.

8b. An explanation for the exile which is here out of place. Nor is the idiom of the last phrase (lit. 'ate them in my anger') typical of Ezekiel.

9. idolatry: same word as harlotry as in verse 7.

10–11. that they ... iniquities does not fit and was added by a later traditionist to give a moral intent to the portrayal. A similar accretion obtains in **And if ... done.** RSV follows G. in reading **its appearance and its plan** for MT's peculiar 'and they shall measure the proportion'. MT 'the form of the temple' is better than **portray the temple.** The original thus should read, 'And you, son of man, describe to the house of Israel the temple, its appearance and plan, the form of the temple, its arrangement, its exits and its entrances. . . .'

11. and its whole form is otiose; it was probably a marginal note. MT also has this for **all its laws** in the last clause, but RSV rightly follows G.

12. G. rightly omits the doublet **Behold . . . temple.** The verse was probably intended to be a title for what follows. The regulations in the remainder of the book are intended to ensure that the entire Temple complex will be kept in a most holy state.

C. The Altar and its Consecration 43.13–27

The section is in two parts: verses 13–17 describe the dimensions of the altar, and verses 18–27 its consecration. The entire section is of later origin as its ill-fitting context shows.

(a) The Description of the Altar 43.13–17
Later traditionists prepared a detailed description of the measurements of the altar, probably on the basis of the altar of burnt offering in the second Temple (cf. 2 Chr. 4.1). The description begins abruptly and it is not clear why the editor should have placed it here.

It has often been pointed out that the prototype of the square-tiered altar is the Babylonian ziggurat. Nothing is said of its materials though dressed stone would seem likely. The description makes use of architectural terms (**base, ledge,** and **altar hearth**) not used elsewhere, and some uncertainty must remain. **base** means lit. 'bosom' and finds an analogy in the term 'bosom of the earth' used in Akkadian to describe the platform on which Nebuchadrezzar's palace stood in Babylon. **ledge** is a technical term referring to the tiers below the top one. The top layer was 12 cubits square; it rested on the upper ledge which was 14 cubits square, which in turn rested on the lower ledge which was 16 cubits square. The altar as a whole stood in a **base**, 1 cubit deep and 18 cubits square. It might be preferable to substitute 'layer' for **ledge** throughout.

13. The words in parentheses define the measure of length as being the long cubit (*c.* 21 in.). **high** is lacking in MT and 'deep' is what was meant. The base had a 4-in. rim or border, probably to protect the trench of the base.

14. base on the ground is lit. 'bosom of the earth' (cf. above), and could better be rendered 'base in the ground'. The lowest layer is called **the smaller ledge** since it was only 2 cubits high, whereas the middle (as well as the upper) was 4. Successively each layer upwards was 1 cubit less on each side.

15. altar hearth represents MT *hr'l* or *'r'yl*, verse 16, the former being vocalized to mean 'mountain of God', and the latter as 'lion of God', neither of which is appropriate. The translation is based on Arabic. It is a technical term for the top layer of the altar. At each of the four corners were **horns,** or projections upward. Altar horns are well known from archaeological sites in Palestine. The height of the horns (**one cubit**) is not given in MT, but is based on G. (which, however, does not mention their number).

17. The dimensions of the lower ledge are not given and must have fallen out after **fourteen broad.** Add 'and the lower ledge also shall be square, sixteen cubits long by sixteen broad'. The reference to the rim that follows should be preceded by that of the base. The rim was on the base, not on the ledge (cf. verse 13*b*). Since the stair ascent was on the east the officiant would face the Temple westward.

(b) THE CONSECRATION OF THE ALTAR **43.18–27**
This section is dependent on the preceding and is therefore not earlier. In its present form it is composite in character. This can be seen from (a) its artificial oracular character as opposed to the expected **These are the ordinances for the altar**; cf. the similar introduction in verse 13; (b) the mixture of 2nd singular and 3rd plural and even some 2nd plural references; and (c) the inconsistent references to Yahweh in 1st (verses 19, 27) and 3rd (verse 24) person.

Since these are simply regulations for the altar consecration the oracular form is artificial, a later attempt to vest these ordinances with divine authority. The introductory formula in verse 18 is thus secondary. This immediately renders the 1st person references in verses 19 and 27 suspect as well. Both of these verses contain oracle conclusion formulae also. The context in verse 19, which must be secondary, is **to the Levitical priests . . . GOD,** which leaves the simple command **you shall give a bull for a sin offering** as original. This must be original since reference to the bull is made anaphorically in verse 20. Verse 27 is in a context of 3rd and 2nd plural references, all of which are secondary. Verse 26 is also in 3rd plural and is a further interpretation of verse 25, which was the original ending. (The last verb *y'św* is plural but is intended as an indefinite passive; this may have given the impulse to plural accretions.) Verses 22*b* and 24*b* are 3rd plural and secondary. The former is an interpretative addition to verse 22*a*. Verse 21 may also be secondary. The verb in verse 21*b* is 3rd masc. singular. The later traditionist in line with P realized that the sin offering was to be burnt outside the holy area; cf. Lev. 8.17; 9.11; 16.27, but contrast Lev. 10.16–18. The original description is thus to be found in verses 18*aβ*, *b*, 19*aα**, *b*, 20, 22*a*, 23, 24*a*, and 25. The close affinity of this passage with P is clear from Exod. 29.36*b*–37.

18. For **Lord GOD**, as in verses 19, 27, cf. on 2.4. A dual use of the altar is given. Throwing blood against the altar is often ordered in P; thus at priestly ordination (Exod. 29.16, 20); of burnt offerings (Lev. 1.5, 11; 9.12), and peace offerings (Lev. 3.2, 8; 9.18). The custom was much earlier, however; cf. Exod. 24.6, where the blood symbolized the covenant. Since the life-force was thought to be in the blood, its use was especially efficacious in sacrifice.

19. The later traditionist insists on the distinction between the Zadokites and other Levites (cf. 40.45–46). Actually the Zadokites were historically probably not Levites at all but descendants of Zadok who became one of David's two priests after the capture of Jerusalem (2 Sam. 8.17). For sin offering cf. on 40.39.

20. By putting some of the blood of the sin offering on its extremities the altar was translated from a profane to a holy realm. **cleanse the altar** is lit. 'make sin offering for it'. Sin attaches itself as a substance and even the altar had to have it removed. It had to be purged, i.e. atonement had to be made for the altar. Atonement here means the removal of taint or sin.

21. Precisely where **the appointed place** was is not known since the word thus rendered only occurs elsewhere in Neh. 3.31 as the name of one of the city gates; it was certainly outside the sacred area (cf. Lev. 8.17; 9.11; 16.27).

22–23. Apparently beginning with the second day of the seven-day consecration, a he-goat was to be used for the sin offering, after which a bull and a ram were to be sacrificed. Verse 22*b* adds that the sin offering is to be offered in the manner of the first day's sacrifice (verses 19–21).

24. The use of **salt** for animal sacrifice is not attested elsewhere in O.T., but it is for the cereal offering (Lev. 2.13). Later it was to become common; cf. the late addition to the text of Mk 9.49. The reason for it is unknown.

26. **and so consecrate it** is lit. 'and fill its hand', an idiom usually used to denote installation into office. As applied to the altar, it means make it ready for use.

27. After the seven days of purificatory rites are completed, the altar can be used for regular sacrifices. **peace offerings** were also animal sacrifices, but in contrast to the burnt offerings were not completely burned. Parts of the flesh were eaten by priests and/or the offerers, and they are usually thought to emphasize communion between Deity and worshippers. Less likely is the notion that these represented payment of debt to the Deity.

D. THE OUTER EAST GATE CLOSED **44.1–5**

This section continues in the vision style of 43.1–7*a*. The angelic guide brings the prophet from the inner court, 43.5, back to the outer east gate, which was not closed. Since the glory of Yahweh had entered it, it was to remain shut to symbolize Yahweh's perpetual presence. Verse 3, by its peculiar text and its introduction of the prince, shows its secondary character, based in part on 46.2, 8. Also secondary is the misinterpretation by which MT (and the Versions) add Yahweh instead of the guide as subject of **said** in verse 2.

Verses 4-5 present a special problem since they repeat earlier materials. Verse 4 reintroduces the glory of Yahweh filling the Temple and the prophet's reaction (cf. 43.3*b*, 5). That it is an accretion is clear from the geographical error. The guide leads the prophet by the north inner gate in view of the closed east gate which would be the normal entrance, forgetting that that gate was the outer, not the inner, one. The reaction of the prophet is to fall on his face, as in 1.28*b* and 43.3*b*, but in those instances there was a natural response (cf. 2.1 and 43.5*a*), whereas verse 5 simply orders the prophet to **see with your eyes**. Verse 5 is also an accretion. Formally it is a parallel to 40.4, on which it is in part based, but here the verse is not particularly fitting to what follows. The words from **concerning** to the end of the verse are based on 43.11, where the Temple ordinances and laws as well as its entrances and exits (not **those who may be admitted,** and **those who are to be excluded**; the emended text would be more appropriate to what follows, but there is no evidence to warrant it) are also mentioned. These verses are editorial expansions possibly intended for the large section 44.6-46.18, after which the guide again conducts the prophet. It should also be noted that, contrary to the vision style, Yahweh speaks rather than the guide, which however, as in verse 2, may be a later change.

1. The prophet is brought into the outer court (not outside the east gate) to the east gate.

2. The gate is to remain closed showing that the glory of Yahweh will remain in the Temple.

3. MT begins the verse with, 'As for the prince, a prince, he may sit.' The word 'a prince' is a dittograph. To **eat bread before the LORD** means to eat the sacrificial meal of the offerings one makes; cf. 46.2, particularly of the peace offerings (cf. on 43.27).

4. The **north gate** is the inner one leading to the inner court **(front of the temple).**

E. THE TWO PRIESTLY RANKS 44.6-16

This section is put in the form of an oracle, with the prophetic invective in verses 6*b*-8 in 2nd plural giving the reason for the demotion of the non-Zadokite priests, and the 'therefore' oracle of verses 9-16 giving the divine mandate for the distinction in ranks, i.e. the ministry of the sanctuary and the ministry of the altar. The 'therefore' oracle is in 3rd plural in contrast to the usual oracular form in Ezekiel. The section has nothing to do with the vision; whether a core of material comes from the prophet himself cannot be determined. If so, it was separate from the vision and editorially inserted here.

The invective is a charge of admitting foreigners to the sanctuary. The Gibeonites had traditionally performed menial services for the 'house of my God' and for 'the altar of Yahweh' (Jos. 9.23, 27), but this is hardly what is meant here. Reference is made in Neh. 13.4–9 to Tobiah the Ammonite being thrown out of the Temple since he was a foreigner, whereupon the Temple had to be cleansed. Some have seen a reference here to prisoners of war presented to the Temple, but this is highly unlikely. Possibly this reflects memories of the foreign Temple guard (2 Kg. 11.4–19) and of the Nethinim or Temple servants (1 Chr. 9.2), who were of foreign extraction and served as menials in the Temple. That within the invective accretions exist is clear from the 3rd plural reference in 'They have broken' in verse 7, which RSV changes to 'You have broken'.

The oracle itself prohibits such foreigners from entering the Temple complex; the work which these had hitherto performed is now to be done by the Levites as punishment for their former idolatry (cf. on verse 10). The Zadokites, having been faithful, will continue as priests. Verses 12–14 probably represent a later addition to the text. Verse 12 is a doublet to verse 10; similarly verse 13 is the negative counterpart to verse 11, and verse 14 is a summarizing parallel to verse 11.

6. For **Lord GOD** as in verses 9, 12, 15, cf. on 2.4. RSV rightly follows G. in adding **house** to **rebellious.** That the verse is not from Ezekiel is clear from the usage of **abominations** as permitting foreigners in the sanctuary (rather than as idolatry).

7. MT has 'my house' after **profaning it,** a late explanatory gloss on **it** omitted by G. For **uncircumcised in heart,** cf. Dt. 10.16 and often in Jeremiah. Spiritual circumcision is meant in contrast to physical (**flesh**). For **blood** in sacrifice, cf. on 43.18. The fat was normally burned as the Deity's share even in the peace offerings, cf. the P legislation in Lev. 3.

8. G. omits verse 8a, a late gloss. MT has 'them' rather than **foreigners**; this refers to **abominations** in verse 7b by which the foreigners are meant.

9. RSV rightly took the last word in verse 8 (*lkm*, 'for you') as an error for *lkn*, **Therefore,** with G. The ban on foreigners in the sanctuary is especially characteristic of the post-exilic age. In the Herodian Temple non-Jews were forbidden to enter the inner court on pain of death.

10. G. omits 'going astray' as a late gloss, i.e. render: 'when Israel went astray from me after . . .'. In the D Code, cult at the high places was prohibited and so the Levites had the right to offer sacrifice at the central sanctuary (Dt. 18.6–8). This obviously was impractical since there were far too many. Furthermore they had been priests at the illegitimate high places (**went far from me**). For this they are to bear their punishment.

11. This punishment is to be demotion from the office of priesthood to that of Temple servant, a position formerly occupied by the foreigners, cf. above. They were to serve as Temple porters and as the official butchers for private sacrifice (in contrast to P legislation where the people slew their own, e.g. Lev. 1.5, 11), but might not 'attend on' Yahweh, i.e. sacrifice on the altar.

12. The secondary character of the verse is apparent from the fact that it introduces an invective, a 'therefore' judgment, and an oracle conclusion formula in the middle of the oracle. The invective refers to the cult of the high places in monarchical times. For **have sworn**, cf. on 20.5.

13. and the things . . . sacred: a gloss on the preceding phrase. Here **abominations** refers to idolatry.

15. For sons of Zadok, cf. on 43.19. The Zadokites were the priests of the Jerusalem sanctuary in the former days of idolatry, and thus had not been priests of the high places. In the early post-exilic age the Zadokites were the official priests, and very few Levites returned from Babylon according to the list in Ezr. 2 (cf. verse 40 with verses 36–39). **come near** and **attend** refer to the privilege of performing the sacrifice on the altar.

16. The oracle conclusion formula at the end of verse 15 renders this verse suspect; it is a supplement giving the Zadokite privileges in greater detail, i.e. enter the sanctuary, and attend to the table of the bread of the presence (and presumably eat it).

F.   REGULATIONS FOR PRIESTS 44.17-31

That verse 17 begins a new section is clear from the literary form; the oracular style is now abandoned; a 1st person reference does not occur until verse 28. The section comprises various regulations about priests: their dress, verses 17–19; personal conduct, verses 20–22; duties, verses 23–24; purification after mourning, verses 25–27; and their benefits, verses 28–31. Since this is a corpus of regulations the oracle conclusion formula in verse 27 is out of place and secondary.

The corpus is clearly composite in origin. Verses 20–24 constitute a small group of rules of single composition, as their legal form shows. Each begins with a verb modifier, with 3rd plural verb following, even in instances when the subject is singular as in verse 21. Verses 17–19, though of a slightly different literary type, none the less may have belonged to the collection. Verses 25–27 are supplemental laws all dealing with a single theme; their involved style shows diverse origin, as does the uncertain use of number; thus in verse 25 the first verb is singular, and the second, plural; verses 26–27 are singular in construction, though the verb in verse 26 is plural (the indefinite plural as passive). Verses 28–30 also are supplemental (for the corrupt text of verse 28*a*, cf. below). The legal style of the corpus as a whole is completely abandoned in verse 28, and Yahweh is the speaker and Israel is addressed in verses 28*b* and 30. Still later is the concluding clause at the end of verse 30, **that . . . house,** which is in 2nd masc. singular. Verse 31 is quite separate in type from verses 28–30; it is a regulation much like those of verses 20–24 but was not originally part of that collection as the designation of subject, **priests,** shows.

Little can be said about the date of the collection. It differs in part from P legislation, e.g. in verse 22. Verse 31 is puzzling since its regulation was mandatory on all Israelites in Lev. 7.24 (cf. 4.14). Thus the latest supplement must have been added before the time of P.

17. G. omits the late gloss **and within.** Linen vestments for priests were ritually clean in contrast to wool, which was an animal product. The custom was ancient; cf. 1 Sam. 2.18 and 2 Sam. 6.14, for linen ephod.

18. This verse was probably not original to the law concerning dress. The detailing of two of the priestly garments to be worn in verse 18a seems foreign to the general point of the laws of verses 17–19, viz. keeping priestly garments rigidly apart from profane garments. Verse 18b seems like a rationalizing explanation for the interdict on wearing wool.

19. MT repeats by error **into the outer court. holy chambers** are those described in 42.1–14 (cf. especially verse 14), thus later than Ezekiel's vision, since that passage is secondary. In post-exilic times holiness was considered to be almost a material thing, and like a communicable disease could infect people simply by touch.

20. Shaving the head was a mourning sign, whereas letting the hair grow was a sign of the Nazirite vow; though why the latter should be forbidden for the priest is not clear. For special prohibitions on cutting hair for priests in H, cf. Lev. 21.5.

21. For priests not allowed to drink wine before cultic duties, cf. Lev. 10.9.

22. Special marriage laws for priests were intended to keep them ritually pure. The prohibition against marrying a widow applies in H only to the chief priest (cf. Lev. 21.14 and 7), but Ezekiel never recognized the office of High Priest.

23. Priestly instruction mainly concerned ritual matters (cf. Lev. 10.10, 11).

24. The institution of the sanctuary judge was an ancient one. Eli and Samuel were both priests and judges (1 Sam. 1.9 and 4.18; 9.12–13 and 7.15–17). It was ordered in the D Code as well (Dt. 17:8–9; 19.17; 21.5). The stress on feasts and sabbaths betrays strong emphasis on cultic observance in post-exilic Israel.

25. MT has 'He shall not defile himself . . .'. The verse has the same rules on mourning as H in Lev. 21.1–3. Neither list of exceptions includes a wife, probably because she is not a blood relative. That contact with a corpse renders one ritually unclean was a widespread, primitive notion not at all peculiar to the Hebrews.

26–27. For detailed laws concerning purificatory rites after mourning in P, cf. Num. 19.11–19.

26. MT has 'cleansed' for **defiled,** whereas RSV follows the rationalizing S. Ordinary people could be cleansed in seven days, but a priest had to wait another seven days before being allowed to exercise his priestly functions. RSV also follows the paraphrasing S. by adding **and then he shall be clean.**

27. For **Lord GOD,** cf. on 2.4. G. omits the late gloss **into the holy place.** For **sin offering,** cf. on 40.39.

28. The opening clause of MT is corrupt, reading 'And it shall become an inheritance for them' with no cross-reference for 'it', unless the words 'I am their inheritance' be taken as the subject. V.'s *non erit*, which RSV follows, makes much better sense. That the priests should have no land in Palestine is in line with the old traditions that the priestly tribe had no tribal allotment but lived among the other tribes. This tradition is in contradiction of the allotments of 45.1–5 and 48.8–14.

29. Priestly portions of the sacrifices agree fully with P legislation; cf. especially Lev. 6 and 7. **cereal offerings** were offerings of grain intended as gift or tribute to the Deity. **devoted thing** is something dedicated to the Deity and thus banned for profane use. This was usually the result of a vow, though in ancient practice it was often a ban of extermination in connection with holy wars.

30. By **first** of the first fruits, the choice first fruits are meant. The **offering** is described in some detail in 45.13–15a. It apparently was used for anything specially set aside. **coarse meal** is obscure; equally plausible is the rendering 'dough cakes'.

G. The Holy District and Various Regulations 45.1–25

The literary history of this section is complicated; the chapter consists of snippets of varied origins and with only vague relations to each other. Thus verses 1–8a detail the dimensions of the sacred area of Temple, priests, Levites, and city. Attached to this is an old oracle of Ezekiel against the princes of Israel which from its contents is clearly from the period before the fall of Jerusalem. Verses 10–12 deal with various weights and measures. Verses 13–15 detail the income-tax laws intended for sacred use, whereas verses 16–17 are later accretions showing the prince's relations to the incomes. Verses 18–20 are a parallel to 43.18–27 and concern the cleansing of the sanctuary, and verses 21–25 deal with two of the great feasts. Whether any of the materials of this chapter outside of verse 9 come originally from Ezekiel is doubtful.

(a) Verses 1–8 are a summary version of 48.8–22 and have been editorially placed here as a corrective to 44.28. The area is a square of 25,000 cubits (equals 43,750 ft). This is divided into three strips running east–west: the central strip, 10,000 cubits wide is the area for the priests (Zadokites) with the sanctuary complex in the middle; the north strip also 10,000 cubits wide is for the Levites, and the south strip, 5,000 cubits wide, for the city. The area to the east and the west extending to the borders of the land is the area for the prince. The section is given in 2nd plural, except for the first verb in verse 3, which is, however, a scribal error (*tmwd* for the original *tmdw*). Probably secondary to the section is verse 2, which interrupts the relation between verses 1 and 3 (cf. **in the holy district** which refers not to verse 2 but to verse 1). Verse 8b is in 3rd plural and is unrelated to verses 1–8a. It was editorially added as a transition to verse 9.

(b) Verse 9 contains an oracle as the introductory and concluding formulae show. It was placed here because of the reference in verse 7 to the **prince** (but here **princes**!).

(c) Verses 10–12 are a late tradition specifying the size and weights of measures and weights probably composed in view of the following section. It should be noted that verse 12 may well be later since only measures are involved in verses 13–14, and weights were probably added for completeness.

(d) Verses 13–15 apply to the people as the 2nd plural subject implies. **to make atonement for them** in verse 15 is then either secondary as a parallel to the concluding phrase in verse 17 or was originally in 2nd plural as G. The tax percentages assessed were undoubtedly the Temple tax and thus for the use of priests and Levites.

(e) That verses 16–17 are not part of verses 13–15 is clear both from the content and the style. They are a later corrective of verses 13–15 and assign the incomes not to the Temple but to the prince who in turn is to provide presumably out of this income for the sacrifices. Furthermore the subject is no longer in 2nd plural but 3rd person. Possibly the section verses 10–17 was placed here as a whole since it ends with the position of the prince and so should follow verses 7–9.

(f) Verses 18–20 appear with 2nd singular subject. This is the first in a series of regulations on feasts which end at 46.15. The passage is clearly related to the regulations concerning the consecration of the altar in 43.18–27, though here it concerns the cleansing of the sanctuary. Problematic is the relation of verse 20, which requires the same rite on the seventh of the month. G. has quite a different text here and the text has been corrupted. By analogy to 43.18–27 it would appear that the cleansing rites took seven days and only the first and last days are detailed.

(g) Verses 21–25 prescribe two of the great feasts, Passover and Tabernacles. Again the passage is of diverse authorship. The command to observe is in the 2nd plural, but the main interest is, as in verse 17, in the provisions which the prince is to make for the two feasts. Verse 21*b* appears to be a later accretion though its text is not certain. MT has 'On the Feast of Weeks for days unleavened bread is to be eaten', whereas G. has 'at the feast for seven days you (plural) shall eat unleavened bread'. The notion that unleavened bread is to be eaten for seven days on Passover may be based on P's account in Num. 28.17*b*. The word 'Weeks' rather than 'seven' may represent a later attempt to add the third annual feast to this calendar.

1. MT repeats **long** by error and has 'ten' for **twenty. portion** is rendered as 'offering' in 44.30, which may further have occasioned the placement of this section here. Though the entire area is a square, only this allotment is a holy district intended for the clergy and the sanctuary. As such it could not be sold or transferred.

2. For dimensions of the sanctuary, cf. 42.15–20. For **open space**, cf. on 48.17.

3. In verse 4 **It shall be the holy portion** is a scribal error omitted by G. and the following **of the land** should be added to verse 3. The sanctuary is the most holy (and central) place of the land in the ideal community of the future.

4. The antecedent of **it** is **section** of verse 3, not **sanctuary. and a . . . sanctuary** is an attempt to reproduce MT's 'and a sanctuary for the sanctuary', a copyist's error by dittography. It should simply read 'and for the sanctuary'. The central area contained both priestly dwellings and, at the centre, the sanctuary complex.

5. cities to live in with G. for MT's corrupt 'twenty chambers'; why their dwelling places should be called cities is not clear; possibly it is a denial of the notion of Levitical cities.

6. The city, i.e. Jerusalem, is only a quarter the size of the holy district, and is not to belong to any tribe but to the entire community.

7. That this passage is a summary of 48.8–22 is clear from the phraseology, which is similar to 48.8, 21. The prince's domain is in two parts, a strip from the eastern boundary of the land (cf. 47.18) to the central square of verses 1–5 (cf. also 48.22b), and from the square westwards to the sea, strips 25,000 cubits wide.

8. G. rightly has 'the princes of Israel' for **my princes**. The editor means the princes of the restored community.

9. For **Lord GOD**, as in verses 15, 18, cf. on 2.4. By **princes** is meant leaders of the people, as in 21.12(MT 17); 22.6. **cease** is the same as 'set apart' in verse 1. This verb and the noun **portion** or **offering** (verse 13) are leitmotifs throughout verses 1–17 and may have conditioned the editor in his arrangement.

10–11. The standard measure was the **homer** (a word related to and probably derived from ḥmwr, 'ass', since it designated a normal ass's load). Its capacity as a dry measure has been variously measured from 3·8 to 6·5 bushels, and a calculation of roughly 5 bushels might be in order. Since the **ephah** was $\frac{1}{10}$ of a homer, this would be approximately $\frac{1}{2}$ a bushel or 2 pecks. **bath** was a liquid measure of about $5\frac{1}{2}$ gal.; thus the homer as a liquid measure was 55 gal.

12. The text of MT is corrupt and RSV rightly follows G. In the Palestinian system of weights the **shekel** was the standard weight; it in turn was equal to 20 gerahs and to $\frac{1}{50}$ of a mina. The shekel weighed about $\frac{4}{10}$ of an ounce.

13. offering here means tax. Tax on grains was to be $\frac{1}{60}$ of the produce.

14. Corrupt text. MT adds after **oil** 'the bath as to the oil', and repeats 'the homer contains ten baths'. Nor does MT have the words **the cor, like** which RSV has added to make sense. The **cor** is the same as the homer. The tax on oil was 1 per cent.

15. The tax on animals was $\frac{1}{200}$. **families** is based on G., which has rationalized the Hebrew's 'watered land'. Though MT is unusual it ought not be changed. Yahweh's land will be well watered in the ideal future (cf. 47.1–12). For **them** read 'you' with G. The tax is a Temple tax to provide for all the required sacrifices and in this way for the Temple personnel. For **cereal offerings,** cf. on 44.29; **burnt offerings,** on 40.39; **peace offerings,** on 43.27.

16. Omit **of the land** with G. Here the prince is to receive the tax.

17. Verse 17b is repetitive and may well be a late accretion. **drink offerings** or 'libations' regularly accompanied cereal and burnt offerings and probably here offerings of oil are intended (cf. verses 14, 24). For the details of the prince's provisions for feasts, new moons and sabbath, cf. 45.22–46.15.

18–20. This is the only mention of an annual rite of purification of the Temple. The notion of some that the rite was semi-annual is based on G. Apparently the rite involved a week, the offering of a sin offering being repeated in identical fashion on the first and seventh day of the first month, i.e. in the spring (March–April).

19. Not only on the altar, as in 43.20, but also on doorposts of Temple and inner gate (should not this be plural?) is the blood of the sin offering to be put. For **sin offering,** cf. on 40.39.

20. for any one . . . ignorance is what MT means but it may be corrupt. G. has 'you shall take for each one a portion', which also cannot be correct. A reference to a sinner by error or ignorance in connection with Temple cleansing seems bizarre, unless it refers to a priest who has inadvertently violated a tabu in the Temple area.

21. Like the D Code the Passover is to be celebrated at the sanctuary (in contrast to P's account in Exod. 12.1–12; but cf. Num. 28.16–25). According to P the Passover was celebrated on the night of the 14th, and the Feast of Unleavened Bread on the following seven days. Verse 21*b* is a later accretion.

22–23. Unique is the reinterpretation of Passover as a time for a sin offering. Nor is a bullock otherwise used on Passover. Herein Ezekiel is at odds with the Pentateuch.

24. hin is ⅙ of one bath; cf. on verses 10–11.

25. Identical provisions are to be given for the Feast of Tabernacles or ingathering. For elaborate details of its celebration in P, cf. Num. 29.12–38; cf. also Lev. 23.33–36. In P, however, it was an eight-day festival (Num. 29.35–38).

H. VARIOUS REGULATIONS 46.1–18

In verses 1–12 the provisions and position of the prince for various feasts and sacrifices is continued (cf. 45.21–25). Verses 1–3 refer to the opening of the inner east gate on the sabbath and new moons and the relative positions of prince and people during the sacrifices. Verses 4–5 outline the prince's provisions for the sabbath sacrifice, and verses 6–7, for the new-moon sacrifices. Verses 8–10 regulate the entrances and exits for prince and people on feast days. Verse 11 may well be secondary since it repeats the requirements for the cereal offering in exactly the same terms as verse 7. Verse 12 regulates the procedure with the inner east gate for the free-will offering of the prince. The entire section is editorially introduced with an oracle introduction formula because a new subject, that of the gate, is introduced in verse 1.

Verses 13–14, as 45.18–20, are presented in the 2nd·singular in MT. RSV has avoided the difference by following G. in changing 'you' to **he** throughout. What the law intended was the imposition of requirements on the people (not on the prince as RSV) for the daily offerings. The end of verse 14 presents a textual problem since the word 'continual' has by error been added from verse 15. Verse 14*b* should read 'the cereal offering to Yahweh is a perpetual ordinance'. Verse 15 has been added later as a supplement; it not only adds nothing to what has been said (except to introduce the P term **continual burnt offering**) but is also in the 3rd plural.

Verse 16–18 detail regulations concerning transfer of property by the prince. The laws presuppose the allotment of land as shown in 45.7, 8*a*, and/or 48.21–22, and is later. Had it been part of that tradition it would surely have been placed as a supplement after 45.8*a*. It was probably placed here by the editor to end the section beginning at 45.7 in which the prince is often mentioned. As verses 1–15 the section is introduced by an oracle introduction formula.

1. For **Lord GOD**, as in verse 16, cf. on 2.4. The outer east gate was perpetually closed, 44.1–2, but the inner one was to be opened on special occasions: sabbath and new moons (cf. verse 12 for other occasions).

2. The prince proceeds from the outer court to the inner end of the inner gate where he takes his stand. He does not enter the inner court itself or take part in the sacrifice. The festive character of these minor feasts is shown by the gates remaining open for the day.

3. The populace must remain in the outer court.

4–5. The provisions for the sacrifices on the sabbath differ considerably from that of P (cf. Num. 28.9–10). In P the daily offering (Num. 28.3–8) was also required on the sabbath (as well as at the new moon) plus the sabbath sacrifice. For **hin,** cf. on 45.24.

6–7. The later P legislation also differed substantially on the provision for the sacrifices at the new moon; cf. Num. 28.11–15 where a sin offering, as well as a burnt offering, cereal offering, and the daily sacrifices, is required.

8–10. The prince must naturally leave through the east gate since exit by the inner court was forbidden. The people must leave by the gate opposite their gate of entrance.

9. come before the LORD: a technical term for appearing in the sanctuary.

12. G. rightly omits the repetitive **as a freewill offering.** This is a voluntary gift given over and beyond what is prescribed. Such spontaneous sacrifices were not circumscribed; they could be either holocausts or peace offerings.

13–14. Read 'you' for **he** throughout. The daily offering was mandatory on Israel and consisted of burnt offering and cereal offering. The daily offering in P was required twice daily (cf. Num. 28.3–8). In post-exilic Judaism these daily sacrifices became the mark of the true cult of Yahweh. Fine **flour** was the constant ingredient of the cereal offering in P in contrast to earlier custom.

15. Literally MT has 'So that they shall provide . . .', correctly understood by RSV as an indefinite plural for the passive.

16. out of his inheritance with G. for MT's 'as his inheritance'. A prince may transfer some of his allotment (cf. 45.7) to his natural heirs.

17. The prince's land is not permanently transferable out of the family. Any land given to someone other than a natural heir reverted to the family in the year of jubilee, for which cf. Lev. 25.8–17, where return of land to original owners is mandatory on all.

18. For **thrusting them out of their property** G. simply has 'by oppressing them'; **their property** is a dittograph. In contrast to monarchical times the people's lands are also to be inviolate. Cf. the oracle in 45.9.

I. The Temple Kitchens 46.19–24

The form of the original vision is imitated in this passage with the heavenly guide bringing the prophet to the two areas in the inner and outer courts respectively where the sacrificial food was prepared for priests and laity. That it is not part of the original vision is, however, clear. Not only is there no measurement involved, but the passage is dependent on the accretions to the vision in 42.1–14. The original vision had no reference to the chambers for the priests (cf. 42.1–14). This passage was occasioned by the tradition of 42.13 where reference is made to the holy chambers where the priests were to eat. Verses 19–20 describe a place at the western end of the north (south also?) row of priests' chambers where the food for the priests from the sacrifices was prepared. By analogy similar kitchens were necessary for the laity, verses 21–24. These were placed in the four corners of the outer court where the Levites might prepare the food for the people.

19. For **entrance,** cf. 42.9. Which gate was meant is not stated.

20. For **guilt offering** and **sin offering,** cf. on 40.39. For the tabu of **holiness,** cf. on 44.19. It would be dangerous for priests to mix with the people or to have the priestly food contaminated by the profane. Since holiness was itself tabu it would be dangerous for the people to be touched by holy food. **and where they shall bake the cereal offering** is probably a later tradition as its asyndetous form shows (lit. 'who shall bake . . .').

22. small: based on reading *ktnwt* for the obscure *ktrwt* as the Versions. But the kitchen courts were not really small at all; they measured *c.* 70 ft by 52½ ft each. Since the root *ktr* has something to do with the smoke of sacrifice some such neutral rendering as 'sacrificial' would be better.

23. The construction is obscure. Apparently a row of stones encircled the hearths. The row of stones lay around kitchen courts making an inner ring. The hearths were to be found below the floor, lining the inner side of the stone wall.

24. The Levites (**those who minister at the temple**) are to serve as cooks for the popular sacrifices.

J. The River Flowing from the Temple 47.1–12

This section in its original form was the conclusion to Ezekiel's vision and originally continued the vision of 44.1–2. Like the introductory vision in chapter 1, this section was a favourite with later scribes, and apocalyptists have added various accretions until it has become almost impossible to recover the original form. This composite form is evident from doublets, repetitions, and the language. Verses 1 and 2 present the first problem. Both show the guide leading the prophet; both describe water coming out from the east side of the Temple area. It is verse 1 which is secondary, as the language shows. The word for **south** in MT is different from that used in chapter 40. Furthermore the minute details of verse 1*b* render it suspect. In verse 3 the words **with a line in his hand** is not original, as the word in MT for 'line' shows. Verse 5 twice states that the river was impassable; the second **a river that could not be passed** through is a doublet.

With verse 6*b* the prophet is brought to the bank where, in view of verse 5, he must already be. In verse 6*a* the guide speaks, and again in verse 8, and what intervenes prematurely introduces the trees on the bank before the course of the river is fully known. If verses 6*b*–8*aa* (**And he said to me**) are taken as a later accretion, the original narrative appears consistent. Verse 9 is not only verbose; it also reflects the style of P and represents a later tradition to explain what the fresh waters will mean for the Dead Sea. Verse 10 is dependent on verse 9, while verse 11 is an attempt to retain some of the saltiness. It is a tradition quite separate from verses 9–10. Verse 12 represents a tradition similar to that of verses 9–10 and explicates what fresh water means for vegetation.

The notion that living waters find their source in the divine sanctuary is rooted in an old Israelite tradition. Ps. 46.4(MT 5) speaks of a river whose streams gladden the dwelling place of the Most High (cf. also Isa. 8.5–8). In the Garden of Eden story of Gen. 2 Paradise is the source of the four great cosmic rivers. To Ezekiel the ideal state of restored Israel will be such a Paradise regained. The Temple not only lies at the centre of Israel's life, but as the place in which the glory of Yahweh is, it becomes the source of Israel's physical well-being as well. For later developments of this theme, cf. Jl 3(MT 4). 18; Zech. 13.1; 14.8; Rev. 22.1–2.

It is, of course, out of order to criticize this section on geographical grounds. It is part of a visionary experience and as such considerations of space are not germane. As a vision it presents a climax to the entire experience. The Temple has been measured; then the glory of God returned through the east gate, which is thereupon permanently closed since Yahweh will remain with his people. What the divine presence in the Temple means for Israel is symbolically portrayed by the ever-deepening river flowing from the sanctuary and transforming the Dead Sea into fresh water.

1. he brought me back, i.e. from viewing the kitchens in the outer court. The traditionist was dissatisfied with the waters merely flowing from the Temple complex; they must issue from beneath the Temple itself, presumably through inner and outer courts eastward before exiting.

2. MT has two words in **that faces toward the east** which are synonyms: 'towards' and 'facing'. G. rightly omits one. **was coming out** occurs only here and might better be rendered 'was trickling out'. The prophet had to be brought out by the north gate since the east gate was closed.

3–5. The stream begins with a trickle and is only ankle deep after a 1,000 cubits (c. 570 yds), then successively knee deep, waist deep, and finally impassable. The picture is probably based on that of a gradual river bank or a seashore. That this is a vision is obvious since the conception is unrealistic. It is thus out of order to rationalize this stream as fed by the cosmic deep.

6. The question posed is identical to that in 8.12, 15, 17.

7. As I went back: a scribal error based on the verb in verse 6b, and should be 'And behold'.

8. And he said to me: made necessary by the addition of verses 6b–7. The **Arabah** is the geological depression in which the Dead Sea lies and which extends southward to the Gulf of 'Aqaba. By **the sea** is meant the Dead Sea. **when it enters the stagnant waters of the sea** is based on S. MT has 'when it enters the sea, into the sea, those brought forth', an obvious corruption. The second instance of 'sea' should read 'waters' and the phrase originally read 'concerning the waters brought forth', a marginal theme wrongly copied into the text. Read: 'when it enters the sea.' That even the saline waters of the Dead Sea could be rendered sweet by the living waters is the climax of the vision.

9. river: with the Versions for MT's 'two rivers' in verse 9*a*. Phrases reminiscent of P's creation story in Gen. 1 are **living creature, swarms, fish.** Though the verse as a whole is an accretion (lengthy explanations are not characteristic of the original vision), there are doublets in the verse itself, as e.g. the last clause.

10. Engedi: modern *Tell el–Jurn*, was an oasis about midway down the west shore of the Dead Sea. The exact location of **Eneglaim** is uncertain, but '*Ain-Feshkha* seems likely (*c.* 18 miles N. of Engedi and only $1\frac{1}{2}$ miles S. of Khirbet Qumran. For **place . . . nets,** cf. 26.5, 14. The **Great Sea** is the Mediterranean. The salt and minerals of the Dead Sea permit no life in it of any kind; in the ideal age it will miraculously teem with life.

11. Some salt is necessary for life and this the traditionist provided for by retaining salinity for the nearly swamps and marshland areas.

12. Vegetation will be abundant, providing both food and medicinal leaves. This picture of miraculous bounty including that of monthly crops is expanded by later apocalyptic writers (cf. Rev. 22.3). For the picture, cf. Ps. 1.3.

K. The Division of the Holy Land 47.13–48.35

(a) THE BOUNDARIES OF THE LAND 47.13–23

This section is formally presented as an oracle with introductory and concluding formulae, but the oracular style is maintained only in verses 13–14 and 21–23. Inserted is the actual description of the four boundaries, a description which has suffered greatly from textual corruption. The oracular style is artificial, as verse 13 shows. Furthermore the concluding verses 22–23 are secondary; they are a later correction on the passage as a whole, giving to the proselytes a share in the tribal allotments.

The boundaries are obviously ideal ones similar to and arising from the same circles as those of P in Num. 34.1–12. The main difference between the two descriptions is that two and a half tribes were to receive land outside these boundaries (Num. 34.13–15), whereas here all tribes were to receive land within, 48.1–7, 23–29. The ideal borders are not exactly drawn, as might be expected. Roughly the future community was bounded by the Mediterranean and the Jordan on the west and east sides respectively, and by a line from Damascus to the coast on the north, and a line from the southern tip of the Dead Sea to the Wadi-l-'Arish on the south. The individual descriptions of the four borders are stylistically alike. Each ends with a concluding **This shall be the . . . side,** and begins with **On the . . . side.** The description as a whole ends with a concluding summary, verse 21.

13. For **Lord GOD,** as in verse 23, cf. on 2.4. **Joseph . . . portions** is a later accretion by a traditionist noticing that Levi had no tribal portion, and Manasseh and Ephraim each had one. **two** is based on V.T., but is correct.

14. For **I swore,** cf. on 20.5. The oath to the patriarchs that the land of Canaan would be given to Israel was a basic theme in the early sources of the Pentateuch.

15-20. The overall borders, whereas the tribal divisions are given in chapter 48.
15. Cf. Num. 34.7-8. **Hethlon:** uncertain location. *Heitela*, east of Tripoli, is a
favoured suggestion. **Hamath:** modern *Ḥama*; the **entrance of Hamath** would
then refer to the area near Riblah. This seems more probable than the theory that
the northern border was much farther south, since to the school of Ezekiel, Riblah
constituted Israel's border, cf. 6.14. **Zedad** may be modern *Sadad*, south-east of
Homs.

16. Berothah may be modern *Bereitan*, south of Ba'albek. **Hazer-hatticon** is
completely unknown. **Hauran** refers here to the area south of Damascus. The
northern border is hardly a straight west-east line, but bends considerably around
the end of the Antilebanon towards the south-east.

17. MT is corrupt, but RSV probably renders the original intent. On the basis
of this verse Hazerhatticon of verse 16 is often emended to **Hazarenon,** which lay
near the foot of Mount Hermon.

18. MT does not have **Hazarenon,** and it is unnecessary. The eastern border is
only described in general terms. **eastern sea** is the Dead Sea, and **Tamar** (for the
erroneous *tmdw* of MT) was a fortified town at the southern tip of the Dead Sea.

19. The southern border is similarly described in 48.28. For **Meribath-kadesh,**
cf. 'waters of Meribah' in Num. 20.13. Meribah means 'strife' and the account in
Num. 20.2-13 is an aetiological tale. The place was known as Kadesh-barnea,
probably modern *'Ain-el-Qudeirāt*. To the east lay the Wadi-l-'Arish or **Brook of
Egypt.**

20. The ideal western border was the Mediterranean Sea.

22. MT begins oddly with 'And it shall be' omitted by G. and RSV. By **aliens**
are meant the proselytes of post-exilic Judaism rather than the resident aliens of
pre-exilic times. For the position of the proselyte in H, cf. Lev. 19.34; 24.22, and
similarly in P, Num. 15.29, but in neither is he given explicit inheritance rights
equal to those who are native born. Possibly the scarcity of population in post-exilic
Palestine fostered this liberalism; the reference here is to resident proselytes who
have a family.

23. Proselytes were to become members of the tribe where they resided.

(b) THE NORTHERN TRIBES 48.1-7

The allotment of the land whose dimensions were given in 47.13-23 to the twelve
tribes is given in verses 1-7 and 23-29. The intervening verses again describe the
central east-west strip with the holy district at the centre described in 45.1-8a. For
convenience verses 23-29 are described here. Verses 1-7 give the allotment of the
seven tribes north of the central strip, and verses 23-29 the allotment of the five to
the south. Presumably each tribe receives an identical strip of land running parallel
from east to west. The allotments are made in complete disregard of historical
reality, but rather in accordance with some priestly conception of racial purity.
Thus the concubine tribes are farthest removed from the central sanctuary. Though
Dan is located in the extreme north which is historically correct, this is pure

accident. Thus Judah lies on the northern boundary of the central strip and Benjamin immediately to the south, the exact reverse of the facts! To the north of Judah is Reuben (the eldest), then Ephraim and Manasseh (Joseph tribes), and finally Naphtali, Asher, and Dan. South of Benjamin were successively Simeon (second eldest), Issachar, Zebulun, and Gad.

1. MT is extremely corrupt, and RSV probably gives the sense intended. For the northern boundary of Dan, cf. on 47.15–17.

2–7. Each verse is given in the same formula.

(c) THE CENTRAL STRIP 48.8–22

For this section, cf. notes on 45.1–8. Problematic is the relation of this section to its context. It recapitulates in somewhat greater detail 45.1–8, which, however, pre-supposes, as does this section, the tribal allotments. Since 45.1–8 is a summary of the longer account, only the relation of the latter to its context needs discussion. There is no question that verse 8 must have been part of the account of tribal allotments since the central strip is described in the same formulaic terms as in verses 1–7 and 23–29. Verse 23 could not, however, stand as a continuation of verse 8. There is no indication within it that it immediately adjoins the central strip to the south. The Benjamin allotment lacks that part of the formula which states 'adjoining the portion which you shall set apart'. This is unnecessary, solely because of verse 22b. Thus some form of verses 9–22 must have been part of the section 48.1–29.

The section has been expanded by later traditions. Verses 11–12 is an accretion identifying the priests as Zadokites; this represents the same tradition as 44.15. Also intrusive in the context is verse 21b–22a. The context is the territory belonging to the prince, and verse 22b fits perfectly as the conclusion to verse 21a.

8. This can hardly be separated from what follows, since it gives the overall dimensions of the central strip, whereas the remainder gives the details of its division.

9. twenty: as G., is original for MT's 'ten'. Yahweh's portion includes both the land of priests and Levites. length throughout .this section refers to east–west measurements; breadth, to north–south. Cf. 45.1.

10. Cf. 45.3–4.

11. MT incorrectly divides hmkdšm bny, 'the consecrated (priests), the sons of', as hmkdš mbny, which is untranslatable. For this verse, cf. on 44.15.

13. That this is a later accretion is clear since it presupposes verse 13. MT has corrupted wllwym, **the Levites shall have,** to whlwym, 'and the Levites', under the influence of the preceding word. For the verse, cf. 45.5.

14. **They** refers specifically to Levites, but the intention is both Levites and priests. Both territories were **holy to the LORD,** and therefore inalienable. **choice portion** is lit. 'first portion'; cf. on 'first', 44.30.

15. The remaining strip (5,000 cubits wide, on the south side) is for the city in the centre with city lands on both ends. **ordinary use** is lit. 'profane', i.e. non-sacred.

16. its (**dimensions**) refers to the actual city, which is to be 4,500 cubits square.

17. **open land** ('open country' in verse 15) is a strip of uncultivated land, 250 cubits wide surrounding the city on all sides, presumably for popular use (cf. Lev. 25.34; Num. 35.2–7), thereby making the city plus open space a square area of 5,000 cubits.

18. **and it shall be alongside the holy portion** is a dittograph. The city only occupies the middle 5,000 cubits of the 25,000-cubit strip, thus leaving 10,000 cubits at either end as farm land for the city's inhabitants.

19. MT inconsistently has singular subject 'worker' but with plural predicate. **from . . . Israel** may be a later accretion to emphasize the varied tribal origins of the capital city's populace; cf. the situation in Nehemiah's day (Neh. 11.1).

20. MT has 'one fourth' for **square**, which must be a scribal error.

21. Cf. on 45.7. **of the holy portion (to)** is lit. 'of a portion' and is probably a scribal error for 'eastward'. In verse 21b the tautologous **sanctuary of the temple** is highly suspect; one of the nouns must be a gloss.

22. RSV omits MT's 'And the property of the Levites' at the beginning of the verse incorrectly. Verses 21b and 22a state that the three parts: holy part, Levites' part, and that of the city bisect the prince's domains.

(d) THE SOUTHERN TRIBES 48.23–29

Cf. (a) above (pp. 336f.) for discussion. The allotments are fictional, only Simeon having ever been a southern tribe.

28. Cf. on 47.19 for the extreme southern border.

29. A subscription to the entire section 47.13–48.28. For **Lord God**, cf. on 2.4. The oracle formula is artificial. The section is in general not in oracular form.

(e) THE HOLY CITY 48.30–35

That this section is a postscript is clear from the preceding verse. Note also the different listing of tribes. In this supplement Joseph and Levi are listed, whereas in verses 1–29 Manasseh and Ephraim take the place of Joseph, and Levi naturally has no portion. The description is symmetrical, a square city with three gates on each side named after the twelve tribes of Israel. For a later parallel, cf. Rev. 21.12–14.

30–31. There seems to be some disarrangement of the text. **the gates . . . Israel** of verse 31 belongs after **city** in verse 30. The three northern gates are all named after Leah tribes.

32. Joseph and Benjamin are Rachel tribes, whereas Dan was a concubine tribe.

33. All Leah tribes.

34. Three concubine tribes.

35. A circumference of 18,000 cubits would be almost six miles. Ideal Jerusalem will be given a new name in that Utopia of exilic and post-exilic dreams to show that it is the holy city where in days of old Yahweh dwelt for a time but now he will remain for ever.

Index

(N.B. Page references in italics indicate a specific discussion of the item.)

'wpn, 74
'yš, 45

b'h, 63
Baal(ism), *passim*
Baal-meon, *145*
Babylon, 14, 24f., 27, 42, 51, 55, 66f.,
    76f., 80f., 95, 99f., 105, 106f., 112ff.,
    120, 122, 125, 135, 142, 144ff., 151,
    153, 156, 159, 164, 166, 175, 179,
    195, 217, 221
Babylonian, *passim*
Babylonian Chronicle, 43
Balaam, 59
bāmāh, 99, 115, 119
Bashan, 151
bath, *225*
Benjamin, 232, 233
Berothah, *231*
Berry, G. R., 23
Bertholet, A., 24, 40, 115, 200, 205
Beth-jeshimoth, *145*
Beth-togarmah, *152*, 199, 202
bhm, 178
bḳ'h, 53
bmṣdwt, 114
bmsrt, 120
bnhrwtyk, 171
bribery, *130f.*
brwk, 51
Brook of Egypt, 231
bšllḥw, 168
btwk, 183
buckler, *137*
Burrows, M., 23
bw, 49, 141
bw', 179

Cain, 71
calendar, *1ff.*
call to prophecy, 12f., 29, 40ff., *47ff.*,
    52, 124
Cambyses, 165
Canaan, *passim*
Canaanite, 94f., 98, 105, 115
Canneh, 153
canon, 23
Carchemish, 159

casuistic law, 19, 26, 58, 91, 109, 117
Chaldean, *135*, 136f.
Chebar, 24, 42, 51, 66, 76
Cherethites, *146*
cherub(im), 43, 45, 66, 71, *73ff.*, 156,
    157f., 213
Chilmad, 153
Chronicler, 91
Chronicles, 155
chronology, *1ff.*
Cimmerians, 152, 199
clairvoyance, 25
Code of Hammurabi, 51
colophon, 114, 170, 173, 215
command (oracle), *16*, 32, 35, 129, 194,
    200f., 215
commentary, 15, 62, 65, 93, 123, 140,
    171, 201
commercial document, 21f., 150
contributions, *121*
Cooke, G. A., 78, 113, 157
copyist, 23, 51, 57, 87, 100, 102, 126f.,
    131, 139, 142, 144, 151, 153, 160,
    161, 167, 170, 178, 180, 182, 197,
    205, 207, 224
cor, *225*
Cornhill, C. H., 30, 87, 88, 165, 175
cosmic tree, *167ff.*
covenant, 79f., 90, 94f., 106f., 108, 120,
    126, 164, 184, 185, 192, 196, 198,
    218
covenant, new 80, 103, 192f., 196f., 198
Covenant Code, 110, 130, 205
covenant renewal, feast of, 108
creation, 195
Cretans, 164
Cush, 202

Damascus, *passim*
Dan, 232, 233
Daniel, 26, 62, 90f., 117, 155
dates, *1ff.*, 23, 42f., 67, 116, 140, 148,
    151, 159f., 162, 166, 168, 170f., 174,
    179, 194, 209
David, 71, 95, 126, 146, 155, 159, 181,
    184, 187, 197f., 218
Davidic dynasty, 33f., 104ff., 107, 113,
    132, 163, 198